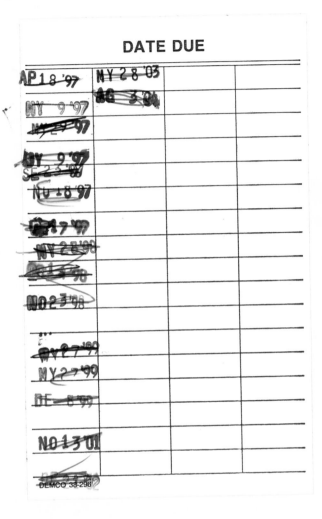

DATE DUE

AP 18 '97	MY 28 '03		
MY 9 '97	AG 3 '04		
~~MY 97~~			
MY 9 '97			
SE 23 '97			
NO 18 '97			
DE 17 '97			
MY 28 '98			
~~98~~			
NO 23 '98			
MY 27 '99			
MY 27 '99			
DE 8 '99			
NO 13 01			

Why does crime persist over generations, within families, and within certain individuals? Is crime the manifestation of an inherited latent trait or the result of a failure of socialization and norm-setting processes? Why do youth commit crimes? *Delinquency and Crime* contains essays by nine leading criminologists that seek to answer these and other questions by describing current theories of crime and the research evidence that supports them.

Research has revealed that a wide range of factors, from broad societal influences to individual characteristics, are associated with increased risk for crime. The authors' views on crime causation go beyond traditional criminological theories of strain, cultural deviance, social control, differential association, and social learning to present emerging and integrated models of the origins of crime, including antisocial peer socialization, social development, interactional theory, behavior genetics, and community determinants. These essays seek to link factors at different levels in internally consistent theories of crime. Each essay explores the practical implications of the authors' theoretical work for crime prevention and control.

Delinquency and Crime

Cambridge Criminology Series

Editors
Alfred Blumstein, *Carnegie Mellon University*
David Farrington, *University of Cambridge*

This new series publishes high quality research monographs of either theoretical or empirical emphasis in all areas of criminology, including measurement of offending, explanations of offending, police courts, incapacitation, corrections, sentencing, deterrence, rehabilitation, and other related topics. It is intended to be both interdisciplinary and international in scope.

Other title in the series

Simon Singer
Recriminalizing Delinquency: Violent Juvenile Crime and Juvenile Justice Reforms

Delinquency and Crime

CURRENT THEORIES

Edited by

J. David Hawkins
University of Washington

CAMBRIDGE
UNIVERSITY PRESS

University of Cambridge
Cambridge CB2 1RP
1-4211, USA
e 3166, Australia

© Cambridge University Press 1996

First published 1996

Printed in the United States of America

Library of Congress Cataloging-in-Publication Data

Delinquency and crime : current theories / edited by J. David Hawkins.
   p. cm. – (Cambridge criminology series)
   ISBN 0-521-47322-5. – ISBN 0-521-47894-4 (pbk.)
   1. Juvenile delinquency – Research. 2. Juvenile delinquency –
Prevention. 3. Adolescent psychology. I. Hawkins, J. David. II. Series.
HV9069.D43   1996
364.3'6 – dc20   95-6529

A catalog record for this book is available from the British Library

ISBN 0-521-47322-5 Hardback
       0-521-47894-4 Paperback

Contents

Introduction   vii
J. DAVID HAWKINS

Contributors   xiii

1   Developmental Continuity, Change, and   1
Pathways in Male Juvenile Problem
Behaviors and Delinquency
ROLF LOEBER

2   Delinquent Friends and Delinquent Behavior: 28
Temporal and Developmental Patterns
DELBERT S. ELLIOTT AND SCOTT MENARD

3   The Explanation and Prevention of Youthful   68
Offending
DAVID P. FARRINGTON

4   The Social Development Model: A Theory   149
of Antisocial Behavior
RICHARD F. CATALANO AND J. DAVID HAWKINS

5   Empirical Support for Interactional Theory: 198
A Review of the Literature
TERENCE P. THORNBERRY

6   The Use of Contextual Analysis in Models   236
of Criminal Behavior
ROBERT J. BURSIK, JR. AND HAROLD G. GRASMICK

7   An Adaptive Strategy Theory of Crime   268
and Delinquency
DAVID C. ROWE

Author Index   315
Subject Index   325

Introduction

J. DAVID HAWKINS

WHY DOES CRIME PERSIST OVER GENERATIONS, within families, and within certain individuals? Is crime the manifestation of an inherited latent trait or the result of a failure of socialization and norm-setting processes? Does crime result from interaction with delinquent peers, or is it simply a spurious correlate of the adolescent peer culture? If crime is the product of interactions between individuals and their social environments, what are the mechanisms by which social contexts affect individual behaviors?

Many of these questions have interested criminologists since the field began. Yet they remain among the current questions of criminology. They are questions that require explanations, questions that require theory, an internally consistent set of assumptions and propositions that organizes the evidence on the wide range of predictors of crime. This is a book of theory.

It is elegant to assume that crime is the manifestation of a single latent construct, such as low self-control, which varies across, but not within individuals, and explains all deviant behavior (Gottfredson & Hirschi, 1990). But this, of course, raises other questions: What are the causes of and the constraints on the operation of low self-control? Ineffective child rearing, that is, failure to set clear expectations for behavior, failure to monitor children, and excessively severe and inconsistent disciplinary practices, clearly contributes to delinquent behavior (Patterson, DeBarysh, & Ramsey, 1989; Dodge, Bates, & Pettit, 1990). In Gottfredson and Hirschi's single-factor theory of crime, ineffective child rearing is also a cause of crime – a cause that operates indirectly through the mediation of low self-control (1990, p. 97). Differences in opportunities for personal gain in various societies are also causes of crime in Gottfredson and Hirschi's theory (p. 177). They influence crime rates observed across different cultures by affecting the opportunities for crime available to those with low self-control. Clearly, more is needed than low self-control to explain crime in a general theory of crime.

Research has revealed that a wide range of factors, from broad societal influences to individual characteristics, are associated with increased risk for crime. How can these factors at different levels be linked in internally consistent theories of crime that explain what we know? This is the challenge to which each of the theories in this book proposes an answer. I invited essays from these authors because each has been engaged in theory construction to explain how multiple factors interact to produce crime and delinquency. This integration of the evidence into a consistent theory of crime is the mission of each of these authors. Their approaches differ.

To illustrate, in their essay Robert J. Bursik, Jr. and Harold G. Grasmick review evidence that the neighborhood contexts in which individuals live affect criminal recidivism. They suggest the end-to-end integration (Liska, Krohn, & Messner, 1989) of micro- and macrolevel theories that include consideration of the indirect effects of neighborhoods on the criminal behavior of the people who live in them. In stark contrast, David C. Rowe advances the proposition that broad ecological, economic, social, and cultural forces reinforce two different styles of behavior, one emphasizing procreation and crime, and the other emphasizing parenting and non-crime, and that these, in turn, have become encoded over generations as genetically produced individual differences in criminal behavior. These perspectives have vastly different implications for policy on what we should do to prevent and reduce crime. Yet ultimately, prevention should be guided by an internally consistent and coherent theory that organizes the available evidence. To this end, the authors of these essays have sought to explicate both the support for their current understanding of criminal offending and the implications of their theories for policy and practice. The chapters included in this volume advance the authors' theories of crime and present the evidential support for these theories.

Chapter 1 is Rolf Loeber's "Developmental Continuity, Change, and Pathways in Male Juvenile Problem Behaviors and Delinquency." This essay addresses important questions about the extent to which various forms of delinquent behavior can be predicted from earlier conduct problems, the relationships among these behaviors, unique versus common behavioral paths to delinquency, and implications of this knowledge for intervention focused on delinquency reduction. This chapter coalesces Loeber's current theoretical thinking and reflections on its implications for social policy. Piece by piece, block by block, Loeber creates an edifice of explanation for the consistency of problem behaviors across the life span.

Chapter 2 is Delbert S. Elliott and Scott Menard's empirically based retort to their critics regarding "Delinquent Friends and Delinquent Behavior: Temporal and Developmental Patterns." The authors analyze data from the National Youth Survey to demonstrate the hypothesis proposed in

Explaining Delinquency and Drug Use (Elliott, Huizinga, & Ageton, 1985) that peers play an important role in delinquency causation, not just in delinquency covariation, as charged by some critics of that book. There continues to be debate in the field regarding whether peer associations and influences play a predictive and causal role in the etiology of delinquency or whether they are simply covariates with delinquent behavior. Because delinquency often occurs in groups, some have charged that delinquent peer associates are simply indicators of delinquent behavior itself. Elliott and Menard have reanalyzed the National Youth Study data, and they argue here that these reanalyses provide a definitive answer to this question.

Chapter 3 is David P. Farrington's "The Explanation and Prevention of Youthful Offending." Farrington, of Cambridge University, has previously been tentative in theorizing from his rich array of data gathered in the Cambridge Study in Delinquent Development. In this chapter, he fully explicates his theory of crime causation, which has emerged from his extensive analyses of the Cambridge data. This chapter builds on Loeber's chapter regarding continuity of offending and examines a wide range of factors that have been shown to be precursors of offending. The review of predictors of offending is followed by Farrington's reasoned and meticulous explanation of how this information has been considered in putting together a theory of offending that can orient work in prevention and treatment of crime. The theory hypothesizes *antisocial tendency* as a key underlying construct, but explicates how offending depends on "energizing, directing, inhibiting, decision-making, and social learning processes." Farrington concludes with a review of approaches to prevention and treatment of youthful offending based on the empirical and theoretical evidence and the strong assertion that delinquency prevention efforts must be implemented as early in a child's life as possible.

Chapter 4, by Richard F. Catalano and myself, is "The Social Development Model: A Theory of Antisocial Behavior." The chapter shows how we have integrated the evidence regarding risk and protective factors for youthful offending into a developmental theory of crime. This theory specifies empirically and theoretically based points for interventions to prevent and reduce delinquency. The chapter is our effort to apply current knowledge to the task of developing grounded interventions for preventing delinquency.

Chapter 5, "Empirical Support for Interactional Theory: A Review of the Literature," by Terence P. Thornberry of the State University of New York at Albany, summarizes the author's interactional model of delinquency and crime and reviews the results of recent longitudinal panel studies that bear on the empirical adequacy of the theory. Thornberry (1987) has postulated both developmental and reciprocal effects in the initiation, maintenance, and termination of delinquency. Here, he assesses the extent to which existing evidence supports the specific hypotheses of the interactional model with regard to bonding and learning variables. He clearly reviews and summarizes the extent of support and nonsupport for the importance of including reciprocal causal effects in models of delinquency and in explicitly considering developmental change in delinquency theories. He also identifies gaps in the existing data with respect to key hypotheses of interactional theory. In this regard, Thornberry's chapter is the definitive statement of the degree of empirical support for interactional theory and a model of using existing research results to test theoretically derived hypotheses.

Chapter 6, "The Use of Contextual Analysis in Models of Criminal Behavior" by Robert J. Bursik, Jr. and Harold G. Grasmick, University of Oklahoma, expands the discussion to consider how broad societal factors influence criminal behavior and can be adequately specified in criminological theory. Their chapter investigates macro community influences, or *contextual effects,* on criminal behavior. They suggest that an adequate theory of the effects of structural and contextual variables on crime requires resolution of continuing theoretical issues. These include specification of the mechanisms by which contextual variables affect individual behavior; delineation of the specific social, structural, or economic contexts hypothesized to affect criminal behavior; and specification of the properties of the social context, as distinct from the aggregate of characteristics of the individuals participating in that social context, which are hypothesized to affect criminal behavior. Bursik and Grasmick review three general contextual models of crime and the evidence regarding each. Reading this chapter stimulated our research group to rescue, from the depths of the Seattle School District's Computer Management Division, geocoded data on residential and school demographic variables for our own longitudinal data sets.

Chapter 7 is David C. Rowe's "An Adaptive Strategy Theory of Crime and Delinquency," presenting a theory of delinquent behavior as biological and genetic adaptation. Rowe, a behavior geneticist at the University of Arizona, has explicated an elegant theory of evolutionary biology that seeks to integrate our existing understandings of the biological and social bases of crime. The chapter provides explicit attention to the genetic and biological foundations of criminal behavior. Its propositions are controversial and worthy of discussion.

This volume should interest criminological researchers who seek to understand, explain, and predict delinquency and crime, policy makers who seek to prevent and reduce crime and delinquency, and students who seek to understand current theory and research in criminology.

REFERENCES

Dodge, K. A., Bates, J. E., & Pettit, G. (1990). Mechanisms in the cycle of violence. *Science, 250,* 1678–1683.

Elliott, D. S., Huizinga, D., & Ageton, S. S. (1985). *Explaining delinquency and drug use.* Beverly Hills, CA: Sage.

Gottfredson, M. R., & Hirschi, T. (1990). *A general theory of crime.* Stanford, CA: Stanford University Press.

Liska, A. E., Krohn, M. D., & Messner, S. F. (1989). Strategies and requisites for theoretical integration in the study of crime and deviance. In S. F. Messner, M. D. Krohn, & A. E. Liska (Eds.), *Theoretical integration in the study of deviance and crime: Problems and prospects* (pp. 1–19). Albany, NY: State University of New York Press.

Patterson, G. R., DeBarysh, B. D., & Ramsey, E. (1989). A developmental perspective on antisocial behavior. *American Psychologist, 44,* 329–335.

Thornberry, T. P. (1987). Toward an interactional theory of delinquency. *Criminology, 25,* 863–891.

I thank the authors who have been included here for their patience with me. I am especially grateful to David Farrington and Al Blumstein for their sustained interest in this collection of essays and to Rick Catalano for keeping this project on my list. Thanks are also due to the Safeco Corporation for sponsoring the Safeco Lectureship in Crime and Delinquency at the University of Washington, which started the idea for this book.

Contributors

Robert J. Bursik, Jr., is professor and chair of the Department of Sociology at the University of Oklahoma. His primary research interests pertain to the relationship between neighborhood dynamics and crime rates and to the formal and informal mechanisms of social control at the local community level that inhibit illegal behavior. He is the author of *Neighborhoods and Crime* (1993, Lexington), along with Harold Grasmick.

Richard F. Catalano is a professor in the School of Social Work and associate director of the Social Development Research Group at the University of Washington, Seattle. He received his B.A. degree (1973) from the University of Wisconsin in sociology and his M.A. (1976) and Ph.D. degrees (1982) from the University of Washington in sociology.

Dr. Catalano's main research and program development activities have been in the areas of drug abuse and delinquency. His work has focused on discovering risk and protective factors and on designing and evaluating programs to address these factors. He is principal investigator and co-investigator on a number of federal grants in this area of research.

Dr. Catalano has served on the National Institute on Drug Abuse's Epidemiology and Prevention Review Committee, the National Academy of Sciences Panel on Needle Exchange and Bleach Distribution Program, and the Washington State Advisory Committee for Alcohol and Substance Abuse. He is coauthor of two books, *Preparing for the Drug (Free) Years* (1987) and *Communities That Care: Action for Drug Abuse Prevention* (1992), and author of many journal articles.

Delbert S. Elliott is a professor in the Department of Sociology and director of the Center for the Study and Prevention of Violence, Institute of Behavioral Science, University of Colorado. Professor Elliott's scholarly work involves both theory development and testing, primarily in the areas of delinquency and violent behavior, but also relative to other forms of problem behavior. His books include *Delinquency and Dropout* (1975, with H. Voss), *The Social Psychology of Runaways* (1978, with T. Brennan and D. Huizinga), *Explaining Delinquency and Drug Use* (1985, with D. Huizinga and S. Ageton), and *Multiple Problem Youth: Delinquency, Substance Use, and Mental Health Problems* (1989, with D. Huizinga and S. Menard). Professor Elliott served as chair for the Criminal and Violent Behavior Review Committee (NIMH) from 1983 to 1986 and as a member of the National Research Council Panel on Criminal Careers (1983–85); he is currently a member of the MacArthur Foundation Research Program on Successful Adolescent Development and the National Academy of Sciences/Institute of Medicine Committee on Youth Development. He is a Fellow of the American Society of Criminology and served as President of the American Society of Criminology in 1992–93.

David P. Farrington is professor of Psychological Criminology at Cambridge University, where he has been on staff since 1969, and acting director of the Institute of Criminology. His major research interest is in the longitudinal study of delinquency and crime, and he is director of the Cambridge Study in Delinquent Development, a prospective longitudinal survey of over 400 London males from age 8 to age 40, funded by the Home Office. He is also co-principal investigator of the Pittsburgh Youth Survey, a prospective longitudinal study of over 1500 Pittsburgh males from age 7 to age 20. In addition to over 170 published papers on criminology and psychological topics, he has published 14 books, one of which (*Understanding and Controlling Crime*, 1986) won the prize for distinguished scholarship of the American Sociological Association Criminology Section. He is president-elect of the European Association of Psychology and Law, a member of the advisory boards of the U.S. National Juvenile Court Data Archive and the Netherlands Institute for the Study of Criminality and Law Enforcement, joint editor of the Cambridge University Press book series on Research in Criminology and Criminal Behaviour and Mental Health, and a member of the editorial boards of several journals. He has been president of the British Society of Criminology, chair of the Division of Criminological and Legal Psychology of the British Psychological Society, vice-chair of the U.S. National Academy of Sciences Panel on Law and Justice, a member of the U.S. National Academy of Sciences Panel on Criminal Career Research, and a member of the national Parole Board for England and Wales. He is a Fellow of the British Psychological Society and of the American Society of Criminology. He received B.A., M.A., and Ph.D. degrees in psychology from Cambridge University, and the Sellin-Glueck Award of the American Society of Criminology for international contributions to criminology.

Harold G. Grasmick is a professor in the Department of Sociology at the University of Oklahoma. In addition to his work with Robert Bursik pertaining to neighborhoods and crime, his research interests include the incorporation of social norms and values into a rational choice theory of crime, and the relationship between attribution styles and attitudes toward punishment.

J. David Hawkins is a professor in the School of Social Work and director of the Social Development Research Group at the University of Washington, Seattle. He received his B.A. degree (1967) from Stanford University in sociology and his M.A. (1969) and Ph.D. degrees (1975) from Northwestern University in sociology.

His research focuses on understanding and preventing child and adolescent health and behavior problems. Since 1981, he has been conducting the Seattle Social Development Project, a longitudinal prevention study that is testing a risk reduction strategy based on his theoretical work. He is coauthor of *Preparing for the Drug (Free) Years* (1987), a prevention program that empowers parents to reduce the risks for drug abuse in their families while strengthening family bonding, and of *Communities that Care: Action for Drug Abuse Prevention* (1992).

Professor Hawkins has served as a member of the Epidemiology, Prevention, and Services Research Review Committee of the National Institute on Drug Abuse, as a member of the Office for Substance Abuse Prevention's National Advisory Committee on Substance Abuse Prevention, and as a member of the Committee on Prevention of Mental Disorders of the Institute of Medicine, National Academy of Sciences. He also serves on the National Education Goals Panel Resource Group on Safe and Drug-Free Schools. He is committed to translating theory and research into effective practice and policy to reduce crime.

Rolf Loeber is a clinical psychologist and is professor in Psychiatry, Psychology, and Epidemiology at the Medical School of the University of Pittsburgh in Pittsburgh, PA. He is co-director with his wife, Magda Stouthamer-

Loeber, of the Life History Studies Program. Under the aegis of this program, two major longitudinal studies, the Pittsburgh Youth Study and the Developmental Trends Study, have been underway now for eight years. In his spare time, he writes about art history, colonial history, and fiction.

Scott Menard is a research associate in the Institute of Behavioral Science at the University of Colorado, Boulder. He received his A.B. at Cornell University and his Ph.D. at the University of Colorado, both in sociology. His primary interests are in applied statistics and the longitudinal study of drug use and other forms of illegal behavior. Dr. Menard's publications include the Sage Quantitative Applications in the Social Sciences monographs *Longitudinal Research* (1991) and *Applied Logistic Regression Analysis* (1995), and the books *Multiple Problem Youth* (with Delbert S. Elliott and David Huizinga, 1989) and *Juvenile Gangs* (with Herbert C. Covey and Robert J. Franzese, 1992).

David C. Rowe is professor of Family Studies at the University of Arizona. He received his A.B. degree in social relations from Harvard University and his Ph.D. in psychology from the University of Colorado. In graduate school, he received training in behavior genetics at the Institute for Behavioral Genetics under the supervision of Robert Plomin. With Plomin, he conducted an observational twin study of shyness in toddler children. He is author of *The Limits of Family Influence* and has written over 90 chapters and articles in behavioral science. In his recent work, he has focused on genetic and environmental influences on adolescent transition behaviors such as sexual intercourse, drinking, and delinquency. In his study of 265 twin pairs, he examined genetic and environmental influences on delinquency. He is also known for early studies of the genetics of the family environment (i.e., looking at the heritability of parenting styles). In another line of work, he has applied the mathematics of infectious disease epidemics to understand the spread of adolescent transition behaviors. He lives in Tucson, Arizona with his wife and son.

Terence P. Thornberry is a professor and former dean at the School of Criminal Justice, University at Albany, State University of New York. Prior to moving to Albany, he held faculty positions at the University of Georgia and the University of Pennsylvania. Professor Thornberry received his M.A. in criminology and his Ph.D. in sociology from the University of Pennsylvania. He is the author of a number of books, including *The Criminally Insane* and *From Boy to Man – From Delinquency to Crime,* as well as numerous articles and book chapters. Professor Thornberry is currently the director of the

Rochester Youth Development Study, an ongoing panel study examining the causes and correlates of serious delinquency and drug use. His research interests focus on the longitudinal examination of the development of delinquency and crime, as well as the construction of an interactional theory to explain these behaviors. Professor Thornberry is the recipient of numerous awards, including the American Bar Association's Gavel Award Certificate of Merit and the President's Award for Excellence in Research at the University at Albany, and he is a Fellow of the American Society of Criminology.

CHAPTER ONE

Developmental Continuity, Change, and Pathways in Male Juvenile Problem Behaviors and Delinquency

ROLF LOEBER

ABSTRACT: There is a growing consensus that major dimensions of early child problem behaviors can be distinguished, and that problem behaviors develop in an orderly sequence over time. Also, there is now also an impressive body of longitudinal data on the continuity of problem behaviors over time. It is less well known, however, whether some problem behaviors may serve as catalysts, in that their presence leads to worsening behavior, while their absence facilitates improvement. It also remains to be seen which classification scheme of child problem behaviors has the highest predictive yield in forecasting long-term negative (and positive) outcomes. Least explored are "dynamic" classifications or pathways, in which youth are classified according to their history and sequence of problem behaviors as those behaviors unfold over time. Moreover, relatively little is known about the diversification of problem behavior over time, but it is more certain that diversification is inversely related to desistance.

This chapter reviews these issues and shows that relevance for intervention studies. It does not attempt to cover the multitude of risk factors that may influence children's development, such as family and peer variables (for which, see Loeber, 1990), but instead, concentrates on the development of child problem behaviors as they unfold over time during childhood and adolescence.

The author is much indebted to JoAnn Koral for her editorial comments. The work on this chapter was supported by grant no. 86-JN-CX-0009 and NIMH grant MH48890. The points of view or opinions in this essay are those of the author and do not necessarily represent the official position or policies of the U.S. Department of Justice and the National Institute of Mental Health.

Dimensions of Problem Behaviors

To what extent can different dimensions of problem behavior be distinguished, and is there "coherence across different manifestations" of child problem behavior (Sroufe, 1979), or are most of these behaviors only marginally related to each other?

To address this question, Loeber and Schmaling (1985a) performed a meta-analysis of the factor analyses based on these ratings from 28 studies covering over 11,000 youngsters. Using a multidimensional scaling technique, they found that antisocial child behavior can be represented on one dimension with two poles. On one extreme, there are primarily confronta-

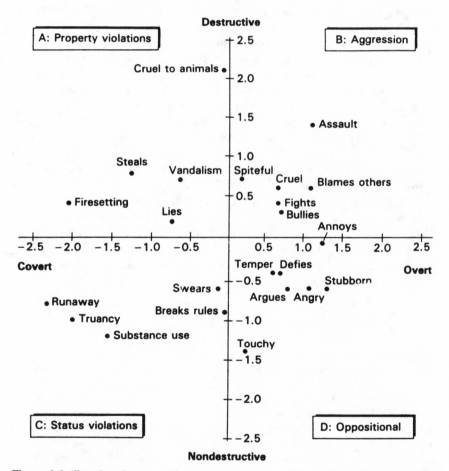

Figure 1.1. Results of meta-analysis of parent and teacher ratings of child problem behaviors using multidimensional scaling. (Frick et al., 1993)

tional or overt behaviors, while the other extreme mainly consists of nonaggressive, concealing, or covert behaviors. More recently, the meta-analysis has been repeated by Frick et al. (1993) on an expanded sample of factor analyses ($N = 60$) covering over 28,000 children. Their results replicated the overt–covert dimension of disruptive behaviors, but also showed a destructive–nondestructive dimension (Figure 1.1). The distance between the behaviors in Figure 1.1 represents the likelihood that behaviors loaded on the same factor. The farther the distance between behaviors in Figure 1.1, the less likely the behaviors are to be found loaded on one factor. Note that disobedient behaviors such as "defiance" and "breaks rules" are positioned close to the intersection of the two axes. This implies that these behaviors are shared by the covert–overt and the destructive–nondestructive dimensions. The results of the Frick et al. (1993) analyses were not substantially different for males and females.

In summary, analysis of the factor-analytic data indicates two dimensions of child problem behaviors, covert–overt and destructive–nondestructive, with disobedient behaviors being shared by the two dimensions. It should be noted that these results are based on parent and teacher ratings, and do not include youngsters' self-reports of delinquent acts, which often are concealed from adults. Moreover, the ratings usually did not include the more serious forms of delinquency found in self-reported delinquency measures or in measures of official offending. Also, the results of the meta-analysis were cross-sectional in nature and did not address developmental continuity of different problem behaviors over time.

Developmental Continuity

Three aspects of the developmental continuity of delinquency will be stressed here: different manifestations of the problems from childhood to adulthood, the persistence of problem behavior, and the impact of behavioral catalysts on the continuity or discontinuity of behavior problems.

Developmental Sequences in Problem Behavior. The basic premise here is that youngsters of different ages have different capabilities and behavioral repertoires for the expression of problematic behavior. Certain developmental changes in problem behavior are more obvious than others. Figure 1.2 shows a developmental ordering of problematic behaviors from early childhood to late adolescence, according to the earliest age at which particular behaviors manifest themselves (Loeber, 1990). The ordering of problem behaviors in Figure 1.2 is only a rough approximation of developmental priority, and may not equally apply to all children.

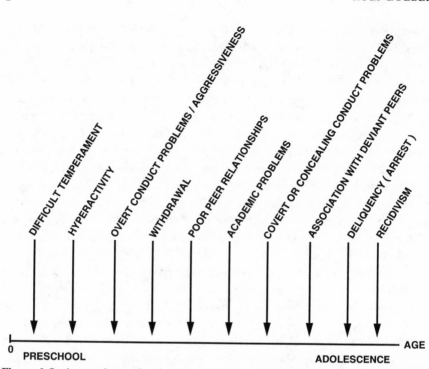

Figure 1.2. Approximate developmental ordering of problem behaviors from childhood to adult. (Loeber, 1990)

One manifestation of problem behaviors in the life cycle is difficult temperament. This refers to a child's style of responding to the environment, such as rhythmicity, adaptability, and quality of mood, rather than specific child behaviors (Thomas, Chess, & Birch, 1968).

Although temperament measures often include a measure of activity level as well, the syndrome of hyperactivity (with its associated problems of impulsivity and attention problems) is usually not measurable until the second or third year of life.

The ability to crawl or walk usually opens up many new avenues of mischief. Improved physical strength may become a weapon, initially in a minor way by enabling the child to physically attack siblings or adult caretakers. As soon as children learn to speak, verbal aggression may be added to their behavioral repertoire. Aggression may then be reinforced by children's cognitions, leading them to misattribution of hostile motives in others. Social withdrawal may also become apparent during the preschool years.

Once youngsters enter preschool or kindergarten, there is not only a new setting in which problems may be exhibited, but the availability of peers may generate new problems or reinforce the aggressive problems that were already apparent with siblings. During the elementary school period, more concealing problem behaviors may emerge, such as truancy, theft, and association with deviant peers. At any point in elementary school, middle school, or high school, youngsters may begin to associate with deviant peers and/or begin to commit minor crimes. For a proportion of children this will be a passing phenomenon, but for others it will be a stepping-stone to the frequent commission of more serious delinquent acts. Children's contacts with police tend to accelerate in early adolescence, as does recidivist offending.

It can be argued that the preceding variety of problem behaviors are often temporary in nature, and that low stability over time may undermine the notion that there is coherence across different manifestations of the problem behaviors.

The Persistence of Early Problem Behaviors. Opinions have been divided about the degree to which certain problem behaviors are stable over time. Studies show that externalizing behaviors tend to have higher stability over time than internalizing behaviors (e.g., Rutter, 1982; Kohlberg, Ricks, & Snarey, 1984). Children's problems with peers during the preschool period, however, do not appear very stable, judging from the Richman, Stevenson, and Graham study (1982), but may improve during the elementary school age years. Juvenile aggression is one of the acting out behaviors that has a relatively high degree of stability over time. Olweus (1979), in his overview of longitudinal studies on aggression, concluded that the degree of longitudinal consistency in aggression is much greater than has generally been assumed. He stated that "Aggressive behavior at ages 12 and 13 may show a high or very high degree of stability for periods of 1 to 5 years (from 50% to more than 90% of the variance accounted for). Also for periods as long as 10 years, the stability is high (some 45% of the variance accounted for)" (p. 869). This is not to say that prediction coefficients for aggression are uniform across all ages. At age 8 these coefficients are comparatively small and increase with age. Longitudinal studies tend to show that serious juvenile aggression becomes more stable over time from early adolescence onward, independent of the length of the follow-up (Loeber, 1982). Around this period test–retest correlations are much higher than at earlier periods, indicating that fewer youngsters who are aggressive tend to subsequently grow out of these acts (in other words, most children will outgrow aggression prior to adolescence). This is in agree-

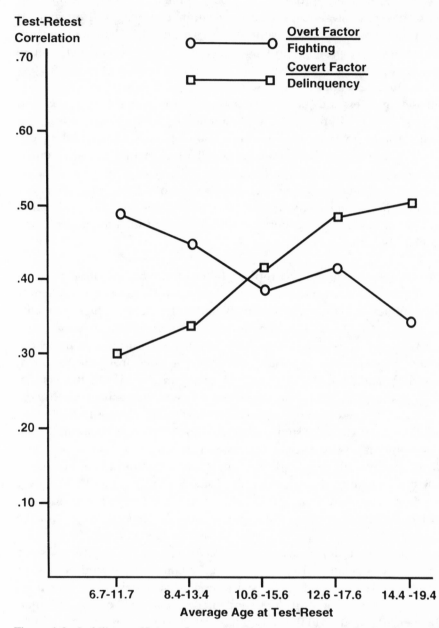

Figure 1.3. Stability coefficients for overt and covert problem behavior factors for different age cohorts over five years. (Based on Gersten et al., 1976)

ment with surveys on the prevalence of aggression during the adolescent years (Loeber, 1982; Moskowitz, Schwartzman, & Ledingham, 1985).

Whether children direct their aggression at adults and peers, there is considerable evidence of continuity for these specific forms of conflict. Studies of sibling conflict show that such conflict is often not only stable from the preschool years to elementary school age (e.g., Richman et al., 1982), but is evident throughout adolescence (Gersten, Langner, Eisenberg, Simcha-Fagan, & McCarthy, 1976; Olweus, 1979). For example, Gersten and her colleagues found an average correlation of 0.48 over a 5-year span. The same study demonstrated that youngsters' conflict with parents averaged about the same correlation. When broken down by different age cohorts, however, the correlations show a decline from the midadolescence onward, which may be attributed to youngsters leaving home. The 5-year test–retest correlations for youngsters' fighting similarly decrease with age, as is shown in Figure 1.3, particularly between age 6 and age 19.

In contrast, the test–retest correlations for delinquent acts in the same study tended to increase over time (Figure 1.3). This increase is almost linear from age 6 to age 19, and accounted for about three times as much variance in late adolescence as compared with late childhood.

Changes in continuity appear to be specific to certain behaviors. For example, hyperactivity is a common problem in preschoolers and is reasonably stable over time (Campbell, Schleifer, & Weiss, 1978; Chamberlin, 1977; Glow, Glow, & Rump, 1982; Richman et al., 1982). A cross-sectional study, however, shows that the prevalence of high activity level appears to be highest in the first 3 years of life, and then declines afterward (Routh, Schroeder, & O'Tuama, 1974). Calculation of desistance rates in the longitudinal study by Richman et al. (1982) shows that desistance is $3\frac{1}{2}$ times higher between ages 3 and 4 than between ages 4 and 8 (see also Campbell & Werry, 1986; La Greca & Quay, 1982).[1] Recently, Hart et al. (1993) reported longitudinal findings showing that particularly hyperactivity and impulsivity declined with age, but that attention problems had a higher stability over time.

In summary, stability coefficients differ in magnitude for different child problem behaviors and may vary with age, increasing for some problem behaviors and decreasing for other problem behaviors. Therefore, the maximum stability coefficient is not achieved at the same age period for all

---

[1] These figures should be interpreted with caution because they refer to change scores that, because of compounded reliability of the pre- and postmeasures, inherently are problematic.

problem behaviors. There is a lack of consensus as to the earliest age at which different behaviors become stable.

Catalysts for the Continuity of Problem Behaviors. Studies of continuities of child behavior often have examined particular categories of behavior problems (e.g., aggression, theft) in isolation rather than looking at whether the continuity of one behavior is influenced by the presence of another behavior. It is hypothesized here that certain behaviors function as *catalysts* in that other behaviors are only prone to persist when the catalyst is present; conversely, when the catalyst is absent, the problematic behavior tends to become less likely over time. Two examples will be given: hyperactivity and substance use.

Hyperactivity. It has long been recognized that hyperactivity (and associated impulsivity and attention problems) and disruptive behaviors often co-occur (Hinshaw, 1987). To what extent, however, is hyperactivity a catalyst for the development of disruptive behavior? And is hyperactivity directly associated with later serious outcomes, or is the relationship conditional on the emergence of early and less serious forms of disruptive behavior?

Several early studies suggested that conduct disorder is more severe and persistent when children also score high on an index of hyperactivity/ attention problems (August & Stewart, 1983; Magnusson, 1988; Offord, Sullivan, Allen, & Abrams, 1979; Schachar, Rutter, & Smith, 1981). For example, Rutter and his associates in the Isle of Wight study (Schachar et al., 1981) found that when 10-year-old conduct-disordered boys and girls were followed up until the age of 14, 66.7% of those with pervasive hyperactivity (as rated by parents) tended to persist over time in conduct disorder compared with about 8.3% of those without hyperactivity at time 1.[2] Subsequent longitudinal studies have replicated this finding for different age groups of males, such as preschoolers who were followed up until the middle of elementary school (Carey & McDevitt, 1978; Richman, Stevenson, & Graham, 1985). Similarly, Gittelman, Mannuzza, Shenker, and Bonagura (1985), who followed up 6- to 12-year-old hyperactive boys until age 16, found that those who continued to be hyperactive were far more likely to show antisocial or substance use disorder than those whose attention deficit disorder abated. Thus, the continuity of several forms of problem behavior depended on the presence or persistence of symptoms of hyperactivity.

The question is, however, to what extent hyperactivity without conduct

___

[2] When teacher ratings were used, the figures were 33.3% and 7.7% respectively.

problems is sufficient to generate conduct problems. Evidence for this is contradictory. Only one study reported that attention-deficit hyperactivity disorder (ADHD) *alone* could serve as a precursor to antisocial personality disorder in adulthood (Mannuzza, Klein, Bessler, Malloy, & LaPadula, 1993). In that same study, ADHD has also been postulated as a risk factor for later criminality, but only when mediated by conduct disorder (Mannuzza, Klein, Konig, & Giampino, 1989). Farrington, Loeber, and Van Kammen (1990) reported that hyperactivity and conduct problems at age 8–10 each predicted chronic offending (i.e., six or more convictions by age 24). Cadoret and Stewart (1991), in a cross-sectional study of antisocial personality disorder (APD) in adoptees, found that ADHD was not directly related to APD, "but indirectly through a set of aggressive behaviors" (p. 79). Thus, the evidence is contradictory that hyperactivity by itself is associated with later serious disruptive behavior.

Could it be that hyperactivity is associated with an early onset of disruptive behavior? Recently, Farrington et al. (1990) reported that hyperactivity predicted an early onset of convictions (ages 10–13) better than conduct problems. Similarly, Loeber, Green, Keenan, and Lahey (1994) found that *only* a diagnosis of ADHD predicted the *early* onset of conduct disorder (i.e., delinquency) in clinic-referred boys. If the age of onset was not taken into account, the best behavioral predictors of the onset of conduct disorder was a combination of oppositional defiant disorder *and* physical aggression.

In summary, most of the evidence indicates the catalytic role of hyperactivity in the development of serious disruptive behavior in childhood and adolescence. It should be understood that hyperactivity is often accompanied by impulsivity and attention problems, and that probably the impulsive element in hyperactivity is of most relevance for the associated onset of disruptive behaviors during childhood and adolescence. The following developmental sequence is plausible. Hyperactivity may stimulate an early onset of disobedience, conduct problems, and delinquency. The risk of serious conduct problems and delinquency may become more acute when physical aggression accompanies disobedience at an early age. Whether a decrease in hyperactivity is associated with a decrease in problem behavior is less certain.

Substance Use. Concurrent studies have shown that the more serious the substance use the higher the likelihood that individuals will engage in serious forms of delinquency (see Loeber, 1988 for a review). Concurrent studies, however, do not indicate the direction of effect, or whether a decrease in substance use is followed by a decrease in delinquent activities.

Studies on the direction of effect have shown that substance use may be associated with an increase in delinquency, but the reverse may also apply (Loeber, 1988). For example, longitudinal analyses reported by Van Kammen and Loeber (1994) on a sample of boys who were followed up from ages 13 to 16 showed that onset of drug use (marijuana use or hard drug use) and drug dealing in adolescent males was associated with a subsequent increase in person-related offenses and carrying of a concealed weapon. The increase was more pronounced for drug dealing than for drug use. In addition, drug dealing was associated with an increase in car- and fraud-related crimes. It can be argued, however, that delinquency may also activate substance use. This was confirmed by Van Kammen and Loeber (1994), who found that previous involvement in property offenses increased the subsequent risk of the onset of illegal drug use. Also, previous involvement in both property- and person-related offenses increased the risk of the onset of drug dealing.

If drug involvement and delinquency are intertwined, does this also mean that a decrease in drug use is followed by a decrease in delinquent activities? There is evidence for this in interview studies of narcotic addicts: When individuals began using hard drugs less frequently, their criminal involvement also decreased (Ball, Shaffer, & Nurco, 1983; Nurco, Shaffer, Ball, & Kinlock, 1985). This is not surprising in light of the decreased need to illegally obtain funds to purchase the drugs. Results from treatment studies demonstrate similar effects on delinquency (see, e.g., Savage & Simpson, 1981). Longitudinal analyses on juveniles (Van Kammen & Loeber, 1994) also showed that discontinuation of illegal drug use (or drug selling) was associated with a decrease in delinquent activities. The extent that a decrease in delinquency is associated with a subsequent decrease in drug involvement, however, is not clear from the available studies.

In summary, hyperactivity and drug involvement may act as catalysts in the development of disruptive behaviors, but the evidence is far from complete. Future studies need to demonstrate that catalysts operate *independently* from third factors, such as impulsivity, aggression, or peer influences.

Classification of Children's Problem Behaviors and the Prediction of Later Outcomes

Given the emergence of different problem behaviors during childhood and adolescence (Figure 1.2), it follows that children in different life stages may be classified differently on the basis of their prevailing problem behavior. Each classification can be related to differential risk for later handicaps, of which delinquency can be one.

Starting with temperament, investigators have classified children as temperamentally "easy" or "difficult" (Thomas et al., 1968). Information on the long-term predictability of temperament on antisocial outcomes is sparse but supportive (e.g., Werner, 1987). Undoubtedly, highly aggressive children are already distinguishable from nonaggressive problem children during the preschool period (see, e.g., Fagot, 1984). Increasingly, studies have been able to demonstrate the importance of boys' aggression from as early as the preschool period as a predictor of later delinquency and conduct problems (Charlebois, Le Blanc, Gagnon, Larivée, & Tremblay, 1993; Loeber, Tremblay, Gagnon, & Charlebois, 1989; Spivack, 1983).

As mentioned, hyperactivity is another important factor in the development of disruptive behavior. It is less clear, however, to what extent this applies to hyperactivity during the preschool period, when the distinction between hyperactive and nonhyperactive children is more difficult to make (e.g., Campbell, Breaux, Ewing, & Szumowski, 1984; Matheny, 1983). The link between hyperactivity and later delinquency, however, now rests largely upon studies with elementary school age or older children as subjects (e.g., Magnusson, 1988).

Difficult peer relations may be used to classify children. For example, Dodge, Coie, and Brakke (1982) studied elementary school age children and, on the basis of their relationships with peers, classified them as popular, rejected, or controversial (i.e., seen as popular by some and rejected by others). This classification was differentially predictive of later problem behavior (Coie & Dodge, 1983; Kupersmidt & Coie, 1990). Other studies also have firmly established a strong link between children's problem behaviors as seen by their peers and later aggression and delinquency (Eron, Walder, & Lefkowitz, 1971; Huesmann, Eron, Lefkowitz, & Walder, 1984; Johnston & Pelham, 1986; Roff, 1986; Roff, Sells, & Golden, 1972; West & Farrington, 1977).

Turning to studies on juvenile problem behavior during the elementary school age period, youngsters have been classified by their teachers as aggressive, troublesome, or as having some other problematic behavior. Especially from age 8 onward, these behaviors have been connected to both self-reported delinquency and official records of arrest or conviction (Loeber & Stouthamer-Loeber, 1987; West & Farrington, 1977). Although concealing, nonaggressive disruptive behaviors such as truancy and theft may already be evident during the preschool period (Stouthamer-Loeber, 1991), it is not known at what ages these behaviors begin to predict later delinquency (Farrington, 1981; Mitchell & Rosa, 1981).

There has been a continuing debate in delinquency studies about whether juvenile delinquency is a homogeneous phenomenon or whether discrete subgroups of juvenile delinquents can be distinguished. On the one hand, there have been proponents of a "cafeteria style" of offending (Klein, 1984). On the other hand, there have been others who distinguish between various groups, such as property and violent offenders (Blumstein, Cohen, Roth, & Visher, 1986). In the areas of juvenile justice and psychiatric care, efforts to classify youngsters have focused on severely impaired populations – gang members, incarcerated juveniles, or juveniles in psychiatric institutions. Epidemiological surveys on samples that include less impaired youngsters similarly constitute a working ground for classification studies. Each can be expected to produce different results. Typically, the former type of study has provided evidence for multi-problem youngsters, whose offending appeared generalized rather than specialized or limited to particular types of offenses (Klein, 1971). The latter type of study, although finding low rates of generalists, found other more specialized groups, who often were not referred to the courts or the clinics.

Frick et al. (1993) innovatively classified clinic-referred boys using two dimensions of problem behavior (see Figure 1.1). Each subject's vector scores from the two-dimension graph were subjected to a k-means cluster analysis in order to identify homogeneous profiles of behavior. This resulted in three clusters: nondeviant boys; boys with an elevation on quadrant D (oppositional behavior) and quadrant B (aggression); and boys with an elevation on quadrant A (property violation), quadrant D (oppositional behavior), and quadrant B (aggression). One of the validity tests of the classification showed a substantial but imperfect overlap between the empirically derived clusters of deviant boys and conceptually derived classification of oppositional defiant disorder and conduct disorder according to *DSM-III-R* (American Psychiatric Association, 1980, 1987). The diagnosis of oppositional defiant disorder refers to nondelinquent disruptive behaviors, while the diagnosis of conduct disorder mostly refers to delinquent acts.

In summary, although various classification schemes have been used in this area of research, their differential utility is far from clear in predicting delinquency. In general, studies comparing the utility of different classification schemes on the *same* subjects are wanting. There is a lack of consensus, however, as to the earliest age at which different classification schemes can be reliably measured and reach optimal utility in predicting negative or positive long-term outcomes.

A Comparison between Different Classifications
of Children at Risk for Delinquency

In order to explore the differential utility of different classification schemes, Loeber and Stouthamer-Loeber (1986) have executed several comparisons, using data initially collected with G. R. Patterson and his associates at the Oregon Social Learning Center. The sample studied consisted of over 200 boys. The sample was followed up over 5 years, and the boys were classified in two ways. A first classification, based on earlier work by Loeber and Dishion (1984), focused on the settings in which aggression occurred: (a) boys who fought at home only, (b) boys who fought at school only, (c) boys who fought at home and school, and (d) remaining nonfighting boys. A second classification, based on earlier work by Loeber and Schmaling (1985b), concentrated on both aggression and theft and distinguished among (a) boys who fought (as rated by the mother and the teacher) but were not involved in theft (exclusive fighters), (b) boys who stole but did not fight (exclusive stealers), (c) boys who stole and fought (versatiles), and (d) the remaining boys.

The question raised by Loeber and Stouthamer-Loeber (1986) was the utility of the aggression-setting classification and the aggression-theft classification in differentially predicting theft, aggression, or arrest rates 5 years later. Briefly, this was indeed the case; analyses of variance showed that the fighting-setting classification predicted later aggression, self-reported theft, and yearly arrest rate. Those who fought at home and school showed the highest scores in each outcome measure compared with those who fought only at home or only at school. Post hoc analyses revealed that youngsters' fighting at school accounted for most of the effect in later antisocial behavior; fighting at home only was distinctly less predictive of antisocial outcomes.

For the aggression-theft classification, the analyses of variance showed a significant effect for self-reported theft, delinquent lifestyle, and rate of arrest, but *not* for various indicators of aggression at time 2. Post hoc tests revealed that the versatile youngsters (those who fought and stole), compared with all others, were most delinquent. The magnitude of effects for the same categories of delinquent behavior were considerably higher in the fighting and theft classification than in the fighting-setting classification. This resulted in different predictive yields, with fighting-setting better explaining later aggression and violence, and fighting-stealing accounting more for later delinquency and theft.

In summary, different classification schemes may have different yields and are likely to produce different interpretations about the relative importance of certain early child behaviors as predictors of specific outcomes. There is a need to expand these analyses to include other classification schemes and compare their predictive utility as well.

Classification schemes discussed so far, however, have been cross-sectional and static in nature. A more promising approach would be to examine a more dynamic classification of children on the basis of their *development* of problem behavior over time.

Dynamic Classification of Problem Behaviors: Developmental Pathways toward Serious Forms of Delinquency

In criminology, it has become common practice to classify youngsters on the basis of their first offense (e.g., Thomas, 1976). From a developmental perspective, it can be argued that classification on the basis of a single behavior is extremely limited, and does not necessarily reflect essential characteristics of the delinquent career. A developmental approach favors a classification based on the youngster's developmental history. Such a "dynamic classification" (Huizinga, 1979) has the advantage of being based on the mix of past problem behaviors rather than a single act, thus forming a better basis for the prediction of future delinquency or risk for psychopathology.

Although few studies have classified developmental histories or pathways (see, e.g., Frum, 1958), a review of longitudinal studies has provided evidence that there is more than one pathway to crime (Loeber, 1988). A pathway represents a group of individuals who experience behavioral development that is distinct from the behavioral development of other group(s) of individuals. A key feature of the concept of a pathway is that it takes into account individuals' history and temporal sequence of problem behavior on a continuum of increasing seriousness of problem behavior over time. Thus, the concept of a pathway allows individuals with varying degrees of deviance to be placed on one or more developmental trajectories.

Loeber et al. (1993) investigated pathways in the two oldest samples of the Pittsburgh Youth Study, who were studied between the ages of 10 and 16. The authors used retrospective data on onset (reported by the child and mother), combined with prospective data over six data waves. They found that the results best fitted three pathways (Figure 1.4): (1) the *overt pathway*, which represented an escalation from minor aggression (annoying others, bullying) to physical fighting, and eventually to violence (robbery,

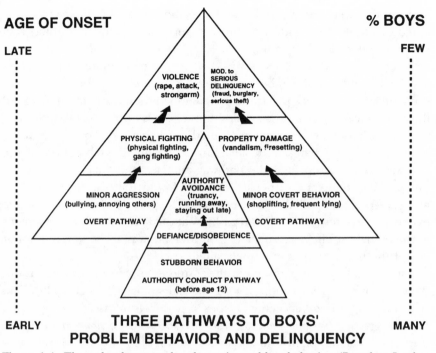

Figure 1.4. Three developmental pathways in problem behavior. (Based on Loeber et al., 1993)

rape, etc.); (2) the *covert pathway,* consisting first of minor covert acts (shoplifting and frequent lying), then property damage (fire setting, vandalism), and then more serious forms of theft (e.g., breaking and entering); and (3) the *authority conflict pathway,* which had as its first step stubborn behavior, followed by serious disobedience and defiance, and finally by authority avoidance before the age of 12 in the form of staying out late at night, truancy, or running away. A proportion of youth were classified as not fitting in more than one pathway, but a substantial group showed problem behavior characteristic of only a single pathway. Typically, the onset of authority conflict preceded the onset of overt or covert behavior (Loeber et al., 1993).

The three pathways were validated against the frequency of self-reported delinquency and the frequency of court petitions for delinquent acts. The rates of self-reported and official delinquency were the lowest for youth who were only in a single pathway. Youth simultaneously in two pathways, those in the overt and covert pathways and those in the covert and authority conflict pathways, had significantly higher rates of delinquency than those in the overt and authority conflict pathways. Those who were simultaneously in all three pathways (overt, covert, and authority conflict) also had high rates of delinquency.

It can be argued that boys vary in their involvement in disruptive behavior. Some exhibit problem behavior once or twice or only for a short time, while others show more persisting problem behavior. It can also be argued that the concept of pathways applies more to boys who persist than to boys who experiment but turn away from these behaviors. For that reason, Loeber, Keenan, Zhang, and Sieck (in press), in an elaboration of the pathway concept, repeated the pathway analyses while distinguishing between experimenters and persisters. They found that the three pathway models especially applied to the persisters. The persisters, more so than the experimenters, tended to enter a pathway at the first rather than later steps in the pathways. The percentage of nonfitters, that is, those who did not fit any of the pathways, was extremely small.

The formulation of pathways in these studies approximates conclusions drawn from an earlier review of longitudinal studies (Loeber, 1988). This review distinguished between two types of pathways in disruptive behavior: (a) an *aggressive/versatile pathway*, and (b) an exclusive *nonaggressive pathway*. The former explains the emergence of chronic offenders involved in both violent and property crime. Individuals in this group can be thought of as being in both the overt and covert pathways according to the empirically based formulation proposed by Loeber et al. (1993). In contrast, individuals in the nonaggressive pathway are thought to correspond to those in the covert pathway only.

In summary, the evidence pointed to multiple pathways rather than a single pathway in the development of disruptive problem behaviors in boys. The concept of pathways helped quantify different manifestations of problem behavior along dimensions of severity, while taking into account individuals' history of past problem behavior. The knowledge of pathways is important because it can help identify, at an early stage, juveniles who appear to be at highest risk for later maladjustment and can distinguish them from youth with minor and/or more transient problem behavior. Pathways can also aid in the specification of the type of problem behaviors that certain risk groups of youth are likely to experience next. Lastly, once pathways have been formulated, risk and causal variables can explain why some youth do not initiate problem behavior at all, why others get into less serious problem behavior temporarily and do not progress, and why a proportion of youth escalate in problem behavior and become seriously affected.

Diversification of Problem Behaviors over Time

The developmental perspective of problem behaviors implies that a group of youngsters will display exclusive problem behaviors, that is, those that occur in the absence of other categories of problematic behavior. The opposite is often the case, however; children often add new problem behaviors to their existing ones. This aggregation or "stacking" of disruptive behaviors is not uncommon, although its incidence may depend upon the behaviors in question. For example, the likelihood that hyperactive children, who have attention problems, will have chronic difficulties with academic tasks is probably higher than in the case of withdrawn children who do not have attention problems. It is very likely that hyperactive children are particularly at risk for the stacking of other problematic behaviors. This is schematically shown in Figure 1.5. It is thought that hyperactive children have a high risk of becoming oppositional, in part because obedience training by adults requires more intensive and longer-term efforts with hyperactive than with nonhyperactive children. A proportion of hyperactive/oppositional children are at risk of becoming aggressive as well; this, in turn, will impede their development of social skills. Each of these behav-

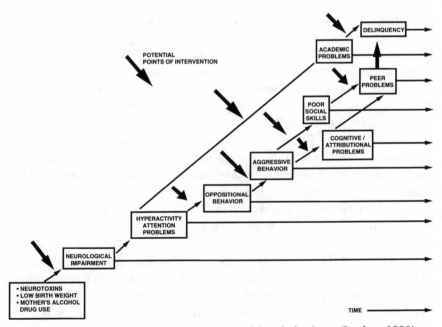

Figure 1.5. Developmental stacking of problem behaviors. (Loeber, 1990)

iors, once established, has a reasonably high stability in and of itself. It is thought that certain cognitive/attributional processes can also play into this, such as children's thinking others are out to get them and/or a slight provocation justifies hitting the other person. Aggression coupled with these cognitive strategies often influence these youngsters' peer relationships and impede normal classroom functioning, which may already be impaired by the attention problems. Eventually, repeated rule breaking and pushing of limits may evolve into delinquent acts.

It is probable that the direction of diversification of problem behavior is not random. For example, Loeber et al. (1993) in their analyses of developmental pathways found that boys in the overt pathway had a much higher likelihood of entering the covert pathway than the reverse. This suggests that aggressive boys are more at risk to diversify (and escalate) into concealing behaviors and delinquent types of activities, and that nonaggressive boys are likely to diversify (and escalate) in aggressive acts.

The stacking of problem behaviors implies that, given the stability of individual problem behaviors, some children diversify their problem behaviors over time. Typically, problem behaviors that develop later in the deviant developmental sequence are added onto developmentally earlier behaviors rather than replacing earlier behaviors.

Diversification and Desistance. The degree of stacking or diversification of problem behaviors has direct implications for the likelihood of desistance over time. Findings show that a high variety of disruptive behaviors is more predictive of the persistence of the problems than is a low variety. This thesis is supported in several studies, irrespective of whether the area examined is delinquent acts, disruptive behaviors, or substance use (Farrington, 1973; Kandel & Faust, 1975; Loeber, 1982, 1988; Robins, 1966). For example, data collected by Robins (1966), shown in Figure 1.6, demonstrates that when the number of juvenile conduct problem symptoms is less than three, the desistance rate in adult sociopathy or antisocial personality is nearly 35%, but this rate is less than 5% when the number of juvenile behaviors is 10 or more. The relationship is clearly nonlinear and accelerating with the number of early problem behaviors.

Transactional Effects among Problem Behaviors. It remains to be explained why the risk of adult antisocial behavior does not follow a linear relationship with the number of early disruptive behaviors. It is hypothesized here that the emergence of a particular problem behavior is often functionally related to preexisting problem behaviors, and that transac-

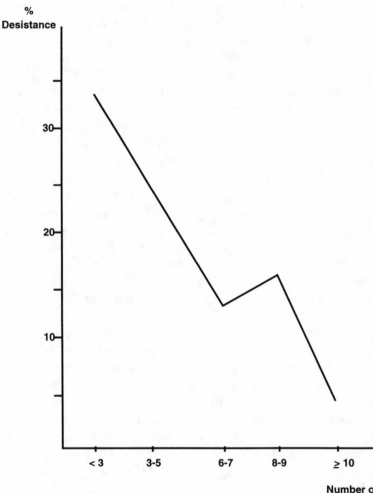

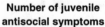

Figure 1.6. Percent desistance in adult sociopathy as a function of the number of juvenile problem behaviors. (Based on Robins, 1966, p. 143)

tions among the behaviors may help account for this effect. Transactional effects take place when an individual's practicing of one problem behavior reliably enhances the probability that he or she will also display another category of problem behavior. For example, studies in the area of children's aggression have shown that coercive interactions among children and between children and adults may escalate and lead to highly aggressive interchanges (Patterson, 1982). In this type of escalation, diverse behaviors take place, such as humiliation of others, arguing, and physical aggression.

In some families the observed frequency of the coercive interchanges can be extremely high and is thought to constitute many instances that seem to gradually improve the child's aggressive skills. Although the direct observations rarely reveal criminally violent acts, studies on assaultive adolescents show that they behaved more aggressively and were more domineering in the family home than any other family member, including the parents (Loeber, Weismann, & Reid, 1983; Madden & Harbin, 1983).

Turning to concealing or covert disruptive behaviors, the picture is more speculative due to the scarcity of behavioral analyses. It has now been well established that use of marijuana increases the probability of the use of hard drugs, such as heroin (Kandel, 1982). From this, the conclusion may be drawn that marijuana use "causes" heroin use. As has been pointed out by O'Donnell (1985), this is an incorrect inference. One possibility, not yet fully proven, is that individuals' marijuana use increases the likelihood that they will meet others who introduce them to other illegal drug use. Again, it is likely that transactional effects, probably involving a number of intervening variables, can help account for why some individuals who use marijuana regularly progress to heroin use and others do not.

Different transactional processes may apply to children's lying as it relates to other problem behaviors. A youngster who steals may cover up the theft by lying about his or her innocence, the whereabouts of the goods, and the like. Repeated lying may initially occur on a trial-and-error basis, and through repeated practice may develop into improved, difficult-to-detect lying in some youngsters. Frequent lying not only increases the positive benefits of theft, but may eventually facilitate future theft. For example, youngsters may begin lying to enable them to steal with minimal chance of detection.

Problem behaviors differ in terms of their potential transactional impact on other problem behaviors. For example, lying can facilitate the initiation and maintenance of a broad range of antisocial acts, including truancy, underage drinking, and the selling of stolen goods.

In short, there is much to be learned about factors that increase the probability of the stacking of problem behaviors. Except for studies on aggression, there is a scarcity of careful event-by-event analyses of the types of transactions among covert problem behaviors that increase the likelihood of the adoption of novel problem behaviors. Part of this scarcity has to do with the concealing nature and the relatively low base rate of many covert acts, which makes them difficult to study systematically. Diary methods and systematic, repeated interviews may be suitable tools for measuring the transactional aspects of these behaviors.

Some Conclusions about the Relationship between Behavioral Development and Intervention

The preceding review contains a number of implications for prevention and treatment, some obvious, others less so, which remain to be verified through systematic evaluation:

1. Although intervention can be aimed at stable problem behaviors, it can be argued that this requires more intensive effort than intervention aimed at an earlier developmental stage with lower stability of problem behavior.
2. The optimal period for intervention probably differs from one problem behavior to another, and should take into account when behaviors become more stable over time.
3. The choice of target behavior for intervention may depend in part on different manifestations of problem behaviors that emerge successively over time.
4. Early intervention necessarily has to rely on early risk indicators. Different classifications of these indicators can be made at different stages of children's development. Certain combinations of risk factors appear to bode ill for particular patterns of maladjustment later, and for that reason are relevant for use with specific rather than generic aims.
5. Intervention aimed at remission of all problem behaviors will have a higher probability of success when the number of problem behaviors is small rather than large.
6. Intervention will be more successful when applied to behaviors that are key to a number of other problem behaviors in a transactional or catalytic sense.
7. There are probably specific developmental pathways to the different antisocial outcomes. Interventions based on an appraisal of an individual's position on developmental pathways will be more informed and, therefore, may be more effective than interventions that ignore such information.

These tentative conclusions may appear rather abstract. A slightly more concrete example is shown in Figure 1.5, which graphically displays the development of hyperactivity, aggression, and a number of other problematic behaviors (Loeber, 1990). Each of the individual behaviors is thought to be relatively stable over time, resulting in a stacking of diversification of the problem behaviors.

Treatment can take place on several levels. Because of the diversification process in disruptive behaviors, an ideal treatment would need to deal with most, if not all, of the problem behaviors. At the same time, such intervention would probably combine treatment and prevention, in that it would also attempt to prevent novel problem behaviors that would typically emerge during the course of antisocial development.

Preventative interventions can take place at different points, as indicated by the bold arrows in Figure 1.5. For instance, one type of prevention may aim at reducing the likelihood of academic problems in hyperactive children. Another type of prevention could be directed to those children who are at risk for becoming chronically oppositional or aggressive as well. In either treatment or prevention, interventions can be optimized by a more precise knowledge of the course of antisocial development than is currently available.

It goes without saying that the discussion of possible points for intervention was limited by the focus in this chapter on the child's behavior only, and excluded many other possible risk factors, such as in the realms of family and peer relationships (see Loeber, 1990). A more precise delineation of the child's behavioral development, however, is seen here as a condition sine qua non for improving distinctions between risk factors and causes (Loeber & Le Blanc, 1990). It is through a better understanding of causes that we can expect a higher yield from interventions.

REFERENCES

American Psychiatric Association. (1980). *Diagnostic and statistical manual of mental disorders* (3rd ed.). Washington, DC: Author.

American Psychiatric Association. (1987). *Diagnostic and statistical manual of mental disorders* (3rd rev. ed.). Washington, DC: Author.

August, G. J., & Stewart, M. A. (1983). Familial subtypes of childhood hyperactivity. *Nervous and Mental Disease, 171,* 362–368.

Ball, J. C., Shaffer, J. W., & Nurco, D. (1983). Day to day criminality of heroin addicts in Baltimore – A study in the continuity of offense rates. *Drug and Alcohol Dependence, 12,* 119–142.

Blumstein, A., Cohen, J., Roth, J. A., & Visher, C. A. (Eds.). (1986). *Criminal careers and "career criminals."* Washington, DC: National Academy of Sciences.

Cadoret, R. J., & Stewart, M. A. (1991). An adoption study of attention deficit hyperactivity, aggression and their relationships to adult antisocial personality. *Comprehensive Psychiatry, 32,* 73–82.

Campbell, S. B., Breaux, A. M., Ewing, L. W., & Szumowski, E. K. (1984). A one-year follow-up study of parent-referred hyperactive preschool children. *Journal of the American Academy of Child Psychiatry, 23,* 243–249.

Campbell, S. B., Schleifer, M., & Weiss, G. (1978). Continuities in maternal reports and child behaviors over time in hyperactive and comparison groups. *Journal of Abnormal Child Psychology, 6,* 33–45.

Campbell, S. B., & Werry, J. S. (1986). Attention deficit disorder (Hyperactivity). In H. C. Quay & J. S. Werry (Eds.), *Psychopathological disorders of childhood* (3rd ed., pp. 111–155). New York: Wiley.

Carey, M. B., & McDevitt, S. C. (1978). Stability and change in individual temperament diagnoses from infancy to early childhood. *Journal of the American Academy of Child Psychiatry, 17,* 331–337.

Chamberlin, R. W. (1977). Can we identify a group of children at age two who are at high risk for the development of behavior or emotional problems in kindergarten and first grade? *Pediatrics, 59,* 971–981.

Charlebois, P., Le Blanc, M., Gagnon, C., Larivée, S., & Tremblay, R. (1993). Age trends in early behavioral predictors of serious antisocial behaviors. *Journal of Psychopathology and Behavioral Assessment, 15,* 23–41.

Coie, J. D., & Dodge, K. A. (1983). Continuities and changes in children's social status: A five-year longitudinal study. *Merrill-Palmer Quarterly, 29,* 261–282.

Dodge, K. A., Coie, J. D., & Brakke, N. P. (1982). Behavior patterns of socially rejected and neglected preadolescents: The roles of social approach and aggression. *Journal of Abnormal Child Psychology, 10,* 349–410.

Eron, L. D., Walder, L. O., & Lefkowitz, M. M. (1971). *Learning of aggression in children.* Boston: Little, Brown.

Fagot, B. I. (1984). The consequents of problem behavior in toddler children. *Journal of Abnormal Child Behavior, 12,* 385–395.

Farrington, D. P. (1973). Self-reports of deviant behavior: Predictive and stable? *Journal of Criminal Law and Criminology, 64,* 99–110.

Farrington, D. P. (1981). The prevalence of convictions. *British Journal of Criminology, 21,* 173–175.

Farrington, D. P., Loeber, R., & Van Kammen, W. B. (1990). Long-term criminal outcomes of hyperactivity-impulsivity-attention deficit and conduct problems in childhood. In L. Robins & M. Rutter (Eds.), *Straight and devious pathways to adulthood* (pp. 62–81). New York: Cambridge University Press.

Frick, P. J., Lahey, B. B., Loeber, R., Tannenbaum, L., Van Horn, Y., Christ, M. A. G., Hart, E. A., & Hanson, K. (1993). Oppositional defiant disorder and conduct disorder: A meta-analytic review of factor analyses and cross-validation in a clinic sample. *Clinical Psychology Review, 13,* 319–340.

Frum, H. S. (1958). Adult criminal offense trends following juvenile delinquency. *Journal of Criminal Law, Criminology, and Police Science, 49,* 29–49.

Gersten, J. C., Langner, T. S., Eisenberg, J. G., Simcha-Fagan, O., & McCarthy, E. D. (1976). Stability and change in types of behavioral disturbances of children and adolescents. *Journal of Abnormal Child Psychology, 4,* 111–127.

Gittelman, R., Mannuzza, S., Shenker, R., & Bonagura, N. (1985). Hyperactive boys almost grown up. *Archives of General Psychiatry, 42,* 937–947.

Glow, R. A., Glow, P. H., & Rump, E. E. (1982). The stability of child behavior disorders: One year test–retest study of Adelaide versions of the Conners Teacher and Parent Rating Scales. *Journal of Abnormal Child Psychology, 10,* 33–60.

Hart, E. L., Lahey, B. B., Loeber, R., Applegate, B., Green, S., & Frick, P. J. (1993). *Developmental change in attention-deficit hyperactivity disorder in boys: A four-year longitudinal study.* Unpublished manuscript. Yale Child Study Center, Yale University, New Haven, CT.

Hinshaw, S. P. (1987). On the distinction between attentional deficits/hyperactivity and conduct problems/aggression in child psychopathology. *Psychological Bulletin, 101,* 443–463.

Huesmann, L. R., Eron, L. D., Lefkowitz, M. M., & Walder, L. O. (1984). The ability of aggression over time and generations. *Developmental Psychology, 20,* 1120–1134.

Huizinga, D. (1979, April). *Dynamic typologies.* Paper presented at the 10th annual meeting of the Classification Society, Gainesville, FL.

Johnston, C., & Pelham, W. E. (1986). Teacher ratings predict peer ratings of aggression at 3-year follow-up in boys with attention deficit disorder with hyperactivity. *Journal of Consulting and Clinical Psychology, 59,* 571–572.

Kandel, D. B. (1982). Epidemiological and psychosocial perspectives on adolescent drug use. *Journal of the American Academy of Child Psychiatry, 21,* 328–347.

Kandel, D. B., & Faust, R. (1975). Sequence and stages in patterns of adolescent drug use. *Archives in General Psychiatry, 32,* 923–932.

Klein, M. W. (1971). *Street gangs and street workers.* Englewood Cliffs, NJ: Prentice-Hall.

Klein, M. W. (1984). Offense specialization and versatility among juveniles. *British Journal of Criminology, 24,* 185–194.

Kohlberg, L., Ricks, D., & Snarey, J. (1984). Childhood development as a predictor of adaptation in adulthood. *Genetic Psychology Monographs, 110,* 91–172.

Kupersmidt, J. B., & Coie, J. D. (1990). Preadolescent peer status, aggression, and school adjustment as predictors of externalizing problems in adolescence. *Child Development, 61,* 1350–1362.

La Greca, A. M., & Quay, H. C. (1982). Behavior disorders of children. In N. S. Endler & J. M. V. Hunt (Eds.), *Personality and behavior disorders* (2nd ed.). New York: Wiley.

Loeber, R. (1982). The stability of antisocial and delinquent child behavior: A review. *Child Development, 53,* 1431–1446.

Loeber, R. (1988). Natural histories of conduct problems, delinquency, and associated substance use. In B. B. Lahey & A. E. Kazdin (Eds.), *Advances in clinical child psychology* (Vol. 11, pp. 73–124). New York: Plenum.

Loeber, R. (1990). Development and risk factors of juvenile antisocial behavior and delinquency. *Clinical Psychology Review, 10,* 1–41.

Loeber, R., & Dishion, T. J. (1984). Boys who fight: Familial and antisocial correlates. *Journal of Consulting and Clinical Psychology, 52,* 759–768.

Loeber, R., Green, S. M., Keenan, K., & Lahey, B. B. (1994). *Early predictors of the onset of conduct disorder in a four-year longitudinal study.* Unpublished manuscript. Western Psychiatric Institute and Clinic, University of Pittsburgh, PA.

Loeber, R., Keenan, K., Zhang, Q., & Sieck, W. (in press). *Boys' experimentation and persistence in developmental pathways toward serious delinquency. Development and Psychopathology.*

Loeber, R., & Le Blanc, M. (1990). Toward a developmental criminology. In M. Tonry & N. Morris (Eds.), *Crime and justice* (Vol. 12, pp. 375–473). Chicago: University of Chicago Press.

Loeber, R., & Schmaling, K. B. (1985a). Empirical evidence for overt and covert patterns of antisocial conduct problems: A meta-analysis. *Journal of Abnormal Child Behavior, 13,* 337–352.

Loeber, R., & Schmaling, K. B. (1985b). The utility of differentiating between mixed and pure forms of antisocial child behavior. *Journal of Abnormal Child Psychology, 13,* 315–336.

Loeber, R., & Stouthamer-Loeber, M. (1986). Unpublished data. Western Psychiatric Institute and Clinic, University of Pittsburgh, Pittsburgh, PA.

Loeber, R., & Stouthamer-Loeber, M. (1987). Prediction. In H. Quay (Ed.), *Handbook of juvenile delinquency* (pp. 325–382). New York: Wiley.

Loeber, R., Tremblay, R. E., Gagnon, C., & Charlebois, P. (1989). Continuity and desistance in disruptive boys' early fighting in school. *Development and Psychopathology, 1,* 39–50.

Loeber, R., Weismann, W., & Reid, J. B. (1983). Family interaction of assaultive adolescents, stealers, and nondelinquents. *Journal of Abnormal Child Psychology, 11,* 1–14.

Loeber, R., Wung, P., Keenan, K., Giroux, B., Stouthamer-Loeber, M., Van Kammen, W. B., & Maughan, B. (1993). Developmental pathways in disruptive child behavior. *Development and Psychopathology, 5,* 101–132.

Madden, D. J., & Harbin, H. T. (1983). Family structures of assaultive adolescents. *Journal of Marital and Family Therapy, 9,* 311–316.

Magnusson, D. (1988). *Individual development from an interactional perspective: A longitudinal study.* Hillsdale, NJ: Erlbaum.

Mannuzza, S., Klein, R. G., Bessler, A., Malloy, P., & LaPadula, M. (1993). Adult outcome of hyperactive boys. Educational achievement, occupational rank, and psychiatric status. *Archives of General Psychiatry, 50,* 565–576.

Mannuzza, S., Klein, R. G., Konig, P. H., & Giampino, T. (1989). Hyperactive boys almost grown up. IV. Criminality and its relationship to psychiatric status. *Archives of General Psychiatry, 46,* 1073–1079.

Matheny, A. P. (1983). A longitudinal twin study of stability of components from Bayley's infant behavior record. *Child Development, 54,* 356–360.

Mitchell, S., & Rosa, P. (1981). Boyhood behavior problems as precursors of criminality: A fifteen year follow-up study. *Journal of Child Psychology and Psychiatry, 22,* 19–33.

Moskowitz, D. S., Schwartzman, A. E., & Ledingham, J. E. (1985). Stability and change in aggression and withdrawal in middle childhood and early adolescence. *Journal of Abnormal Psychology, 94,* 30–41.

Nurco, D. N., Shaffer, J. W., Ball, J. C., & Kinlock, T. W. (1985). Trends in the commission of crime among narcotic addicts over successive periods of addiction and nonaddiction. *American Journal of Drug and Alcohol Abuse, 10,* 481–490.

O'Donnell, J. A. (1985). Interpreting progression from one drug to another. In L. N. Robins (Ed.), *Studying drug abuse.* New Brunswick, NJ: Rutgers University Press.

Offord, D. R., Sullivan, K., Allen, N., & Abrams, N. (1979). Delinquency and hyperactivity. *Journal of Nervous & Mental Disorder, 167,* 734–741.

Olweus, D. (1979). Stability of aggressive reaction patterns in males: A review. *Psychological Bulletin, 86,* 852–857.

Patterson, G. R. (1982). *Coercive family interactions.* Eugene, OR: Castalia Press.

Richman, N., Stevenson, J., & Graham, P. J. (1982). *Preschool to school: A behavioral study.* London: Academic Press.

Richman, N., Stevenson, J., & Graham, P. (1985). Sex differences in outcome of pre-school behavior problems. In A. R. Nicol (Ed.), *Longitudinal studies in child psychology and psychiatry.* New York: Wiley.

Robins, L. N. (1966). *Deviant children grow up: A sociological and psychiatric study of sociopathic personality.* Baltimore: Williams & Wilkins.

Roff, J. D. (1986). Identification of boys at high risk for delinquency. *Psychological Reports, 58,* 615–618.

Roff, M., Sells, S. B., & Golden, M. M. (1972). *Social adjustment and personality development in children.* Minneapolis: University of Minnesota Press.

Routh, D. K., Schroeder, C. S., & O'Tuama, L. (1974). Development of activity level in children. *Developmental Psychology, 10,* 163–168.

Rutter, M. (1982). Epidemiological-longitudinal approaches to the study of development. In W. A. Collins (Ed.), *The concept of development.* Hillsdale, NJ: Erlbaum.

Savage, L. J., & Simpson, D. D. (1981). Drug use and crime during a four-year post-treatment follow up. *American Journal of Drug and Alcohol Abuse, 8,* 1–16.

Schachar, R., Rutter, M., & Smith, A. (1981). The characteristics of situationally and pervasively hyperactive children: Implications for syndrome definition. *Journal of Child Psychology and Psychiatry*, 22, 375–392.

Spivack, G. (1983). *High risk early behaviors indicating vulnerability to delinquency in the community and school – a 15-year longitudinal study.* Report to the Office of Juvenile Justice and Delinquency Prevention. Philadelphia: Hahnemann University.

Sroufe, L. A. (1979). The coherence of individual development. *American Psychologist*, 34, 834–841.

Stouthamer-Loeber, M. (1991). Young children's verbal misrepresentations of reality. In K. J. Rotenberg (Ed.), *Children's interpersonal trust: Sensitivity to lying, deception, and promise violation* (pp. 20–42). New York: Springer-Verlag.

Thomas, C. W. (1976). Are status offenders really different? *Crime and Delinquency*, 22, 438–455.

Thomas, A., Chess, S., & Birch, H. G. (1968). *Temperament and behavior disorders in children.* New York: New York University Press.

Van Kammen, W. B., & Loeber, R. (1994). Are fluctuations in delinquent activities related to the onset and offset of juvenile illegal drug use and drug dealing? *Journal of Drug Issues*, 24, 9–24.

Werner, E. E. (1987). Vulnerability and resiliency in children at risk for delinquency: A longitudinal study from birth to young adulthood. In J. D. Burchard & S. N. Burchard (Eds.), *Prevention of delinquent behavior* (pp. 16–43). Newbury Park: Sage.

West, D. J., & Farrington, D. P. (1977). *The delinquent way of life.* London: Heinemann.

CHAPTER TWO

Delinquent Friends and Delinquent Behavior:
TEMPORAL AND DEVELOPMENTAL PATTERNS

DELBERT S. ELLIOTT
SCOTT MENARD

ABSTRACT: The relationship between delinquent peer group association and delinquent behavior is examined in detail, beginning with an analysis of the onset of delinquent behavior and the onset of having delinquent friends. It appears from this analysis that the onset of exposure to delinquent friends typically precedes the onset of one's own illegal behavior. Next, the developmental progression of delinquent behavior and association with delinquent peers over the adolescent years (ages 11–20) is examined. This analysis indicates that adolescents tend to gradually become more involved with more delinquent friends, and to gradually become more involved in more delinquent behavior, from early to middle adolescence, and then to become less involved in both delinquent peer groups and delinquent behavior as they enter young adulthood. Some association with delinquent peers typically precedes initiation of minor delinquent behavior, but it also appears to be the case that after onset, some illegal behavior precedes involvement in more delinquent peer groups. These patterns are further confirmed in a structural equation model of the relationship among delinquent peer group bonding (a product of the delinquency of one's friends and the amount of time one spends with one's friends), belief that it is wrong to commit illegal acts, and delinquent behavior. The structural equation model indicates that the influence of delinquent peer group bonding on delinquent behavior is consistently stronger than the influence of delinquent behavior on delinquent peer group bonding. These results are more consistent with social learning theory than with either control theory or interactional theory.

This research was supported by grants from the Antisocial and Violent Behavior Branch, National Institute of Mental Health (MH27552), and the National Institute for Juvenile Justice and Delinquency Prevention, Office of Juvenile Justice and Delinquency Prevention, U.S. Department of Justice (78-JN-AX-003).

28

Delinquent Friends and Delinquent Behavior: Temporal and Developmental Patterns

One of the most stable and well-established findings in delinquency research is that the delinquent behavior of an individual is positively related to the actual or perceived delinquent behavior of that individual's friends (Akers, Krohn, Lanza-Kaduce, & Radosevich, 1979; Elliott, Huizinga, & Ageton, 1985; Elliott, Huizinga, & Menard, 1989; Elliott & Voss, 1974; Erickson & Empey, 1965; Hardt & Peterson, 1968; Jensen, 1972; Kandel, 1973; Kercher, 1988; Krohn, 1974; Matsueda, 1982; Matsueda & Heimer, 1987; Menard & Morse, 1984; Reiss & Rhodes, 1964; Short, 1957; Voss, 1964). Scholars disagree, however, about the proper interpretation of this relationship. Explanations that have been proposed for this relationship include: (1) the suggestion that delinquent behavior and having delinquent friends are really different measures of the same thing (Farrington, 1986b; Gottfredson & Hirschi, 1987; Loeber, 1987; West, 1985); (2) the social learning theory explanation that exposure to delinquent friends leads to delinquent behavior (Akers, 1985; Bandura & Walters, 1963; Burgess & Akers, 1966; Elliott, Ageton, & Canter, 1979; Sutherland, 1947); and (3) the social control theory explanation that delinquent behavior leads to the acquisition of delinquent friends (Glueck & Glueck, 1950; Gottfredson & Hirschi, 1987; Hirschi, 1969).

Rationales for the second and third explanations follow directly from social learning and social control theory, respectively, and may be found in the sources cited above. The argument that delinquent behavior and delinquent peers are two indicators of the same phenomenon (delinquency) has been raised by several authors and involves both conceptual and measurement issues. Conceptually, the issue is whether delinquency refers to an observable class of illegal behaviors or to some underlying, unobservable, individual predisposition to deviance, for example, what Farrington (1988) calls a "criminal potential." If one is interested in an unobservable individual potential for deviance, then one might employ both association with delinquent peers and delinquent behavior (and perhaps other variables as well) as indicators of this latent trait. This is essentially what Farrington suggests. Given this conceptualization, the interesting theoretical question about a possible causal role of delinquent peers in the onset of delinquent behavior is dismissed by definition.[1]

---

[1] We respect the right of each investigator to define her or his research questions, but we do not believe this conceptualization of delinquency will advance our

On the other hand, if delinquency is conceptualized as involvement in an observable class of illegal behaviors, one's own involvement in delinquency is conceptually distinct from her or his friends' involvement in delinquent acts and the question of the causal relationship between these variables remains a viable question that can be examined empirically as long as these two conceptual variables can be measured independently. Our interest in this essay is in delinquency defined as an observable class of illegal behavioral acts, not as an indicator of some unobservable individual predisposition to illegal behavior. We can thus entertain the hypothesis that involvement with delinquent friends is a cause of delinquent behavior without danger of tautology.

The question remains whether these two conceptual variables can be measured independently. This is the primary issue raised by Hirschi (1987) and Gottfredson and Hirschi (1987). If both measures are obtained from self-reports from respondents, if respondents report on both their own and their friends' delinquency, Gottfredson and Hirschi claim that the only way respondents can know about their friends' delinquency is by (1) their co-involvement in the delinquent acts, (2) the imputation of their own behavior to their friends, (3) the imputation of friendship to people like themselves, or (4) by "hearsay." They thus conclude that "self-reported peer delinquency is just another measure of self-reported delinquency" (Gottfredson & Hirschi, 1987, p. 597). It is curious that Gottfredson and Hirschi do not allow for the possibility of witnessing a friend's involvement in delinquent acts without being a participant. They also dismiss reports based upon the respondent's having been told by eyewitnesses about a friend's delinquent behavior or the friend's own credible (and perhaps verified by others) admission to the respondent of involvement in delin-

---

understanding of its etiology. Given this conceptualization and operationalization, one may not use "crime potential" as an explanation for delinquent behavior, for any such statement would be a tautology. Further, by definition, this approach dismissed long-standing theoretical propositions about major explanatory variables in the etiology of delinquency, rendering empirical tests of these theoretical claims impossible. Finally, we suspect that the conceptualization of delinquency as an unobservable or latent variable is sometimes the substitution of available methodology for theoretical conceptualization – a case of the methodological tail wagging the theoretical dog. We have no objection to the use of a latent construct of delinquency or delinquent lifestyle if that conceptualization is theoretically grounded. Our concern is that the methodology not dictate the theory.

quent acts as invalid data. Nevertheless, this is an important measurement issue that must be addressed.

Those who claim that the respondents' reports of their friends' delinquent behavior and their own delinquent behavior are measures of the same thing base this assertion on the fact that measures of these two variables are consistently and strongly correlated, together with the claim that most delinquent behavior is group behavior. Logically, the correlation may indicate a direct, indirect, or spurious causal relationship, as well as a conceptual or empirical unity. Instead of being indicators of the same concept or of an unobservable latent variable, we may view delinquent behavior and having delinquent friends as indicators of two observable, conceptually distinct variables, one of which causes the other (mutual causation is also possible) or both of which share a common antecedent cause.

With regard to the argument that delinquency is group behavior, we believe the case is overstated. Studies of the group nature of delinquency provide mixed evidence at best. Some offenses, such as substance use, are committed primarily in groups, but others, such as assaults (Erickson & Jensen, 1977), burglaries, and robberies (Reiss, 1986) are primarily solitary offenses. Four of the 10 criminal offenses examined by Erickson and Jensen (excluding substance use offenses) involved as much or more solitary offending as co-offending. Further, rates of solitary as opposed to group offending appear to vary by age, race, and gender (Reiss, 1986). Reiss also cited evidence that the modal size of "groups" in group offending is only two or three, and Miller (1982) estimated that two-thirds of all collectively executed youth crimes are committed by two individuals.[2] Based on these patterns, the presence of others is clearly not a necessary condition for delinquent behavior, and any of the three explanations for the relationship between delinquent behavior and having delinquent friends may be plausible.

Progress toward resolution of the disagreement among the three alternative explanations can be greatly facilitated by a knowledge of the temporal order in which onset and changes in delinquent behavior and having

[2] Our own data on co-offending for 19 separate offenses included on the self-reported delinquency (SRD) measure for wave 6 of the National Youth Survey indicate that for 11 of these offense types, the majority of reported offenses involved no co-offenders. With the exception of burglary, the proportion of reported offenses with no co-offending were 40% or greater for all of the remaining offense types. For burglary, only 29% of the self-reported offenses involved no co-offending.

delinquent friends occur. Because a cause must temporally as well as logically precede an effect (see, e.g., Williamson, Karp, Dalphin, & Gray, 1982, pp. 218–219), knowledge of the temporal order of onset of delinquency and having delinquent friends would help us decide between the social learning (delinquent friends come first) and social control (delinquent behavior comes first) theoretical explanations. In addition, knowledge of the temporal order in which changes occur in the two variables may reveal developmental patterns that further specify the relationship between the two variables.

Until recently, longitudinal data that would allow a direct test of these three competing explanations for the relationship between delinquent peers and delinquent behavior have been either unavailable or unused, and tests of the control and learning theory hypotheses have been performed by using statistical techniques to infer causal order from cross-sectional data. Hepburn (1976) used partial correlation analysis and found support for the sequence postulated by control theory. Matsueda (1982) used LISREL and found support for the ordering suggested by learning (differential association) theory. Both Hepburn and Matsueda acknowledged the limitations of their cross-sectional methods, and Matsueda indicated that longitudinal data were needed to conclusively establish the correct temporal order. Gottfredson and Hirschi (1987) cited the absence of longitudinal research on the temporal order of delinquent peers and delinquent behavior as evidence of the sterility of longitudinal research to date. The issue is a critical one for deciding among competing theories of delinquent behavior. As Hirschi (1987, p. 198) stated, "A major point of contention between control and learning theories is the causal ordering of delinquency and involvement with delinquent friends. Control theory says delinquency comes first."

Yet another perspective suggests that both social learning and social control theories are each half right. Thornberry's (1987) interactional perspective asserts that delinquent behavior and delinquent peer group association mutually reinforce each other; each is both cause and effect. At each stage of adolescence (early, middle, and late), according to interactional theory, delinquent behavior has a positive influence on association with delinquent peers, and association with delinquent peers has a positive influence on delinquent behavior. Thornberry (1987, p. 872) explicitly suggests that "An attempt to resolve the somewhat tedious argument over the temporal priority of associations and behavior is less productive theoretically than capitalizing on the interactive nature of human behavior and treating the relationship as it probably is: a reciprocal one."

Whether the relationship between delinquent peer group association and delinquent behavior reflects a single concept, a unidirectional causal relationship, or a reciprocal, bidirectional causal relationship remains an empirical question. In the present study, we use longitudinal data to evaluate the relative amount of support for control theory, learning theory, interactional theory, and the equivalence hypothesis, and to identify and describe developmental patterns involving delinquent behavior and having delinquent friends.

Data, Analysis, and Measurement

Data for this study were taken from the National Youth Survey (NYS), a prospective longitudinal study that has been described in detail elsewhere (Elliott & Ageton, 1980; Elliott & Huizinga, 1983; Elliott et al., 1985). The NYS follows a national probability sample of 1,725 youth, aged 11–17 in 1976, and provides data on self-reported delinquency, delinquency of friends, involvement with friends, and other variables relevant to the study of delinquent behavior. The analysis reported here is based upon the first six waves of data covering the years 1976–80 and 1983.

Our analysis proceeds in three stages. First, we analyze the onset of delinquent behavior and exposure to delinquent friends. This first analysis focuses on the beginning of the process of delinquent behavior and delinquent peer group association, in an effort to determine which comes first, exposure or delinquency. Second, we provide an extended examination of developmental patterns of delinquent behavior and exposure to delinquent friends, culminating in a description of the sequencing of changes in delinquent behavior and exposure to delinquent friends in adolescence. Although the developmental patterns described in this second analysis are age-related, they are not determined by age, and the focus is on the *stage* of involvement in delinquent behavior and exposure to delinquent friends, with age as a secondary consideration. Third and finally, we present the results of a structural equation model of the relationships among delinquent behavior, exposure to delinquent friends, and beliefs that it is wrong to engage in illegal behaviors. This third analysis places the results of our earlier analysis within a somewhat broader theoretical context, and helps resolve some questions of causal influence raised in the analysis of developmental processes.

Delinquent Behavior

We used three measures of delinquent behavior in this study. *Index offending* is a scale described in Elliott et al. (1985) that includes burglary, theft of over $50, motor vehicle theft, strongarm robbery, sexual assault, aggravated assault, and gang fighting.[3] *Minor offending* is a subset of the 22-item general delinquency scale described in Elliott et al. (1985). In the present study, minor offending excludes index offenses and also excludes status offenses, acts such as runaway and sexual intercourse, which would not be illegal if committed by adults. It includes such non-index offenses as larceny less than $50, receiving stolen goods, prostitution, selling marijuana or hard drugs, simple assault, joyriding, and disorderly conduct. All the offenses in both the index and minor offense scales are offenses that would be illegal if committed by an adult. *General offending* is here defined as minor delinquency plus index offending plus marijuana and hard drug (heroin, cocaine, amphetamine, barbiturate, hallucinogen) use. As a summary measure that incorporates both of the other measures of delinquency, general offending is used only in the analysis of temporal priority. The analysis of developmental patterns focuses on minor and index offending, and excludes different types of substance use, because our principal concern is with delinquency. Also, we know that the onset of delinquency consistently precedes the onset of substance use for the NYS sample (Elliott et al., 1989; Huizinga, Menard, & Elliott, 1989).

For purposes of analyzing transitions among offense types, we have categorized respondents in each year as either *nonoffenders* (no minor offenses and no index offenses), *minor offenders* (at least one minor offense, but no index offenses), or *index offenders* (at least one index offense, regardless of the number of minor offenses). A small proportion of the sample in each year (0.4% to 1.3%) reported committing at least one index offense but no minor offenses. Because this proportion was so small, they were included with respondents who reported committing both index and minor offenses, rather than examining them as a separate category. Most of the individuals classified as index offenders therefore have reported committing both index and minor offenses.[4]

[3] The inclusion of gang fighting in the index offense scale is justified primarily because follow-up questions about these offenses indicated that 66% involved either serious injury or the use of a weapon. For a more detailed justification, see Elliott, Ageton, Huizinga, Knowles, & Canter (1983). Note that one may be involved in gang fights without naming others involved in gang fights as friends (for our measure of exposure).

[4] Our use of the broad minor, general, and index offense scales reflects the concerns raised by Skogan (1981), who argued against the use of specific-item measures and in favor of broader conceptual categories because the specific-item

Peer Group Types, Exposure, and Delinquent Peer Group Bonding

Exposure to delinquent peers was measured with an 8-item scale that asked respondents what proportion of their friends had committed a variety of delinquent acts: (1) vandalism, (2) theft of less than $5, (3) theft of more than $50, (4) assault, (5) burglary, (6) selling hard drugs, (7) suggesting that the respondent break the law, and (8) marijuana use. Scale scores potentially ranged from 8 (no friends committing any of the eight acts) to 40 (all friends committing all eight acts). The response set for the eight items in this measure involved a 5-point scale: 1 = none, 2 = few, 3 = some, 4 = most, 5 = all. For the structural equation model in the last analysis in this essay, we used the variable *delinquent peer group bonding*, as described in Elliott et al. (1989). Delinquent peer group bonding is the product of exposure to delinquent peers and involvement with peers, thus measuring both how delinquent one's friends are and how much time one spends with those friends. For more detail on this measure, see Elliott et al. (1989).

To analyze developmental patterns, we constructed a typology of peer groups using a slightly longer version of the exposure scale that included alcohol use and cheating on school tests. Five peer group types were identified. *Saints* (with apologies to Chambliss 1973) are respondents who report having two or more friends, *none* of whom are known to be involved in any of the acts described in the 10-item scale of exposure to delinquent peers. Respondents in *prosocial* peer groups report a score from 11 to 15 on the 10-item scale, indicating a very low level of exposure to delinquency (e.g., from at least a few friends involved in one offense to all friends involved in no more than one offense). *Mixed* peer group types are indicated by a score from 16 to 24, a more substantial level of known delinquency on the part of friends (e.g., at least a few involved in six of the listed offenses or most friends involved in at least two offenses). Respondents in *delinquent* peer groups (indicated by a score of 25 or more) have high levels of exposure to delinquency by peers (e.g., involvement in more than half of the scale behaviors by all of one's friends, or involvement in all of the behaviors by some of one's friends). Not all youth are in one of the above peer groups,

---

measures are more susceptible to measurement error. We should note that the offense types here are not the same as those used previously (Dunford & Elliott, 1984; Elliott, Dunford, & Huizinga, 1987) for studying patterned or career offenders. The present study uses a different typology, first because the focus in the present study is not on career offending, and second to more clearly specify the onset of both minor and index offending.

however. Respondents who reported that they had no friends, or had only one friend, were classified as *isolates*. Isolates have minimal ties to peers. Because they typically report having no friends, we have no peer bonding scores for respondents classified as isolates.

A potential drawback of both exposure to delinquent peers scales is that they are probably too conservative in detecting exposure to delinquent behavior. Our measures of delinquency include a total of 30 separate items (24 excluding illicit drug use), representing 19 separate offenses (17 excluding illicit drug use; three items each were used for larceny, robbery, and simple assault, two items were used for sale of illicit drugs, and six items were used in the general offending scale for illicit drug use, one to represent marijuana use and five to represent hard drug use). Exposure to friends involved in delinquent behavior as measured above does not include exposure to offenses such as rape, sale of marijuana, use of hard drugs, disorderly conduct, carrying a hidden weapon, or receiving stolen goods, all of which are included among our delinquency measures. In addition, we asked only about the delinquency of a specific set of nominated friends. Exposure to delinquency could also occur as a result of exposure to the illegal behavior of parents or other relatives, especially brothers or sisters.[5] These two limitations to our measures of exposure to delinquent others potentially bias our data toward finding delinquent behavior prior to exposure to delinquency.

Belief

The belief scale consists of nine items, which ask how wrong it is (very wrong; wrong; a little bit wrong; or not wrong at all) to commit each of nine illegal acts. With the exception of how wrong it is to encourage someone to break the law (which was not a question that NYS respondents were asked), the belief scale items are identical to the items in the exposure to delinquency scale. Because the focus of this study is on the relationship between exposure to delinquent peers and delinquent behavior, the belief variable plays no role in most of the analyses in this chapter, but in the final analysis,

---

[5] It is possible that exposure to parents' or siblings' illegal behavior plays little role in the etiology of illegal behavior (Sampson & Laub, 1993). In some contexts, however, there is substantial evidence for intrafamilial transmission of illegal behavior. Examples include Hispanic gangs in Los Angeles (Vigil, 1988), the intergenerational transmission of domestic violence (Widom, 1989), and the relationship between the drug use of parents and their children (Dembo, Grandon, LaVoie, Schmeidler, & Burgos, 1986).

it is important to include belief when we analyze a multivariate model of the relationship between exposure to delinquent peers and delinquent behavior.[6]

Onset of Delinquent Behavior and Exposure to Delinquent Friends

The first analysis focuses on a strong test (Platt 1964) of three competing hypotheses about the relationship between delinquent behavior and association with delinquent peers. Hypothesis 1 states that respondents' reports of their own delinquent behavior and that of their friends are empirically indistinct. The operational consequence of this hypothesis is that onset or initiation of the respondent's own delinquent behavior should occur at the same time or in the same measurement interval (in this case, in the same year) as the reported onset of association with delinquent peers. If this is true, we should not be able to ascertain which comes first, exposure to delinquent peers or one's own delinquent behavior. Hypothesis 2 is the learning theory hypothesis that exposure to delinquent friends precedes onset of delinquent behavior. Hypothesis 3 is the control theory hypothesis that onset of delinquent behavior precedes the onset of exposure to delinquent friends. Operationally, if onset of delinquency typically precedes exposure to delinquent friends, then hypotheses 1 and 2 are falsified; if exposure to delinquent friends typically precedes onset of delinquent behavior, then hypotheses 1 and 3 are falsified; and if we are unable to determine any temporal sequencing, we cannot rule out hypothesis 1 and no empirical test of hypotheses 2 and 3 is possible.

To test these competing hypotheses, we examined the sequence of onset of exposure to delinquent peers and the onset of delinquent behavior. Onset of exposure to delinquent peers is defined as the earliest report of being in a peer group in which *any* member of the peer group engages in

---

[6] According to Elliott et al. (1989), belief appears to have no direct effect on illegal behavior, and Matsueda (1989) found that delinquency affects belief more than belief affects delinquency. Our own analyses, some of them unpublished, suggest that the direct effect of belief on delinquency is weak and sometimes not statistically significant, but aside from delinquent peer group bonding, it is the variable most predictive of illegal behavior, especially illicit drug use, and the strongest predictor of illegal behavior to emerge from the control theory perspective. We include belief in the present model, risking the possibility that it is unnecessary, in order to avoid the more serious danger (Berry & Feldman, 1985) of excluding from the model a variable that should be included.

any of the eight delinquent acts used in constructing the exposure scale. This is equivalent to being a member of any peer group type other than the saints. Because we have no data on the delinquency of the friends (if any) of respondents classified as isolates, isolates are excluded as a valid peer group type in this analysis. Less than 5% of the sample are lost by excluding isolates from this analysis; all others report membership in at least one of the other peer group types between 1976 and 1983.

We consider the onset of delinquency in general as the initial reporting of any delinquent act (general offending). The onset of serious delinquency involves the initial reporting of an index offense. In this analysis, for both onset of exposure and onset of delinquency, we have adopted an absolute standard: *any* exposure or *any* delinquency constitutes onset, if there has been no previous exposure or delinquent behavior, respectively. These are strict criteria, but no other definition would be clearer or less arbitrary. Temporal order is determined by comparing the year of onset of exposure with the year of onset of delinquency. Note that although we have restricted our measure of exposure and delinquent behavior to acts that would be criminal if committed by an adult, there is nothing in principle that would prohibit inclusion of status offenses in both measures. We choose to focus here, however, on offenses for which illegality does not depend on the age of the actor.

Temporal Priority and Censoring

Left censoring is a problem that occurs when an event of interest, in this case the onset of delinquent behavior or exposure to delinquent peers, occurs prior to the initial wave of data collection. Specific to the present study, exposure to delinquent friends and delinquent behavior is already present for a substantial number of respondents in 1976, the first wave (year) of data collection in the NYS, when the respondents were 11 to 17 years old. For these cases we cannot ascertain the temporal priority of exposure and delinquency, although we know the onset of both occurred prior to or during 1976. We also have some *right censoring*, respondents who initiated neither exposure to delinquent peers nor delinquent behavior over the 7-year period of observation (1976–83), but who may initiate either or both at some time in the future. Again, we cannot ascertain the temporal order for these cases.[7] Levels of each type of censoring vary with the measure of

---

[7] While the most apparent form of left censoring involves respondents who report-

delinquent behavior used in the analysis and are reported in the tables. Right censoring is minimal (2%) but left censoring is often substantial (from 18% to 60%).

The critical issue with censored data is whether these unobserved sequences are the same as the sequences we observe during the study. Given the low level of right censoring in the data, this form of censoring does not appear to be a significant problem. For left censoring, this problem appears more serious. As a partial check on the effects of left censoring, we present the sequences of onset for our two youngest birth cohorts (ages 11 and 12 in 1976) and for two of our older birth cohorts (ages 15 and 16 in 1976) in addition to the sequence for the sample in general. It is unlikely that we have completely missed these events for 11- and 12-year-old respondents; that is, it is unlikely that 11- to 12-year-old respondents have experienced both the *onset* and the *termination* of delinquent behavior and exposure to delinquent peers prior to wave 1 of the study. The experiencing of both onset and termination of both delinquent behavior and exposure to delinquent peers prior to the first wave of data collection is more likely to arise for our older cohorts (e.g., respondents age 15 and 16 in 1976). Further, assuming minimal cohort differences, we can use the experience of these two age cohorts over the first four waves of the study to approximate the unobserved (censored) experience of the 15- and 16-year-old cohorts. Should the onset sequences for these younger and older cohorts be markedly different, this would indicate that the sequence is age-dependent, and would complicate the interpretation of the sequence observed in the general sample. As it turns out, however, the sequences for older and younger cohorts are quite similar, suggesting that the sequences may not be age-dependent.

Results

Table 2.1 presents the results of the temporal order analysis for the full NYS sample and for the younger and older cohorts. Five sequential patterns are

---

ed *both* exposure to delinquent peers and delinquent behavior at wave 1 (1976), it is also possible that both the onset and termination of exposure and delinquent behavior have occurred for some respondents prior to the start of the study, and neither is reported at any time during the study period. In our analysis these respondents would appear as right censored cases when in reality they are left censored cases. The likelihood of this type of left censoring might be substantial for respondents who were 17 at wave 1 but it should be extremely low for respondents who were 11 or 12 at wave 1.

presented in each section of the table. The first row in each part of the table indicates the number and percent of respondents who initiated neither exposure nor delinquency (of a given type, as indicated in the columns) over the study period. For these respondents, temporal order is not ascertainable because neither exposure nor delinquency has occurred between 1976 and 1983. The first category is thus a measure of right censoring in the data. The second row in each table includes all of the respondents who were both exposed to delinquent peers and committed delinquent acts in 1976, the first year of the survey. These respondents may have initiated either or both, exposure or delinquency, *in* or *before* 1976. The second category gives us an indication of the extent of left censoring in our data.

The third category represents respondents who initiated exposure and delinquency *after* 1976, but who nonetheless did so in the same year. For these respondents, one behavior may be initiated as much as 11 months prior to the other, but because our data are collected on an annual basis, we cannot tell which was initiated first. If hypothesis 1 (conceptual equivalence of delinquent behavior and exposure to delinquent peers) were correct, all or most of the respondents who do not fall into the first two categories should fall into the third. The fourth category consists of respondents who initiated exposure in one year, and who either initiated delinquency in a subsequent year or who did not initiate delinquency at all from 1977 to 1983.[8] If hypothesis 2 (learning theory) were correct, this is

---

[8] In this analysis, the initiation of one behavior (either exposure or delinquent behavior) is considered evidence of the temporal priority of this behavior in the sequence, whether the other behavior occurs subsequently or not, since the *reverse* ordering is clearly ruled out, and if the respondent was followed over a more extended period, the second event might be observed (i.e., the failure to observe the "effect" may be the result of right censoring). For example, this is quite likely for respondents reporting the initial behavior at the last wave of the study when there are no data for the subsequent year. This procedure is the same as the procedure used in developmental studies of temporal order (e.g., Yamaguchi & Kandel, 1984). However, we have also examined these two sequences (categories 4 and 5 in Table 2.1), limiting the analysis to respondents who reported *both* exposure *and* delinquent behavior at some point *during* the study period. In this more restricted analysis, the onset of one behavior is *always* followed by the onset of the other. The results of this analysis are essentially the same as the results reported here (Menard & Elliott, 1990a). Approximately one-third of respondents in categories 4 and 5 (Table 2.1) initiated one of these behaviors and not the other after 1976.

Table 2.1. *Temporal priority of onset of exposure to delinquent friends and own delinquent behavior*

Age in 1976	Sequential pattern	Index of offending			Minor nondrug offending			General offending		
		N	% total sample	% uncensored	N	% total sample	% uncensored	N	% total sample	% uncensored
11–17	Neither initiated	24	1.7		13	0.8		14	0.9	
	Both in first year	302	21.1		848	53.5		892	54.7	
	Both in same year (after first)	76	5.3	6.9	226	14.3	31.3	205	12.6	28.2
	Exposure before delinquency	1,011	70.7	91.7	373	23.5	51.6	409	25.1	56.3
	Delinquency before exposure	16	1.1	1.5	124	7.8	17.2	112	6.9	15.4
11–12	Neither initiated	8	1.8		5	1.1		5	1.0	
	Both in first year	79	18.2		212	45.4		224	46.4	
	Both in same year (after first)	28	6.4	8.0	77	16.5	30.8	67	13.9	26.4
	Exposure before delinquency	313	72.0	89.9	133	28.5	53.2	151	31.3	59.4
	Delinquency before exposure	7	1.6	2.1	40	8.6	16.0	36	7.5	14.2
15–16	Neither initiated	8	2.0		4	0.9		5	1.1	
	Both in first year	91	22.9		256	56.9		273	59.0	
	Both in same year (after first)	19	4.8	6.4	59	13.1	31.1	56	12.1	30.3
	Exposure before delinquency	277	69.8	93.0	90	20.0	47.4	96	20.7	51.9
	Delinquency before exposure	2	0.5	0.7	41	9.1	21.6	33	7.1	17.8

where we would expect to find most of the respondents who did not fall into categories 1 and 2. The fifth category consists of respondents who initiated delinquency in one year, and who either initiated exposure in a subsequent year or who did not initiate exposure at all from 1977 to 1983. If hypothesis 3 (control theory) is correct, this is where we would expect to find most of the respondents who were not in categories 1 and 2.[9]

In the first category, regardless of age, only 1% of the total sample initiated neither exposure to delinquent friends nor general or minor offending, and less than 2% initiated neither exposure nor index offending. Right censoring thus does not appear to be a significant problem in the present analysis. Turning to the second category, left censoring appears to be a problem for about half of the total sample for general and minor offending, and for about one-fifth of the sample for index offending. Predictably, the percentage of respondents who have already initiated both exposure and delinquency is smaller for the younger cohorts (age 11 or 12 in 1976) than for the older cohorts (age 15 or 16 in 1976). Neither of these first two categories has any direct bearing on the three hypotheses (equivalence, learning, control) we are examining, but the second category does indicate the extent to which a more complete examination of the three hypotheses may require data on respondents of even younger ages.

If hypothesis 1 (equivalence) is true, most or all of the cases that did not fall into the first two categories should fall into the third. The design of the study, particularly the long (1 year) measurement intervals, is somewhat biased in the direction of this hypothesis, since actual lagged onsets of up to 1 year are treated as nonlagged simultaneous events. For index offending, only 5% of the total cases, or 7% of uncensored cases, fall into this third category. The rates are higher for general and minor offending: 13% to 14% of the total respondents, or 28% to 31% of the uncensored cases, fall into the third category. Depending on the type of delinquency and cohort (age), however, between 69% and 92% of the cases involving initiation of exposure to or delinquency after 1976 have a discernible temporal order in their exposure to delinquent peers and their own delinquency. Virtually identical percentages of younger (11–12) and older (15–16) cohorts reported both exposure and delinquency in the same year after 1976. On the basis of these data and the observation that these rates probably

[9] Thornberry's (1987) interactional theory offers no guidance about whether exposure or delinquency should be initiated first. Any of the aforementioned patterns or an approximately even division among delinquency first, exposure first, and simultaneous initiation would thus not be inconsistent with interactional theory.

overstate the number of truly simultaneous events (because the events may occur at distinctly different times during the same year), we may reject the hypothesis of equivalence between exposure to delinquent peers and one's own involvement in delinquent behavior.

If hypothesis 2 (learning theory) is correct, most or all of the cases that did not fall into the first two categories should fall into the fourth category, exposure before delinquency. For index offending, exposure precedes delinquency in about 70% of the total cases in the general sample and for each age group. Excluding censored cases, over 90% of cases fall into the fourth category, exposure prior to index offending. Only 1% to 2% initiate index offending prior to exposure. For the remaining 6% to 8%, both exposure and index offending are initiated within the same year. These results are strong enough to indicate that serious forms of delinquent behavior such as index offending rarely, if ever, precede exposure to delinquent friends. Instead, in the vast majority of cases, exposure precedes index offending.

For both minor and general offending in the total sample, about one-fourth of the total number of cases and a little over one-half of the uncensored cases experience exposure prior to the onset of delinquency. The percentage who initiate exposure prior to delinquency is *highest* for the youngest cohorts. The relationship is thus strongest for the respondents for whom the problem of left censoring is least severe. Bear in mind, too, that these results are obtained despite the inherent bias in the data *against* finding exposure prior to delinquency, as discussed previously, relative to the measurement of exposure. It therefore appears inappropriate to reject the learning theory explanation for the relationship between delinquent behavior and exposure to delinquent friends.

If hypothesis 3 (control theory) is correct, most or all of the cases that did not fall into the first two categories should fall into the fifth category, delinquency before exposure. The evidence in favor of hypothesis 3, however, is even weaker than the evidence in favor of hypothesis 1 (equivalence). Less than 18% of the total sample initiated general or minor offending before the onset of exposure to delinquent friends. Only 1% initiated index offending prior to exposure to delinquent friends. For uncensored cases, 15% initiated general offending, 17% initiated minor offending, and less than 2% initiated index offending prior to exposure to delinquent friends. It is worth noting that respondents who were 11 or 12 in 1976, for whom left censoring is less of a problem than for other respondents, have the *lowest* percentages of initiating general or minor offending prior to exposure. Tentatively, we may reject the control theory explanation for the relationship between delinquent behavior and exposure to delinquent friends. Delinquent behavior typically does *not* appear to come first.

Even having tentatively ruled out both hypothesis 1 (equivalence) and hypothesis 3 (control), it is appropriate to directly compare the strength of the evidence for hypotheses 2 (learning) and 3 (control). This may be done by calculating the ratio of cases or percentage of cases demonstrating ordered sequences that support each of the two hypotheses. For index offending, considering only those cases for which temporal order is ascertainable (categories 4 and 5), the learning theory ordering is favored by ratios of 45:1 to 140:1. In other words, 98% to 99% of the cases indicate exposure to delinquent peers prior to the onset of their own index offending. For minor non–drug offending, learning theory is favored by ratios of 2:1 to 3:1. Here, 69% to 77% of the cases favor learning theory, and the strength of learning theory relative to control theory is strongest for the youngest cohorts. For general offending, learning theory is favored by ratios of 2:1 to 4:1; 74% to 81% of the cases favor learning theory, and again the relationship is strongest for the youngest cohorts.[10]

Developmental Patterns

The concern over onset or initiation of association with delinquent friends and initiation of delinquent behavior involves only one aspect of the relationship between these two variables. In further analysis, we seek to elaborate this relationship by tracing both developmental progressions over the adolescent and early adult phases of the life cycle. To this end, we begin by considering exposure to delinquent friends and committing delinquent acts in parallel but separate developmental progressions. First, we describe the age distribution of particular peer group and offense types. Next we examine age-specific transition rates among peer group and offense types.

[10] Similar analyses, not reported in detail here, were undertaken in which the 10-item exposure scale (including alcohol use and cheating on tests) was used (Menard & Elliott, 1990a). While differing somewhat in the precise percentages or ratios (sometimes higher, sometimes lower), this analysis produced the same substantive conclusions as the results presented in Table 2.1. When the 10-item scale is used, the evidence for the sequence postulated by social learning theory is even stronger: there are *no* respondents who initiate delinquent behavior prior to exposure to delinquent peers. The slight difference in outcome between the 8- and 10-item exposure scales is primarily the result of including alcohol use in the scale.

Then we consider the temporal order of different types of peer group exposure, the temporal order of different types of delinquent behavior, and the interaction between changing exposure to delinquent peers and changing involvement in delinquent behavior.

Age, Peer Group Type, and Delinquency

Table 2.2 presents the percent of respondents in each age group who are in each peer group type. For ages 11, 22, 23, and 24, only 1 year of data (for a single birth cohort) was available, so ages 11 and 12 are aggregated, as are ages 22 to 24, within the table. For each of the remaining ages, the estimates in the table are each based on two to five cohorts. The aggregated figures have the advantage of mitigating the impact of random error that might occur in any given year, and are thus more reliable than single-year (or single-cohort) estimates.

The percentage of respondents with no exposure to delinquency on the part of their friends, the "saints," declines steadily from age 11 to age 17, then stabilizes and increases slightly after age 21. The percentage of respondents in prosocial peer groups has a pattern similar to the pattern for the saints: a decline until age 17, followed by relative stability until age 21, then an increase after age 21. These developmental patterns, both for predominantly prosocial and completely nondelinquent peer groups, are consistent with the suggestion that a sort of "maturational reform" (Menard & Elliott, 1990b) occurs in late adolescence.

Predictably, the patterns for mixed and delinquent peer groups are the reverse of the patterns in saint and prosocial peer groups, again consistent with maturational reform. The percentage in delinquent peer groups increases up to age 15, remains stable until age 18, then declines from age 19 onward. Eventually the percentage in delinquent peer groups is as low at ages 22 to 24 as it was at ages 11 to 12. The percentage in mixed peer groups increases to ages 16 and 17, remains fairly constant until age 21, then appears to decline slightly. In contrast to saint, prosocial, and delinquent peer groups, the percentage in mixed peer groups shows a net increase from ages 11 to 12 to ages 21 to 24, approximately doubling in size.

Until age 18, the percentage of isolates remains fairly stable, with a slight increase around age 17. Between ages 17 to 18 and 19 to 20, there is an increase in the proportion classified as isolates, which probably corresponds to a combination of peer groups breaking up with the departure from high school of most respondents and the formation of primarily

Table 2.2. Age, peer group type, and delinquency

Age	Saint	Prosocial	Mixed	Delinquent	Isolate	Nonoffender	Minor offender	Index offender
11–12	13	51	19	3	14	43	40	17
13	9	44	26	6	15	43	40	16
14	8	39	31	9	14	41	44	15
15	6	35	33	13	14	42	40	19
16	4	29	38	14	16	39	43	18
17	3	25	42	14	17	41	42	18
18	3	24	43	13	17	48	40	13
19	3	23	41	8	26	53	36	11
20	3	25	40	7	25	53	37	9
21	3	25	41	6	25	56	34	10
22–24	4	29	36	3	27	66	28	6

monogamous heterosexual relationships. From ages 19 to 24, the percentage of isolates appears to be fairly stable, perhaps increasing slightly after age 22.

Some important considerations emerge from the relationship between age and peer group types. First, although involvement in prosocial or saint peer groups indicates little or no exposure to delinquency in these groups for a particular year or at a particular age, this does not necessarily imply that there has been no exposure to delinquent peers at earlier years or ages. For respondents just entering the adolescent years (ages 11–12), it may not be unreasonable to assume no prior exposure to delinquent behavior on the part of friends, but this is not a reasonable assumption for respondents in saint and prosocial groups at later ages, since there is considerable movement among different types of peer groups during the adolescent years. A tracking of individual respondents over time indicates that at least one-fourth of respondents in purely nondelinquent peer groups after age 21 have had at least some prior exposure to delinquent behavior. Second and similarly, at least some of the respondents classified as isolates after age 18 are qualitatively different from respondents classified as isolates before age 17. Although exit from school and entry into adult relationships probably provide the main reason for the increase in the percentage of isolates after age 19, it is unlikely that these factors are operative for respondents 11 to 14 years old.

Third, prosocial groups are the dominant type of peer group until age 15, but after age 15 mixed peer groups dominate until age 23. This change in levels of exposure to illegal behavior in the peer group is slightly earlier if we consider the proportion in saint and prosocial groups as compared to mixed and delinquent groups. At age 15, 46% of respondents are in mixed and delinquent peer groups, compared to 41% in saint and prosocial groups, and from age 15 onward, substantially more respondents are in mixed and delinquent peer groups than in saint and prosocial peer groups. Not until age 24 does this pattern appear to reverse itself, with 37% of respondents in saint/prosocial and 32% in mixed/delinquent peer groups. (Note that these estimates are based on single birth cohorts and should be viewed with some caution). That period in the life span with the highest levels of exposure to illegal behavior in the peer group (typically involving a majority of respondents in mixed or delinquent groups) is the period from age 15 to age 18. This is the period generally considered to be the period of greatest risk for involvement in delinquent behavior.

Finally, the increased percentages in less delinquent groups (saint and prosocial) and the declining percentages in more delinquent groups (mixed and delinquent) during the late adolescent and early adult years are consistent with the maturational reform hypothesis. Although it is not clear from the data presented here, a separate analysis of age, period, and cohort effects (Elliott et al., 1989; Menard & Elliott, 1990b) indicates that the prevalence and frequency of delinquent behavior peak at about age 16 for general delinquency and age 15 for index offenses. This suggests that prevalence and frequency of delinquent behavior may begin to decline prior to the decline in exposure to delinquent friends. Whether this occurs in anticipation of leaving the group, or whether departure from the group is precipitated by conflicts over the continuing delinquency of group members, or whether the respondents' perceptions of friends' desistance lags behind their actual desistance, remains to be examined. From this and other evidence (Menard, 1992) it appears that changes in the distribution of peer group types largely account for the observed age gradients in rates of delinquent behavior, that is, for the maturation effect.

Turning to age-specific offender types (Table 2.2), the relationship between age and offender type reflects the typical (e.g., Farrington, 1986a) pattern, with the prevalence of both minor and index offenders reaching its highest level (as a percent of age group) in midadolescence, minor offenders at age 14 and index offenders at age 15. Correspondingly, the percent of respondents who are nonoffenders is lowest in midadolescence, at age 16. After age 17 or 18, the percent of nonoffenders increases, and the percent of both minor and index offenders declines, so that by ages 22 to 24, two-thirds of the sample are nonoffenders. Bear in mind that all of the offenses in this typology would be criminal if committed by an adult, so the observed decline in offender types does not reflect changes associated with status offenses.

Transitions among Peer Group Types

Transition matrices among peer group types were calculated for 1976–77, 1977–78, 1978–79, and 1979–80 for respondents 11 to 12 years old and for respondents 15 to 16 years old in 1976 (the same division of respondents present in Table 2.1). Taken together, these two age groups form a *synthetic cohort* (Shryock & Siegel, 1976; Newell, 1988), and provide information on transitions among peer group types throughout adolescence, from ages 11–12 to ages 19–20. To test whether the two groups could properly be aggregated into a single synthetic cohort, a 3-year transition matrix was calculated for each group for ages 15–16 to ages 18–19, the only ages for which overlapping data were available for the two age groups. A test for the homogeneity of the two 3-year transition matrices (Markus 1979) indicated

Table 2.3. *Age-specific peer group type transition matrices*

	11–12 to 12–13					12–13 to 13–14				
	S	P	I	M	D	S	P	I	M	D
Saints	**.274**	.548	.145	.016	.016	**.340**	.447	.128	.085	.000
Prosocial	.084	**.578**	.116	.211	.012	.097	**.529**	.097	.252	.025
Isolate	.078	.328	**.422**	.156	.016	.089	.266	**.494**	.139	.013
Mixed	.040	.343	.141	**.404**	.071	.038	.267	.067	**.467**	.162
Delinquent	.063	.250	.063	.188	**.438**	.000	.053	.158	.211	**.579**
	n = 492					n = 488				

	13–14 to 14–15					14–15 to 15–16				
	S	P	I	M	D	S	P	I	M	D
Saints	**.227**	.477	.227	.068	.000	**.536**	.321	.107	.036	.000
Prosocial	.063	**.603**	.085	.238	.011	.083	**.572**	.463	.224	.030
Isolate	.041	.270	**.459**	.189	.041	.060	.224	**.463**	.224	.030
Mixed	.024	.202	.089	**.565**	.121	.007	.176	.051	**.618**	.147
Delinquent	.000	.114	.057	.171	**.657**	.000	.000	.150	.325	**.525**
	n = 466					n = 451				

	15–16 to 16–17					16–17 to 17–18				
	S	P	I	M	D	S	P	I	M	D
Saints	**.348**	.304	.174	.130	.043	**.250**	.509	.050	.150	.000
Prosocial	.063	**.486**	.077	.345	.028	.054	**.509**	.089	.321	.027
Isolate	.067	.167	**.367**	.350	.050	.000	.167	**.470**	.258	.106
Mixed	.000	.167	.077	**.625**	.131	.000	.095	.125	**.635**	.145
Delinquent	.000	.026	.218	.346	**.410**	.000	.000	.138	.362	**.500**
	n = 471					n = 456				

	17–18 to 18–19					18–19 to 19–20				
	S	P	I	M	D	S	P	I	M	D
Saints	**.333**	.444	.222	.000	.000	**.231**	.538	.154	.077	.000
Prosocial	.101	**.506**	.146	.247	.000	.025	**.588**	.188	.188	.013
Isolate	.000	.087	**.623**	.203	.087	.011	.159	**.568**	.216	.045
Mixed	.010	.155	.140	**.637**	.057	.011	.167	.126	**.661**	.034
Delinquent	.000	.031	.172	.375	**.422**	.000	.000	.209	.372	**.419**
	n = 492					n = 488				

Two separate cohort-specific samples are involved in these matrices. The first four matrices involve 11- to 12-year-olds in 1976 over four subsequent annual transitions; the second four matrices involve 15- to 16-year-olds in 1976 over four subsequent annual transitions. The n for the 1976 11- to 12-year-old subsample is 507, and for the 15- to 16-year-old subsample is 489. The number of cases for each matrix reflects the number of cases with data for each of the two-year periods involved.

no significant departure from homogeneity ($X^2 = 12.29$, $df = 16$, $p \geq .70$), indicating that the two groups are sufficiently homogeneous to be aggregated into a single synthetic cohort. The age-specific transition matrices are presented in Table 2.3.

The most likely transition from one year to the next is to remain in the same type of peer group. The exception to this pattern occurs for the saints, who, at most ages, are more likely to move into prosocial peer groups than to remain in saint peer groups. During midadolescence, however, saints appear most likely to stay within saint peer groups from one year to the next. For saints, then, the most likely transitions are to remain in a totally nondelinquent peer group or to move into a prosocial peer group. With one exception (ages 16–17 to 17–18), the third most likely transition for saints is to become isolates. For every age, the least likely transition for saints is to a delinquent peer group, and for six of the eight transitions, the probability of going from a saint peer group to a delinquent peer group is zero.

At the opposite end of the continuum, respondents in delinquent peer groups are most likely to remain in delinquent peer groups. Except for ages 11–12 to 12–13, the second most likely transition is to a mixed peer group, and this probability is relatively high beginning with the 14–15 to 15–16 transition. In six of the eight transition matrices, delinquents are least likely to become saints, and in seven of the eight transition matrices, the probability of this transition is zero.

For respondents in prosocial peer groups, the most frequent transition is to remain in a prosocial peer group, followed in turn by transitions to mixed, isolate, and saint types. The least probable transition for someone in a prosocial peer group is the transition to a delinquent peer group. This pattern holds at every age. For respondents in mixed peer groups, the pattern varies by age. For all ages, respondents in mixed peer groups are most likely to stay in mixed peer groups, and least likely to move into totally nondelinquent saint peer groups. For ages 11–12 to 12–13, the second, third, and fourth most likely transitions are to prosocial, isolate, and delinquent types, respectively. For ages 12–13 to 16–17, the second, third, and fourth most probable transitions are to prosocial, delinquent, and isolate types. For ages 16–17 to 17–18, the order is delinquent, then isolate, then prosocial. For ages 17–18 to 19–20, the pattern returns to that observed for ages 11–12: prosocial, followed by isolate, then delinquent.

For respondents classified as isolates, at every age, the most likely transition is to remain isolates. The next most likely transition is to move into one of the intermediate (prosocial or mixed) peer group types, and the least likely transition is to move into one of the extreme (saint or delinquent) peer group types. At earlier ages, isolates are more likely to move into the less delinquent of the intermediate or extreme peer group types; at later ages, they are more likely to move into the more delinquent of the intermediate or extreme peer group types.

The image that emerges is one of considerable stability from one year to the next. When a change in peer group type occurs, it most often involves a gradual transition from one peer group type to a type not too dissimilar from the first. The isolate type may be an intermediate step in gradual patterns of transition, or it may be a sort of temporary detour out of peer group involvement. The higher probability of transition into the isolate type, which is evident at the older ages for all peer group types (see, particularly, the transition matrices for ages 17–18 to 18–19 and 18–19 to 19–20, compared with earlier transition matrices), probably reflects the characteristic exit from peer groups and entry into adult monogamous relationships upon graduation from high school. The general pattern of gradual transitions and the pattern of increased transition into isolate status at the older ages appear to be the dominant general patterns of transitions among peer group types. Although there are some minor exceptions (in both directions), the delinquent and mixed groups appear to be as stable across the adolescent period as the prosocial group. There is no evidence here that associations with delinquent peers are less stable or enduring than associations with prosocial peers. No other patterns are clearly evident in the transition matrices.

Transitions among Offense Types

Parallel to our presentation of transitions among peer group types, Table 2.4 presents the age-specific transitions among offense types. The transition matrices in Table 2.4 are less complex than the transition matrices in Table 2.3, and may be summarized with three generalizations. First, the most probable transition from one year to the next is to remain in a given offense type. The one exception to this rule occurs in the transition matrix from ages 17–18 to 18–19, in which index offenders are slightly more likely to become minor offenders than to remain index offenders. Second, transition to an adjacent category (specifically, minor offending for both nonoffenders and index offenders) is more likely than transition to a nonadjacent category (between nonoffending and index offending). This difference is particularly dramatic when transitions involving an escalation in the seriousness of offending are examined. Rarely do respondents initi-

Table 2.4. *Age-specific offense type transition matrices*

	11–12 to 12–13			12–13 to 13–14		
	N	M	I	N	M	I
Nonoffender	**.65**	.29	.06	**.72**	.25	.04
Minor	.38	**.51**	.10	.31	**.61**	.09
Index	.19	.34	**.47**	.13	.44	**.44**
	n = 474			*n* = 481		

	13–14 to 14–15			14–15 to 15–16		
	N	M	I	N	M	I
Nonoffender	**.74**	.21	.06	**.77**	.30	.03
Minor	.30	**.56**	.14	.33	**.53**	.14
Index	.11	.29	**.60**	.20	.29	**.51**
	n = 461			*n* = 447		

	15–16 to 16–17			16–17 to 17–18		
	N	M	I	N	M	I
Nonoffender	**.68**	.31	.01	**.76**	.21	.03
Minor	.24	**.63**	.14	.31	**.59**	.10
Index	.14	.34	**.53**	.09	.42	**.50**
	n = 466			*n* = 450		

	17–18 to 18–19			18–19 to 19–20		
	N	M	I	N	M	I
Nonoffender	**.77**	.21	.02	**.81**	.17	.02
Minor	.32	**.58**	.11	.37	**.55**	.08
Index	.12	.45	**.43**	.09	.33	**.58**
	n = 420			*n* = 398		

Two separate cohort-specific samples are involved in these matrices. The first four matrices involve 11- to 12-year-olds in 1976 over four subsequent annual transitions; the second four matrices involve 15- to 16-year-olds in 1976 over four subsequent annual transitions. The *n* for the 1976 11- to 12-year-old subsample is 507, and for the 15- to 16-year-old subsample is 489. The number of cases for each matrix reflects the number of cases with data for each of the 2-year periods involved.

ate offending with index offenses. Third, subject to the first two generalizations, transition to a less delinquent category is more likely than transition to a more delinquent category. Minor offenders are more likely to become nonoffenders than to become index offenders, and index offenders are more likely to become nonoffenders than nonoffenders are likely to become index offenders.[11]

Ever-Prevalence of Peer Group and Offense Types

Of the total sample, 37% are ever in saint peer groups, 78% in prosocial peer groups, 82% in mixed peer groups, 44% in delinquent peer groups, and 61% report having no friends or only one friend in at least 1 year (isolates). Addition of these figures indicates that NYS respondents report involvement in an average of three different peer group types (including isolates) over the 8 years spanned by the data. Clearly, peer group membership is not static, but changes considerably over the adolescent phase of the life span.

Of the respondents 11 to 12 years old in 1976 ($n = 346$), 91% have ever committed at least one minor offense and 47% have ever committed at least one index offense. Only one respondent reported having ever committed one or more index offenses, but never a minor offense. All of the others who report having committed index offenses reported having committed minor offenses as well, and *all* of them reported having committed minor offenses in a reporting period prior to ($n = 148$) or at the same time as ($n = 198$) the one in which they reported committing their first index offense. (For a further discussion of this sequencing pattern, see Elliott et al., 1989.)

The Temporal Pattern of Transitions between Peer Group Types Relative to Transitions between Types of Delinquent Behavior

Table 2.5 presents the typical patterns of temporal priority involving both peer group type and offending type transitions. In the first half of the table, we present the transitions that occur for the general sample. In the second

---

[11] We also considered temporal sequences in types of peer groups. The general pattern in early adolescence is one of movement from less delinquent to more delinquent peer group types. In later adolescence (ages 15 to 16 in 1976), movement tends to be reversed from the delinquent peer group type to other types.

Table 2.5. *Temporal priority of transitions among peer group types and onset of types of delinquent behavior*

Sample	Transitions	Concordant		Discordant		Indeterminate	
		N	percent	N	percent	N	percent
General[c]	Exposure to delinquency[a] before onset of minor delinquency	466	27.0	35	2.0	1,224	71.0
	Exposure to delinquency before onset of index delinquency	1,079	62.6	6	0.3	640	37.1
	Onset of minor delinquency before increased peer group delinquency[b]	408	23.7	200	11.6	1,117	64.8
	Increased peer group delinquency before onset of index delinquency	783	45.4	86	5.0	856	49.6
	Onset of minor delinquency before membership in delinquent peer group type	653	37.9	14	0.8	1,058	61.3
	Onset of index delinquency before membership in delinquent peer group type	251	14.6	165	9.6	1,309	75.9
Ever-active only[c]	Exposure to delinquency[a] before onset of minor delinquency	304	20.9	35	2.4	1,116	76.7
	Exposure to delinquency before onset of index delinquency	299	44.0	6	0.9	374	54.8
	Onset of minor delinquency before increased peer group delinquency[b]	334	26.8	123	9.9	790	63.3
	Increased peer group delinquency before onset of index delinquency	209	33.0	71	11.2	354	55.8
	Onset of minor delinquency before membership in delinquent peer group type	238	50.7	10	2.1	221	47.1
	Onset of index delinquency before membership in delinquent peer group type	117	34.4	53	15.6	170	50.0

[a]Prosocial, mixed, or delinquent (as opposed to saints) peer group type; usually means membership in prosocial peer group type.
[b]Mixed or delinquent (as opposed to saints or prosocial) peer group type; usually means membership in mixed peer group type.

half of the table, data are presented for the ever-active sample, respondents who have initiated both the type of peer group and the type of delinquency listed on that row. The first half of the table thus refers to making a transition *prior to or in the absence of* making the other transition, and the second half of the table refers to making a transition *strictly prior to* (not in the absence of) the other transition in the specified row. The first half of the table assumes, in effect, that the second of the two transitions in any row will be made at a later date; the second half of the table assumes, in effect, that if a transition had not been made by the last year of data used in this analysis, that the transition will never occur. These are two extremes between which the actual future pattern must lie. It is evident from Table 2.5 that these opposite assumptions produce the same substantive conclusion: only the strength of the relationship, not its direction (the temporal order of the two transitions) changes between the first and second part of Table 2.5. As in Table 2.1, isolates are excluded from this analysis.

Table 2.5 indicates the predominant order of the transitions between delinquent peer group types and offense types. The first column (concordant) lists the number and percent of respondents who made the transitions in the order indicated. The second column (discordant) lists the number and percentage of respondents who made the two transitions in the order opposite to the order indicated. The last column (indeterminate) indicates the number and percentage of respondents for whom the order of the two transitions was indeterminate, either because the respondent had made neither transition (neither more delinquent friends nor more delinquent behavior; right censoring), because the respondent had made both transitions in or before 1976 (left censoring), or because the respondent made both transitions in the same year (after 1976). Most of the cases listed in the indeterminate column are there because of left censoring.

As detailed earlier (Table 2.1), the transition from friends who are completely nondelinquent (saints) to friends who are at least slightly delinquent (prosocials) typically precedes the transition from no illegal behavior to minor offending. This is consistent with a social learning theory perspective (Akers, 1985; Bandura & Walters, 1963; Elliott et al., 1979; Sutherland, 1947) and with previous findings from the NYS (Elliott et al., 1985; Elliott et al., 1989). Although there are some respondents who make the two transitions in the opposite order, the ratio of concordant to discordant cases is from 9:1 to 13:1, depending on whether the general or ever-active sample is used. Similarly, by ratios of 50:1 to 180:1, the transition from a completely nondelinquent to a somewhat delinquent peer group type precedes the transition from no delinquency or minor delinquency to index delinquency.

Before one moves from nondelinquent or only weakly delinquent peer group types (saint or prosocial) to more delinquent peer group types (mixed or delinquent), one typically moves from nondelinquency to minor offending, but the ratio of concordant to discordant cases is only 2:1 or 3:1. Movement to more delinquent peer groups does, however, precede movement to index offending, by ratios of 24:1 to 47:1, and index offending precedes membership in delinquent peer group types by ratios of 2:1 to 4:1. From Tables 2.3–2.5, the typical sequence appears to be:

1. from saint to prosocial peer group type; then
2. from nonoffending to minor offending; then
3. from prosocial to mixed peer group type; then
4. from minor offending to index offending; and lastly,
5. from mixed to delinquent peer group type.

This sequence is diagrammed in Figure 2.1. Not everyone completes this sequence, and some may deviate from it, but it is the most frequent pattern among respondents for whom temporal order is ascertainable.

Discussion: Developmental Patterns

For both delinquent peer group association and delinquent behavior, there appears to be a gradual pattern of increasing delinquency as one moves into midadolescence, and then a pattern of decreasing delinquency and exposure to delinquent peers in late adolescence and early adulthood. Early adolescence is a time of moving into increasingly delinquent peer groups; late adolescence and early adulthood involve not only movement away from more delinquent peer groups, but also movement out of peer groups altogether, most likely into dyadic, monogamous relationships. The movement typically appears to be gradual, one step at a time, rather than abrupt.

Given these developmental progressions, it is logically possible that the causal influences, if any, operate only in parallel, with the temporal priority of transitions only an artifact of the timing of transitions in exposure to delinquent peers and delinquent behavior. In other words, minor delin-

Saints/ ➡ Prosocial ➡ Minor ➡ Mixed ➡ Index ➡ Delinquent
Nonoffenders   peer group   offending   peer group   offending   peer group

Figure 2.1. Sequencing of peer group type and offender type transitions.

quency may lead with some probability to index offending, and association with slightly delinquent peers may lead with some probability to association with more delinquent peers, but delinquency does not cause association and association does not cause delinquency. It is also possible that the causal influence between exposure to delinquent peers and delinquent behavior is unidirectional (and if so, it is more likely that having delinquent friends influences delinquent behavior than the reverse) or bidirectional, with delinquent behavior and exposure to delinquency influencing one another. If the relationship is bidirectional, it would be interesting to know which of the two influences, exposure leads to delinquency or delinquency leads to exposure, is stronger. In an attempt to further resolve these issues, we present the results of a causal model that permits either unidirectional or bidirectional causal paths (or neither) between delinquent behavior and exposure to delinquent peers.

A Structural Equation Model: Exposure, Belief, and Delinquent Behavior

In an analysis presented in more detail elsewhere (Menard & Elliott, 1994), we constructed a three-wave, three-variable structural equation model based on the integrated theory presented in Elliott et al. (1979; 1985; 1989). The three variables in the model are illegal behavior, indicated first by minor offending and then by index offending; delinquent peer group bonding, a product (as described in Elliott et al., 1989) of exposure to delinquent peers and involvement with friends, which captures both the level of delinquency in the peer group and the extent of involvement with the peer group; and belief that it is wrong to violate the law, as described in Elliott et al. (1989) and earlier in this chapter. The inclusion of belief in this model is consistent with the integrated theory of Elliott et al. (1979) and is necessary in order to avoid serious misspecification of the causal model. This model places the relationship between exposure to delinquent peers and delinquent behavior within a slightly broader context that is consistent with both social learning and social control theories. A similar analysis was undertaken by Thornberry, Lizotte, Krohn, Farnworth, and Jang (1994) to test Thornberry's interactional theory. In the present analysis, six hypotheses are built into the structural equation model:

Hypothesis 1: Delinquent bonding has a direct, positive effect on illegal behavior.

Hypothesis 2: Belief has either a weak direct negative effect, or an indirect negative effect, on illegal behavior.

Hypothesis 3: Belief has a direct negative effect on delinquent bonding.
Hypothesis 4: Delinquent bonding has a direct negative effect on belief.
This hypothesis is implicit in Elliott et al. (1979), who posited that bonding and peer groups should mutually influence one another, but it has not been systematically explored in previously published work on the NYS by Elliott et al. This hypothesis may also be derived from the interactional theory of Thornberry (1987).

Two additional hypotheses are based on Thornberry's (1987) interactional theory:

Hypothesis 5: Illegal behavior has a direct positive effect on subsequent delinquent bonding.
Hypothesis 6: Illegal behavior has a direct negative effect on subsequent belief.

In the structural equation model, simultaneous effects are permitted between delinquency and delinquent bonding (which are measured for the same time interval). Belief, which is measured for a single point in time, is placed in the correct temporal order relative to delinquent bonding and delinquent behavior. The resulting temporal ordering of the variables is diagrammed in Figure 2.2. The models themselves are presented in Figure 2.3 (for minor offending) and Figure 2.4 (for index offending).

The structural equation models were tested using LISREL 7 (Jöreskog & Sörbom, 1989). In both Figure 2.3 and Figure 2.4, coefficients that were not statistically significant (one-tailed $p \leq 0.05$) are enclosed in parentheses. For minor offending, the four hypotheses derived from the integrated theory of Elliott et al. are all supported. Hypothesis 6 is also supported; delinquent behavior does have a weak negative effect on subsequent belief.

JAN-DEC 1978	JAN 1979	JAN-DEC 1979	JAN 1980	JAN-DEC 1980
MINOR AND INDEX OFFENDING (3)		MINOR AND INDEX OFFENDING (4)		MINOR AND INDEX OFFENDING (5)
DELINQUENT BONDING (3)		DELINQUENT BONDING (4)		DELINQUENT BONDING (5)
	BELIEF (3)		BELIEF (4)	

Numbers in parentheses refer to wave of the National Youth Survey in which the data were collected.

Figure 2.2. Temporal order of measurement in the NYS.

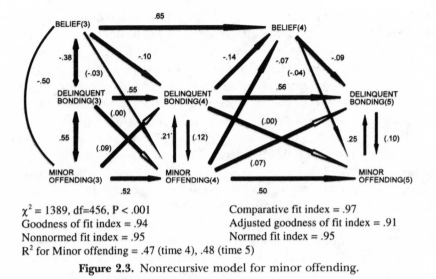

$\chi^2 = 1389$, df=456, P < .001   Comparative fit index = .97
Goodness of fit index = .94   Adjusted goodness of fit index = .91
Nonnormed fit index = .95   Normed fit index = .95
R^2 for Minor offending = .47 (time 4), .48 (time 5)

Figure 2.3. Nonrecursive model for minor offending.

Hypothesis 5, however, is not supported; for both lagged and simultaneous effects, we are unable to reject the null hypothesis that there is no effect of minor offending on delinquent peer group bonding.

In Figure 2.4, a somewhat different story emerges. For index offending, the four hypotheses derived from the integrated theory of Elliott et al. are

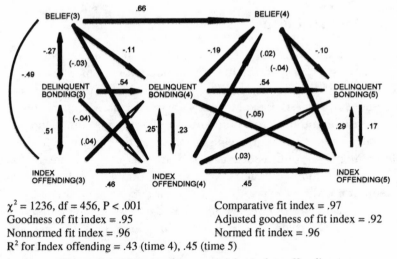

$\chi^2 = 1236$, df = 456, P < .001   Comparative fit index = .97
Goodness of fit index = .95   Adjusted goodness of fit index = .92
Nonnormed fit index = .96   Normed fit index = .96
R^2 for Index offending = .43 (time 4), .45 (time 5)

Figure 2.4. Nonrecursive model for index offending.

again supported. (The direct effect of belief on index offending is not statistically significant, but the integrated theory indicates that the effect of belief on delinquency may be indirect.) This time, however, hypothesis 5 receives some support; index offending does affect delinquent peer group bonding, though not as strongly as delinquent peer group bonding affects index offending. Hypothesis 6, however, is not supported in this analysis; the effect of delinquent behavior on belief is not statistically significant.

These findings are consistent with the findings from the analysis of transitions among peer group types and offense types. First, they suggest that exposure to delinquent peers (here in the form of delinquent peer group bonding) has a stronger effect on illegal behavior than illegal behavior has on exposure to delinquent peers. Second, at relatively low levels of delinquency (minor offending), exposure to delinquent peers comes first in the causal sequence; it influences, but is not influenced by, delinquent behavior. Third, at more advanced levels of delinquency (index offending), exposure to delinquent peers and delinquent behavior influence one another; each amplifies the other. This is consistent with the alternating sequence of escalation in peer group type and delinquent behavior, with emphasis on the fact that change in peer group appears to precede change in behavior. This also suggests that the simple reciprocal pattern suggested by Thornberry's (1987) interactional theory may be oversimplified. Based on these results, it *does* matter which comes first, delinquency or exposure to delinquent peers, and, contrary to control theory, exposure comes first.

Theoretical Implications

For the adolescent years, ages 12 to 18, the preponderance of the evidence regarding onset clearly favors the developmental sequence postulated by learning theory over the sequences suggested by control theory or the equivalence hypothesis as explanations for the relationship between delinquent behavior and having delinquent friends. (Because interactional theory is silent about the sequencing of onset of delinquent behavior and delinquent peer group association, the analysis of onset has no direct implications for interactional theory.) Among those respondents for whom the temporal order of exposure and delinquency is ascertainable, even if we were to include respondents who initiated exposure and delinquency in the same year as having all initiated delinquency first, the majority of respondents initiate some exposure prior to delinquency. With respect to serious forms of delinquency, the evidence for this developmental sequence appears to be quite compelling. For minor forms of delinquency, however, there is reason to be more cautious.

In the analysis involving minor forms of delinquent behavior, there was a substantial amount of left censoring. For the 11- to 12-year-old cohort, 45% reported both minor delinquent acts and some exposure to peer delinquency at the initial wave of data collection. Since we have not observed the behavior–exposure sequence for individuals prior to age 11, it is logically possible that the sequence prior to age 11 is different from the sequence observed after age 11. While it is possible that the influence of peers operates differently before and after age 11, such a finding would not necessarily result in a reversal of the exposure–behavior sequence postulated by learning theory and observed in this analysis. If peers are not causally implicated prior to age 11, exposure to illegal behavior on the part of siblings, parents, or other family members whose influence is presumed to be relatively strong prior to age 11 may still precede the onset of delinquent behavior. Furthermore, in the absence of a theoretical or empirical argument for such an age-specific effect applicable to both family members and peers, or data clearly demonstrating this effect, the most reasonable guess seems to be that the sequencing before ages 11 to 12 is as consistent with the sequencing for 11- to 12-year-olds as the sequencing for ages 11 to 12 is with the sequencing for older respondents, like the 15- to 16-year-old respondents in the present study. We are skeptical of the possibility that the delinquent exposure–behavior sequence is any different prior to age 11, but we acknowledge that this is a logical possibility. Until longitudinal data are available for a sample of respondents at younger ages (e.g., 7–10), it may not be possible to resolve this issue.

Our measure of exposure to delinquent peers, as noted above, was biased *against* finding exposure prior to delinquency. Nevertheless, this was the predominant finding. We were able to reject the hypothesis suggested by Farrington (1986b), West (1985), Loeber (1987), and Gottfredson and Hirschi (1987) that exposure to delinquent friends and one's own delinquent behavior really measure the same thing. We were able to reject the control theory hypothesis suggested by Hirschi (1969; 1987) and by Glueck and Glueck (1950) that the onset of delinquent behavior typically precedes the onset of exposure to or association with delinquent friends during adolescence. We were *not* able to reject the learning theory hypothesis that the onset of exposure to delinquent others typically precedes the onset of delinquent behavior. Instead, we found that exposure to delinquent peers preceded minor delinquent behavior in a majority of cases, and serious delinquency in nearly all cases where some order could be determined.

These findings are further reinforced by the more detailed analysis of the sequencing of transitions among peer group and delinquent behavior types, and by the structural equation models. Transitions from one type of peer group to another more delinquent type are more likely to precede transitions from lower to higher levels of delinquency than the transitions in delinquency are likely to precede the transitions in peer group type. The influence of delinquent bonding on delinquent behavior is stronger than the influence of delinquent behavior on delinquent bonding, especially for the early stages of delinquent behavior, as represented by the analysis involving minor delinquency. Contrary to both control and interactional theory, for minor offending, illegal behavior does not appear to influence delinquent peer group association; instead, at the early stages of delinquency, the causal relationship appears to be unidirectional, in the direction suggested by social learning theory. It is only at the later stages of delinquency that the relationship between delinquent bonding and delinquent behavior becomes reciprocal, and even then the relationship hypothesized by social learning theory, exposure leads to delinquency, predominates.

Although the temporal order suggested by learning theory predominates, it is not the only pattern evident in the data. For a significant minority, the control theory pattern holds with respect to minor delinquency. Two possible explanations for this may be suggested. First, if our measure of exposure to delinquent behavior on the part of friends were as exhaustive in its coverage of possible offenses as our measure of the respondent's own delinquent behavior, and if it included exposure to criminal behavior on the part of parents and siblings (and perhaps other relatives) as well as friends, we might well find that fewer individuals, or perhaps even no one, initiated delinquent behavior prior to exposure to delinquent behavior on the part of significant others, including relatives as well as friends. Alternatively, Elliott et al. (1979) may have been correct in suggesting that there are alternative etiological paths to delinquent behavior, and that while infrequent, there are causal paths in which delinquency is initiated prior to any exposure to delinquent behavior in the peer group. If this is so, the pertinent question may be whether it is control theory or, as suggested by Elliott et al., strain theory that best explains those cases in which delinquency precedes exposure.

The findings here suggest the following scenario. First, for most adolescents, exposure to delinquent peers precedes delinquent behavior. Most typically, the initial exposure to delinquency is limited, probably to a few, relatively rare, relatively minor delinquent acts. Next comes delinquent behavior, but again represented by a few minor offenses. Escalation may stop here, and at this stage, infrequent participation in relatively minor offenses is not enough to limit one's choices of peer groups, either by exclusion from relatively nondelinquent peer groups or by deliberate selection of highly delinquent friends. This is consistent with both the order of transition in the temporal order analysis and with the structural equation model for minor offending. Further escalation may result in exclusion from relatively less delinquent peer groups, or may lead to a deliberate choice of more delinquent friends (as suggested by control theory), but the strength of the influence of exposure to delinquent peers on delinquent behavior remains stronger than the influence of delinquent behavior on exposure to delinquent peers. Having delinquent friends and being involved in delinquent behavior may influence one another, but the influence is not symmetric; the influence of exposure on delinquency begins earlier in the sequence, and remains stronger throughout the sequence, than the influence of delinquency on exposure.

Conclusion

A critical difference among competing theoretical approaches has been the explanation of the role of exposure to or association with delinquent peers relative to one's own delinquent behavior. Some authors have argued that the two, exposure and delinquent behavior, are just different measures of delinquency. Other authors, from a control theory perspective, have argued that the onset of delinquent behavior comes first. Still others, from a learning theory perspective, have argued that the onset of exposure comes first. With respect to the *onset* of delinquency (particularly serious forms of delinquency) the preponderance of the evidence in this study is in favor of the sequence suggested by learning theory. Insofar as evidence exists that is inconsistent with learning theory, this evidence may reflect either bias against learning theory in our measure of exposure or the existence of multiple etiological paths to delinquent behavior.

For changing levels of involvement in delinquent behavior and exposure to delinquent peers *after* onset, our results appear most consistent with a bidirectional causal explanation that is consistent with both control and learning theories, and with Thornberry's interactional theory. The results of the developmental analysis and the structural equation model indicate that control theory or Thornberry's interactional theory may be more valid after the onset of both exposure and delinquency, rather than in the early stages of the emergence of delinquent behavior and exposure to delinquent peers. These conclusions seem fairly well supported for the adolescent phase of the life span, but further research on younger age groups needs to be undertaken to provide a more complete test of learning versus control theory explanations. Such an analysis should include preadolescent subjects, exposure measured for a wider range of delinquent behaviors, and exposure to criminal or delinquent relatives as well as to criminal or delinquent friends.

REFERENCES

Akers, R. L. (1985). *Deviant behavior: A social learning approach* (3rd ed.). Belmont, CA: Wadsworth.

Akers, R. L., Krohn, M. K., Lonza-Kaduce, L., & Radosevich, M. (1979). Social learning and deviant behavior: A specific test of a general theory. *American Sociological Review, 44,* 636–655.

Bandura, A., & Walters, R. (1963). *Social learning and personality development.* New York: Holt, Rinehart & Winston.

Berry, W. D., & Feldman, S. (1985). *Multiple regression in practice.* Beverly Hills, CA: Sage.

Burgess, R. L., & Akers, R. L. (1966). A differential association-reinforcement theory of criminal behavior. *Social Problems, 14,* 128–147.

Chambliss, W. J. (1973). The saints and the roughnecks. *Society, 11,* 24–31.

Dembo, R., Grandon, G., LaVoie, L., Schmeidler, J., & Burgos, W. (1986). Parents and drugs revisited: Some further evidence in support of social learning theory. *Criminology, 24,* 85–104.

Dunford, F. W., & Elliott, D. S. (1984). Identifying career offenders using self-reported data. *Journal of Research in Crime and Delinquency, 21,* 57–86.

Elliott, D. S., & Ageton, S. S. (1980). Reconciling race and class differences in self-reported and official estimates of delinquency. *American Sociological Review, 45,* 95–110.

Elliott, D. S., Ageton, S. S., & Canter, R. J. (1979). An integrated theoretical perspective on delinquent behavior. *Journal of Research in Crime and Delinquency, 16,* 3–27.

Elliott, D. S., Ageton, S. S., Huizinga, D., Knowles, B. A., & Canter, R. J. (1983). *The prevalence and incidence of delinquent behavior: 1976–1980.* Boulder, CO: Behavioral Research Institute.

Elliott, D. S., Dunford, F. W., & Huizinga, D. (1987). The identification and prediction of career offenders utilizing self-reported and official data. In J. D. Burchard & S. N. Burchard (Eds.), *Prevention of delinquent behavior* (pp. 90–121). Newbury Park, CA: Sage.

Elliott, D. S., & Huizinga, D. (1983). Social class and delinquent behavior in a national youth panel. *Criminology, 2,* 149–177.

Elliott, D. S., Huizinga, D., & Ageton, S. S. (1985). *Explaining delinquency and drug use.* Beverly Hills, CA: Sage.

Elliott, D. S., Huizinga, D., & Menard, S. (1989). *Multiple problem youth: Delinquency, drug use, and mental health problems.* New York: Springer-Verlag.

Elliott, D. S., & Voss, H. (1974). *Delinquency and dropout.* Lexington, MA: D. C. Heath.

Erickson, M. L., & Empey, L. T. (1965). Class position, peers and delinquency. *Sociology and Social Research, 49,* 268–282.

Erickson, M. L., & Jensen, G. F. (1977). Delinquency is still group behavior! Toward revitalizing the group premise in the sociology of deviance. *Journal of Criminal Law and Criminology, 68,* 262–273.

Farrington, D. P. (1986a). Age and crime. In M. Tonry & N. Morris (Eds.), *Crime and justice: An annual review of research* (Vol. 7, pp. 189–250). Chicago: University of Chicago Press.

Farrington, D. P. (1986b). Review of *Explaining delinquency and drug use* by Delbert S. Elliott, David Huizinga and Suzanne S. Ageton. *British Journal of Addiction, 81,* 433.

Farrington, D. P. (1988). Studying changes within individuals: The causes of offending. In M. Rutter (Ed.), *Studies of psychosocial risk: The power of longitudinal data* (pp. 158–183). Cambridge: Cambridge University Press.

Glueck, S., & Glueck, E. (1950). *Unraveling juvenile delinquency.* Cambridge, MA: Harvard University Press.

Gottfredson, M., & Hirschi, T. (1987). The methodological adequacy of longitudinal research in crime and delinquency. *Criminology, 25,* 581–614.

Hardt, R. H., & Peterson, S. J. (1968). Arrests of self and friends as indicators of delinquency involvement. *Journal of Research in Crime and Delinquency, 5,* 44–51.

Hepburn, J. R. (1976). Testing alternative models of delinquency causation. *Journal of Criminal Law and Criminology, 67,* 450–460.

Hirschi, T. (1969). *Causes of delinquency.* Berkeley: University of California Press.

Hirschi, T. (1987). Review of *Explaining delinquency and drug use* by Delbert S. Elliott, David Huizinga and Suzanne S. Ageton. *Criminology, 25,* 193–201.

Huizinga, D. H., Menard, S., & Elliott, D. S. (1989). Delinquency and drug use: Temporal and developmental patterns. *Justice Quarterly, 6,* 419–455.

Jensen, G. F. (1972). Parents, peers and delinquent action: A test of the differential association perspective. *American Journal of Sociology, 78,* 562–575.

Jöreskog, K. G., & Sörbom, D. (1989). *LISREL 7: A guide to the program and applications* (2nd ed.). Chicago: SPSS Inc.

Kandel, D. B. (1973). Adolescent marijuana use: Role of parents and peers. *Science, 181,* 1067–1070.

Kercher, K. (1988). Criminology. In E. F. Borgatta & K. S. Cook (Eds.), *The future of sociology* (pp. 294–316). Newbury Park, CA: Sage.

Krohn, M. D. (1974). An investigation of the effect of parental and peer associations on marijuana use: An empirical test of the differential association theory. In M. Riedel & T. P. Thornberry (Eds.), *Crime and delinquency: Dimensions of deviance* (pp. 75–87). New York: Praeger.

Loeber, R. (1987). Review of *Explaining delinquency and drug use* by Delbert S. Elliott, D. Huizinga and Suzanne S. Ageton. *Aggressive Behavior, 13,* 97–99.

Markus, G. B. (1979). *Analyzing panel data.* Beverly Hills, CA: Sage.

Matsueda, R. L. (1982). Testing control theory and differential association: A causal modeling approach. *American Sociological Review, 47,* 489–504.

Matsueda, R. L. (1989). The dynamics of moral beliefs and minor deviance. *Social Forces, 68,* 428–457.

Matsueda, R. L., & Heimer, K. (1987). Race, family structure and delinquency: A test of differential association and control theories. *American Sociological Review, 52,* 826–840.

Menard, S. (1992). Demographic and theoretical variables in the age-period-cohort analysis of illegal behavior. *Journal of Research in Crime and Delinquency, 29,* 178–199.

Menard, S., & Elliott, D. S. (1990a). Longitudinal and cross-sectional data collection and analysis in the study of crime and delinquency. *Justice Quarterly, 7,* 11–55.

Menard, S., & Elliott, D. S. (1990b). Self-reported offending, maturational reform and the Easterlin hypothesis. *Journal of Quantitative Criminology, 6,* 237–267.

Menard, S., & Elliott, D. S. (1994). Delinquent bonding, moral beliefs, and illegal behavior: A three-wave panel model. *Justice Quarterly, 11,* 173–188.

Menard, S., & Morse, B. J. (1984). A structuralist critique of the IQ–delinquency hypothesis. *American Journal of Sociology, 89,* 1347–1378.

Miller, W. B. (1982). Gangs, groups and youth crime. In R. Giallombardo (Ed.), *Juvenile delinquency: A book of readings* (4th ed., pp. 311–328). New York: Wiley.

Newell, C. (1988). *Methods and models in demography.* New York: Guilford.

Platt, J. R. (1964). Strong inference. *Science, 146,* 347–353.

Reiss, A. J., Jr. (1986). Co-offender influences on criminal careers. In A. Blumstein, J. Cohen, J. A. Roth, & C. A. Visher (Eds.), *Criminal careers and "career criminals"* (Vol. 2, pp. 121–160). Washington, DC: National Academy Press.

Reiss, A. J., Jr., & Rhodes, A. L. (1964). An empirical test of differential association theory. *Journal of Research in Crime and Delinquency, 1,* 13–17.

Sampson, R. J., & Laub, J. H. (1993). *Crime in the making: Pathways and turning points through life.* Cambridge, MA: Harvard University Press.

Short, J. F. (1957). Differential association and delinquency. *Social Problems, 4,* 233–239.

Shryock, H. S., Siegel, J. S., et al. (1976). *The methods and materials of demography.* Condensed edition by E. G. Stockwell. New York: Academic Press.

Skogan, W. G. (1981). Assessing the behavioral context of victimization. *Journal of Criminal Law and Criminology*, 72, 727–742.

Sutherland, E. H. (1947). *Principles of criminology*. (4th ed.). Philadelphia: J. B. Lippincott.

Thornberry, T. P. (1987). Toward an interactional theory of delinquency. *Criminology*, 25, 863–891.

Thornberry, T. P., Lizotte, A. J., Krohn, M. D., Farnworth, M., & Jang, S. J. (1994). Delinquent peers, beliefs and delinquent behavior: A longitudinal test of interactional theory. *Criminology*, 32, 47–84.

Vigil, J. D. (1988). *Barrio gangs*. Austin, TX: University of Texas Press.

Voss, H. L. (1964). Differential association and reported delinquent behavior: A replication. *Social Problems*, 12, 78–85.

West, D. J. (1985). Review of *Explaining delinquency and drug use* by Delbert S. Elliott, David Huizinga and Suzanne S. Ageton. *Journal of Adolescence*, 8, 376–377.

Widom, C. S. (1989). The cycle of violence. *Science*, 244, 160–166.

Williamson, J. B., Karp, D. A., Dalphin, J. R., & Gray, P. S. (1982). *The research craft: An introduction to social research methods*. Boston: Little, Brown.

Yamaguchi, K., & Kandel, D. B. (1984). Patterns of drug use from adolescence to young adulthood. II. Sequences of progression. *American Journal of Public Health*, 74, 668–672.

CHAPTER THREE

The Explanation and Prevention
of Youthful Offending

DAVID P. FARRINGTON

ABSTRACT: The main aim of this chapter is to summarize the most important empirically supported propositions that should be included in a comprehensive theory of youthful offending, and to derive some implications about prevention and treatment. Most of the implications concern primary prevention early in life. There is now broad agreement about many of the predictors and correlates of offending, and consistent results have been obtained in a variety of studies carried out in different settings. There is less agreement about what theory explains these results most adequately, or about the most important implications that might be drawn about how to reduce youthful offending.

Toward an Empirically Based Theory

Knowledge about Offending

Theories and empirical results are only likely to be true within certain boundary conditions. The theories and results discussed here are applicable to male offending in the United States and England in the past 30 years or so. They are almost certainly applicable to other Western democracies such as Canada, Australia, New Zealand, Germany, Holland, and the Scandinavian countries. They may be equally applicable to female offending, but this is not certain because of the lack of comparable research on female offending. Most research has concentrated on offending by males, since this is generally more frequent and serious than offending by females (e.g., Farrington, 1987a).

Within a single chapter, it is obviously impossible to review everything that is known about the development of offending. Rutter and Giller (1983), Wilson and Herrnstein (1985), Hollin (1992), and Blackburn (1993) have provided more detailed reviews of risk factors. I will be very selective in focusing on some of the more important and replicable findings obtained in some of the more methodologically adequate studies – especially longitudinal studies of large community samples. In studying the development and predictors of offending, it is essential to carry out prospective longitudinal surveys.

I will refer especially to knowledge gained in the Cambridge Study in Delinquent Development, which is a prospective longitudinal survey of over 400 London males from age 8 to age 32 (Farrington & West, 1990). However, similar results have been obtained in projects elsewhere in England (e.g., Kolvin, Miller, Fleeting, & Kolvin, 1988; Kolvin, Miller, Scott, Gatzanis, & Fleeting, 1990), in the United States (e.g., McCord, 1979; Robins, 1979), in the Scandinavian countries (e.g., Wikstrom, 1987; Pulkkinen, 1988), and in New Zealand (e.g., Moffitt & Silva, 1988a).

The Cambridge study found that the typical offender – a male property offender – tends to be born in a low-income, large-sized family and to have criminal parents. When he is young, his parents supervise him rather poorly, use harsh or erratic child-rearing techniques, and are likely to be in conflict and to separate. At school, he tends to have low intelligence and attainment, is troublesome, hyperactive, and impulsive, and often truants. He tends to associate with friends who are also delinquents.

After leaving school, the offender tends to have a low-status job record punctuated by periods of unemployment. His deviant behavior tends to be versatile rather than specialized. He not only commits property offenses such as theft and burglary but also engages in violence, vandalism, drug use, excessive drinking, reckless driving, and sexual promiscuity. His likelihood of offending reaches a peak during his teenage years and then declines in his 20s, when he is likely to get married or cohabit with a woman.

By the time he is in his 30s, the offender is likely to be separated or divorced from his wife and separated from his children. He tends to be unemployed or to have a low-paying job, to move frequently, and to live in rented rather than owner-occupied accommodations. His life is still characterized by more evenings out, more heavy drinking and drunk driving, more violence, and more drug taking than his contemporaries'. Hence, the typical offender tends to provide the same kind of deprived and disrupted family background for his own children that he himself experienced, thus perpetuating from one generation to the next a range of social problems, of which offending is only one element.

Similar conclusions have been reached by other researchers. Robins (1979) argued that there is an "antisocial personality" that arises in childhood and persists into adulthood, and this idea is embodied in the *DSM-IV* diagnosis of antisocial personality disorder (American Psychiatric Association, 1994). According to Robins, the antisocial adult male generally fails to maintain close personal relationships with anyone, tends to perform poorly in his jobs, tends to be involved in crime, fails to support himself and his dependents without outside aid, and tends to change his plans impulsively and to lose his temper in response to minor frustrations. As a child, he tended to be restless, impulsive, and lacking in guilt, performed badly in school, truanted, ran away from home, was cruel to animals or people, and committed delinquent acts.

Robins (1986) has consistently shown how a constellation of indicators of childhood antisocial behavior predicts a constellation of indicators of adult antisocial behavior. In several longitudinal studies, the number of different childhood symptoms predicted the number of different adult symptoms, rather than there being a linkage between any specific childhood and adult symptoms (Robins & Wish, 1977; Robins & Ratcliff, 1978, 1980).

The main difficulty of interpretation is that all types of social problems tend to be interrelated, making it difficult to know what causes what, and when and how it is best to intervene to try to interrupt the developmental sequence from childhood to adult antisocial behavior.

Concepts of Offending

The focus in this chapter is on youthful offending rather than juvenile delinquency. The legal category of juvenile delinquency ends at an arbitrary age boundary (the 18th birthday in most cases) that is close to the peak age of offending (Farrington, 1986a). Hence, a strict focus on legally defined delinquency would cover only the first part of offending careers. In contrast, the study of youthful offending up to the mid-20s requires theories that cover the major part of offending careers, and explanations not only of why offending begins, continues, or escalates, but also of why offending decreases or ceases.

Criminal career research has been important in establishing basic knowledge about the development of offending from childhood to adulthood (Blumstein, Cohen, Roth, & Visher, 1986; Blumstein, Cohen, & Farrington, 1988; Farrington, 1992a). A *criminal career* is defined as the longitudinal sequence of offenses committed by an individual offender. *Offenses* in this chapter are defined as the most common types of crime that predominate in the official criminal statistics, including theft, burglary, robbery, violence, vandalism, and drug use. White-collar crime is not included here, partly because it is not usually a youthful crime and partly because there has been little attempt as yet to study its predictors, causes, or development from childhood to adulthood.

A criminal career has a beginning (onset), end (desistance), and career length in between (duration). Only a certain proportion of the population (prevalence) has a criminal career and commits offenses. During their careers, offenders commit offenses at a certain rate (frequency) while they are at risk of offending in the community (e.g., not incarcerated or hospitalized). For offenders who commit several offenses, it is possible to investigate how far they specialize in certain types of offense and how far the seriousness of their offending escalates over time.

The criminal career approach (e.g., Blumstein & Cohen, 1987; Blumstein et al., 1986) emphasizes the need to investigate such questions as why people start offending, why they continue offending, why offending becomes more frequent or more serious, and why people stop offending. The factors influencing onset may differ from those influencing other criminal career features such as persistence, escalation, and desistance, if only because the different processes occur at different ages. Indeed, Farrington and Hawkins (1991) found that there was no relationship among factors influencing prevalence (official offenders versus nonoffenders), those influencing early versus later onset, and those influencing desistance after age 21; and Loeber, Stouthamer-Loeber, Van Kammen, and Farrington (1991) in the Pittsburgh Youth Study reported no relationship between factors influencing onset and those influencing escalation.

In order to understand the causes of offending it is important to study developmental processes such as onset, persistence, escalation, and desistance. However, it is also important not to restrict this study narrowly to offending, but also to study the onset, persistence, escalation, and desistance of related types of antisocial behavior. Loeber and Le Blanc (1990) used many other concepts to describe developmental processes in antisocial careers, including acceleration and deceleration, diversification, switching, stabilization, escalation and deescalation. For example, retention (escalating to serious acts while still committing trivial acts) seems more common than innovation (escalating and giving up trivial acts).

The criminal career approach is essentially concerned with human development over time. Therefore, it is important to investigate developmental sequences over time, for example, where one behavior facilitates or acts as a kind of stepping-stone to another. It is desirable to identify noncriminal behaviors that lead to criminal behaviors, and long-term developmental sequences including types of offending. For example, hyperactivity at age 2 may lead to cruelty to animals at 6, shoplifting at 10, burglary at 15, robbery at 20, and eventually spouse assault, child abuse and neglect, alcohol abuse, and employment and accommodation problems later in life. Typically, a career of childhood antisocial behavior leads to a criminal career, which often coincides with a career of teenage antisocial behavior and leads to a career of adult antisocial behavior. The criminal career is a legally defined subset of a longer-term and more wide-ranging antisocial career. A deeper understanding of the development of the criminal career requires a deeper understanding of the wider antisocial career.

Basic Theoretical Ideas

Offending is a type of behavior, similar in many respects to other types of antisocial or deviant behavior. Hence, the theories, methods, and knowledge of other types of antisocial behavior can be applied to the study of crime. It is plausible to argue that, like other types of behavior, criminal behavior results from the interaction between a person (with a certain degree of criminal potential or antisocial tendency) and the environment (which provides criminal opportunities). Some people will be consistently more likely to commit offenses than others (in various environments), and conversely the same person will be more likely to commit offenses in some environments than in others. Hence, human behavior is, to a considerable degree, consistent and predictable.

In any theory, there is an important distinction between empirical variables or behavioral manifestations such as offending and underlying theoretical constructs. A key issue centers on the generality or specificity of the underlying constructs. A theory could focus on violence potential, criminal potential, or antisocial tendency, for example. A major problem in any theory is to explain the development of individual differences in an underlying construct such as criminal potential, or conversely in the strength of internal inhibitions against offending. Generally, I will assume that offenses and other types of antisocial acts are behavioral manifestations of the underlying theoretical construct of *antisocial tendency*.

An underlying antisocial tendency may lead to offending in some circumstances and to other types of antisocial acts in other circumstances, forcing attention to interactive effects of influencing factors. In particular, there will be different antisocial manifestations at different ages from birth to adulthood. For example, the antisocial child may be troublesome and disruptive in school, the antisocial teenager may steal cars and burgle houses, and the antisocial adult male may beat his wife and neglect his children. The variation in antisocial behavior with age is one of the key issues that any theory needs to explain.

In view of the consistency within individuals of antisocial tendency across situations and its continuity over time, it is important to include individual difference factors in any theory. In general, the antisocial child tends to become the antisocial teenager and the antisocial adult, just as the antisocial adult then tends to produce another antisocial child. The relative ordering of any cohort of people on antisocial tendency is significantly consistent over time (Farrington, 1991a).

Measurement of Offending

The prevalence of offenders varies according to the definition of offending and the method of measurement (official records or self-reports, usually). For example, in the Cambridge study, 96% of a sample of inner-city London males admitted committing at least one of 10 common offenses (including theft, burglary, violence, vandalism, and drug abuse) at some time between ages 10 and 32, whereas only 33% of them had been convicted of at least one of these offenses during this age range (Farrington, 1989c). In order to compare offenders and nonoffenders, it is important to set a sufficiently high criterion for "offending" (e.g., in terms of frequency, seriousness, or duration, or in terms of arrests or convictions) so that the vast majority of the male population are not classified as offenders.

When the high rate of admission of minor offenses first became widely known in the 1960s, this led some sociologists to argue that there were no differences between offenders and nonoffenders (since "everybody does it"), and hence that the marked differences seen in the official statistics (especially in social class) reflected selection biases by the police or courts. However, more recent reviews (e.g., Hindelang, Hirschi, & Weis, 1981) show that, with comparable criteria of seriousness of offending, official statistics and self-reports yield quite concordant results, and both demonstrate numerous significant differences between offenders and nonoffenders. This chapter focuses on these differences.

Officially recorded offenders and nonoffenders (or, in self-report studies, more and less serious offenders) are significantly different – before, during, and after their offending careers. This is basically because of consistent individual differences in underlying criminal potential or antisocial tendency. Generally, the worst offenders according to self-reports (taking account of frequency and seriousness) tend also to be the worst offenders according to official records (Farrington, 1973; Huizinga & Elliott, 1986). For example, in the Cambridge study, 11% of the males between ages 15 and 18 admitted burglary, and 62% of these males were convicted of burglary (West & Farrington, 1977). The correlates of official and self-reported offending are very similar (Farrington, 1992c). Hence, conclusions about individual characteristics of offenders can be drawn validly from both convictions and self-reports. In this chapter, *offenders* will generally refer to officially recorded offenders, unless otherwise stated.

Natural History of Offending

The prevalence of offending increases to a peak in the teenage years and then decreases in the 20s. This pattern is seen both cross-sectionally and longitudinally (Farrington, 1986a). The peak age of official offending for English males was 15 until 1987, but it increased to 18 in 1988 as a result of a decrease in detected juvenile shoplifting offenders (Barclay, 1990; Farrington & Burrows, 1993). The peak age for females was 14 until 1985 but then increased to 15. In the Cambridge study, the rate of convictions increased to a peak at age 17 and then declined (Farrington, 1992a). The median age of conviction for most types of offense (burglary, robbery, theft of and from vehicles, shoplifting) was 17, while it was 20 for violence and 21 for fraud. Similarly, in the Philadelphia cohort study of Wolfgang, Thornberry, and Figlio (1987), the arrest rate increased to a peak at age 16 and then declined.

Self-report studies also show that the most common types of offending decline from the teens to the 20s. In the Cambridge study, the prevalence of burglary, shoplifting, theft of and from vehicles, theft from slot machines, and vandalism all decreased from the teens to the 20s, but the same decreases were not seen for theft from work, assault, drug abuse, and fraud (Farrington, 1989c). For example, burglary (since the last interview) was admitted by 13% at age 14, 11% at age 18, 5% at age 21, and 2% at both ages 25 and 32. In their American National Youth Survey, Elliott, Huizinga, and Menard (1989) found that self-reports of the prevalence of offending increased from 11 to 13 to a peak at 15 to 17 and then decreased by 19 to 21.

Many theories have been proposed to explain why offending peaks in the teenage years (see Farrington, 1986a). For example, offending has been linked to testosterone levels in males, which increase during adolescence and early adulthood and decrease thereafter, and to changes in physical abilities or opportunities for crime. The most popular explanation focuses on social influence. From birth, children are under the influence of their parents, who generally discourage offending. However, during their teenage years, juveniles gradually break away from the control of their parents and become influenced by their peers, who may encourage offending in many cases. After age 20, offending declines again as peer influence gives way to a new set of family influences hostile to offending, originating in spouses and cohabitees.

Versatility of Offending

Juvenile delinquents are predominantly versatile rather than specialized in their offending (e.g., Klein, 1984; Farrington, Snyder, & Finnegan, 1988c). In other words, people who commit one type of offense have a significant tendency also to commit other types. For example, in the Cambridge study, 86% of convicted violent offenders also had convictions for nonviolent offenses (Farrington, 1991b).

Just as offenders tend to be versatile in their types of offending, they also tend to be versatile in their antisocial behavior generally. In the Cambridge study, convicted delinquents tended to be troublesome and dishonest in their primary schools, tended to be frequent liars and aggressive at ages 12 to 14, and tended to be bullies at age 14. By age 18, delinquents tended to be antisocial in a wide variety of respects, including heavy drinking, heavy smoking, using prohibited drugs, and heavy gambling. In addition, they tended to be sexually promiscuous, often beginning sexual intercourse before age 15, having several sexual partners by age 18, and usually having unprotected intercourse (West & Farrington, 1977). Because of this versatility, any prevention method that succeeds in reducing delinquency is likely also to reduce these associated social problems.

West and Farrington (1977) argued that delinquency (which is dominated by crimes of dishonesty) is only one element of a larger syndrome of antisocial behavior that arises in childhood and usually persists into adulthood. They developed a scale of "antisocial tendency" at age 18, based on factors such as an unstable job record, heavy gambling, heavy smoking, drug use, drunk driving, sexual promiscuity, spending time hanging around on the street, antisocial group activity, violence, and antiestablishment attitudes. Their aim was to devise a scale that was not based on the types of act (thefts and burglaries) that usually led to convictions, and they showed that the convicted males were usually antisocial in several other respects. For example, two-thirds (67%) of the males convicted up to age 18 had four or more of these antisocial features, compared with only 15% of the unconvicted males.

Farrington (1991a) developed more comprehensive scales of "antisocial personality" at ages 10, 14, 18, and 32, based on offending and other types of antisocial behavior. For example, the scale at age 14 included convictions, high self-reported delinquency, stealing outside the home, regular smoking, sexual intercourse, bullying, frequent lying, frequent disobedience, hostility to police, frequent truancy, daring, and poor concentration/restlessness. All these measures tended to be interrelated. However, the last two measures, of impulsivity, are arguably causes of antisocial behavior rather than indicators of it. They were included for consistency with psychiatric criteria of antisocial personality disorder, but impulsivity will be reviewed as a possible cause of offending later in this chapter. It is often difficult to distinguish between causes and indicators.

These results are consistent with findings obtained in numerous other studies. For example, in a St. Louis survey of black males, Robins and Ratcliff (1980) reported that juvenile delinquency tended to be associated with truancy, precocious sex, drinking, and drug use. In two American studies separated by 13 years, Donovan, Jessor, and Costa (1988) concluded that a single common factor accounted for the positive correlations among a number of adolescent antisocial behaviors, including problem drinking, marijuana use, precocious sexual intercourse, and delinquent behavior. Hence, as Jessor and Jessor (1977) argued, there is a syndrome of problem behavior in adolescence. In the literature on childhood psychopathology, it is also customary to find a single broad-band syndrome of externalizing problems, including stealing, lying, cheating, vandalism, substance use, running away from home, and truancy (Achenbach, Verhulst, Baron, & Althaus, 1987). As already stated, I will assume in this chapter that the key underlying theoretical construct is antisocial tendency.

Offending tends to be concentrated in certain people and certain families. In the Cambridge study, while about one-third of the males were convicted of criminal offenses, it was nevertheless true that only 5% of the sample – the chronic offenders – accounted for about half of all the convictions (Farrington & West, 1990). Similarly, chronic offenders were disproportionately likely to commit other types of antisocial behavior. In numerous other projects, such as the Philadelphia cohort study of Wolfgang et al. (1987) and the Finnish research of Pulkkinen (1988), there was a similar concentration of offending in a small proportion of the sample.

Magnusson and Bergman (1988) argued for a person-oriented rather than variable-oriented approach. In their Swedish longitudinal survey, they noted the clustering of risk factors such as aggressiveness, restlessness, poor concentration, and underachievement among boys at age 13, and of outcomes such as crime, alcohol abuse, and psychiatric illness up to age 23. Single risk factors such as aggressiveness significantly predicted single outcomes such as crime and alcohol abuse. However, when they excluded the

13% of boys with multiple risk factors from their analyses, these significant relationships disappeared. This suggests that many of the results obtained in variable-oriented research might be produced by a small minority of chronically antisocial people.

Continuity in Offending

Generally, there is significant continuity between offending in one age range and offending in another. In the Cambridge study, nearly three-quarters (73%) of those convicted as juveniles at ages 10 to 16 were reconvicted at ages 17 to 24, in comparison with only 16% of those not convicted as juveniles (Farrington, 1992a). Nearly half (45%) of those convicted as juveniles were reconvicted at ages 25 to 32, in comparison with only 8% of those not convicted as juveniles. Furthermore, this continuity over time did not merely reflect continuity in police reaction to crime. Farrington (1989c) showed that, for 10 specified offenses, the significant continuity between offending in one age range and offending in a later age range held for self-reports as well as official convictions.

Other studies (e.g., McCord, 1991) show similar continuity. For example, in Sweden, Stattin and Magnusson (1991) reported that nearly 70% of males registered for crime before age 15 were registered again between ages 15 and 20, and nearly 60% were registered between ages 21 and 29. Also, the number of juvenile offenses is an effective predictor of the number of adult offenses (Wolfgang et al., 1987). Farrington and Wikstrom (1994) showed that there was considerable continuity in offending between ages 10 and 25 in both London and Stockholm.

It is not always realized that relative continuity is quite compatible with absolute change. In other words, the relative ordering of people on some underlying construct such as antisocial tendency can remain significantly stable over time, even though the absolute level of antisocial tendency declines on average for everyone. For example, Farrington (1990a) in the Cambridge study showed that the prevalence of self-reported offending declined significantly between ages 18 and 32, but that there was a significant tendency for the worst offenders at 18 also to be the worst offenders at 32.

Numerous studies show that childhood conduct problems predict later offending and antisocial behavior (e.g., Loeber & Le Blanc, 1990). For example, Spivack, Marcus, and Swift (1986) in Philadelphia discovered that troublesome behavior in kindergarten (ages 3–4) predicted later police contacts; and Ensminger, Kellam, and Rubin (1983) in Chicago and Tremblay, LeBlanc, and Schwartzman (1988) in Montreal showed that ratings of aggressiveness by teachers and peers in the first grade (ages 6–7) predicted self-reported offending at ages 14 to 15.

Similarly, in the Cambridge study there was evidence of continuity in antisocial behavior from childhood to the teenage years. The antisocial personality scale at age 10 correlated 0.50 with the corresponding scale at age 14 and 0.38 with the scale at age 18 (Farrington, 1991a). The second best predictor of the antisocial tendency scale at age 18 was childhood troublesomeness (getting into trouble at school, e.g., for bad behavior or laziness) at ages 8 to 10, rated by peers and teachers (Farrington, 1993a); the best predictor was having a convicted parent by age 10. In regard to specific types of antisocial behavior, troublesomeness at ages 8 to 10 significantly predicted bullying at both ages 14 and 18 (Farrington, 1993d). Again, troublesomeness at ages 8 to 10 was the best predictor of both truancy and aggression at ages 12 to 14 in the secondary schools (Farrington, 1980, 1989a).

There is also continuity in antisocial behavior at younger ages. For example, Rose, Rose, and Feldman (1989) in New York City found that externalizing problems on the Achenbach Child Behavior Checklist were significantly correlated ($r = 0.57$) between ages 2 and 5. Furthermore, a mother's ratings of her boy's difficult temperament at age 6 months significantly predicted ($r = 0.31$) his externalizing problems at age 8 in the Bloomington longitudinal survey (Bates, Bayles, Bennett, Ridge, & Brown, 1991). It might possibly be argued that these kinds of relationships reflected the stability of the parent's personality rather than of the child's behavior, but similar results were obtained even with different data sources (parents at an earlier age and teachers later).

In Outer London, Richman, Stevenson, and Graham (1985) reported that behavior problems tended to persist between ages 3 and 8, and in New Zealand, White, Moffitt, Earls, Robins, and Silva (1990) showed that externalizing problems and being difficult to manage at age 3 predicted antisocial behavior at age 11. Also, in Washington State, Lerner, Inui, Trupin, and Douglas (1985) found that aggression and hyperactivity at age 4 predicted various psychiatric disorders up to age 16. The fact that antisocial behavior in the first few years of life predicts later antisocial behavior and delinquency is a strong argument for implementing prevention efforts as early in a child's life as possible.

There is also continuity in antisocial behavior from the teenage to the adult years. In the Cambridge study, a measure of adult social dysfunction was developed at age 32, based on (in the previous 5 years) convictions, self-reported offending, poor home conditions, poor cohabitation history, child problems, poor employment history, substance abuse, violence, and poor mental health (a high score on the General Health Questionnaire; see Farrington, Gallagher, Morley, St. Ledger, & West, 1988a, 1988b; and Farrington, 1989b). This measure of adult social dysfunction at age 32 was significantly predicted by the antisocial tendency measure at age 18 (Farrington, 1993a). Similarly, a measure of antisocial personality was developed at age 32 that was comparable with the earlier antisocial personality measures. Antisocial personality at age 18 correlated 0.55 with antisocial personality at age 32 (Farrington, 1991a).

Expressing this another way, 60% of the most antisocial quarter of males at age 18 were still in the most antisocial quarter 14 years later at age 32. Bearing in mind the very great environmental changes between ages 18 and 32, as the males left their parental homes, went through a period of unstable living arrangements, and eventually settled down in marital homes, this consistency over time seems likely to reflect consistency in the individual's personality rather than consistency in the environment. It is often found that about half of any sample of antisocial children persist to become antisocial teenagers, and that about half of any sample of antisocial teenagers persist to become antisocial adults. Comparing the 0.55 correlation between ages 18 and 32 with the 0.38 correlation between ages 10 and 18, it is interesting that there was increasing stabilization of antisocial personality with age.

Zoccolillo, Pickles, Quinton, and Rutter (1992), in a follow-up of children who had been in care, also demonstrated the continuity between childhood conduct disorder (at ages 9–12) and adult social dysfunction (at age 26) in areas of work and social and sexual relationships. For example, 81% of those with three or more symptoms of conduct disorder showed adult dysfunction in two or more areas, compared with only 21% of those with zero to two symptoms of conduct disorder. Approaching half (40%) of the males with three or more symptoms of conduct disorder showed persistent antisocial behavior after age 18 and fulfilled the psychiatric criteria for adult antisocial personality disorder.

The continuity in antisocial personality does not mean that it is not desirable to study influences on criminal career features such as onset and desistance. Unlike Gottfredson and Hirschi (1990), I would not argue that all criminal career features reflect only one underlying construct of criminal potential. Also, the persistence of antisocial personality does not mean that there is no scope for change. The correlations between measures of antisocial personality at different ages (e.g., the 0.55 correlation between

ages 18 and 32), and the fact that only about half of antisocial children
become antisocial adults, show that a great deal of relative change is occurring. This makes it possible to investigate factors that might encourage
antisocial children to become less antisocial as they grow older, or that
might foster early desistance of offending.

There is specific as well as general continuity in offending from the
teenage to the adult years. In the Cambridge study, Farrington (1990a)
developed measures of absolute change and relative consistency between
ages 18 and 32. For example, the prevalence of marijuana use declined
significantly, from 29% at age 18 to 19% at age 32. However, there was a
significant tendency for the users at age 18 also to be users at age 32 (44%
of users at age 18 were users at age 32, whereas only 8% of nonusers at age
18 were users at age 32). Other researchers (e.g., Ghodsian & Power, 1987)
have also reported significant consistency in substance use between adolescence and adulthood.

There is also specific continuity in aggression and violence from the
teenage to the adult years. In the Cambridge study, aggression at ages 16 to
18 was the best predictor of fighting at age 32 (Farrington, 1989a). Spouse
assault at age 32 was significantly predicted by teacher-rated aggression at
ages 12 to 14, and by the antisocial personality measures at ages 14 and 18,
but not (surprisingly) by aggression at age 18 (Farrington, 1994). Bullying
at 32 was specifically predicted by bullying at 14 and 18 independently of
the continuity between aggression at 14 and 18 and aggression at 32 (Farrington, 1993d). Furthermore, a male's bullying at 14 and 18 predicted
bullying by his child when he was 32, showing that there was intergenerational continuity in bullying. In their New York study, Eron and Huesmann
(1990) also found that a boy's aggression at age 8 predicted not only his
aggression and spouse assault at age 30 but also the aggressiveness of his
child.

Notwithstanding the continuity between specific types of offense, I will
focus on the general continuity in antisocial tendency, in the interests of
simplicity.

Risk Factors and Causes

This chapter reviews risk factors that influence the development of offending. Fortunately or unfortunately, there is no shortage of factors that are
significantly correlated with offending and antisocial behavior; indeed,
literally thousands of variables differentiate significantly between official
offenders and nonoffenders and correlate significantly with reports of anti-

social behavior by teenagers, peers, parents, and teachers. In this chapter, it is only possible to review briefly some of the most important risk factors for offending and antisocial behavior: prenatal and perinatal factors such as low birth weight, individual difference factors such as high impulsivity and low intelligence, family influences such as poor child rearing and antisocial parents, socioeconomic deprivation, peer influences such as having delinquent friends, school factors, community characteristics such as social disorganization, and situational factors. These factors often have additive, interactive, or sequential effects, but I will consider them one by one.

Risk factors are prior factors that increase the risk of occurrence of events such as the onset, frequency, persistence, or duration of offending. Longitudinal data are required to establish the ordering of risk factors and criminal career features, and to avoid retrospective bias in measurement. The focus in this chapter is on risk factors for the onset or prevalence of offending and antisocial behavior. Few studies have examined risk factors for persistence or duration. However, in the Cambridge study, Farrington and Hawkins (1991) investigated factors that predicted whether convicted offenders before age 21 persisted or desisted between ages 21 and 32. The best independent predictors of persistence included the boy rarely spending leisure time with his father at age 11–12, low intelligence at age 8–10, employment instability at age 16, and heavy drinking at age 18. Indeed, nearly 90% of the convicted males who were frequently unemployed and heavy drinkers as teenagers went on to be reconvicted after age 21.

Few projects have explicitly investigated why offenders desist. However, in the Cambridge study, both getting married and moving out of London fostered desistance (Osborn, 1980; West, 1982). Shover (1985) explicitly asked retrospective questions about desistance to older men who had given up offending. The main reasons advanced for desistance focused on the increasing costs of crime (long prison sentences), the importance of intimate relationships with women, increasing satisfaction with jobs, and becoming more mature, responsible, and settled with age. Some policy implications of desistance research are that ex-offenders should be helped to settle down in stable marital relationships and in stable jobs, and helped to break away from their criminal associates.

It is often difficult to decide if any given risk factor is an indicator (symptom) or a possible cause of antisocial behavior. The problems raised by impulsivity have already been mentioned. As other examples, do heavy drinking, truancy, unemployment, and divorce measure antisocial tendency, or do they cause (an increase in) it? It is important not to include a measure of the dependent variable as an independent variable in causal analyses, because this will lead to false (tautological) conclusions and an overestimation of explanatory or predictive power (see, e.g., Amdur, 1989).

It is not unreasonable to argue that some factors may be both indicative and causal. For example, long-term variations *between* individuals in antisocial tendency may be reflected in variations in alcohol consumption, just as short-term variations *within* individuals in alcohol consumption may cause more antisocial behavior during the heavier drinking periods. The interpretation of other factors may be more clear-cut. For example, being exposed as a child to poor parental child-rearing techniques might cause antisocial tendency but would not be an indicator of it; and burgling a house might be an indicator of antisocial tendency but would be unlikely to cause it (although it might be argued that, when an antisocial act is successful in leading to positive reinforcement, this reinforcement causes an increase in the underlying antisocial tendency).

Cross-sectional studies make it impossible to distinguish between indicators and causes, since they can merely demonstrate correlations between high levels of one factor (e.g., unemployment) and high levels of another (e.g., offending). However, longitudinal studies can show that offending is greater (within individuals) during some periods (e.g., of unemployment) than during other periods (e.g., of employment). Because within-individual studies have greater control over extraneous influences than between-individual studies, longitudinal studies can demonstrate that changes in unemployment within individuals cause offending with high internal validity in quasi-experimental analyses (Farrington, 1988; Farrington, Gallagher, Morley, St. Ledger, & West, 1986b). Longitudinal studies can also establish whether factors such as unemployment have the same or different effects on offending when they vary within or between individuals. Implications for prevention and treatment, which require changes within individuals, cannot necessarily be drawn from effects demonstrated only in between-individual (cross-sectional) research.

Because of the difficulty of establishing causal effects of factors that vary only between individuals (e.g., gender and ethnicity), and because such factors have no practical implications for prevention (e.g., it is not practicable to change males into females), unchanging variables will not be reviewed in this chapter. In any case, their effects on offending are usually explained by reference to other, changeable, factors (Farrington, 1987a). For example, gender differences in offending have been explained on the basis of different socialization methods used by parents with boys and girls, or different opportunities of males and females for offending.

It is unfortunate that a static model of relationships between independent and dependent variables has dominated research and theories of offending. This model may have a veneer of plausibility in a cross-sectional study, at least if problems of causal order are neglected. However, it is not easily applied to longitudinal or criminal career data, where explanatory constructs and measures of offending change continuously within individuals over different ages. Relationships between an explanatory factor in one age range and a measure of offending in another age range may vary a great deal according to the particular age ranges, and this needs to be systematically investigated by researchers.

Influences on Offending

Loeber and Dishion (1983) and Loeber and Stouthamer-Loeber (1987) extensively reviewed the predictors of male offending. The most important predictors were poor parental child management techniques, childhood antisocial behavior, offending by parents and siblings, low intelligence and educational attainment, and separation from parents. All of these influences will be reviewed in this chapter. In contrast, low socioeconomic status was a rather weak predictor, in agreement with other research casting doubt on the importance of this factor (e.g., Hindelang et al., 1981). I will begin with the earliest influences on behavior, during the prenatal and perinatal time periods.

Prenatal and Perinatal Factors

At least in Western industrialized countries, early childbearing, or teenage pregnancy, predicts many undesirable outcomes for the children, including low school attainment, antisocial school behavior, substance use, and early sexual intercourse (Furstenberg, Brooks-Gunn, & Morgan, 1987a, 1987b). The children of teenage mothers are also more likely to become offenders. For example, Morash and Rucker (1989) analyzed results from four surveys in the United States and England (including the Cambridge study) and found that teenage mothers were associated with low-income families, welfare support, and absent biological fathers, that they used poor child-rearing methods, and that their children were characterized by low school attainment and delinquency. However, the presence of the biological father mitigated many of these adverse factors and generally had a protective effect. In Newcastle-upon-Tyne, Kolvin et al. (1990) reported that mothers who married as teenagers (a factor strongly related to teenage childbearing) were twice as likely to have sons who became offenders by age 32 (49% as opposed to 23%). Baker and Mednick (1984) in Copenhagen also concluded that children of teenage mothers tended to be more aggressive and to have low school attainment.

Substance use (smoking, drinking, and drug use) during pregnancy is also associated with the later undesirable development of children. For example, Streissguth (1986) showed that smoking during pregnancy was associated with low birth weight, small height, and low school attainment. Steinhausen, Willms, and Spohr (1993) found that excessive alcohol consumption during pregnancy (the fetal alcohol syndrome) predicted hyperactivity, low intelligence, and speech disorders in children. Trad (1993) reported that infants of cocaine-abusing mothers tended to have low birth weight and small head circumference, and to be small for their gestational age. Of course, none of these results necessarily prove causal effects; for example, smoking and low school attainment could both be caused by a deprived background. Prevention experiments trying to change a risk factor are the best means of proving causal effects.

A low-birth-weight, relatively small baby and perinatal complications (such as forceps delivery, asphyxia, a long duration of labor, or toxemia during pregnancy) also predict later conduct problems and delinquency of children, although the low prevalence of such complications in representative community samples makes it difficult to establish their effects. For example, in Cleveland (Ohio), Breslau, Klein, and Allen (1988) found that males with low birth weight were more aggressive, hyperactive, and delinquent at age 9 (on the Achenbach Child Behavior Checklist) than other males, independently of differences in intelligence. In Ontario (Canada), Szatmari, Reitsma-Street, and Offord (1986) reported that pregnancy and birth complications were more common in antisocial adolescents than in their siblings. However, perinatal complications were rather weak predictors of offending in the surveys by Werner (1986) in Hawaii and Denno (1990) in Philadelphia.

It may sometimes be difficult to detect the effects of perinatal complications because they vary with other factors such as the quality of the home environment. For example, Kolvin et al. (1990) in Newcastle-upon-Tyne found that neonatal injuries significantly predicted offending up to age 32 only for boys who were in deprived families (low-income or disrupted) at age 5. In Dunedin (New Zealand), McGee, Silva, and Williams (1984) reported that children who were small at birth for their gestational age significantly tended to be badly behaved at age 7, especially if they were also exposed to family adversities. In later research on the same survey,

Moffitt (1990a) showed that perinatal complications predicted delinquency, but only among boys who were also hyperactive.

The most extensive studies of the link between perinatal complications and later delinquency have been carried out in Copenhagen. Kandel and Mednick (1991) and Brennan, Mednick, and Mednick (1993) showed that delivery complications significantly predicted later violent offending for males (12% as opposed to 3% had recorded offenses up to age 21), but only if the males had a psychiatric (psychopathic or schizophrenic) parent. Pregnancy complications tended to predict property offenses. Baker and Mednick (1984) found that "medical risk" (a combination of physical health at birth and motor development at 12 months) predicted later aggression and bullying in school, but only for children from broken families. As Morash and Rucker (1989) also suggested, coming from an intact family (having the biological father present) may act as a protective factor. The key link in the chain between perinatal complications and delinquency may be injury to the brain and neurological dysfunction; Rivara and Farrington (1995) have extensively reviewed the effects of brain injury on delinquency and violence. Brain-imaging techniques should be used to establish neurological dysfunctions in more detail (Chandola, Robling, Peters, Melville-Thomas, & McGuffin, 1992).

Hyperactivity and Impulsivity

Hyperactivity is an important psychological construct that predicts later delinquency. It usually begins before age 5 and often before age 2, and it tends to persist into adolescence (Taylor, 1986). It is associated with restlessness, impulsivity, and a short attention span, and for that reason has been termed the "hyperactivity-impulsivity-attention deficit" or HIA syndrome (Loeber, 1987). Related concepts include a poor ability to defer gratification (Mischel, Shoda, & Rodriguez, 1989) and a short future time perspective (Stein, Sarbin, & Kulik, 1968). Pulkkinen (1986) has usefully reviewed the various concepts and measures of hyperactivity and impulsivity.

HIA may be an early stage in a causal or developmental sequence leading to offending. For example, in the Cambridge study, Farrington, Loeber, and Van Kammen (1990) showed that HIA at ages 8 to 10 significantly predicted juvenile convictions independently of conduct problems at ages 8 to 10. Hence, it might be concluded that HIA is not merely another measure of antisocial tendency. Other projects have also concluded that hyperactivity and conduct disorder are different constructs (Blouin, Conners, Seidel, & Blouin, 1989; Taylor, Schachar, Thorley, & Wieselberg, 1986). Similar constructs to HIA, such as sensation seeking, are also associated with offending (Farley & Sewell, 1976; White, Labouvie, & Bates, 1985). In the Cambridge study, the rating of daring or risk taking at ages 8 to 10 by parents and peers significantly predicted convictions up to age 32 independently of all other variables (Farrington, 1990b, 1993a), and poor concentration or restlessness was the most important predictor of convictions for violence (Farrington, 1994).

It has been suggested that HIA might be a behavioral consequence of a low level of physiological arousal (Ellis, 1987). Offenders have a low level of arousal according to their low alpha frequency (brain) waves on the EEG, or according to autonomic nervous system indicators such as heart rate, blood pressure, or skin conductance, or they show low autonomic reactivity (Venables & Raine, 1987). For example, violent offenders in the Cambridge study had significantly low heart rates (Farrington, 1987b). The causal links between low autonomic arousal, consequent sensation seeking, and offending are brought out explicitly in Mawson's (1987) theory of transient criminality.

In the Cambridge study, being shy, nervous, or withdrawn was the main factor that protected boys from criminogenic backgrounds against becoming offenders (Farrington et al., 1988a, 1988b). In Boston, Kagan, Reznick, and Snidman (1988) classified children as inhibited (shy, fearful, socially avoidant) or uninhibited at age 2 on the basis of observations of how they reacted to unfamiliar people or objects. This classification of inhibited or uninhibited children remained significantly stable up to age 7 and was independent of social class and intelligence. Furthermore, the inhibited children had a higher resting heart rate and a greater increase in their heart rate in the unfamiliar situation. Hence, just as low arousal may be conducive to impulsivity, sensation seeking, and offending, high arousal may be conducive to shyness and may act as a protective factor against offending.

Intelligence and Attainment

As Hirschi and Hindelang (1977) showed in their review, intelligence is an important correlate of offending – at least as important as social class or ethnicity. Intelligence can be measured very early in life. For example, in a prospective longitudinal survey of about 120 Stockholm males, intelligence measured at age 3 significantly predicted officially recorded offending up to age 30 (Stattin & Klackenberg-Larsson, 1993). Frequent offenders (with four or more offenses) had an average IQ of 88 at age 3, whereas nonoffenders had an average IQ of 101. Official offending was also significantly predicted by language development at 6, 18, and 24 months. All of these results held up after controlling for social class. Also, in the Perry preschool project in Michigan, intelligence at age 4 significantly predicted the number of arrests up to age 27 (Schweinhart, Barnes, & Weikart, 1993).

In the Cambridge study, West and Farrington (1973) found that twice as many of the boys scoring 90 or less on a nonverbal intelligence test (Raven's Progressive Matrices) at ages 8 to 10 were convicted as juveniles than of the remainder. Low nonverbal intelligence was highly correlated with low verbal intelligence (vocabulary, word comprehension, verbal reasoning) and with low school attainment, and all of these measures predicted juvenile convictions to much the same extent. In addition to their poor school performance, delinquents tended to be frequent truants, to leave school at the earliest possible age (which was then 15), and to take no school examinations.

Low nonverbal intelligence was especially characteristic of the juvenile recidivists and those first convicted at the earliest ages (10–13). Furthermore, low nonverbal intelligence predicted juvenile self-reported offending to almost exactly the same degree as juvenile convictions, suggesting that the link between low intelligence and delinquency was not caused by the less intelligent boys having a greater probability of being caught. Also, measures of intelligence predicted measures of offending independently of other variables such as family income and family size. Similar results have been obtained in other projects (Lynam, Moffitt, & Stouthamer-Loeber, 1993; Moffitt & Silva, 1988a; Wilson & Herrnstein, 1985). It has also been argued that high intelligence is a protective factor against offending for children from high-risk backgrounds (Kandel et al., 1988; White, Moffitt, & Silva, 1989). Delinquents often do better on nonverbal performance tests, such as object assembly and block design, than on verbal tests (Walsh, Petee, & Beyer, 1987), suggesting that they find it easier to deal with concrete objects than with abstract concepts.

Intelligence may lead to delinquency through the intervening factor of school failure, as Hirschi and Hindelang (1977) suggested. The association between school failure and offending has been demonstrated consistently in longitudinal surveys (e.g., Polk et al., 1981; Wolfgang, Figlio, & Sellin, 1972). In their longitudinal survey of over 200 African-American males, Robins and Hill (1966) reported that truancy and school failure were both related to early official delinquency (before age 15). They showed how the probability of offending increased according to the presence of truancy, school failure, and low socioeconomic status. Where none of these factors was present, only 3% of the boys became delinquent, compared with 36% when all three factors were present.

A more plausible explanatory factor underlying the link between intelligence and offending is the ability to manipulate abstract concepts. People who are poor at this tend to do badly in intelligence tests such as the Matrices and in school attainment, and they also tend to commit offenses, mainly because of their poor ability to foresee the consequences of their offending and to appreciate the feelings of victims (i.e., their low empathy). Certain family backgrounds are less conducive than others to the development of abstract reasoning. For example, lower-class, poorer parents tend to live for the present and to have little thought for the future, and tend to talk in terms of the concrete rather than the abstract, as Cohen (1955) pointed out many years ago. A lack of concern for the future is also linked to the concept of impulsivity.

Modern research is studying not just intelligence but also detailed patterns of cognitive and neuropsychological deficit. For example, in a New Zealand longitudinal study of over 1,000 children from birth to age 15, Moffitt and Silva (1988b) found that self-reported offending was related to verbal, memory, and visual-motor integration deficits, independently of low social class and family adversity. Neuropsychological research might lead to important advances in knowledge about the link between brain functioning and delinquency. For example, the "executive functions" of the brain, located in the frontal lobes, include sustaining attention and concentration, abstract reasoning and concept formation, anticipation and planning, self-monitoring of behavior, and inhibition of inappropriate or impulsive behavior (Moffitt, 1990b). Deficits in these executive functions are conducive to low measured intelligence and to offending. Moffitt and Henry (1989) found deficits in these executive functions especially for delinquents who were both antisocial and hyperactive.

Parental Supervision, Discipline, and Attitude

Loeber and Stouthamer-Loeber (1986) completed an exhaustive review of family factors as correlates and predictors of juvenile conduct problems and delinquency. They found that poor parental supervision or monitoring, erratic or harsh parental discipline, parental disharmony, parental rejection of the child, and low parental involvement in the child's activities (as well as antisocial parents and large family size) were all important predictors of offending. Similar conclusions were drawn by Snyder and Patterson (1987) in another detailed review. Utting, Bright, and Henricson (1993) have provided perhaps the most recent extensive review of the literature on family factors in offending.

In the Cambridge–Somerville study in Boston, McCord (1979) reported that poor parental supervision was the best predictor of both violent and property crimes. Parental aggressiveness (which included harsh discipline, shading into child abuse at the extreme) and parental conflict were significant precursors of violent but not property crimes, while the mother's attitude (passive or rejecting) was a significant precursor of property but not violent crimes. Robins (1979), in her long-term follow-up studies in St. Louis, also found that poor supervision and discipline were consistently related to later offending, and Shedler and Block (1990) in San Francisco reported that hostile and rejecting mothers when children were age 5 predicted their children's frequent drug use at age 18.

Other studies also show the link between supervision and discipline and delinquency. In a Birmingham survey, Wilson (1980) followed up nearly 400 boys in 120 large intact families, and concluded that the most important correlate of convictions, cautions, and self-reported delinquency was lax parental supervision at age 10. In their English national survey of juveniles aged 14–15 and their mothers, Riley and Shaw (1985) found that poor parental supervision was the most important correlate of self-reported delinquency for girls, and that it was the second most important for boys (after delinquent friends). Also, in their follow-up of nearly 700 Nottingham children in intact families, the Newsons reported that physical punishment by parents at ages 7 and 11 predicted later convictions (Newson & Newson, 1989).

In the Cambridge study, West and Farrington (1973) found that harsh or erratic parental discipline, cruel, passive, or neglecting parental attitude, poor supervision, and parental conflict, measured at age 8, all predicted later juvenile convictions. Generally, the presence of any of these adverse family background features doubled the risk of later juvenile conviction. Furthermore, poor parental child-rearing behavior (a combination of discipline, attitude, and conflict) and poor parental supervision both predicted juvenile self-reported as well as official offending (Farrington, 1979). Poor parental child-rearing behavior was related to early rather than later offending, and it predicted early convictions between ages 10 and 13 independently of all other factors (Farrington, 1984, 1986b). However, it was not characteristic of those first convicted as adults (West & Farrington, 1977). In contrast, poor parental supervision predicted both juvenile and adult convictions (Farrington, 1992b).

Offenders tend to have difficulties in their personal relationships. The juvenile offenders tended to be in conflict with their parents at age 18. Both juvenile and adult offenders tended to have a poor relationship with their wife or cohabitee at age 32, or had assaulted her, and they also tended to be divorced and/or separated from their children (Farrington, 1992c).

There seems to be significant intergenerational transmission of aggressive and violent behavior from parents to children, as McCord's (1979) research suggested. This is also demonstrated in Widom's (1989) retrospective study of over 900 abused children in Indianapolis. Children who were physically abused up to age 11 were significantly likely to become violent offenders in the next 15 years. Similarly, harsh discipline and attitude of parents when the boys were age 8 significantly predicted later violent as opposed to nonviolent offenders up to age 21 in the Cambridge study (Farrington, 1978). More recent research (Farrington, 1991b) showed that harsh discipline and attitude predicted both violent and persistent offending up to age 32. Of course, the mechanisms underlying the intergenerational transmission of violence could be genetic as well as environmental (DiLalla & Gottesman, 1991).

Broken Homes

Inspired by psychoanalytic ideas, Bowlby (1951) popularized the theory that broken homes cause delinquency. In his research, he found that delinquents were significantly more likely than comparison children to have suffered a complete and prolonged separation from their mothers during their first 5 years of life. He argued that mother love in infancy and childhood was just as important for mental health as were vitamins and proteins for physical health. He thought that it was essential that a child should experience a warm, loving, and continuous relationship with a mother figure. If a child suffered a prolonged period of maternal deprivation during the first 5 years of life, this would have irreversible negative effects, including delinquency. Such deprived children tended to become "affectionless characters," failing to develop loving ties with other children or with adults, and hence having no close friendships and no deep emotional feelings in their relationships.

Later researchers (Andry, 1960; Rutter, 1981b) have emphasized the complexity of the concept of maternal deprivation and the importance of separation from the father as well as from the mother. Many of the children identified as suffering maternal deprivation in Bowlby's research and other early studies were children who had been brought up in institutions. They had suffered not only maternal but also paternal deprivation, and they had also had a constantly changing stream of caretakers. The development of affectionless characters and delinquency may have more to do with the lack of a continuous, unbroken, loving relationship with one person than with the loss of the mother specifically. It is important to distinguish separation from a biological or operative parent after a loving relationship has been built up, attributable to different causes such as death or parental disharmony, from the complete lack of contact with a biological parent. Modern research, inspired by Bowlby's work, on offending and childhood conduct disorder focuses especially on the attachment of the child to the mother (Erickson, Sroufe, & Egeland, 1985; Sroufe, 1986).

Most studies of broken homes have focused on the loss of the father rather than the mother, simply because the loss of a father is much more common. In the Newcastle Thousand Family Study, Kolvin et al. (1988) reported that marital disruption (divorce or separation) in a boy's first 5 years predicted his later convictions up to age 32. McCord (1982) in Boston carried out an interesting study of the relationship between homes broken by loss of the natural father and later serious offending. She found that the prevalence of offending was high for boys reared in broken homes without affectionate mothers (62%) and for those reared in united homes characterized by parental conflict (52%), irrespective of whether they had affectionate mothers. The prevalence of offending was low for those reared in united homes without conflict (26%) and – importantly – equally low for boys from broken homes with affectionate mothers (22%).

These results suggest that it is not so much the broken home that is criminogenic as the parental conflict that often causes it. They also suggest that a loving mother might in some sense be able to compensate for the loss of a father. The importance of the cause of the broken home is also shown in the English national longitudinal survey of over 5,000 children born during a selected week of 1946 (Wadsworth, 1979). Illegitimate children were excluded from this survey, so all the children began life with two married parents. Boys from homes broken by divorce or separation had an increased likelihood of being convicted or officially cautioned up to age 21, in comparison with those from homes broken by death or from unbroken homes. Homes broken while the boy was between birth and age 4 especially predicted delinquency, while homes broken while the boy was between age 11 and age 15 were not particularly criminogenic. Remarriage (which happened more often after divorce or separation than after death) was also associated with an increased risk of delinquency, suggesting a possibly negative effect of step-parents. The meta-analysis by Wells and Rankin (1991) also shows that broken homes are more strongly related to delinquency when they are caused by parental separation or divorce rather than by death.

In the Cambridge study, both permanent and temporary (more than one month) separations before age 10 (usually from the father) predicted convictions and self-reported delinquency, providing that they were not caused by death or hospitalization (Farrington, 1992c). However, homes broken at an early age (under age 5) were not unusually criminogenic (West & Farrington, 1973). Separation before age 10 predicted both juvenile and adult convictions (Farrington, 1992b) and convictions up to age 32 independently of all other factors such as low family income or poor school attainment (Farrington, 1990b, 1993a).

In a survey of over 1,000 adults carried out for the British *Sunday Times* (November 14, 1993), the majority (63%) thought that it was vital for a child to grow up with both a mother and a father. Indeed, growing up in a single-parent, female-headed household has predicted offending in American research (e.g., Ensminger et al., 1983). In Canada, the large-scale Ontario Child Health Study of 3,300 children aged 4–16 reported that single-parent families tended to have conduct-disordered and substance-abusing children (Blum, Boyle, & Offord, 1988; Boyle & Offord, 1986). However, the researchers found it difficult to disentangle the effects of single-parent families from the effects of low-income families, because most single-parent families were living in poverty. The analyses of Morash and Rucker (1989) suggest that teenage childbearing combined with a single-parent female-headed household is particularly conducive to later offending by children.

Parental Criminality

Criminal, antisocial, and alcoholic parents also tend to have delinquent sons, as Robins (1979) found. Robins, West, and Herjanic (1975) followed up over 200 black males in St. Louis and found that arrested parents (the study's subjects) tended to have arrested children, and that the juvenile records of the parents and children showed similar rates and types of offense. McCord (1977), in her 30-year follow-up of about 250 treated boys in the Cambridge–Somerville study, also reported that convicted sons (her subjects) tended to have convicted fathers. Whether there is a specific relationship in her study between types of conviction of parents and children is not clear. McCord found that 29% of fathers convicted for violence had sons convicted for violence, in comparison with 12% of other fathers, but this may reflect the general tendency for convicted fathers to have convicted sons rather than any specific tendency for violent fathers to have violent sons. Wilson (1987) in Birmingham also showed that convictions of parents predicted convictions and cautions of sons; more than twice as many sons of convicted parents were themselves convicted.

In the Cambridge study, the concentration of offending in a small number of families was remarkable. West and Farrington (1977) discovered that less than 5% of the families were responsible for about half of the criminal convictions of all members (fathers, mothers, sons, and daughters) of all 400 families. West and Farrington (1973) showed that having convicted mothers, fathers, and brothers by a boy's 10th birthday significantly predicted his own later convictions. Furthermore, convicted parents and delinquent siblings were related to self-reported as well as to official offending (Farrington, 1979).

Unlike most early precursors, a convicted parent was related less to offending of early onset (age 10–13) than to later offending (Farrington, 1986b). Also, a convicted parent predicted which juvenile offenders went on to become adult criminals and which recidivists at age 19 continued offending rather than desisted (West & Farrington, 1977), and predicted convictions up to age 32 independently of all other factors (Farrington, 1990b, 1993a). As many as 59% of boys with a convicted parent were themselves convicted up to age 32 (Farrington, 1990b).

It is not entirely clear why criminal parents tend to have delinquent children. In the Cambridge study, there was no evidence that criminal parents directly encouraged their children to commit crimes or taught them criminal techniques. On the contrary, criminal parents were highly critical of their children's offending; for example, 89% of convicted men at age 32 disagreed with the statement that "I would not mind if my son/daughter committed a criminal offense." Also, it was extremely rare for a parent and a child to be convicted for an offense they had committed together (Reiss & Farrington, 1991).

There was some evidence that having a convicted parent increased a boy's likelihood of being convicted, over and above his actual level of misbehavior (West & Farrington, 1977). However, the fact that a convicted parent predicted self-reported offending as well as convictions shows that the labeling of children from known criminal families was not the only reason for the intergenerational transmission of criminality. It is possible that there is some genetic factor in this transmission (Mednick, Gabrielli, & Hutchings, 1983). However, the main link in the chain between criminal parents and delinquent children that we could discover in the Cambridge study was the markedly poor supervision by criminal parents.

Just as early family factors predict the early onset or prevalence of offending, later family factors predict later desistance. For example, it is often believed that male offending decreases after marriage, and there is some evidence in favor of this (Bachman, O'Malley, & Johnston, 1978). In the Cambridge study, there was a clear tendency for convicted males who got married at age 22 or earlier to be reconvicted less in the next 2 years than comparable convicted males who did not get married (West, 1982). However, in the case of both the males and their fathers, convicted males tended to marry convicted females, and convicted males who married convicted females continued to offend at the same rate after marriage as matched unmarried males. Offenders who married convicted females incurred more convictions after marriage than those who married unconvicted females, independently of their conviction records before marriage. Hence, it was concluded that the reformative effect of marriage was lessened by the tendency of male offenders to marry females who were also offenders. Rutter (1989) has drawn attention to the importance of studying turning points in people's lives, such as marriage, in studying human development.

Large Family Size

Many studies show that large families predict delinquency (Fischer, 1984). For example, in the National Survey of Health and Development, Wadsworth (1979) found that the percentage of boys who were officially delinquent increased from 9% for families containing one child to 24% for families containing four or more children. The Newsons in their Nottingham study also concluded that large family size was one of the most important predictors of offending (Newson, Newson, & Adams, 1993), and similar results were reported by Kolvin et al. (1988) in Newcastle-upon-Tyne and Ouston (1984) in Inner London.

In the Cambridge study, if a boy had four or more siblings by his 10th birthday, this doubled his risk of being convicted as a juvenile (West & Farrington, 1973). Large family size predicted self-reported delinquency as well as convictions (Farrington, 1979), and adult as well as juvenile convictions (Farrington, 1992b). Large family size was the most important independent predictor of convictions up to age 32 in a logistic regression analysis (Farrington, 1993a); 58% of boys from large families were convicted up to this age.

There are many possible reasons why a large number of siblings might increase the risk of delinquency. Generally, as the number of children in a family increases, the amount of parental attention that can be given to each child decreases. Also, as the number of children increases, the household will tend to become more overcrowded, possibly leading to increases in frustration, irritation, and conflict. In the Cambridge study, large family size did not predict delinquency for boys living in the least crowded conditions, with two or more rooms than there were children (West & Farrington, 1973). More than 20 years earlier, Ferguson (1952) drew a similar conclusion in his study of over 1,300 Glasgow boys, suggesting that an overcrowded household might be an important intervening factor between large family size and delinquency.

Socioeconomic Deprivation

Most delinquency theories assume that offenders disproportionately come from lower-class social backgrounds, and aim to explain why this is so. For example, Cohen (1955) proposed that lower-class boys found it hard to succeed according to the middle-class standards of the school, partly because lower-class parents tended not to teach their children to delay immediate gratification in favor of long-term goals. Consequently, lower-class boys joined delinquent subcultures by whose standards they could succeed. Cloward and Ohlin (1960) argued that lower-class children could not achieve universal goals of status and material wealth by legitimate means and consequently had to resort to illegitimate means.

Generally, the social class or socioeconomic status (SES) of a family has been measured primarily according to rankings of the occupational prestige of the family breadwinner. Persons with professional or managerial jobs are ranked in the highest class, while those with unskilled manual jobs are ranked in the lowest. However, these occupational prestige scales may not correlate very highly with real differences among families in socioeconomic circumstances. The scales often date from many years ago, when it was more common for the father to be the family breadwinner and for the mother to be a housewife. Because of this, it may be difficult to derive a realistic measure of SES for a family with a single parent or with two working parents (Mueller & Parcel, 1981).

Over the years, many other measures of social class have become popular, including family income, educational levels of parents, type of housing, overcrowding in the house, possessions, and dependence on welfare benefits. These may all reflect more meaningful differences in socioeconomic deprivation among families than occupational prestige does. For example, in his California self-report survey of over 4,000 children, Hirschi (1969) concluded that offending was related to the family being on welfare and the father being unemployed, but not to the occupational or educational status of the father.

In many criminological research projects, offenders and nonoffenders are matched on SES, or SES is controlled first in regression analyses. This reflects a widespread belief in the overriding importance of SES, but of course it often prevents the correctness of this belief from being tested. Unfortunately, as Thornberry and Farnworth (1982) pointed out, the voluminous literature on the relationship between SES and offending is characterized by inconsistencies and contradictions, and some reviewers (e.g., Hindelang et al., 1981) have concluded that there is no relationship between SES and either self-reported or official offending.

Beginning with the pioneering self-report research of Short and Nye (1957), it was common in the United States to argue that low social class was related to official offending but not to self-reported offending, and hence that the official processing of offenders was biased against lower-class youth. However, British studies have reported more consistent links between low social class and offending. In the British national survey, Douglas, Ross, Hammond, and Mulligan (1966) showed that the prevalence of official juvenile delinquency in males varied considerably according to the occupational prestige and educational background of their parents, from 3% in the highest category to 19% in the lowest.

Numerous indicators of SES were measured in the Cambridge study, both for the study male's family of origin and for the male himself as an adult, including occupational prestige, family income, housing, and employment instability. Most of the measures of occupational prestige (based on the registrar general's scale) were not significantly related to offending. However, in a reversal of the American results, low SES of the family when the male was aged 8–10 significantly predicted his later self-reported but not his official delinquency. Should we therefore conclude that official processing is biased in favor of lower-class youth?

More consistently, low family income and poor housing predicted official and self-reported, juvenile and adult, offending (Farrington, 1992c, 1992d). Low family income at age 8 was the best independent predictor of adult social dysfunction (Farrington, 1989b, 1993a). Low-income families also tended to have conduct-disordered children in the Ontario Child Health Study (Offord, Boyle, & Racine, 1989).

Socioeconomic deprivation of parents is usually compared with offending by sons. However, when the sons grow up, their own socioeconomic deprivation can be related to their own offending. In the Cambridge study, official and self-reported delinquents tended to have unskilled manual jobs and an unstable job record at age 18. Just as an erratic work record of his father predicted the later offending of the study male, an unstable job record of the male at age 18 was one of the best independent predictors of his convictions between ages 21 and 25 (Farrington, 1986b). Also, having an unskilled manual job at age 18 was an important independent predictor of adult social dysfunction and antisocial personality at age 32 (Farrington, 1993a, 1995). Between ages 15 and 18, the study males were convicted at a higher rate when they were unemployed than when they were employed (Farrington et al., 1986b), suggesting that unemployment in some way causes crime, and conversely that employment may lead to desistance from offending. Since crimes involving material gain (e.g., theft, burglary, robbery) especially increased during periods of unemployment, it seems likely that financial need is an important link in the causal chain between unemployment and crime.

It seems clear that socioeconomic deprivation is an important risk factor for offending and antisocial behavior. However, low family income and poor housing are better measures and produce more reliable results than low occupational prestige.

Peer Influences

The reviews by Zimring (1981) and Reiss (1988) show that delinquent acts tend to be committed in small groups (of two or three people, usually) rather than alone. In the Cambridge study, most officially recorded juvenile and young adult offenses were committed with others, but the incidence of co-offending declined steadily with age from age 10 onward. Burglary, robbery, and theft from vehicles were particularly likely to involve co-offenders, who tended to be similar in age and sex to the study males and lived close to the boys' homes and to the locations of the offenses.

The study males were most likely to offend with brothers when they had brothers who were similar in age (Reiss & Farrington, 1991). In a study of delinquent boys and girls in Ottawa, Jones, Offord, and Abrams (1980) proposed that there was male potentiation and female suppression of delinquency by boys. This theory was intended to explain why they found that male delinquents had relatively more brothers than sisters. However, this result was not obtained in the Cambridge study, where the number of sisters was just as closely related to a boy's delinquency as the number of brothers (West & Farrington, 1973).

The major problem of interpretation is whether young people are more likely to commit offenses while they are in groups than while they are alone, or whether the high prevalence of co-offending merely reflects the fact that, whenever young people go out, they tend to go out in groups. Do peers tend to encourage and facilitate offending, or is it just that most kinds of activities out of the home (both delinquent and nondelinquent) tend to be committed in groups? Another possibility is that the commission of offenses encourages association with other delinquents, perhaps because "birds of a feather flock together" or because of the stigmatizing and isolating effects of court appearances and institutionalization. It is surprisingly difficult to decide among these various possibilities, although most researchers argue that peer influence is an important factor.

There is clearly a close relationship between the delinquent activities of a young male and those of his friends. Both in the United States (Hirschi, 1969) and in the United Kingdom (West & Farrington, 1973), it has been found that a boy's reports of his own offending are significantly correlated with his reports of his friends' delinquency. In the American National Youth Survey of Elliott, Huizinga, and Ageton (1985), having delinquent peers was the best independent predictor of self-reported offending in a multivariate analysis. However, it is unclear how far this association reflects co-offending.

In the Cambridge study, association with delinquent friends at age 14 was a significant independent predictor of convictions at the young adult ages (Farrington, 1986b). Also, the recidivists at age 19 who ceased offending differed from those who persisted, in that the desisters were more likely to have stopped going around in a group of male friends. Furthermore, spontaneous comments by the youth indicated that withdrawal from the delinquent peer group was seen as an important influence on ceasing to offend (West & Farrington, 1977). Therefore, continuing to associate with delinquent friends may be a key factor in determining whether juvenile delinquents persist in offending as young adults or desist.

School Influences

It is clear that the prevalence of offending varies dramatically among different secondary schools, as Power, Alderson, Phillipson, Shoenberg, and Morris (1967) showed many years ago in London. However, what is far less clear is how much of this variation should be attributed to differences in school organization, climate, and practices, and how much to differences in the composition of the student body.

In the Cambridge study, Farrington (1972) investigated the effects of secondary schools on offending by following boys from their primary schools to their secondary schools. The best primary school predictor of juvenile offending in this study was the rating of troublesomeness at ages 8 to 10 by peers and teachers, showing the continuity in antisocial behavior. The secondary schools differed dramatically in their official offending rates, from one school with 21 court appearances per 100 boys per year to another where the corresponding figure was only 0.3. Moreover, going to a secondary school with a high delinquency rate was a significant predictor of later convictions (Farrington, 1993a).

It was, however, very noticeable that the most troublesome boys tended to go to schools with high delinquency rates, while the least troublesome boys tended to go to schools with low delinquency rates. Furthermore, it was clear that most of the variation among schools in their delinquency rates could be explained by differences in their intakes of troublesome boys. The secondary schools themselves had only a very small effect on the boys' offending.

The most famous study of school effects on offending was also carried out in London, by Rutter, Maughan, Mortimore, and Ouston (1979). They studied 12 comprehensive schools, and again found big differences in official delinquency rates among them. Schools with high delinquency rates tended to have high truancy rates, low-ability pupils, and low-class parents. However, the differences among the schools in delinquency rates could not be entirely explained by differences in the social class and verbal reasoning scores of the pupils at intake (age 11). Therefore, they must have been caused by some aspect of the schools themselves or by other, unmeasured factors.

In trying to discover which aspects of schools might be encouraging or inhibiting offending, Rutter et al. (1979) developed a measure of "school process" based on school structure, organization, and functioning. This was related to children's misbehavior in school, academic achievement, and truancy independently of intake factors. However, it was not significantly related to delinquency independently of intake factors. The main school factors that were associated with delinquency were a high amount of punishment and a low amount of praise given by teachers in class. Unfortunately, it is difficult to know whether much punishment and little praise are causes or consequences of antisocial school behavior, which in turn is probably linked to offending outside school. Therefore, it is not clear what school factors are conducive to delinquency. However, in regard to other outcome measures, Rutter (1983) argued that academic emphasis, good classroom management, the careful use of praise and punishment, and student participation were important features of successful schools.

Community Influences

Offending rates vary systematically with area of residence. For example, Clark and Wenninger (1962) compared four areas in Illinois and concluded that self-reported offending rates were highest in the inner city, less in a lower-class urban area, less still in an upper middle-class urban area, and lowest of all in a rural farm area. In their national survey of American juveniles, Gold and Reimer (1975) also found that self-reported offending was highest for males living in the city centers and lowest for those living in rural areas. More recently, Shannon (1988) documented how police contact rates over a long period were highest in the inner city (of Racine, Wisconsin) and lowest in the more peripheral areas.

The classic studies by Shaw and McKay (1942, 1969) in Chicago and other American cities also showed that juvenile delinquency rates (based on where offenders lived) were highest in inner-city areas characterized by physical deterioration, neighborhood disorganization, and high residential mobility. A large proportion of all offenders came from a small proportion of areas, which tended to be the most deprived. Furthermore, these relatively high delinquency rates persisted over time, despite the effect of successive waves of immigration and emigration of different national and ethnic groups in different areas. Shaw and McKay concluded that the delinquency-producing factors were inherent in the community. Areas had persistently high offending rates partly because of the cultural transmission of antisocial values and norms from one generation to the next and partly because of the ineffective socialization processes to which children were exposed in deprived areas. Both of these were consequences of the social disorganization of an area, or the poor ability of local institutions to control the behavior of local residents (Bursik, 1988).

Jonassen (1949) criticized Shaw and McKay's conclusions about the unimportance of national and ethnic origins. He pointed out that it was desirable not only to compare delinquency rates of the same ethnic group in different areas (as Shaw and McKay did) but also of different ethnic groups in the same area. Jonassen argued that Shaw and McKay's published data showed that Northern and Western Europeans had lower delinquency rates than Southern and Eastern Europeans living in the same areas of

Chicago. Jonassen also noticed that Shaw and McKay had found that Asians had low delinquency rates even when they lived in the most deteriorated areas of the city, whereas African-Americans had high delinquency rates in all areas where they lived (see also Gold, 1987).

Later work has tended to cast doubt on the consistency of offending rates over time. Bursik and Webb (1982) tested Shaw and McKay's cultural transmission hypothesis using more recent data in Chicago and more sophisticated quantitative methods. They concluded that the ordering of area delinquency rates was not stable after 1950, but reflected demographic changes. Variations in delinquency rates in different areas were significantly correlated with variations in the percentage of nonwhites, the percentage of foreign-born whites, and the percentage of overcrowded households. The greatest increase in offending in an area occurred when African-Americans moved from the minority to the majority, as indeed Jonassen (1949) and Short (1969) had noticed earlier. These results suggested that Shaw and McKay's ideas about community values that persisted irrespective of successive waves of immigration and emigration were incorrect. It was necessary to take account both of the type of area and of the type of individuals living in the area (e.g., Simcha-Fagan & Schwartz, 1986).

Similar ecological studies have been carried out in the United Kingdom (for a review, see Baldwin, 1979). For example, Wallis and Maliphant (1967) in London showed that official offender rates correlated with rates of local authority renting, percentage of land used industrially or commercially, population density, overcrowded households, the proportion of non-white immigrants, and the proportion of the population under age 21. However, offender rates were negatively related to suicide and unemployment rates and not related to illegitimacy or mental illness rates. Power, Benn, and Morris (1972) carried out a similar study in one lower-class London borough and found that official delinquency rates varied with rates of overcrowding and fertility and with the social class and type of housing of an area.

In Wallis and Maliphant's (1967) project, it was generally true that crime rates were higher in the inner city, and it is important to investigate why this is so. One of the most significant studies of inner-city and rural areas is the comparison by Rutter et al. (1975a, 1975b) of 10-year-old children in Inner London and in the Isle of Wight. They found a much higher incidence of conduct disorder in their Inner London sample. However, they also showed that the differences between the inner-city and rural areas disappeared after they controlled for family adversity (based on parental conflict, family breakdown, criminal parents, and large family size). Rutter

(1981a) concluded that rates of conduct disorder were higher in Inner London purely because family adversities were more common there. Any effects of inner-city residence on children's antisocial behavior were indirect and sequential: communities affected families, which in turn affected children.

It is not invariably true that offender rates are highest in inner-city areas. Baldwin and Bottoms (1976) in Sheffield found that the key factor influencing where offenders lived was the type of housing. Offender rates were lowest in owner-occupied areas and highest in areas of council housing and private renting, and the high crime areas were not all near the center of the city. They concluded that council housing allocation policies played a role in creating high offender rate areas. This again raises the issue of how far offender rates reflect the influence of the area or the kinds of individuals who happen to be living there. In the Cambridge study, offenders significantly tended to be living in rented accommodation rather than owner-occupied homes (Farrington, 1989b).

Reiss (1986) pointed out that a key question was why crime rates in communities changed over time, and to what extent this was a function of changes in the communities or in the individuals living in them. Answering this question requires longitudinal research in which both communities and individuals are followed up. The best way of establishing the impact of the environment is to follow people who move from one area to another, thus using each person as his or her own control. For example, Osborn (1980) in the Cambridge study found that moving out of London led to a significant decrease in convictions and self-reported offending. This decrease may have occurred because moving out led to a breaking up of co-offending groups, or because there were fewer opportunities for crime outside London. Also, Rutter (1981a) showed that the differences between Inner London and the Isle of Wight held even when the analyses were restricted to children reared by parents who had been reared in the same area. This result suggests that the movement of problem families into problem areas cannot be the whole explanation for area differences in offending.

Clearly, there is an interaction between individuals and the communities in which they live. Some aspect of an inner-city neighborhood may be conducive to offending, perhaps because the inner city leads to a breakdown of community ties or neighborhood patterns of mutual support, or perhaps because the high population density produces tension, frustration, or anonymity. There may be many interrelated factors. As Reiss (1986) argued, high crime areas often have a high concentration of single-parent female-headed households with low incomes, living in low-cost, poor housing. The weakened parental control in these families – partly caused by the fact that the mother had to work and left her children unsupervised – meant that the children tended to congregate on the streets. In consequence, they were influenced by a peer subculture that often encouraged and reinforced offending. This interaction of individual, family, peer, and neighborhood factors may be the rule rather than the exception.

Situational Influences

While most psychologists have aimed to explain the development of offending people, some have tried to explain the occurrence of offending events. Because offenders are predominantly versatile rather than specialized, it seems unnecessary to develop a different theory for each type of offender in studying characteristics of offenders. In contrast, in trying to explain why certain offenses occur, the situations are so diverse and specific to particular crimes that it probably is necessary to have different explanations for different types of offense.

The most popular theory of offending events is a rational choice theory, suggesting that they occur in response to specific opportunities when expected benefits (e.g., stolen property, peer approval) outweigh expected costs (e.g., legal punishment, parental disapproval). For example, Clarke and Cornish (1985) outlined a theory of residential burglary that included such influencing factors as whether a house was occupied, whether it looked affluent, whether there were bushes to hide behind, whether there were nosy neighbors, and whether the house had a burglar alarm or contained a dog. A related theory is the "routine activities" idea of Cohen and Felson (1979). They argued that predatory crime rates were influenced by routine activities that satisfied basic needs such as food and shelter. Changes in routine activities led to changing opportunities for crime. For example, the increased number of working women meant that more homes were left unattended during the day.

In the Cambridge study, the most common reasons given for offending were rational ones, suggesting that most property crimes were committed because the offenders wanted the items stolen (Farrington, 1993c). The next most common reasons focused on seeking excitement or enjoyment or relieving boredom. In Montreal, Le Blanc and Frechette (1989) also reported that most offenses (e.g., burglary, theft, drug trafficking) were motivated by the utilitarian need for material goods, while others (e.g., shoplifting, vandalism, joy riding) were predominantly committed for excitement.

In agreement with the idea of deterrence, a number of cross-sectional surveys have shown that low estimates of the risk of being caught were correlated with high rates of self-reported offending (Erickson, Gibbs, & Jensen, 1977). Unfortunately, the direction of causal influence is not clear in cross-sectional research, since committing delinquent acts may lead to lower estimates of the probability of detection as well as the reverse. Farrington and Knight (1980) carried out a number of studies, using experimental, survey, and observational methods, which suggested that stealing involved risky decision making. Hence, it is plausible to suggest that opportunities for delinquency, the immediate costs and benefits of delinquency, and the probabilities of these outcomes all influence whether people offend in any situation.

Explaining the Development of Offending

Summarizing the Major Risk Factors

The major risk factors for offending include socioeconomic deprivation, poverty, poor housing, and living in public housing in inner-city, socially disorganized communities. Other risk factors are poor parental child-rearing techniques (including poor supervision, harsh or erratic discipline, parental conflict, and separation from a biological parent), impulsivity (which may be linked to low physiological arousal), and low intelligence (which may reflect a poor ability to manipulate abstract concepts and deficits in the "executive functions" of the brain). It seems likely that communities influence parenting, and that parenting influences the development of impulsivity and low intelligence, although both of these may have a large biological or genetic component.

Other risk factors are probably linked to poverty, poor parenting, and impulsivity/intelligence. For example, teenage mothers tend to live in poverty, to use poor child-rearing techniques, and to have impulsive children with low intelligence. Perinatal complications, in combination with other risk factors, may cause neurological dysfunction, which in turn causes impulsivity or low intelligence. Large family size may lead to poor parenting because of the problem of dividing attention among several children at once. Criminal parents may be poor supervisors of children and disproportionately separated, or alternatively there may be genetic transmission of a biological factor linked to offending. The links between delinquent peers and delinquent schools and offending are less clear. However, it is likely that the occurrence of offenses depends on situational factors such as costs, benefits, and opportunities.

In explaining the development of offending, a major problem is that most risk factors tend to coincide and be interrelated. For example, adolescents living in physically deteriorated and socially disorganized neighborhoods disproportionately tend also to come from families with poor parental supervision and erratic parental discipline and tend also to have high impulsivity and low intelligence. The concentration and co-occurrence of these kinds of adversities make it difficult to establish their independent, interactive, and sequential influences on offending and antisocial behavior. Hence, any theory of the development of offending is inevitably speculative in the present state of knowledge.

It is important to establish which factors predict offending independently of other factors. In the Cambridge study, it was generally true that each of six categories of variables (impulsivity, intelligence, parenting, antisocial family, socioeconomic deprivation, child antisocial behavior) predicted offending independently of each other category (Farrington, 1990b). For example, Farrington and Hawkins (1991) reported that the independent predictors of convictions between ages 10 and 20 included high daring, low school attainment, poor parental child rearing, convicted parents, poor housing, and troublesomeness. Hence, it might be concluded that impulsivity, low intelligence, parenting, antisocial family, and socioeconomic deprivation, despite their interrelations, all contribute independently to the development of offending. In addition, of course, there is significant continuity in offending and antisocial behavior from childhood to adulthood, even though the prevalence of offending peaks in the teenage years. Any theory needs to give priority to explaining these results.

Building on Previous Theories

In proposing any new theory, it is important to build on previous theories that have not been disproved. As already mentioned, the classic delinquency theories of Cohen (1955) and Cloward and Ohlin (1960) aimed to explain why offenders disproportionately came from deprived, lower-class backgrounds. Cohen focused on the factors of poor parenting and impulsivity, while Cloward and Ohlin proposed that lower-class children adopted illegitimate means because they could not achieve their goals legitimately. Shaw and McKay (1969) aimed to explain why offenders disproportionately came from deprived inner-city areas, and focused on ineffective socialization processes and cultural transmission of antisocial values. Sutherland and Cressey (1974) also proposed that children learn to offend if they are surrounded by antisocial values, emphasizing the role of criminal families, delinquent peers, delinquent schools, and criminal areas.

In contrast to classic sociological theories that aim to explain why people learn to offend, classic psychological theories aim to explain why people are inhibited from offending. As they may be less familiar to criminologists, I will review them in some detail. According to these theories, children learn to inhibit their antisocial tendencies and build up internal inhibitions against offending in a conditioning or social learning process as a result of the way their parents react to their transgressions. Conditioning theories focus on reinforcement and punishment, whereas social learning theories focus on modeling and thinking processes as well.

One of the most influential conditioning theories was propounded by Trasler (1962). This theory suggests that when a child behaves in a socially disapproved way, the parent will punish the child. This punishment causes an anxiety reaction. After a number of pairings of the disapproved act and the punishment, the anxiety becomes classically conditioned to the act and to the sequence of events preceding the act. Consequently, when the child contemplates the disapproved act, the conditioned anxiety automatically arises and tends to block the tendency to commit the act, so the child becomes less likely to do it. Also, the anxiety generalizes to similar acts, so the child tends to feel anxious when contemplating similar acts. Hence, as Eysenck (1977) also argued, conscience is essentially a conditioned anxiety response.

However, whereas Eysenck emphasized individual, constitutional differences in conditionability, Trasler emphasized differences in parental child-rearing behavior as the major source of differences in criminal tendencies (conditioned anxiety). Children are unlikely to build up the link between disapproved behavior and anxiety unless their parents supervise them closely, use punishment consistently, and make punishment contingent on disapproved acts. Hence, poor supervision, erratic or inconsistent discipline, and conflict between parents are all conducive to offending by children. It is also important for parents to explain to children why they are being punished, so that they can identify precisely the behavior that is disapproved.

Trasler argued that middle-class parents were more likely to explain to children why they were being punished and to be concerned with long-term character building and the inculcation of general moral principles. This was linked to the greater facility of middle-class parents with language and abstract concepts. In contrast, lower-class parents supervised their children less closely and were more inconsistent in their use of discipline. Generally, middle-class parents used love-oriented discipline, relying on withdrawal of love as the main sanction, whereas lower-class parents used much more physical punishment. Trasler contended that lower-class children committed more crimes because lower-class parents used less effective methods of socialization.

More recent learning theories tend to be cognitive social learning theories, which emphasize the role of modeling, instruction, thought processes, and interpersonal problem solving strategies (Bandura, 1977; Nietzel, 1979; Sarason, 1978). The individual is viewed as an information-processor whose behavior depends on cognitive processes (thinking, problem solving) as well as the history of rewards and punishments. Ross and Ross (1988) explicitly linked offending to cognitive deficits, arguing that offenders tended to be impulsive, egocentric, concrete rather than abstract in their thinking, and poor at interpersonal problem solving because they failed to understand how other people were thinking and feeling (Chandler, 1973). Many other scholars have argued that offenders are deficient in their thinking processes (e.g., Guerra, 1989). Whether they are also deficient in interpersonal social skills is less clear (Dishion, Loeber, Stouthamer-Loeber, & Patterson, 1984; Hollin, 1990; Tisdelle & St. Lawrence, 1986).

Some modern criminological theories also aim to explain the development of internal inhibitions against offending. For example, Wilson and Herrnstein (1985) suggested that people differed in their underlying criminal tendency, and that whether a person chose to commit a crime in any situation depended on whether the expected benefits of offending outweighed the expected costs. The benefits of offending, including material gain, peer approval, and sexual gratification, tended to be contemporaneous with the crime. In contrast, many of the costs of offending, such as the risk of being caught and punished and the possible loss of reputation or employment, were uncertain and long-delayed. Other costs, such as pangs of conscience (or guilt), disapproval by onlookers, and retaliation by the victim, were more immediate.

As in many psychological theories, Wilson and Herrnstein emphasized the importance of the conscience as an internal inhibitor of offending, and suggested that it was built up in a process of classical conditioning according to parental reinforcement or punishment of childhood transgressions. Nevertheless, the key individual difference factor in the Wilson–Herrnstein theory is the extent to which people's behavior is influenced by immediate as opposed to delayed consequences. As in other theories, they suggested that individuals varied in their ability to think about or plan for the future, and that this was linked to intelligence. The major determinant of offending was a person's impulsivity. More impulsive people were less influenced by the likelihood of future consequences and hence were more likely to commit crimes.

Gottfredson and Hirschi (1990) castigated criminological theorists for ignoring the fact that people differ in underlying criminal propensities and that these differences appeared early in life and remained stable over much of the life course. The key individual difference factor in their theory is low self-control, which refers to the extent to which individuals are vulnerable to the temptations of the moment. People with low self-control are impulsive, take risks, have low cognitive and academic skills, are egocentric, have low empathy, and have short time horizons. Hence, they find it hard to defer gratification and their decisions to offend are insufficiently influenced by the possible future painful consequences of offending.

Gottfredson and Hirschi argued that crimes were part of a larger category of deviant acts (including substance abuse, heavy smoking, heavy drinking, heavy gambling, sexual promiscuity, truanting, and road accidents) that were all behavioral manifestations of the key underlying theoretical construct of low self-control. They conceded that self-control, as an internal inhibitor, was similar to the conscience, but preferred the term "self-control" because the idea of the conscience was less applicable to some of the wider category of acts that they were concerned with (e.g., accidents). Their theory easily explains the considerable versatility of antisocial behavior.

They argued that between-individual differences in self-control were present early in life (by ages 6 to 8), were remarkably stable over time, and were essentially caused by differences in parental child-rearing practices. Much parenting was concerned with suppressing impulsive behavior, with making children consider the long-range consequences of their acts, and with making them sensitive to the needs and feelings of others. Poor parental supervision contributed to low self-control, and poor parental supervision was more common in large families, with single parents, or with criminal parents. Ambitiously, Gottfredson and Hirschi aimed to present a theory that applied to all kinds of crimes in all kinds of cultures.

The Farrington Theory

The modern trend is to try to achieve increased explanatory power by integrating propositions derived from several earlier theories (e.g., Elliott et al., 1985; Hawkins & Weis, 1985; Pearson & Weiner, 1985). My own theory of offending and antisocial behavior (Farrington, 1986b, 1992b, 1993c) is also integrative, and it distinguishes explicitly between the long-term development of antisocial tendency and the immediate occurrence of offenses and other antisocial acts. The level of antisocial tendency depends on energizing, directing, and inhibiting processes. The occurrence of offenses and other antisocial acts depends on the interaction between the individual (with a certain degree of antisocial tendency) and the social environment, in a decision-making process.

The main energizing factors that ultimately lead to variations in antisocial tendency are desires for material goods, status among intimates, and excitement; boredom; frustration; anger; and alcohol consumption. The desire for excitement may be greater among children from poorer families, perhaps because excitement is more highly valued by lower-class people than by middle-class ones, because poorer children think they lead more boring lives, or because poorer children are less able to postpone immediate gratification in favor of long-term goals (which could be linked to the emphasis in lower-class culture on the concrete and present as opposed to the abstract and future).

In the directing stage, these motivations lead to an increase in antisocial tendency if socially disapproved methods of satisfying them are habitually chosen. The methods chosen depend on maturation and behavioral skills; for example, a 5-year-old would have difficulty stealing a car. Some people (e.g., children from poorer families) are less able to satisfy their desires for material goods, excitement, and social status by legal or socially approved methods, and so tend to choose illegal or socially disapproved methods. The relative inability of poorer children to achieve goals by legitimate methods could be because they tend to fail in school and to have erratic, low-status employment histories. School failure in turn may often be a consequence of the unstimulating intellectual environment that lower-class parents tend to provide for their children, and their lack of emphasis on abstract concepts.

In the inhibiting stage, antisocial tendencies can be reduced (or increased) by internalized beliefs and attitudes that have been built up in a social learning process as a result of a history of rewards and punishments. The belief that offending is wrong, or a strong conscience, tends to be built up if parents are in favor of legal norms, if they exercise close supervision of their children, and if they punish socially disapproved behavior using love-oriented discipline. Antisocial tendency can also be inhibited by empathy, which may develop as a result of parental warmth and loving relationships. There are individual differences in the development of these internal inhibitions. Because of associated neurological dysfunctions, children with high impulsivity and low intelligence are less able to build up internal inhibitions against offending, and therefore they tend to have a high level of antisocial tendency.

The level of antisocial tendency can also be increased in a social learning process if children are surrounded by antisocial models (criminal parents and siblings, delinquent peers, in delinquent schools and criminal areas). The belief that offending is legitimate, and antiestablishment attitudes generally, tend to be built up if children have been exposed to attitudes and behaviors favoring offending (e.g., in a modeling process), especially by members of their family, by their friends, and in their communities.

In the decision-making stage, which specifies the interaction between the individual and the environment, whether a person with a certain degree of antisocial tendency commits an antisocial act in a given situation depends on opportunities, costs and benefits, and the subjective probabilities of the different outcomes. The costs and benefits include immediate situational factors such as the material goods that can be stolen and the likelihood and consequences of being caught by the police, as perceived by the individual. They also include social factors such as likely disapproval by parents or spouses, and encouragement or reinforcement from peers. In general, people tend to make rational decisions. However, more impulsive people are less likely to consider the possible consequences of their actions, especially consequences that are likely to be long-delayed.

The consequences of offending may, as a result of a learning process, lead to changes in antisocial tendency or in the cost–benefit calculation. This is especially likely if the consequences are reinforcing (e.g., gaining material goods or peer approval) or punishing (e.g., legal sanctions or parental disapproval). Also, if the consequences involve labeling or stigmatizing the offender, this may make it more difficult for him or her to achieve aims legally, and hence there may be an increase in antisocial tendency. In other words, events that occur after offending may lead to changes in energizing, directing, inhibiting, or decision-making processes in a dynamic system.

Applying the theory to explain some of the results reviewed here, children from poorer families may be likely to offend because they are less able to achieve their goals legally and because they value some goals (e.g., excitement) especially highly. Children with low intelligence may be more likely to offend because they tend to fail in school and hence cannot achieve their goals legally. Impulsive children, and those with a poor ability to manipulate abstract concepts, may be more likely to offend because they do not give sufficient consideration and weight to the possible consequences of offending. Also, children with low intelligence and high impulsivity are less able to build up internal inhibitions against offending.

Children who are exposed to poor parental child-rearing behavior, disharmony, or separation may be likely to offend because they do not build up internal inhibitions against socially disapproved behavior, while children from criminal families and those with delinquent friends tend to build up antiestablishment attitudes and the belief that offending is justifiable. The whole process is self-perpetuating, in that poverty, low intelligence, and early school failure lead to truancy and a lack of educational qualifications, which in turn lead to low-status jobs and periods of unemployment, both of which make it harder to achieve goals legitimately.

It is important to try to explain the onset, persistence, and desistance of offending. The onset of offending might be caused by increasing motivation (an increasing need for material goods, status, and excitement), an increasing likelihood of choosing socially disapproved methods (possibly linked to a change in dominant social influences from parents to peers), increasing facilitating influences from peers, increasing opportunities (because of increasing freedom from parental control and increasing time spent with peers), or an increasing expected utility of offending (because of the greater importance of peer approval and lesser importance of parental disapproval).

Persistence depends on the stability of the underlying antisocial tendency that is built up in a long-term learning process. The relative ordering of people on antisocial tendency generally stays relatively constant over time, because energizing, directing, and inhibiting factors are built up in childhood and thereafter change rather slowly. Desistance from offending could be linked to an increasing ability to satisfy desires by legal means (e.g., obtaining material goods through employment, obtaining sexual gratification through marriage), increasing inhibiting influences from spouses and cohabitees, decreasing opportunities (because of decreasing time spent with peers), and a decreasing expected utility of offending (because of the lesser importance of peer approval and the greater importance of disapproval from spouses and cohabitees).

The prevalence of offending may increase to a peak between ages 14 and 20 because boys (especially lower-class school failures) have high impulsivity, high desires for excitement, material goods, and social status between these ages, little chance of achieving their desires legally, and little to lose (since legal penalties are lenient and their intimates – male peers – often approve of offending). In contrast, after age 20, desires become attenuated or more realistic, there is more possibility of achieving these more limited goals legally, and the costs of offending are greater (since legal penalties are harsher and their intimates – wives or girlfriends – disapprove of offending).

Prevention and Treatment

Risk Factors, Causes, and Prevention

Methods of preventing or treating antisocial behavior should be based on empirically validated theories about causes. In this section, implications about prevention and treatment are drawn from some of the risk factors and likely causes of antisocial behavior. I will focus more on risk factors than on my theory, although my theory aims to explain the risk factors and is concordant with the prevention implications. The major emphasis is on the early prevention of offending. Gordon and Arbuthnot (1987), Kazdin (1985, 1987), and McCord and Tremblay (1992) have provided more extensive reviews of this topic. My focus is on randomized experiments with reasonably large samples and with outcome measures of offending because the effect of any intervention on offending can be demonstrated most convincingly in such experiments (Farrington, 1983; Farrington, Ohlin, & Wilson, 1986a). Many interesting experiments are not randomized (Jones & Offord, 1989), or do not have outcome measures of offending (Kazdin, Bass, Siegel, & Thomas, 1989; Kazdin, Esveldt-Dawson, French, & Unis, 1987), or are based on very small samples (Shore & Massimo, 1979).

It is difficult to know how and when it is best to intervene, because of the lack of knowledge about developmental sequences, ages at which causal factors are most salient, and influences on onset, persistence, and desistance. For example, if truancy leads to delinquency in a developmental sequence, intervening successfully to decrease truancy should lead to a decrease in delinquency. On the other hand, if truancy and delinquency are merely different behavioral manifestations of the same underlying construct, tackling one symptom would not necessarily change the underlying construct. Experiments are useful in distinguishing between developmental sequences and different manifestations, and indeed Berg, Hullin, and McGuire (1979) found experimentally that decreases in truancy were followed by decreases in delinquency.

An important consequence of the continuity in antisocial behavior over time is that potential offenders can be identified at an early age with a reasonable degree of accuracy. In the Cambridge study, Farrington (1985) developed a prediction scale based on early antisocial behavior, convicted parents, socioeconomic deprivation, low intelligence, and poor parental child-rearing behavior, all measured at ages 8 to 10. This scale was constructed in a randomly chosen half of the sample and validated in the other half, with very little shrinkage in predictive efficiency. The 55 boys with the highest prediction scores included the majority of chronic offenders with six or more convictions up to age 25 (15 out of 23), 22 other convicted males (out of 109 with between one and five convictions) and only 18 unconvicted males (out of 265).

The ideas of early intervention and preventive treatment raise numerous theoretical, practical, ethical, and legal issues. For example, should prevention techniques be targeted narrowly on children identified as potential delinquents or more widely on all children living in a certain high-risk area (e.g., a deprived housing estate)? It would be most efficient to target the children who are most in need of the treatment. Also, some treatments may be ineffective if they are targeted widely, if they depend on raising the level of those at the bottom of the heap relative to everyone else. However, the most extreme group may also be the most resistant to treatment or difficult to engage, so there may be a greater payoff from targeting those who are not quite the most in need. Also, it might be argued that early identification could have undesirable labeling or stigmatizing effects, although the most extreme cases are likely to be stigmatized anyway and there is no evidence that identification for preventive treatment in itself is damaging. The degree of stigmatization, if any, is likely to depend on the nature of the treatment. In order to gain political acceptance, it may be best to target areas rather than individuals.

The ethical issues raised by early intervention depend on the level of predictive accuracy and might perhaps be resolved by weighing the social costs against the social benefits. In the Cambridge study, Farrington et al. (1988a, 1988b) found that three-quarters of vulnerable boys identified at age 10 were convicted. It might be argued that, if preventive treatment had been applied to these boys, the one-quarter who were "false positives" would have been treated unnecessarily. However, if the treatment consisted of extra welfare benefits to families, and if it was effective in reducing the offending of the other three-quarters, the benefits might outweigh the costs and early identification might be justifiable. Actually, the vulnerable boys who were not convicted had other types of social problems, including having few or no friends at age 8 and living alone in poor home conditions at age 32. Therefore, even the unconvicted males in the survey might have needed and benefited from some kind of preventive treatment designed to alleviate their problems. Blumstein, Farrington, and Moitra (1985) developed an explicit method of taking social costs and benefits into account in prediction exercises.

Can Offending Be Prevented and Treated Successfully?

In the 1970s there was a widespread belief, stimulated by influential reviews by Martinson (1974) in the United States and Brody (1976) in England, that existing treatment techniques had no differential effects on the recidivism of detected offenders. This conclusion was substantially endorsed by a National Academy of Sciences panel in an impressive, methodologically sophisticated review (Sechrest, White, & Brown, 1979). However, for a number of reasons, it should not be concluded that "nothing works," nor even that everything works equally well.

Martinson's (1974) conclusions were based on the Lipton, Martinson, and Wilks (1975) review of 231 studies of the effectiveness of correctional treatment between 1945 and 1967. However, Thornton (1987) found that only 38 of these studies met minimum methodological standards, included matched or randomized comparison groups, and had an outcome measure of recidivism. For nearly all of these studies (34 out of 38), the treatment was "psychological" in nature, such as individual counseling, psychotherapy, or casework. Of these 34 psychological studies, 16 showed that the treatment was effective in reducing recidivism, 17 found no significant difference, and only one found that the treatment was harmful. These numbers were more compatible with the hypothesis that psychological treatment had beneficial effects than with the hypothesis that psychological treatment had no effect (since that would have predicted equal numbers of positive and negative results). Other commentators (e.g., Gendreau & Ross, 1979, 1987; Ross & Gendreau, 1980) also argued that there were many examples of effective correctional treatment. Also, Martinson (1979) later rejected his original conclusions about the ineffectiveness of treatment.

In the past decade, reviews of the effectiveness of correctional treatment have increasingly used the technique of meta-analysis (Hedges & Olkin, 1985) to summarize results from a number of studies. This technique requires the calculation of a comparable effect size (ES) in each study, usually defined as the difference between the average score of a treated group and the average score of a control group, expressed in standard deviation units. This ES measure is not very relevant to studies of correctional treatment, where the main interest is usually in the difference between the proportion of a treated group reconvicted and the proportion of a control group reconvicted. However, at least for effect sizes below 1, the difference in proportions is roughly half the ES. Thus, an ES of 0.2 corresponds to a 10% difference in recidivism rates (e.g., 40% versus 50%) between treated and control groups. An ES of 0.2 or greater has considerable practical significance.

The most important meta-analyses all focus on adjudicated juvenile delinquents. In an analysis of 111 institutional treatment studies, Garrett (1985) reported a mean ES of 0.37 for all outcomes of correctional treatment, but only 0.13 for recidivism specifically. Most of her outcome measures were of institutional or psychological adjustment or academic or vocational skills. Behavioral treatments were generally effective in reducing recidivism (mean ES = 0.18), but psychodynamic techniques were not (mean ES = −0.01). In an analysis of 90 community-based treatment studies, Gottschalk, Davidson, Gensheimer, and Mayer (1987) reported an identical mean ES of 0.37 for overall effectiveness in treatment-control comparisons, but a higher ES for recidivism of 0.33. They considered that 56% of treatments had beneficial effects, 43% had no marked effect, and only 1% had harmful effects.

Whitehead and Lab (1989) drew more pessimistic conclusions from their meta-analysis of 50 studies of juvenile correctional treatment, largely because they set a very high criterion (a phi correlation of at least 0.2) for concluding that a treatment was effective. Only 16 of their 50 studies met this criterion for recidivism. This value of the phi correlation approximates to a 20% difference in recidivism rates (Farrington & Loeber, 1989) and to an ES of 0.4. According to Lipsey (1992), their mean ES was 0.25, which has some practical significance. Andrews et al. (1990b) criticized Whitehead and Lab's review and reanalyzed their data, concluding that the mean phi correlation for "appropriate" treatments was 0.3, corresponding to a halving of recidivism rates in many cases. Overall, behavioral treatments had a high mean phi correlation of 0.29 (or a mean ES of about 0.6), whereas nonbehavioral treatments had a mean phi correlation of only 0.04 (Andrews et al., 1990a).

Roberts and Camasso (1991) reviewed 46 studies of juvenile correctional treatment published between 1980 and 1990, and reported a mean ES of 0.36 for recidivism. However, the largest meta-analysis, based on 443 studies, was completed by Lipsey (1992). Overall, he considered that the treatment reduced offending in 64% of studies, increased offending in 30%, and made no difference in 6%. The mean ES for delinquency outcomes in all studies was 0.17, and behavioral and skill-oriented programs were most effective, with mean ESs in the 0.2–0.3 range after various adjustments.

It is reasonable to conclude from the meta-analyses that psychological, and especially behavioral, treatments generally succeed in reducing the recidivism rates of adjudicated juvenile offenders. The effect sizes are not large (on the order of 0.2–0.3), but they correspond to reductions of 10% to 15% in the proportion reconvicted, which to my mind is a decrease of some practical significance. Personally, I prefer more traditional methods of reviewing and summarizing the literature rather than meta-analysis. It seems more useful to identify the most adequate studies methodologically (e.g., randomized experiments with large samples, long follow-up periods, and outcome measures of offending) and to review the best studies in detail rather than try to summarize a large number of projects with varying degrees of methodological adequacy and relevance.

Why do treatments not cause a greater reduction in recidivism? There are many possible reasons for this, including the fact that interventions may not be sufficiently powerful (e.g., averaging only 1 hour per week in the review by Gottschalk et al., 1987) especially in comparison to the overwhelming influence of environmental (e.g., family, peer, community) factors. Another problem is the persistence of offending and antisocial behavior over time. Kazdin (1987) suggested that serious antisocial behavior might be viewed as a chronic disease that requires continuous monitoring and intervention over the life course. It might be desirable to distinguish chronic and less seriously delinquent juveniles, and to apply different types of interventions to these two categories (Le Blanc & Frechette, 1989). If the chronics are the worst 5%, interventions applied to the next 10% may be more successful.

Delinquency Prevention in Pregnancy and Infancy

Adolescent pregnancy prevention programs have been reviewed by Hayes (1987). Most focus on imparting knowledge (e.g., in sex education classes), improving decision-making skills (e.g., through peer counseling), enhancing a girl's life options (e.g., in education or employment), and providing access to contraception (e.g., in school-based clinics). While many programs have been developed and implemented, it is hard to find randomized experiments with rigorous evaluations of effectiveness, although encouraging results have been reported (Brooks-Gunn & Paikoff, 1993; Byrne, Kelley, & Fisher, 1993).

Problems in pregnancy and infancy can be alleviated by home visiting programs designed to help mothers. For example, in New York State, Olds,

Henderson, Chamberlain, and Tatelbaum (1986a, 1986b) randomly allocated 400 mothers either to receive home visits from nurses during pregnancy, or to receive visits both during pregnancy and during the first 2 years of life, or to a control group who received no visits. Each visit lasted about 1¼ hours, and the mothers were visited on average every 2 weeks. The home visitors gave advice about prenatal and postnatal care of the child, about infant development, and about the importance of proper nutrition and avoiding smoking and drinking during pregnancy.

The results of this experiment showed that home visits during pregnancy led to teenage mothers having heavier babies. Also, women who had previously smoked decreased their smoking and had fewer preterm deliveries. In addition, the postnatal home visits caused a decrease in recorded child physical abuse and neglect during the first 2 years of life, especially by poor unmarried teenage mothers; 4% of visited versus 19% of nonvisited mothers of this type were guilty of child abuse or neglect. This latter result is important because of the common observation that being physically abused or neglected as a child predicts later violent offending (Widom, 1989).

Similar results were obtained by Larson (1980) in an experiment in Montreal with over 100 lower-class mothers. The mothers were randomly allocated to receive either home visits both before and after the child's birth, or home visits only after the child's birth, or no visits. The home visitors (child psychologists) provided advice about taking care of the infant and about infant development. The home visits had beneficial effects; the children of visited mothers sustained significantly fewer injuries in the first year of life. The children of mothers visited both before and after birth (the category with the best outcome) had only half as many injuries as the children of nonvisited mothers. Also, the mothers visited both prenatally and postnatally were rated by observers as the most skilled in taking care of the child.

One of the largest early prevention projects was the Infant Health and Development Program, which was carried out with nearly 1,000 low-birth weight infants in eight sites across the United States (Brooks-Gunn, Klebanov, Liaw, & Spiker, 1993). Children were selected at birth and randomly allocated to experimental or control groups. The experimental families received about three home visits per month up to age 3, providing family support and information about health and development. Also, the experimental infants received a free child care program in their second and third years. This treatment had beneficial effects, since the experimental infants had higher intelligence and fewer behavior problems at ages 2 and 3.

Few early prevention experiments have included a long-term follow-up of the children. However, in Houston (Texas), Johnson and Walker (1987) carried out a home-visiting program when children were between 1 and 3 and then followed up about 140 children to age 11. Low-income Mexican-American families with 1-year-old children were randomly assigned to receive home visits or no visits. The home visitors advised the mother about child development and parenting skills, tried to help her develop an affectionate relationship with her child, and also aimed to develop the cognitive skills of the child. At the end of the program (age 3), the visited mothers were rated as more affectionate, as using more praise and less criticism, and as providing a more stimulating home environment. Teachers rated the visited children at age 11 as less aggressive than the controls. Therefore, the early home visits led to improved child behavior.

One of the few prevention experiments beginning in pregnancy and collecting outcome data on delinquency was the Syracuse (New York) Family Development Research Program (Lally, Mangione, & Honig, 1988). The researchers began with a sample of pregnant women and gave them weekly help with child-rearing, health, nutrition, and other problems. In addition, their children received free day care, designed to develop their intellectual abilities, up to age 5. This was not a randomized experiment, but a matched control group was chosen when the children were age 3. The treated children had significantly higher intelligence than the controls at age 3 but were not different at age 5. Ten years later, about 120 treated and control children were followed up to about age 15. Significantly fewer of the treated children (2% as opposed to 17%) had been referred to the juvenile court for delinquency offenses, and the treated girls showed better school attendance and school performance. Hence, this prevention experiment agrees with others in showing that early home visits providing advice and support to mothers can have later beneficial outcomes, including the reduction of offending. (For a review of home-visiting programs, see Olds & Kitzman, 1990).

Reducing Hyperactivity and Impulsivity

Hyperactivity is often treated, at least in the United States, using stimulant drugs such as Ritalin (Whalen & Henker, 1991). However, I will focus on psychological techniques designed to increase self-control. Hyperactivity and impulsivity might be altered using the set of techniques variously termed cognitive-behavioral interpersonal skills training, which have proved to be quite successful (e.g., Michelson, 1987). For example, the methods used by

Ross to treat juvenile delinquents (see Ross, Fabiano, & Ewles, 1988; Ross & Ross, 1988) were solidly based on some of the known individual characteristics of offenders: impulsivity, concrete rather than abstract thinking, low empathy, and egocentricity.

Ross believed that delinquents could be taught the cognitive skills in which they were deficient, and that this could lead to a decrease in their offending. His reviews of delinquency rehabilitation programs (Gendreau & Ross, 1979, 1987) showed that those that were successful in reducing offending generally tried to change the offender's thinking. Ross carried out his own "Reasoning and Rehabilitation" program in Ottawa, Canada, and found (in a randomized experiment) that it led to a significant (74%) decrease in reoffending for a small sample in a short 9-month follow-up period. His training was carried out by probation officers, but he believed that it could be carried out by parents or teachers.

Ross's program aimed to modify the impulsive, egocentric thinking of delinquents, to teach them to stop and think before acting, to consider the consequences of their behavior, to conceptualize alternative ways of solving interpersonal problems, and to consider the impact of their behavior on other people, especially their victims. It included social skills training, lateral thinking (to teach creative problem solving), critical thinking (to teach logical reasoning), value education (to teach values and concern for others), assertiveness training (to teach nonaggressive, socially appropriate ways to obtain desired outcomes), negotiation skills training, interpersonal cognitive problem solving (to teach thinking skills for solving interpersonal problems), social perspective training (to teach how to recognize and understand other people's feelings), role playing and modeling (demonstration and practice of effective and acceptable interpersonal behavior).

The successful social skills training program carried out by Sarason (1978) in Tacoma, Washington, is also worth mentioning here, although it was conducted in a juvenile institution. Nearly 200 male first offenders were randomly allocated to modeling, discussion, or control groups. The modeling and discussion groups focused on prosocial ways of achieving goals, coping with frustrations, resisting temptation, and delaying gratification. A 5-year follow-up showed that the proportion of recidivists was halved in the modeling and discussion groups compared with the control group.

Preschool Intellectual Enrichment Programs

If low intelligence and school failure are causes of offending, then any program that leads to an increase in school success should lead to a decrease in offending. One of the most successful delinquency prevention programs has been the Perry preschool project carried out in Ypsilanti (Michigan) by Schweinhart and Weikart (1980). This was essentially a Head Start program targeted at disadvantaged black children, who were allocated (approximately at random) to experimental and control groups. The experimental children attended a daily preschool program, backed up by weekly home visits, usually lasting 2 years (covering ages 3–4). The aim of the program was to provide intellectual stimulation, to increase cognitive abilities, and to increase later school achievement.

About 120 children in the two groups were followed up to age 15, using teacher ratings, parent and youth interviews, and school records. As demonstrated in several other Head Start projects, the experimental group showed gains in intelligence that were rather short-lived. However, they were significantly better in elementary school motivation, school achievement at 14, teacher ratings of classroom behavior at 6 to 9, self-reports of classroom behavior at 15, and self-reports of offending at 15. Furthermore, a later follow-up of this sample by Berrueta-Clement, Schweinhart, Barnett, Epstein, and Weikart (1984) showed that, at age 19, the experimental group was more likely to be employed, more likely to have graduated from high school, more likely to have received college or vocational training, and less likely to have been arrested.

By age 27, the experimental group had accumulated only half as many arrests on average as the controls (Schweinhart et al., 1993). Also, they had significantly higher earnings and were more likely to be homeowners. More of the experimental females were married, and fewer of their children had been born out of wedlock. Hence, this preschool intellectual enrichment program led to decreases in school failure, offending, and other undesirable outcomes.

The Perry project is admittedly only one study based on relatively small numbers. However, its results become more compelling when viewed in the context of 10 other similar American Head Start projects followed up by the Consortium for Longitudinal Studies (1983) and other preschool programs such as the Carolina Abecedarian Project, which began at age 3 months (Horacek, Ramey, Campbell, Hoffmann, & Fletcher, 1987). With quite impressive consistency, all studies show that preschool intellectual enrichment programs have long-term beneficial effects on school success, especially in increasing the rate of high school graduation and decreasing the rate of special education placements. The Perry project was the only one to study offending, but the consistency of the school success results in all projects suggests that the effects on offending might be replicable.

Parent Management Training

If poor parental supervision and erratic child-rearing behavior are causes of delinquency, it seems likely that parent training might succeed in reducing offending. Many different types of family therapy have been used (Kazdin, 1987; Tolan, Cromwell, & Brasswell, 1986), but the behavioral parent management training developed by Patterson (1982) in Oregon is one of the most hopeful approaches. His careful observations of parent–child interaction showed that parents of antisocial children were deficient in their methods of child rearing. These parents failed to tell their children how they were expected to behave, to monitor the behavior to ensure that it was desirable, and to enforce rules promptly and unambiguously with appropriate rewards and penalties. The parents of antisocial children used more punishment (such as scolding, shouting, or threatening), but failed to make it contingent on the child's behavior.

Patterson attempted to train these parents in effective child-rearing methods, namely, noticing what a child is doing, monitoring behavior over long periods, clearly stating house rules, making rewards and punishments contingent on behavior, and negotiating disagreements so that conflicts and crises did not escalate. His treatment was shown to be effective in reducing child stealing and antisocial behavior over short periods in small-scale studies (Dishion, Patterson, & Kavanagh, 1992; Patterson, Chamberlain, & Reid, 1982; Patterson, Reid, & Dishion, 1992).

Another parenting intervention, termed "functional family therapy," was evaluated by Alexander and his colleagues (Alexander & Parsons, 1973; Alexander, Barton, Schiavo, & Parsons, 1976; Klein, Alexander, & Parsons, 1977). This therapy aimed to modify patterns of family interaction by modeling, prompting, and reinforcement, to encourage clear communication of requests and solutions among family members, and to minimize conflict. Essentially, all family members were trained to negotiate effectively, to set clear rules about privileges and responsibilities, and to use techniques of reciprocal reinforcement with each other. This technique halved the recidivism rate of status offenders in comparison with other approaches (client-centered or psychodynamic therapy). Its effectiveness with more serious offenders was confirmed in a replication study using matched groups (Barton, Alexander, Waldron, Turner, & Warburton, 1985).

A combination of interventions may be more effective than a single method. For example, Kazdin, Siegel, and Bass (1992) found that a combination of parent management training and problem-solving skills training was more effective in reducing self-reported delinquency than either method alone. Also, more complex individualized techniques including several different elements may be effective. For example, Henggeler, Melton, and Smith (1992) and Henggeler, Melton, Smith, Schoenwald, and Hanley (1993) showed that "multisystemic therapy," targeting the relationships between children and families, peers and schools, was effective in reducing rearrests in a 2-year follow-up period, compared with the usual probation.

One of the most important prevention experiments was carried out in Montreal by Tremblay et al. (1991, 1992). They identified about 250 disruptive (aggressive/hyperactive) boys at age 6 for a prevention experiment. Between ages 7 and 9, the experimental group received training to foster social skills and self-control. Coaching, peer modeling, role playing, and reinforcement contingencies were used in small-group sessions on such topics as "how to help," "what to do when you are angry," and "how to react to teasing." Also, their parents were trained using the parent management training techniques developed by Patterson (1982). Parents were trained to notice what a child is doing, to monitor the child's behavior over long periods, to state house rules clearly, to reward prosocial behavior, to punish behavior consistently and contingently, and to negotiate disagreements.

This prevention program was quite successful. By age 12, the experimental boys committed less burglary and theft, were less likely to get drunk, and were less likely to be involved in fights than the controls. Also, the experimental boys were higher in school achievement. Interestingly, the differences in antisocial behavior between experimental and control boys increased as the follow-up progressed.

Reducing Socioeconomic Deprivation

If socioeconomic deprivation causes offending, then providing increased economic resources for the more deprived families should lead to a decrease in offending by their children. The major problem is to identify the active ingredient to be targeted. Low income and poor housing are interrelated, but the causal chain linking these factors with offending is unclear. Experiments are needed that target each of these factors separately. It seems likely that relative rather than absolute income and housing quality are important, since there have been great changes in recent years in the absolute values of these variables.

The most relevant studies are probably the income maintenance experiments carried out in the United States, which provided extra income for

poor families. However, the only evaluation of the effect of income maintenance on children's behavior (Groeneveld, Short, & Thoits, 1979) did not
yield positive results. There were no significant differences between the
experimental and control groups in the later official offending records of
children who were ages 9 to 12 at the time of the treatment. Nevertheless,
there is some evidence that extra welfare benefits given to ex-prisoners can,
in some instances, lead to a decrease in their offending (Rossi, Berk, &
Lenihan, 1980). In light of the clear link between socioeconomic deprivation and antisocial behavior, it is surprising that more prevention experiments targeting this factor have not been conducted.

Peer Influences

If having delinquent friends causes offending, then any program that reduces their influence or increases the influence of prosocial friends could
have a reductive effect on offending. Feldman, Caplinger, and Wodarski
(1983) carried out an experimental test of this prediction in St. Louis. Over
400 boys (age about 11) who were referred because of antisocial behavior
were randomly assigned to two types of activity group, each comprising
about 10 to 12 adolescents. The groups consisted either totally of referred
youths or of one or two referred youths and about 10 nonreferred (prosocial) peers. The focus was on group-level behavior modification. On the
basis of systematic observation, self-reports by the youth, and ratings by
group leaders, it was concluded that the antisocial behavior of the referred
youth with prosocial peers decreased relative to that of the referred youth
in homogeneously antisocial groups.

Several studies show that schoolchildren can be taught to resist peer
influences encouraging smoking, drinking, and marijuana use. (For detailed reviews of these programs, see Botvin, 1990; Hawkins, Catalano, &
Miller, 1992a.) For example, Telch, Killen, McAlister, Perry, and Maccoby
(1982) in California employed older high school students to teach younger
ones to develop counterarguing skills to resist peer pressure to smoke,
using modeling and guided practice. This approach was successful in decreasing smoking by the younger students, and similar results were reported by Botvin and Eng (1982) in New York City. Murray, Luepker, Johnson,
and Mittelmark (1984) in Minnesota used same-aged peer leaders to teach
students how to resist peer pressures to begin smoking, and Evans et al.
(1981) in Houston used films.

Using high-status peer leaders, alcohol and marijuana use can be reduced as well as smoking (e.g., Klepp, Halper, & Perry, 1986; McAlister,

Perry, Killen, Slinkard, & Maccoby, 1980). Botvin, Baker, Renick, Filazzola, and Botvin (1984) in New York compared the application of a substance use prevention program by teachers and peer leaders. The program aimed to foster social skills and teach students ways of resisting peer pressure to use these substances. They found that peer leaders were effective in decreasing smoking, drunkenness, and marijuana use, but teachers were not. A large-scale meta-analysis of 143 substance use prevention programs by Tobler (1986) concluded that programs using peer leaders were the most effective in reducing smoking, drinking, and drug use. These techniques, designed to counter antisocial peer pressures, could also help decrease offending.

School Programs

Several school programs have been implemented to decrease delinquency. For example, in Charleston (South Carolina), Gottfredson (1986) implemented the Positive Action Through Holistic Education (PATHE) program. The main elements included increasing shared decision making in schools, increasing the competence of teachers, increasing the academic competence of students (e.g., through teaching study skills), and improving the school climate (e.g., through a school pride campaign). An evaluation of the program in seven schools (compared with two control schools) suggested that it caused small decreases in self-reported delinquency and school suspensions. A similar program was also implemented successfully in a school in Baltimore (Gottfredson, 1988).

Another important school-based prevention experiment was carried out in Seattle by Hawkins, Von Cleve, and Catalano (1991) and Hawkins et al. (1992b). This combined parent training, teacher training, and skills training. About 500 first-grade children (age 6) in 21 classes in 8 schools were randomly assigned to be in experimental or control classes. The children in the experimental classes received special treatment at home and school designed to increase their attachment to their parents and their bonding to the school, on the assumption that offending was inhibited by the strength of social bonds. Their parents were trained to notice and reinforce socially desirable behavior in a program called "Catch 'Em Being Good." Their teachers were trained in classroom management – how to provide clear instructions and expectations to children, to reward children for participation in desired behavior, and to teach children prosocial methods of solving problems (Hawkins, Doueck, & Lishner, 1988).

In an evaluation of this program 18 months later, when the children were in different classes, Hawkins et al. (1991) found that the boys who received the experimental program were significantly less aggressive than the control boys, according to teacher ratings. This difference was particularly marked for white boys rather than black boys. The experimental girls were not significantly less aggressive, but they were less self-destructive, anxious, and depressed. By the fifth grade, the experimental children were less likely to have initiated delinquency and alcohol use. It might be expected that a combination of interventions might in general be more effective than a single technique, although combining interventions makes it harder to identify the active ingredient.

There are problems in evaluating school-based programs, because it is rare that investigators can randomly allocate a large number of schools to different conditions. However, in project "ALERT," Ellickson and Bell (1990) randomly allocated 30 schools in California and Oregon to three conditions. This project aimed to decrease adolescent drug use by motivating young people to resist drugs and by helping them acquire resistance skills, using modeling and reinforcement. The program succeeded in decreasing the onset of cigarette and marijuana use among nonusers, but had no effect on alcohol use or on the persistence of substance use among early users. Unfortunately, the beneficial effects had worn off 4 years later (Ellickson, Bell, & McGuigan, 1993).

Community Crime Prevention

If some feature of inner-city areas cause offending, and if that feature could be identified and changed by some kind of community action, then offending might decrease. Unfortunately, the specific causal feature is not known. Also, there are very few well-designed experimental tests of the effectiveness of community influences in preventing offending. The most insightful and extensive discussion of how to evaluate community prevention programs has been provided by Peterson, Hawkins, and Catalano (1992). They were concerned to evaluate the *Communities That Care* strategy (Hawkins & Catalano, 1992), which involves community leaders identifying locally important risk and protective factors and choosing specific family, school, and community interventions.

Shaw and McKay (1969) argued that, since offending was caused by social disorganization, it could be prevented by community organization. This idea led to the Chicago Area Project (for reviews of this, see Short, 1969; Schlossman & Sedlak, 1983). However, the effectiveness of this project, based on physically improving neighborhoods, coordinating community resources, and organizing recreational facilities for young people, was never properly evaluated. Of course, there are methodological and statistical problems raised by community-level interventions targeted at individuals.

More recent attempts to reduce crime by changing community factors have been reviewed by Hope and Shaw (1988). However, most of these projects are targeted at offenses, not offenders, and their success is typically evaluated using measures of crimes committed in neighborhoods (in official records or from victim surveys), rather than crimes committed by residents of neighborhoods. For example, Hope and Foster (1992) evaluated the effects of physically improving part of a council housing estate, and found that this tended to displace crime to other parts of the estate. Generally, these kinds of projects do not provide information directly about the effects of community features on individual offenders.

Situational Prevention

A number of crime prevention methods have been based on situational influences on crime. These methods are typically aimed at specific types of offenses and are designed to change the environment to decrease criminal opportunities (e.g., Clarke, 1983). They include increasing surveillance (e.g., by installing closed-circuit television cameras in subway stations), hardening targets (e.g., by replacing aluminum coin boxes with steel ones in public telephone kiosks), and managing the environment (e.g., by paying wages by check rather than by cash). These techniques have been shown to be effective in reducing crime in time-series studies with before and after measures (Clarke, 1992).

Few controlled experiments have been carried out on situational prevention. However, Farrington et al. (1993) studied the impact of store redesign, electronic tagging, and uniformed guards on shoplifting (measured by systematically counting specified items each day). They had before and after measures in nine experimental and control stores. They found that electronic tagging caused a lasting decrease in shoplifting, store redesign caused a short-lived decrease (because staff continually altered the displays), and the uniformed guard had no effect.

The major difficulty with this approach is displacement. If some people have criminal tendencies, and if one outlet for these is blocked, they will seek other outlets: other types of crimes, other methods of committing crimes, other targets, and so on. Situational prevention is not likely to be effective with chronic offenders, and hence should be targeted at more opportunistic and less committed offenders. Also, as Clarke (1983) pointed out, situational approaches provoke fears of "big brother" forms of state control and of a "fortress society" in which frightened citizens scuttle from their fortified house, in their fortified car, to their fortified workplace, avoiding contact with other citizens. However, it is also argued that many measures are unobtrusive and that some lead to a decrease in the fear of crime. Situational crime prevention is clearly an important approach that holds out the promise of decreasing offending.

As mentioned earlier, situational approaches are often linked to a rational decision-making theory of crime (e.g., Cornish & Clarke, 1986). If offending involves a rational decision in which the costs are weighed against the benefits, it might be deterred by increasing the costs of offending or by increasing the probability of costs (e.g., the risk of detection). Indeed, experimental and quasi-experimental research on drunken driving (e.g., Ross, Campbell, & Glass, 1970), driving with worn tires (e.g., Buikhuisen, 1974), and domestic violence (e.g., Sherman & Berk, 1984) suggests that adults can be deterred in this way. However, the attempt to deter juveniles in the "Scared Straight" program, by having adult prisoners tell them about the horrors of imprisonment, was not successful (e.g., Finckenauer, 1982; Lewis, 1983). Given the "macho" orientation of many young offenders, it may be that these warnings made offending seem more risky and hence more attractive.

Conclusions

A great deal has been learned in the past 20 years, particularly from longitudinal surveys, about risk factors for offending and other types of antisocial behavior. Offenders differ significantly from nonoffenders in many respects, including impulsivity, intelligence, family background, peer influence, socioeconomic deprivation, and residence in deprived inner-city areas. These differences are present before, during, and after criminal careers. Most is known about risk factors for prevalence and onset; more research is needed on risk factors for frequency, duration, escalation, and desistance. While the precise causal chains that link these factors with antisocial behavior, and the ways in which these factors have independent, interactive, or sequential effects, are not known, it is clear that at-risk individuals can be identified with reasonable accuracy.

Offending is one element of a larger syndrome of antisocial behavior that arises in childhood and tends to persist into adulthood, with numerous different behavioral manifestations. However, while there is continuity over time in the relative ordering of people on antisocial behavior, changes are also occurring. It is commonly found that about half of a sample of antisocial children go on to become antisocial teenagers, and about half of antisocial teenagers go on to become antisocial adults. More research is needed on factors that vary within individuals and that predict these changes over time. Research is especially needed on changing behavioral manifestations and developmental sequences at different ages. More efforts should especially be made to identify factors that protect vulnerable children from developing into antisocial teenagers. More longitudinal surveys are needed.

The theory proposed here suggests that the key underlying construct is antisocial tendency and that offending depends on energizing, directing, inhibiting, decision-making, and social learning processes. It aims to explain how individuals interact with situations to produce offenses. In addition to explaining between-individual differences in the prevalence or frequency of offending, theories should explain within-individual changes: why people start offending, why they continue or escalate their offending, and why they stop offending. For example, onset may depend primarily on poor parental child-rearing behavior, persistence may depend on criminal parents and delinquent peers, and desistance may depend on settling down with spouses and cohabitees.

The stability of antisocial behavior from childhood to adulthood suggests that delinquency prevention efforts should be implemented as early in a child's life as possible. Teenage pregnancy, substance use during pregnancy, and perinatal complications (including low birth weight) are risk factors for a variety of undesirable outcomes, including low intelligence and attainment, hyperactivity and impulsivity, and child conduct problems, aggression, and delinquency. Hence, it is important to mount delinquency prevention programs targeting these risk factors, and to follow up the children into adolescence and adulthood to establish the long-term effects on delinquency and crime. Home-visiting programs, which attempt to improve child-rearing methods and parental knowledge about child development, seem to be quite effective. Cognitive-behavioral interpersonal skills training to improve self-control, preschool intellectual enrichment programs to develop cognitive skills, and parent management training also seem to be effective methods of preventing offending.

The interrelationships among social problems make it hard to know which are causes and which are indicators, what causes what, or when and how it is best to intervene. Prevention experiments can be useful in establishing causal effects. Also, because of the link between offending and numerous other social problems, any measure that succeeds in reducing crime will have benefits that go far beyond this. Any measure that reduces crime will probably also reduce alcohol abuse, drunk driving, drug abuse, sexual promiscuity, family violence, truancy, school failure, unemployment, marital disharmony, and divorce. It is clear that problem children tend to grow up into problem adults, and that problem adults tend to produce more problem children. Major efforts to tackle the roots of crime are urgently needed, especially those focusing on early development in the first few years of life.

REFERENCES

Achenbach, T. M., Verhulst, F. C., Baron, G. D., & Althaus, M. (1987). A comparison of syndromes derived from the child behavior checklist for American and Dutch boys aged 6–11 and 12–16. *Journal of Child Psychology and Psychiatry, 28*, 437–453.

Alexander, J. F., Barton, C., Schiavo, R. S., & Parsons, B. V. (1976). Systems-behavioral intervention with families of delinquents: Therapist characteristics, family behavior and outcome. *Journal of Consulting and Clinical Psychology, 44*, 656–664.

Alexander, J. F., & Parsons, B. V. (1973). Short-term behavioral intervention with delinquent families: Impact on family process and recidivism. *Journal of Abnormal Psychology, 81*, 219–225.

Amdur, R. L. (1989). Testing causal models of delinquency: A methodological critique. *Criminal Justice and Behavior, 16*, 35–62.

American Psychiatric Association. (1994). *Diagnostic and statistical manual of mental disorders* (4th ed.). Washington, DC: Author.

Andrews, D. A., Zinger, I., Hoge, R. D., Bonta, J., Gendreau, P., & Cullen, F. T. (1990a). A human science approach or more punishment and pessimism: A rejoinder to Lab and Whitehead. *Criminology, 28*, 419–429.

Andrews, D. A., Zinger, I., Hoge, R. D., Bonta, J., Gendreau, P., & Cullen, F. T. (1990b). Does correctional treatment work? A clinically relevant and psychologically informed meta-analysis. *Criminology, 28*, 369–404.

Andry, R. G. (1960). *Delinquency and parental pathology*. London: Methuen.

Bachman, J. G., O'Malley, P. M., & Johnston, J. (1978). *Youth in transition* (Vol. 6). Ann Arbor, MI: University of Michigan Institute for Social Research.

Baker, R. L., & Mednick, B. R. (1984). *Influences on human development*. Boston: Kluwer-Nijhoff.

Baldwin, J. (1979). Ecological and areal studies in Great Britain and the United States. In N. Morris & M. Tonry (Eds.), *Crime and justice* (Vol. 1, pp. 29–66). Chicago: University of Chicago Press.

Baldwin, J., & Bottoms, A. E. (1976). *The urban criminal*. London: Tavistock.

Bandura, A. (1977). *Social learning theory.* Englewood Cliffs, NJ: Prentice-Hall.

Barclay, G. C. (1990). The peak age of known offending by males. *Home Office Research Bulletin, 28,* 20–23.

Barton, C., Alexander, J. F., Waldron, H., Turner, C. W., & Warburton, J. (1985). Generalizing treatment effects of functional family therapy: Three replications. *American Journal of Family Therapy, 13,* 16–26.

Bates, J. E., Bayles, K., Bennett, D. S., Ridge, B., & Brown, M. M. (1991). Origins of externalizing behavior problems at 8 years of age. In D. J. Pepler & K. H. Rubin (Eds.), *The development and treatment of childhood aggression* (pp. 93–120). Hillsdale, NJ: Erlbaum.

Berg, I., Hullin, R., & McGuire, R. (1979). A randomly controlled trial of two court procedures in truancy. In D. P. Farrington, K. Hawkins, & S. Lloyd-Bostock (Eds.), *Psychology, law and legal processes* (pp. 143–151). London: Macmillan.

Berrueta-Clement, J. R., Schweinhart, L. J., Barnett, W. S., Epstein, A. S., & Weikart, D. P. (1984). *Changed lives.* Ypsilanti, MI: High/Scope.

Blackburn, R. (1993). *The psychology of criminal conduct.* Chichester: Wiley.

Blouin, A. G., Conners, C. K., Seidel, W. T., & Blouin, J. (1989). The independence of hyperactivity from conduct disorder: Methodological considerations. *Canadian Journal of Psychiatry, 34,* 279–282.

Blum, H. M., Boyle, M. H., & Offord, D. R. (1988). Single-parent families: Child psychiatric disorder and school performance. *Journal of the American Academy of Child and Adolescent Psychiatry, 27,* 214–219.

Blumstein, A., & Cohen, J. (1987). Characterizing criminal careers. *Science, 237,* 985–991.

Blumstein, A., Cohen, J., & Farrington, D. P. (1988). Criminal career research: Its value for criminology. *Criminology, 26,* 1–35.

Blumstein, A., Cohen, J., Roth, J. A., & Visher, C. A. (Eds.). (1986). *Criminal careers and "career criminals."* Washington, DC: National Academy Press.

Blumstein, A., Farrington, D. P., & Moitra, S. (1985). Delinquency careers: Innocents, desisters and persisters. In M. Tonry & N. Morris (Eds.), *Crime and justice* (Vol. 6, pp. 187–219). Chicago: University of Chicago Press.

Botvin, G. J. (1990). Substance abuse prevention: Theory, practice and effectiveness. In M. Tonry & J. Q. Wilson (Eds.), *Drugs and crime* (pp. 461–519). Chicago: University of Chicago Press.

Botvin, G. J., Baker, E., Renick, N. L., Filazzola, A. D., & Botvin, E. M. (1984). A cognitive-behavioral approach to substance abuse prevention. *Addictive Behaviors, 9,* 137–147.

Botvin, G. J., & Eng, A. (1982). The efficacy of a multicomponent approach to the prevention of cigarette smoking. *Preventive Medicine, 11,* 199–211.

Bowlby, J. (1951). *Maternal care and mental health.* Geneva, Switzerland: World Health Organization.

Boyle, M. H., & Offord, D. R. (1986). Smoking, drinking and use of illicit drugs among adolescents in Ontario: Prevalence, patterns of use and socio-demographic correlates. *Canadian Medical Association Journal, 135,* 1113–1121.

Brennan, P. A., Mednick, B. R., & Mednick, S. A. (1993). Parental psychopathology, congenital factors and violence. In S. Hodgins (Ed.), *Mental disorder and violence* (pp. 244–261). Newbury Park, CA: Sage.

Breslau, N., Klein, N., & Allen, L. (1988). Very low birthweight: Behavioral sequelae at nine years of age. *Journal of the American Academy of Child and Adolescent Psychiatry, 27,* 605–612.

Brody, S. R. (1976). *The effectiveness of sentencing.* London: Her Majesty's Stationery Office.

Brooks-Gunn, J., Klebanov, P. K., Liaw, F., & Spiker, D. (1993). Enhancing the development of low-birthweight, premature infants: Changes in cognition and behavior over the first three years. *Child Development, 64,* 736–753.

Brooks-Gunn, J., & Paikoff, R. L. (1993). "Sex is a gamble, kissing is a game": Adolescent sexuality and health promotion. In S. G. Millstein, A. C. Peterson, & E. O. Nightingale (Eds.), *Promoting the health of adolescents* (pp. 180–208). New York: Oxford University Press.

Buikhuisen, W. (1974). General deterrence: Research and theory. *Abstracts in Criminology and Penology, 14,* 285–298.

Bursik, R. J. (1988). Social disorganization and theories of crime and delinquency: Problems and prospects. *Criminology, 26,* 519–551.

Bursik, R. J., & Webb, J. (1982). Community change and patterns of delinquency. *American Journal of Sociology, 88,* 24–42.

Byrne, D., Kelley, K., & Fisher, W. A. (1993). Unwanted teenage pregnancies: Incidence, interpretation and intervention. *Applied and Preventive Psychology, 2,* 101–113.

Chandler, M. J. (1973). Egocentrism and antisocial behavior: The assessment and training of social perspective-taking skills. *Developmental Psychology, 9,* 326–332.

Chandola, C. A., Robling, M. R., Peters, T. J., Melville-Thomas, G., & McGuffin, P. (1992). Pre- and perinatal factors and the risk of subsequent referral for hyperactivity. *Journal of Child Psychology and Psychiatry, 33,* 1077–1090.

Clark, J. P., & Wenninger, E. P. (1962). Socio-economic class and area as correlates of illegal behavior among juveniles. *American Sociological Review, 27,* 826–834.

Clarke, R. V. (1983). Situational crime prevention: Its theoretical basis and practical scope. In M. Tonry & N. Morris (Eds.), *Crime and justice* (Vol. 4, pp. 225–256). Chicago: University of Chicago Press.

Clarke, R. V. (Ed.). (1992). *Situational crime prevention.* New York: Harrow & Heston.

Clarke, R. V., & Cornish, D. B. (1985). Modelling offenders' decisions: A framework for research and policy. In M. Tonry & N. Morris (Eds.), *Crime and justice* (Vol. 6, pp. 147–185). Chicago: University of Chicago Press.

Cloward, R. A., & Ohlin, L. E. (1960). *Delinquency and opportunity.* New York: Free Press.

Cohen, A. K. (1955). *Delinquent boys.* Glencoe, IL: Free Press.

Cohen, L. E., & Felson, M. (1979). Social change and crime trends: A routine activity approach. *American Sociological Review, 44,* 588–608.

Consortium for Longitudinal Studies. (1983). *As the twig is bent . . . Lasting effects of pre-school programs.* Hillsdale, NJ: Erlbaum.

Cornish, D. B., & Clarke, R. V. (Eds.). (1986). *The reasoning criminal.* New York: Springer-Verlag.

Denno, D. W. (1990). *Biology and violence.* Cambridge: Cambridge University Press.

DiLalla, L. F., & Gottesman, I. I. (1991). Biological and genetic contributors to violence – Widom's untold tale. *Psychological Bulletin, 109,* 125–129.

Dishion, T. J., Loeber, R., Stouthamer-Loeber, M., & Patterson, G. R. (1984). Skill deficits and male adolescent delinquency. *Journal of Abnormal Child Psychology, 12,* 37–54.

Dishion, T. J., Patterson, G. R., & Kavanagh, K. A. (1992). An experimental test of the coercion model: Linking theory, measurement and intervention. In J. McCord & R. Tremblay (Eds.), *Preventing antisocial behavior* (pp. 253–282). New York: Guilford.

Donovan, J. E., Jessor, R., & Costa, F. M. (1988). Syndrome of problem behavior in adolescence: A replication. *Journal of Consulting and Clinical Psychology, 56,* 762–765.

Douglas, J. W. B., Ross, J. M., Hammond, W. A., & Mulligan, D. G. (1966). Delinquency and social class. *British Journal of Criminology, 6,* 294–302.

Ellickson, P. L., & Bell, R. M. (1990). Drug prevention in junior high: A multi-site longitudinal test. *Science, 247,* 1299–1305.

Ellickson, P. L., Bell, R. M., & McGuigan, K. (1993). Preventing adolescent drug use: Long-term results of a junior high program. *American Journal of Public Health, 83,* 856–861.

Elliott, D. S., Huizinga, D., & Ageton, S. S. (1985). *Explaining delinquency and drug use.* Beverly Hills, CA: Sage.

Elliott, D. S., Huizinga, D., & Menard, S. (1989). *Multiple problem youth.* New York: Springer-Verlag.

Ellis, L. (1987). Relationships of criminality and psychopathy with eight other apparent behavioral manifestations of suboptimal arousal. *Personality and Individual Differences, 8,* 905–925.

Ensminger, M. E., Kellam, S. G., & Rubin, B. R. (1983). School and family origins of delinquency. In K. T. Van Dusen & S. A. Mednick (Eds.), *Prospective studies of crime and delinquency* (pp. 73–97). Boston: Kluwer-Nijhoff.

Erickson, M., Gibbs, J. P., & Jensen, G. F. (1977). The deterrence doctrine and the perceived certainty of legal punishment. *American Sociological Review, 42,* 305–317.

Erickson, M. F., Sroufe, L. A., & Egeland, B. (1985). The relationship between quality of attachment and behavior problems in preschool in a high-risk sample. In I. Bretherton & E. Waters (Eds.), Growing points of attachment theory and research (pp. 147–166). *Monographs of the Society for Research in Child Development, 50* (Serial No. 209).

Eron, L. D., & Huesmann, L. R. (1990). The stability of aggressive behavior – even unto the third generation. In M. Lewis & S. M. Miller (Eds.), *Handbook of developmental psychopathology* (pp. 147–156). New York: Plenum.

Evans, R. I., Rozelle, R. M., Maxwell, S. E., Raines, B. E., Dill, C. A., Guthrie, T. J., Henderson, A. H., & Hill, P. C. (1981). Social modelling films to deter smoking in adolescents: Results of a three-year field investigation. *Journal of Applied Psychology, 66,* 399–414.

Eysenck, H. J. (1977). *Crime and personality* (3rd ed.). London: Routledge & Kegan Paul.

Farley, F. H., & Sewell, T. (1976). Test of an arousal theory of delinquency: Stimulation-seeking in delinquent and nondelinquent black adolescents. *Criminal Justice and Behavior, 3,* 315–320.

Farrington, D. P. (1972). Delinquency begins at home. *New Society, 21,* 495–497.

Farrington, D. P. (1973). Self-reports of deviant behavior: Predictive and stable? *Journal of Criminal Law and Criminology, 64,* 99–110.

Farrington, D. P. (1978). The family backgrounds of aggressive youths. In L. Hersov, M. Berger, & D. Shaffer (Eds.), *Aggression and antisocial behavior in childhood and adolescence* (pp. 73–93). Oxford: Pergamon.

Farrington, D. P. (1979). Environmental stress, delinquent behavior, and convictions. In I. G. Sarason & C. D. Spielberger (Eds.), *Stress and anxiety* (Vol. 6, pp. 93–107). Washington, DC: Hemisphere.

Farrington, D. P. (1980). Truancy, delinquency, the home and the school. In L. Hersov & I. Berg (Eds.), *Out of school: Modern perspectives in truancy and school refusal* (pp. 49–63). Chichester: Wiley.

Farrington, D. P. (1983). Randomized experiments on crime and justice. In M. Tonry & N. Morris (Eds.), *Crime and justice* (Vol. 4, pp. 257–308). Chicago: University of Chicago Press.

Farrington, D. P. (1984). Measuring the natural history of delinquency and crime. In R. A. Glow (Ed.), *Advances in the behavioral measurement of children* (Vol. 1, pp. 217–263). Greenwich, CT: JAI Press.

Farrington, D. P. (1985). Predicting self-reported and official delinquency. In D. P. Farrington & R. Tarling (Eds.), *Prediction in criminology* (pp. 150–173). Albany, NY: State University of New York Press.

Farrington, D. P. (1986a). Age and crime. In M. Tonry & N. Morris (Eds.), *Crime and justice* (Vol. 7, pp. 189–250). Chicago: University of Chicago Press.

Farrington, D. P. (1986b). Stepping stones to adult criminal careers. In D. Olweus, J. Block, & M. R. Yarrow (Eds.), *Development of antisocial and prosocial behavior* (pp. 359–384). New York: Academic Press.

Farrington, D. P. (1987a). Epidemiology. In H. C. Quay (Ed.). *Handbook of juvenile delinquency* (pp. 33–61). New York: Wiley.

Farrington, D. P. (1987b). Implications of biological findings for criminological research. In S. A. Mednick, T. E. Moffitt, & S. A. Stack (Eds.), *The causes of crime: New biological approaches* (pp. 42–64). Cambridge: Cambridge University Press.

Farrington, D. P. (1988). Studying changes within individuals: The causes of offending. In M. Rutter (Ed.), *Studies of psychosocial risk* (pp. 158–183). Cambridge: Cambridge University Press.

Farrington, D. P. (1989a). Early predictors of adolescent aggression and adult violence. *Violence and Victims, 4,* 79–100.

Farrington, D. P. (1989b). Later adult life outcomes of offenders and non-offenders. In M. Brambring, F. Losel, & H. Skowronek (Eds.), *Children at risk: Assessment, longitudinal research, and intervention* (pp. 220–244). Berlin: De Gruyter.

Farrington, D. P. (1989c). Self-reported and official offending from adolescence to adulthood. In M. W. Klein (Ed.), *Cross-national research in self-reported crime and delinquency* (pp. 399–423). Dordrecht, Netherlands: Kluwer.

Farrington, D. P. (1990a). Age, period, cohort, and offending. In D. M. Gottfredson & R. V. Clarke (Eds.), *Policy and theory in criminal justice: Contributions in honor of Leslie T. Wilkins* (pp. 51–75). Aldershot: Avebury.

Farrington, D. P. (1990b). Implications of criminal career research for the prevention of offending. *Journal of Adolescence, 13,* 93–113.

Farrington, D. P. (1991a). Antisocial personality from childhood to adulthood. *The Psychologist, 4,* 389–394.

Farrington, D. P. (1991b). Childhood aggression and adult violence: Early precursors and later life outcomes. In D. J. Pepler & K. H. Rubin (Eds.), *The development and treatment of childhood aggression* (pp. 5–29). Hillsdale, NJ: Erlbaum.

Farrington, D. P. (1992a). Criminal career research in the United Kingdom. *British Journal of Criminology, 32,* 521–536.

Farrington, D. P. (1992b). Explaining the beginning, progress and ending of antisocial behavior from birth to adulthood. In J. McCord (Ed.), *Facts, frameworks and forecasts: Advances in criminological theory* (Vol. 3, pp. 253–286). New Brunswick, NJ: Transaction.

Farrington, D. P. (1992c). Juvenile delinquency. In J. C. Coleman (Ed.), *The school years* (2nd ed., pp. 123–163). London: Routledge.

Farrington, D. P. (1993a). Childhood origins of teenage antisocial behavior and adult social dysfunction. *Journal of the Royal Society of Medicine, 86,* 13–17.

Farrington, D. P. (1993b). Have any individual, family or neighborhood influences on offending been demonstrated conclusively? In D. P. Farrington, R. J. Sampson, & P. O. Wikstrom (Eds.), *Integrating individual and ecological aspects of crime* (pp. 3–37). Stockholm: National Council for Crime Prevention.

Farrington, D. P. (1993c). Motivations for conduct disorder and delinquency. *Development and Psychopathology, 5,* 225–241.

Farrington, D. P. (1993d). Understanding and preventing bullying. In M. Tonry and N. Morris (Eds.), *Crime and justice* (Vol. 17, pp. 381–458). Chicago: University of Chicago Press.

Farrington, D. P. (1994). Childhood, adolescent and adult features of violent males. In L. R. Huesmann (Ed.), *Aggressive behavior: Current perspectives* (pp. 215–240). New York: Plenum.

Farrington, D. P. (1995). Psychosocial influences on the development of antisocial personality. In G. Davies, S. Lloyd-Bostock, M. McMurran, & C. Wilson (Eds.) *Psychology, law and criminal justice: International developments in research and practice.* Berlin: De Gruyter, in press.

Farrington, D. P., Bowen, S., Buckle, A., Burns-Howell, T., Burrows, J., & Speed, M. (1993). An experiment on the prevention of shoplifting. In R. V. Clarke (Ed.), *Crime prevention studies* (Vol. 1, pp. 93–119). Monsey, NY: Criminal Justice Press.

Farrington, D. P., & Burrows, J. N. (1993). Did shoplifting really decrease? *British Journal of Criminology, 33,* 57–69.

Farrington, D. P., Gallagher, B., Morley, L., St. Ledger, R. J., & West, D. J. (1986b). Unemployment, school leaving, and crime. *British Journal of Criminology, 26,* 335–356.

Farrington, D. P., Gallagher, B., Morley, L., St. Ledger, R. J., & West, D. J. (1988a). A 24-year follow-up of men from vulnerable backgrounds. In R. L. Jenkins & W. K. Brown (Eds.), *The abandonment of delinquent behavior* (pp. 155–173). New York: Praeger.

Farrington, D. P., Gallagher, B., Morley, L., St. Ledger, R. J., & West, D. J. (1988b). Are there any successful men from criminogenic backgrounds? *Psychiatry, 51,* 116–130.

Farrington, D. P., & Hawkins, J. D. (1991). Predicting participation, early onset, and later persistence in officially recorded offending. *Criminal Behavior and Mental Health, 1,* 1–33.

Farrington, D. P., & Knight, B. J. (1980). Four studies of stealing as a risky decision. In P. D. Lipsitt & B. D. Sales (Eds.), *New directions in psycholegal research* (pp. 26–50). New York: Van Nostrand Reinhold.

Farrington, D. P., & Loeber, R. (1989). Relative improvement over chance (RIOC) and phi as measures of predictive efficiency and strength of association in 2 x 2 tables. *Journal of Quantitative Criminology, 5,* 201–213.

Farrington, D. P., Loeber, R., & Van Kammen, W. B. (1990). Long-term criminal outcomes of hyperactivity-impulsivity-attention deficit and conduct problems in childhood. In L. N. Robins & M. Rutter (Eds.), *Straight and devious pathways from childhood to adulthood* (pp. 62–81). Cambridge: Cambridge University Press.

Farrington, D. P., Ohlin, L. E., & Wilson, J. Q. (1986a). *Understanding and controlling crime.* New York: Springer-Verlag.

Farrington, D. P., Snyder, H. N., & Finnegan, T. A. (1988c). Specialization in juvenile court careers. *Criminology, 26,* 461–487.

Farrington, D. P., & West, D. J. (1990). The Cambridge study in delinquent development: A long-term follow-up of 411 London males. In H. J. Kerner & G. Kaiser (Eds.), *Criminality: Personality, behavior, life history* (pp. 115–138). Berlin: Springer-Verlag.

Farrington, D. P., & Wikstrom, P-O. H. (1994). Criminal careers in London and Stockholm: A cross-national comparative study. In E. G. M. Weitekamp & H. J. Kerner (Eds.), *Cross-national longitudinal research on human development and criminal behavior* (pp. 65–89). Dordrecht, Netherlands: Kluwer.

Feldman, R. A., Caplinger, T. E., & Wodarski, J. S. (1983). *The St. Louis conundrum.* Englewood Cliffs, NJ: Prentice-Hall.

Ferguson, T. (1952). *The young delinquent in his social setting.* London: Oxford University Press.

Finckenauer, J. O. (1982). *Scared straight.* Englewood Cliffs, NJ: Prentice-Hall.

Fischer, D. G. (1984). Family size and delinquency. *Perceptual and Motor Skills, 58,* 527–534.

Furstenberg, F. F., Brooks-Gunn, J., & Morgan, S. P. (1987a). Adolescent mothers and their children in later life. *Family Planning Perspectives, 19,* 142–151.

Furstenberg, F. F., Brooks-Gunn, J., & Morgan, S. P. (1987b). *Adolescent mothers in later life.* Cambridge: Cambridge University Press.

Garrett, C. J. (1985). Effects of residential treatment on adjudicated delinquents: A meta-analysis. *Journal of Research in Crime and Delinquency, 22,* 287–308.

Gendreau, P., & Ross, R. R. (1979). Effective correctional treatment: Bibliotherapy for cynics. *Crime and Delinquency, 25,* 463–489.

Gendreau, P., & Ross, R. R. (1987). Revivification of rehabilitation: Evidence from the 1980s. *Justice Quarterly, 4,* 349–407.

Ghodsian, M., & Power, C. (1987). Alcohol consumption between the ages of 16 and 23 in Britain: A longitudinal study. *British Journal of Addiction, 82,* 175–180.

Gold, M. (1987). Social ecology. In H. C. Quay (Ed.), *Handbook of juvenile delinquency* (pp. 62–105). New York: Wiley.

Gold, M., & Reimer, D. J. (1975). Changing patterns of delinquent behavior among Americans 13 through 16 years old: 1967–72. *Crime and Delinquency Literature, 7,* 483–517.

Gordon, D. A., & Arbuthnot, J. (1987). Individual, group and family interventions. In H. C. Quay (Ed.), *Handbook of juvenile delinquency* (pp. 290–324). New York: Wiley.

Gottfredson, D. C. (1986). An empirical test of school-based environmental and individual interventions to reduce the risk of delinquent behavior. *Criminology, 24,* 705–731.

Gottfredson, D. C. (1988). An evaluation of an organization development approach to reducing school disorder. *Evaluation Review, 11,* 739–763.

Gottfredson, M., & Hirschi, T. (1990). *A general theory of crime.* Stanford, CA: Stanford University Press.

Gottschalk, R., Davidson, W. S., Gensheimer, L. K., & Mayer, J. P. (1987). Community-based interventions. In H. C. Quay (Ed.), *Handbook of juvenile delinquency* (pp. 266–289). New York: Wiley.

Groeneveld, L. P., Short, J. F., & Thoits, P. (1979). *Design of a study to assess the impact of income maintenance on delinquency.* Final report to the National Institute of Juvenile Justice and Delinquency Prevention, Washington, DC.

Guerra, N. (1989). Consequential thinking and self-reported delinquency in high school youth. *Criminal Justice and Behavior, 16,* 440–454.

Hawkins, J. D., & Catalano, R. F. (1992). *Communities that care.* San Francisco: Jossey-Bass.

Hawkins, J. D., Catalano, R. F., & Miller, J. Y. (1992a). Risk and protective factors for alcohol and other drug problems in adolescence and early adulthood: Implications for substance use prevention. *Psychological Bulletin, 112,* 64–105.

Hawkins, J. D., Catalano, R. F., Morrison, D. M., O'Donnell, J., Abbott, R. D., & Day, L. E. (1992b). The Seattle social development project: Effects of the first four years on protective factors and problem behaviors. In J. McCord & R. Tremblay (Eds.), *Preventing antisocial behavior* (pp. 139–161). New York: Guilford.

Hawkins, J. D., Doueck, H. J., & Lishner, D. M. (1988). Changing teaching practices in mainstream classrooms to improve bonding and behavior of low achievers. *American Educational Research Journal, 25,* 31–50.

Hawkins, J. D., Von Cleve, E., & Catalano, R. F. (1991). Reducing early childhood aggression: Results of a primary prevention program. *Journal of the American Academy of Child and Adolescent Psychiatry, 30,* 208–217.

Hawkins, J. D., & Weis, J. G. (1985). The social development model: An integrated approach to delinquency prevention. *Journal of Primary Prevention, 6,* 73–97.

Hayes, C. D. (Ed.). (1987). *Risking the future.* Washington, DC: National Academy Press.

Hedges, L. V., & Olkin, I. (1985). *Statistical methods for meta-analysis.* Orlando, FL: Academic Press.

Henggeler, S. W., Melton, G. B., & Smith, L. A. (1992). Family preservation using multi-systemic therapy: An effective alternative to incarcerating serious juvenile offenders. *Journal of Consulting and Clinical Psychology, 60,* 953–961.

Henggeler, S. W., Melton, G. B., Smith, L. A., Schoenwald, S. K., & Hanley, J. H. (1993). Family preservation using multi-systemic treatment: Long-term follow-up to a clinical trial with serious juvenile offenders. *Journal of Child and Family Studies, 2,* 283–293.

Hindelang, M. J., Hirschi, T., & Weis, J. G. (1981). *Measuring delinquency.* Beverly Hills, CA: Sage.

Hirschi, T. (1969). *Causes of delinquency.* Berkeley, CA: University of California Press.

Hirschi, T., & Hindelang, M. J. (1977). Intelligence and delinquency: A revisionist review. *American Sociological Review, 42,* 571–587.

Hollin, C. R. (1990). Social skills training with delinquents: A look at the evidence and some recommendations for practice. *British Journal of Social Work, 20,* 483–493.

Hollin, C. R. (1992). *Criminal behavior.* London: Falmer Press.

Hope, T., & Foster, J. (1992). Conflicting forces: Changing the dynamics of crime and community on a "problem" estate. *British Journal of Criminology, 32,* 488–504.

Hope, T., & Shaw, M. (Eds.). (1988). *Communities and crime reduction.* London: Her Majesty's Stationery Office.

Horacek, H. J., Ramey, C. T., Campbell, F. A., Hoffmann, K. P., & Fletcher, R. H. (1987). Predicting school failure and assessing early intervention with high-risk children. *Journal of the American Academy of Child and Adolescent Psychiatry, 26,* 758–763.

Huizinga, D., & Elliott, D. S. (1986). Reassessing the reliability and validity of self-report measures. *Journal of Quantitative Criminology, 2,* 293–327.

Jessor, R., & Jessor, S. L. (1977). *Problem behavior and psychosocial development.* New York: Academic Press.

Johnson, D. L., & Walker, T. (1987). Primary prevention of behavior problems in Mexican-American children. *American Journal of Community Psychology, 15,* 375–385.

Jonassen, C. T. (1949). A re-evaluation and critique of the logic and some methods of Shaw and McKay. *American Sociological Review, 14,* 608–614.

Jones, M. B., & Offord, D. R. (1989). Reduction of antisocial behavior in poor children by non-school skill-development. *Journal of Child Psychology and Psychiatry, 30,* 737–750.

Jones, M. B., Offord, D. R., & Abrams, N. (1980). Brothers, sisters and antisocial behavior. *British Journal of Psychiatry, 136,* 139–145.

Kagan, J., Reznick, J. S., & Snidman, N. (1988). Biological bases of childhood shyness. *Science, 240,* 167–171.

Kandel, E., & Mednick, S. A. (1991). Perinatal complications predict violent offending. *Criminology, 29,* 519–529.

Kandel, E., Mednick, S. A., Kirkegaard-Sorenson, L., Hutchings, B., Knop, J., Rosenberg, R., & Schulsinger, F. (1988). IQ as a protective factor for subjects at high risk for antisocial behavior. *Journal of Consulting and Clinical Psychology, 56,* 224–226.

Kazdin, A. E. (1985). *Treatment of antisocial behavior in children and adolescents.* Homewood, IL: Dorsey Press.

Kazdin, A. E. (1987). Treatment of antisocial behavior in children: Current status and future directions. *Psychological Bulletin, 102,* 187–203.

Kazdin, A. E., Bass, D., Siegel, T., & Thomas, C. (1989). Cognitive-behavioral therapy and relationship therapy in the treatment of children referred for antisocial behavior. *Journal of Consulting and Clinical Psychology, 57,* 522–535.

Kazdin, A. E., Esveldt-Dawson, K., French, N. H., & Unis, A. S. (1987). Effects of parent management training and problem-solving skills training combined in the treatment of antisocial child behavior. *Journal of the American Academy of Child and Adolescent Psychiatry, 26,* 416–424.

Kazdin, A. E., Siegel, T. C., & Bass, D. (1992). Cognitive problem-solving skills training and parent management training in the treatment of antisocial behavior in children. *Journal of Consulting and Clinical Psychology, 60,* 733–747.

Klein, M. W. (1984). Offense specialization and versatility among juveniles. *British Journal of Criminology, 24,* 185–194.

Klein, N. C., Alexander, J. F., & Parsons, B. V. (1977). Impact of family systems intervention on recidivism and sibling delinquency: A model of primary prevention and program evaluation. *Journal of Consulting and Clinical Psychology, 45,* 469–474.

Klepp, K-I., Halper, A., & Perry, C. L. (1986). The efficacy of peer leaders in drug abuse prevention. *Journal of School Health, 56,* 407–411.

Kolvin, I., Miller, F. J. W., Fleeting, M., & Kolvin, P. A. (1988). Social and parenting factors affecting criminal-offense rates: Findings from the Newcastle Thousand Family Study (1947–1980). *British Journal of Psychiatry, 152,* 80–90.

Kolvin, I., Miller, F. J. W., Scott, D. M., Gatzanis, S. R. M., & Fleeting, M. (1990). *Continuities of deprivation?* Aldershot: Avebury.

Lally, J. R., Mangione, P. L., & Honig, A. S. (1988). Long-range impact of an early intervention with low-income children and their families. In D. R. Powell (Ed.), *Parent education as early childhood intervention* (pp. 79–104). Norwood, NJ: Ablex.

Larson, C. (1980). Efficacy of prenatal and postpartum home visits on child health and development. *Pediatrics, 66,* 191–197.

Le Blanc, M., & Frechette, M. (1989). *Male criminal activity from childhood through youth.* New York: Springer-Verlag.

Lerner, J. A., Inui, T. S., Trupin, E. W., & Douglas, E. (1985). Preschool behavior can predict future psychiatric disorders. *Journal of the American Academy of Child Psychiatry, 24,* 42–48.

Lewis, R. V. (1983). Scared straight – California style. *Criminal Justice and Behavior, 10,* 209–226.

Lipsey, M. W. (1992). Juvenile delinquency treatment: A meta-analytic inquiry into the variability of effects. In T. D. Cook, H. Cooper, D. S. Cordray, H. Hartmann, L. V. Hedges, R. J. Light, T. A. Louis, & F. Mosteller (Eds.), *Meta-analysis for explanation* (pp. 83–127). New York: Russell Sage.

Lipton, D., Martinson, R., & Wilks, J. (1975). *The effectiveness of correctional treatment.* New York: Praeger.

Loeber, R. (1987). Behavioral precursors and accelerators of delinquency. In W. Buikhuisen & S. A. Mednick (Eds.), *Explaining criminal behavior* (pp. 51–67). Leiden: Brill.

Loeber, R., & Dishion, T. (1983). Early predictors of male delinquency: A review. *Psychological Bulletin, 94,* 68–99.

Loeber, R., & Le Blanc, M. (1990). Toward a developmental criminology. In M. Tonry & N. Morris (Eds.), *Crime and justice* (Vol. 12, pp. 375–473). Chicago: University of Chicago Press.

Loeber, R., & Stouthamer-Loeber, M. (1986). Family factors as correlates and predictors of juvenile conduct problems and delinquency. In M. Tonry & N. Morris (Eds.), *Crime and justice* (Vol. 7, pp. 29–149). Chicago: University of Chicago Press.

Loeber, R., & Stouthamer-Loeber, M. (1987). Prediction. In H. C. Quay (Ed.), *Handbook of juvenile delinquency* (pp. 325–382). New York: Wiley.

Loeber, R., Stouthamer-Loeber, M., Van Kammen, W. B., & Farrington, D. P. (1991). Initiation, escalation and desistance in juvenile offending and their correlates. *Journal of Criminal Law and Criminology, 82,* 36–82.

Lynam, D., Moffitt, T., & Stouthamer-Loeber, M. (1993). Explaining the relation between IQ and delinquency: Class, race, test motivation, school failure or self-control? *Journal of Abnormal Psychology, 102,* 187–196.

Magnusson, D., & Bergman, L. R. (1988). Individual and variable-based approaches to longitudinal research on early risk factors. In M. Rutter (Ed.), *Studies of psychosocial risk* (pp. 45–61). Cambridge: Cambridge University Press.

Martinson, R. M. (1974). What works? Questions and answers about prison reform. *The Public Interest, 35,* 22–54.

Martinson, R. M. (1979). New findings, new views: A note of caution regarding sentencing reform. *Hofstra Law Review, 7,* 243–258.

Mawson, A. R. (1987). *Transient criminality.* New York: Praeger.

McAlister, A., Perry, C., Killen, J., Slinkard, L. A., & Maccoby, N. (1980). Pilot study of smoking, alcohol and drug abuse prevention. *American Journal of Public Health, 70,* 719–721.

McCord, J. (1977). A comparative study of two generations of native Americans. In R. F. Meier (Ed.), *Theory in criminology* (pp. 83–92). Beverly Hills, CA: Sage.

McCord, J. (1979). Some child-rearing antecedents of criminal behavior in adult men. *Journal of Personality and Social Psychology, 37,* 1477–1486.

McCord, J. (1982). A longitudinal view of the relationship between paternal absence and crime. In J. Gunn & D. P. Farrington (Eds.), *Abnormal offenders, delinquency, and the criminal justice system* (pp. 113–128). Chichester: Wiley.

McCord, J. (1991). Family relationships, juvenile delinquency, and adult criminality. *Criminology, 29,* 397–417.

McCord, J., & Tremblay, R. (Eds.). (1992). *Preventing antisocial behavior.* New York: Guilford.

McGee, R., Silva, P. A., & Williams, S. (1984). Perinatal, neurological, environmental and developmental characteristics of seven-year-old children with stable behavior problems. *Journal of Child Psychology and Psychiatry, 25,* 573–586.

Mednick, S. A., Gabrielli, W. F., & Hutchings, B. (1983). Genetic influences on criminal behavior: Evidence from an adoption cohort. In K. T. Van Dusen & S. A. Mednick (Eds.), *Prospective studies of crime and delinquency* (pp. 39–56). Boston: Kluwer-Nijhoff.

Michelson, L. (1987). Cognitive-behavioral strategies in the prevention and treatment of antisocial disorders in children and adolescents. In J. D. Burchard & S. N. Burchard (Eds.), *Prevention of delinquent behavior* (pp. 275–310). Beverly Hills, CA: Sage.

Mischel, W., Shoda, Y., & Rodriguez, M. L. (1989). Delay of gratification in children. *Science, 244,* 933–938.

Moffitt, T. E. (1990a). Juvenile delinquency and attention deficit disorder: Boys' developmental trajectories from age 3 to age 15. *Child Development, 61,* 893–910.

Moffitt, T. E. (1990b). The neuropsychology of juvenile delinquency: A critical review. In M. Tonry & N. Morris (Eds.), *Crime and justice* (Vol. 12, pp. 99–169). Chicago: University of Chicago Press.

Moffitt, T. E., & Henry, B. (1989). Neuropsychological assessment of executive functions in self-reported delinquents. *Development and Psychopathology, 1,* 105–118.

Moffitt, T. E., & Silva, P. A. (1988a). IQ and delinquency: A direct test of the differential detection hypothesis. *Journal of Abnormal Psychology, 97,* 330–333.

Moffitt, T. E., & Silva, P. A. (1988b). Neuropsychological deficit and self-reported delinquency in an unselected birth cohort. *Journal of the American Academy of Child and Adolescent Psychiatry, 27,* 233–240.

Morash, M., & Rucker, L. (1989). An exploratory study of the connection of mother's age at childbearing to her children's delinquency in four data sets. *Crime and Delinquency, 35,* 45–93.

Mueller, C. W., & Parcel, T. L. (1981). Measures of socioeconomic status: Alternatives and recommendations. *Child Development, 52,* 13–30.

Murray, D. M., Luepker, R. V., Johnson, C. A., & Mittelmark, M. B. (1984). The prevention of cigarette smoking in children: A comparison of four strategies. *Journal of Applied Social Psychology, 14,* 274–288.

Newson, J., & Newson, E. (1989). *The extent of parental physical punishment in the UK.* London: Approach.

Newson, J., Newson, E., & Adams, M. (1993). The social origins of delinquency. *Criminal Behavior and Mental Health, 3,* 19–29.

Nietzel, M. T. (1979). *Crime and its modification.* New York: Pergamon.

Offord, D. R., Boyle, M. H., & Racine, Y. (1989). Ontario Child Health Study: Correlates of disorder. *Journal of the American Academy of Child and Adolescent Psychiatry, 28,* 856–860.

Olds, D. L., Henderson, C. R., Chamberlain, R., & Tatelbaum, R. (1986a). Preventing child abuse and neglect: A randomized trial of nurse home visitation. *Pediatrics, 78,* 65–78.

Olds, D. L., Henderson, C. R., Tatelbaum, R., & Chamberlain, R. (1986b). Improving the delivery of prenatal care and outcomes of pregnancy: A randomized trial of nurse home visitation. *Pediatrics, 77,* 16–28.

Olds, D. L., & Kitzman, H. (1990). Can home visitation improve the health of women and children at environmental risk? *Pediatrics, 86,* 108–116.

Osborn, S. G. (1980). Moving home, leaving London, and delinquent trends. *British Journal of Criminology, 20,* 54–61.

Ouston, J. (1984). Delinquency, family background, and educational attainment. *British Journal of Criminology, 24,* 2–26.

Patterson, G. R. (1982). *Coercive family process.* Eugene, OR: Castalia.

Patterson, G. R., Chamberlain, P., & Reid, J. B. (1982). A comparative evaluation of a parent training program. *Behavior Therapy, 13,* 638–650.

Patterson, G. R., Reid, J. B., & Dishion, T. J. (1992). *Antisocial boys.* Eugene, OR: Castalia.

Pearson, F. S., & Weiner, N. A. (1985). Toward an integration of criminological theories. *Journal of Criminal Law and Criminology, 76,* 116–150.

Peterson, P. L., Hawkins, J. D., & Catalano, R. F. (1992). Evaluating comprehensive community drug risk reduction interventions: Design challenges and recommendations. *Evaluation Review, 16,* 579–602.

Polk, K., Alder, C., Bazemore, G., Blake, G., Cordray, S., Coventry, G., Galvin, J., & Temple, M. (1981). *Becoming adult.* Washington, DC: National Institute of Mental Health (Final Report).

Power, M. J., Alderson, M. R., Phillipson, C. M., Shoenberg, E., & Morris, J. N. (1967). Delinquent schools? *New Society, 10,* 542–543.

Power, M. J., Benn, R. T., & Morris, J. N. (1972). Neighborhood, schools, and juveniles before the courts. *British Journal of Criminology, 12,* 111–132.

Pulkkinen, L. (1986). The role of impulse control in the development of antisocial and prosocial behavior. In D. Olweus, J. Block, & M. R. Yarrow

(Eds.), *Development of antisocial and prosocial behavior* (pp. 149–175). New York: Academic Press.

Pulkkinen, L. (1988). Delinquent development: Theoretical and empirical considerations. In M. Rutter (Ed.), *Studies of psychosocial risk* (pp. 184–199). Cambridge: Cambridge University Press.

Reiss, A. J. (1986). Why are communities important in understanding crime? In A. J. Reiss & M. Tonry (Eds.), *Communities and crime* (pp. 1–33). Chicago: University of Chicago Press.

Reiss, A. J. (1988). Co-offending and criminal careers. In M. Tonry & N. Morris (Eds.), *Crime and justice* (Vol. 10, pp. 117–170). Chicago: University of Chicago Press.

Reiss, A. J., & Farrington, D. P. (1991). Advancing knowledge about co-offending: Results from a prospective longitudinal survey of London males. *Journal of Criminal Law and Criminology, 82,* 360–395.

Richman, N., Stevenson, J., & Graham, P. (1985). Sex differences in the outcome of pre-school behavior problems. In A. R. Nicol (Ed.), *Longitudinal studies in child psychology and psychiatry* (pp. 75–89). Chichester: Wiley.

Riley, D., & Shaw, M. (1985). *Parental supervision and juvenile delinquency.* London: Her Majesty's Stationery Office.

Rivara, F. P., & Farrington, D. P. (1995). Head injury and criminal behavior. In D. Johnson, B. Pentland, & E. Glasgow (Eds.), *Head injury and litigation.* London: Sweet & Maxwell, in press.

Roberts, A. R., & Camasso, M. J. (1991). The effect of juvenile offender treatment programs on recidivism: A meta-analysis of 46 studies. *Notre Dame Journal of Law, Ethics and Public Policy, 5,* 421–441.

Robins, L. N. (1979). Sturdy childhood predictors of adult outcomes: Replications from longitudinal studies. In J. E. Barrett, R. M. Rose, & G. L. Klerman (Eds.), *Stress and mental disorder* (pp. 219–235). New York: Raven Press.

Robins, L. N. (1986). Changes in conduct disorder over time. In D. C. Farran & J. D. McKinney (Eds.), *Risk in intellectual and psychosocial development* (pp. 227–259). New York: Academic Press.

Robins, L. N., & Hill, S. Y. (1966). Assessing the contributions of family structure, class, and peer groups to juvenile delinquency. *Journal of Criminal Law, Criminology and Police Science, 57,* 325–334.

Robins, L. N., & Ratcliff, K. S. (1978). Risk factors in the continuation of childhood antisocial behavior into adulthood. *International Journal of Mental Health, 7,* 96–116.

Robins, L. N., & Ratcliff, K. S. (1980). Childhood conduct disorders and later arrest. In L. N. Robins, P. J. Clayton, & J. K. Wing (Eds.), *The social consequences of psychiatric illness* (pp. 248–263). New York: Brunner/Mazel.

Robins, L. N., West, P. J., & Herjanic, B. L. (1975). Arrests and delinquency in two generations: A study of black urban families and their children. *Journal of Child Psychology and Psychiatry, 16,* 125–140.

Robins, L. N., & Wish, E. (1977). Childhood deviance as a developmental process: A study of 223 urban black men from birth to 18. *Social Forces, 56,* 448–473.

Rose, S. L., Rose, S. A., & Feldman, J. F. (1989). Stability of behavior problems in very young children. *Development and Psychopathology, 1,* 5–19.

Ross, H. L., Campbell, J. T., & Glass, G. V. (1970). Determining the social effects of a legal reform: The British "breathalyzer" crackdown of 1967. *American Behavioral Scientist, 13,* 493–509.

Ross, R. R., Fabiano, E. A., & Ewles, C. D. (1988). Reasoning and rehabilitation. *International Journal of Offender Therapy and Comparative Criminology, 32,* 29–35.

Ross, R. R., & Gendreau, P. (Eds.). (1980). *Effective correctional treatment.* Toronto: Butterworths.

Ross, R. R., & Ross, B. D. (1988). Delinquency prevention through cognitive training. *New Education, 10,* 70–75.

Rossi, P. H., Berk, R. A., & Lenihan, K. J. (1980). *Money, work and crime.* New York: Academic Press.

Rutter, M. (1981a). The city and the child. *American Journal of Orthopsychiatry, 51,* 610–625.

Rutter, M. (1981b). *Maternal deprivation reassessed* (2nd ed.). Harmondsworth: Penguin.

Rutter, M. (1983). School effects on pupil progress: Research findings and policy implications. *Child Development, 54,* 1–29.

Rutter, M. (1989). Psychosocial risk trajectories and beneficial turning points. In S. Doxiadis (Ed.), *Early influences shaping the individual* (pp. 229–239). New York: Plenum.

Rutter, M., Cox, A., Tupling, C., Berger, M., & Yule, W. (1975a). Attainment and adjustment in two geographical areas: I. The prevalence of psychiatric disorder. *British Journal of Psychiatry, 126,* 493–509.

Rutter, M., & Giller, H. (1983). *Juvenile delinquency.* Harmondsworth: Penguin.

Rutter, M., Maughan, B., Mortimore, P., & Ouston, J. (1979). *Fifteen thousand hours.* London: Open Books.

Rutter, M., Yule, B., Quinton, D., Rowlands, O., Yule, W., & Berger, M. (1975b). Attainment and adjustment in two geographical areas. III. Some factors accounting for area differences. *British Journal of Psychiatry, 126,* 520–533.

Sarason, I. G. (1978). A cognitive social learning approach to juvenile delinquency. In R. D. Hare & D. Schalling (Eds.), *Psychopathic behavior* (pp. 299–317). Chichester: Wiley.

Schlossman, S., & Sedlak, M. (1983). The Chicago Area Project revisited. *Crime and Delinquency, 29,* 398–462.

Schweinhart, L. J., Barnes, H. V., & Weikart, D. P. (1993). *Significant benefits.* Ypsilanti, MI: High/Scope.

Schweinhart, L. J., & Weikart, D. P. (1980). *Young children grow up.* Ypsilanti, MI: High/Scope.

Sechrest, L., White, S. O., & Brown, E. D. (1979). *The rehabilitation of criminal offenders: Problems and prospects.* Washington, DC: National Academy of Sciences.

Shannon, L. W. (1988). *Criminal career continuity.* New York: Human Sciences Press.

Shaw, C. R., & McKay, H. D. (1942). *Juvenile delinquency and urban areas.* Chicago: University of Chicago Press.

Shaw, C. R., & McKay, H. D. (1969). *Juvenile delinquency and urban areas* (rev. ed.). Chicago: University of Chicago Press.

Shedler, J., & Block, J. (1990). Adolescent drug use and psychological health. *American Psychologist, 45,* 612–630.

Sherman, L. W., & Berk, R. A. (1984). The specific deterrent effects of arrest for domestic assault. *American Sociological Review, 49,* 261–272.

Shore, M. F., & Massimo, J. L. (1979). Fifteen years after treatment: A follow-up study of comprehensive vocationally oriented psychotherapy. *American Journal of Orthopsychiatry, 49,* 240–245.

Short, J. F. (1969). Introduction to the revised edition. In C. R. Shaw & H. D. McKay (Eds.), *Juvenile delinquency and urban areas* (rev. ed.). Chicago: University of Chicago Press.

Short, J. F., & Nye, F. I. (1957). Reported behavior as a criterion of deviant behavior. *Social Problems, 5,* 207–213.

Shover, N. (1985). *Aging criminals.* Beverly Hills, CA: Sage.

Simcha-Fagan, O., & Schwartz, J. E. (1986). Neighborhood and delinquency: An assessment of contextual effects. *Criminology, 24,* 667–703.

Snyder, J., & Patterson, G. R. (1987). Family interaction and delinquent behavior. In H. C. Quay (Ed.), *Handbook of juvenile delinquency* (pp. 216–243). New York: Wiley.

Spivack, G., Marcus, J., & Swift, M. (1986). Early classroom behaviors and later misconduct. *Developmental Psychology, 22,* 124–131.

Sroufe, L. A. (1986). Bowlby's contribution to psychoanalytic theory and developmental psychology. *Journal of Child Psychology and Psychiatry, 27,* 841–849.

Stattin, H., & Klackenberg-Larsson, I. (1993). Early language and intelligence development and their relationship to future criminal behavior. *Journal of Abnormal Psychology, 102,* 369–378.

Stattin, H., & Magnusson, D. (1991). Stability and change in criminal behavior up to age 30. *British Journal of Criminology, 31,* 327–346.

Stein, K. B., Sarbin, T. R., & Kulik, J. A. (1968). Future time perspective: Its relation to the socialization process and the delinquent role. *Journal of Consulting and Clinical Psychology, 32,* 257–264.

Steinhausen, H-C., Willms, J., & Spohr, H-L. (1993). Long-term psychopathological and cognitive outcome of children with fetal alcohol syndrome. *Journal of the American Academy of Child and Adolescent Psychiatry, 32,* 990–994.

Streissguth, A. P. (1986). Smoking and drinking during pregnancy and offspring learning disabilities: A review of the literature and development of a research strategy. In M. Lewis (Ed.), *Learning disabilities and prenatal risk* (pp. 28–67). Urbana: University of Illinois Press.

Szatmari, P., Reitsma-Street, M., & Offord, D. R. (1986). Pregnancy and birth complications in antisocial adolescents and their siblings. *Canadian Journal of Psychiatry, 31,* 513–516.

Sutherland, E. H., & Cressey, D. R. (1974). *Criminology* (9th ed.). Philadelphia: Lippincott.

Taylor, E. A. (1986). Childhood hyperactivity. *British Journal of Psychiatry, 149,* 562–573.

Taylor, E. A., Schachar, R., Thorley, G., & Wieselberg, M. (1986). Conduct disorder and hyperactivity. I. Separation of hyperactivity and antisocial conduct in British child psychiatric patients. *British Journal of Psychiatry, 149,* 760–767.

Telch, M. J., Killen, J. D., McAlister, A. L., Perry, C. L., & Maccoby, N. (1982). Long-term follow-up of a pilot project on smoking prevention with adolescents. *Journal of Behavioral Medicine, 5,* 1–8.

Thornberry, T. P., & Farnworth, M. (1982). Social correlates of criminal involvement: Further evidence on the relationship between social status and criminal behavior. *American Sociological Review, 47,* 505–518.

Thornton, D. M. (1987). Treatment effects on recidivism: A reappraisal of the "nothing works" doctrine. In B. J. McGurk, D. M. Thornton, & M. Williams (Eds.), *Applying psychology to imprisonment* (pp. 181–189). London: Her Majesty's Stationery Office.

Tisdelle, D. A., & St. Lawrence, J. S. (1986). Interpersonal problem-solving competency: Review and critique of the literature. *Clinical Psychology Review, 6,* 337–356.

Tobler, N. S. (1986). Meta-analysis of 143 drug treatment programs: Quantitative outcome results of program participants compared to a control or comparison group. *Journal of Drug Issues, 16,* 537–567.

Tolan, P. H., Cromwell, R. E., & Brasswell, M. (1986). Family therapy with delinquents: A review of the literature. *Family Process, 25,* 619–649.

Trad, P. V. (1993). Substance abuse in adolescent mothers: Strategies for diagnosis, treatment and prevention. *Journal of Substance Abuse Treatment, 10,* 421–431.

Trasler, G. B. (1962). *The explanation of criminality.* London: Routledge & Kegan Paul.

Tremblay, R. E., LeBlanc, M., & Schwartzman, A. E. (1988). The predictive power of first-grade peer and teacher ratings of behavior: Sex differences in antisocial behavior and personality at adolescence. *Journal of Abnormal Child Psychology, 16*, 571–583.

Tremblay, R. E., McCord, J., Boileau, H., Charlebois, P., Gagnon, C., LeBlanc, M., & Larivee, S. (1991). Can disruptive boys be helped to become competent? *Psychiatry, 54*, 148–161.

Tremblay, R. E., Vitaro, F., Bertrand, L., LeBlanc, M., Beauchesne, H., Boileau, H., & David, L. (1992). Parent and child training to prevent early onset of delinquency: The Montreal longitudinal-experimental study. In J. McCord & R. Tremblay (Eds.), *Preventing antisocial behavior* (pp. 117–138). New York: Guilford.

Utting, D., Bright, J., & Henricson, C. (1993). *Crime and the family*. London: Family Policy Studies Centre.

Venables, P. H., & Raine, A. (1987). Biological theory. In B. J. McGurk, D. M. Thornton, & M. Williams (Eds.), *Applying psychology to imprisonment* (pp. 3–27). London: Her Majesty's Stationery Office.

Wadsworth, M. (1979). *Roots of delinquency*. London: Martin Robertson.

Wallis, C. P., & Maliphant, R. (1967). Delinquent areas in the county of London: Ecological factors. *British Journal of Criminology, 7*, 250–284.

Walsh, A., Petee, T. A., & Beyer, J. A. (1987). Intellectual imbalance and delinquency: Comparing high verbal and high performance IQ delinquents. *Criminal Justice and Behavior, 14*, 370–379.

Wells, L. E., & Rankin, J. H. (1991). Families and delinquency: A meta-analysis of the impact of broken homes. *Social Problems, 38*, 71–93.

Werner, E. E. (1986). A longitudinal study of perinatal risk. In D. C. Farran & J. D. McKinney (Eds.), *Risk in intellectual and psychosocial development* (pp. 3–27). New York: Academic Press.

West, D. J. (1982). *Delinquency: Its roots, careers and prospects*. London: Heinemann.

West, D. J., & Farrington, D. P. (1973). *Who becomes delinquent?* London: Heinemann.

West, D. J., & Farrington, D. P. (1977). *The delinquent way of life*. London: Heinemann.

Whalen, C. K., & Henker, B. (1991). Therapies of hyperactive children: Comparisons, combinations and compromises. *Journal of Consulting and Clinical Psychology, 59*, 126–137.

White, H. R., Labouvie, E. W., & Bates, M. E. (1985). The relationship between sensation seeking and delinquency: A longitudinal analysis. *Journal of Research in Crime and Delinquency, 22*, 197–211.

White, J. L., Moffitt, T. E., Earls, F., Robins, L. N., & Silva, P. A. (1990). How early can we tell? Predictors of child conduct disorder and adolescent delinquency. *Criminology, 28*, 507–533.

White, J. L., Moffitt, T. E., & Silva, P. A. (1989). A prospective replication of the protective effects of IQ in subjects at high risk for juvenile delinquency. *Journal of Consulting and Clinical Psychology, 57,* 719–724.

Whitehead, J. T., & Lab, S. P. (1989). A meta-analysis of juvenile correctional treatment. *Journal of Research in Crime and Delinquency, 26,* 276–295.

Widom, C. S. (1989). The cycle of violence. *Science, 244,* 160–166.

Wikstrom, P. O. (1987). *Patterns of crime in a birth cohort.* Stockholm: University of Stockholm Department of Sociology.

Wilson, H. (1980). Parental supervision: A neglected aspect of delinquency. *British Journal of Criminology, 20,* 203–235.

Wilson, H. (1987). Parental supervision re-examined. *British Journal of Criminology, 27,* 275–301.

Wilson, J. Q., & Herrnstein, R. J. (1985). *Crime and human nature.* New York: Simon & Schuster.

Wolfgang, M. E., Figlio, R. M., & Sellin, T. (1972). *Delinquency in a birth cohort.* Chicago: University of Chicago Press.

Wolfgang, M. E., Thornberry, T. P., & Figlio, R. M. (1987). *From boy to man, from delinquency to crime.* Chicago: University of Chicago Press.

Zimring, F. E. (1981). Kids, groups and crime: Some implications of a well-known secret. *Journal of Criminal Law and Criminology, 72,* 867–885.

Zoccolillo, M., Pickles, A., Quinton, D., & Rutter, M. (1992). The outcome of childhood conduct disorder: Implications for defining adult personality disorder and conduct disorder. *Psychological Medicine, 22,* 971–986.

CHAPTER FOUR

The Social Development Model:
A THEORY OF ANTISOCIAL BEHAVIOR

RICHARD F. CATALANO

J. DAVID HAWKINS

ABSTRACT: This chapter presents a theory of antisocial behavior, the *social development model*, which organizes the results of research on risk and protective factors for delinquency, crime, and substance abuse into hypotheses regarding the development of antisocial and prosocial behavior. The social development model is grounded in tests of prior criminological theory. It hypothesizes similar general processes leading to prosocial and antisocial development, and specifies submodels for four specific periods during childhood and adolescent development.

Theoretical Considerations

The social development model seeks to explain a broad range of distinct behaviors ranging from the use of illegal drugs to homicide. Crime, including violent and nonviolent offending and drug abuse, is viewed as a constellation of behaviors subject to the general principles incorporated in the model. By considering evidence from research on the etiology of both delinquency and drug abuse, it is possible to identify general constructs that predict both types of behavior and to use this knowledge in specifying predictive relationships in the development of antisocial behavior.

As used here, the terms *delinquency* and *drug use* refer to behaviors. All behaviors are subject to influence from a variety of forces. The same principles, factors, or processes that influence one behavior should predict other behaviors. At the least, this suggests that a theory of antisocial behavior should be able to predict both drug use and criminal behavior, whether committed by children or adults. More ambitiously, it suggests a search for universal factors, mechanisms, or processes that predict all behavior. This implies a general theory. Gottfredson and Hirschi (1990), for example, have proposed "A General Theory of Crime," which attributes all criminal

Preparation of this chapter was supported in part by grants from the National Institute on Drug Abuse.

behavior to a single theoretical construct: low self-control. In contrast, developmental psychopathologists call for holistic developmental paradigms of learning, building on notions of hierarchical integration that explicitly recognize the importance of the developing organism's behavioral feedback on its own development (Cicchetti, 1990).

Our goal is to explain and predict the onset, escalation, maintenance, deescalation, and cessation or desistance from patterned behaviors that are of concern to society, namely, crime and illegal drug use. These behaviors, which constitute antisocial behavior as the term is used here, have in common the fact that they are outside the normative consensus regarding acceptable social behavior. We seek to predict antisocial behavior as viewed from the social order. This requires an understanding of how both prosocial and antisocial patterned behaviors evolve in the social order. Given this knowledge, it is possible to hypothesize factors or processes that explain normatively disapproved as well as approved patterned behaviors. The social development model, by seeking to predict and understand both prosocial and antisocial behavior, attempts to identify general processes of human behavior.

Because delinquency and drug use typically are initiated in childhood or adolescence, and because an early onset of both predicts maintenance as well as diversity, seriousness, and persistence in crime and drug use, the social development model specifies causal processes in childhood and adolescence. Because criminal behavior persists for some into early adulthood, and because drug use and drug problems continue to increase into early adulthood (Anthony & Cohler, 1987), the general theory also predicts the maintenance and cessation of crime and drug use in adulthood, although specific developmental models for adulthood are not included in this chapter. (See Farrington & Hawkins, 1991, for a report of the power of social development constructs to predict onset, frequent involvement, and desistance from officially recorded crime. See Catalano & Hawkins, 1985, for a description of the theory of crime maintenance and cessation in adulthood.)

Before this theory of antisocial behavior is presented, the relevance of a developmental model and the importance of including empirical evidence on risk and protective factors in constructing the theory require discussion.

Developmental Perspective

Developmental theories of antisocial behavior have been advocated (Loeber & LeBlanc, 1990), and several criteria for such theories have been advanced. It has been suggested that developmental theory should take into account evidence of "reciprocal effects," that is, the likelihood that past behaviors affect future attitudes and behaviors and that patterned behavior development takes place through social interactions over time (Shaw & Bell, 1992; Thornberry, 1987). For example, there is evidence that belief in the legitimacy of the moral order inhibits the initiation of minor offending, and there is also evidence that involvement in minor delinquent behavior affects belief in the legitimacy of the moral order (Agnew, 1985). Developmental theory should seek to specify how these reciprocal relationships evolve over time. Additionally, Sameroff (1990) and Shaw and Bell (1992) have suggested that developmental theory should be "transactional," specifying how behavior outcomes involving more than one participant and not attributable to either participant alone arise from repeated social interactions. For example, in the social development model, bonding between a mother and child is thought to result from processes of interaction involving both participants. The model specifies processes through which such bonding develops, thereby meeting the transactional criterion for developmental theory.

Finally, it has been suggested that developmental theories of antisocial behavior should be "transformational," specifying how developmental changes in behavior arising from sources other than interaction take on forms not shown in previous stages (Shaw & Bell, 1992). Transformational theory would explicitly identify developmentally specific behavioral outcomes indicative of antisocial behavior during different periods of development and identify the socializing units expected to influence behavior during different developmental periods. There is evidence that different patterns of delinquency and drug use occur at different developmental stages. For most youth, initiation of delinquency occurs in early adolescence, peaks from ages 15 to 17, and declines thereafter (Wolfgang, Thornberry, & Figlio, 1987). For drug use, the usual age of initiation is slightly later and continues to increase until the early 20s, after which prevalence rates decline (Elliott, in press). Drug problems appear to reach their peak during the period from 18 to 29 (Anthony & Cohler, 1987).

There is evidence that different patterns of involvement in these behaviors have different etiological origins (Kandel, 1982) and are associated with different outcomes (Newcomb & Bentler, 1988; Shedler & Block, 1990). The factors leading to occasional involvement are distinct from factors leading to serious and persistent delinquency or the regular use of illicit drugs (Kandel, Simcha-Fagan, & Davies, 1986; Kaplan, Martin, Johnson, & Robbins, 1986; Robins & Przybeck, 1985; Simcha-Fagan, Gersten, & Langner, 1986). Further, there is evidence that there are common as well as distinct predictors for initiation, maintenance, and desistance (Elliott & Menard, 1992, this volume; Farrington & Hawkins, 1991; Menard & Huizinga, 1990). Thus, theory must confront the empirical evidence that predictors of onset, maintenance, and desistance of delinquency and drug use may differ in degree, kind, and period of salience. At the same time, theory must address the evidence that, over the course of development, factors associated with different units of socialization have different predictive power. Moreover, theory should be able to specify causal pathways whereby influences from different social units interact in the etiology of behavior. For example, studies of adolescent delinquency find that parental influences are less strongly predictive of adolescent delinquent behavior than is involvement with delinquent peers (Elliott, Huizinga, & Ageton, 1985). However, poor parental monitoring of children who are age 10 is predictive of antisocial peer involvement by children at age 12 (Dishion, Patterson, Stoolmiller, & Skinner, 1991), suggesting that good family management practices may moderate early involvement with antisocial peers in predicting antisocial behavior. Theory should specify how interactions across time and units of socialization predict behavior.

The social development model posits general processes by which bonding and behavior evolve. At the same time, the model recognizes that the socializing contexts or units in which these processes occur change in salience and importance developmentally as children enter first the family and preschool environments, then the elementary school environment, and so on. This allows for specification of domain- and behavior-specific indicators of the general model constructs appropriate at different developmental periods.

Risk and Protective Factors

There is a growing body of knowledge regarding risk and protective factors for involvement in delinquent behavior and drug use. It is clear empirically that multiple biological, psychological, and social factors at multiple levels in different social domains – that is, within the individual and in the family, school, peer group, and community – all contribute to some degree to the prediction of delinquency and drug use. Risk factors for drug abuse and criminal behavior include community norms favorable to these behaviors, neighborhood disorganization, extreme economic deprivation, family history of drug abuse or crime, poor family management practices, family conflict, low family bonding, parental permissiveness, early and persistent problem behaviors, academic failure, peer rejection in elementary grades, association with drug-using or delinquent peers or adults, alienation and rebelliousness, attitudes favorable to drug use and crime, and early onset of drug use or criminal behavior. (For reviews, see Hawkins, Catalano, & Miller, 1992b; Loeber, Stouthamer-Loeber, Von Kammen, & Farrington, 1991; Simcha-Fagan et al., 1986).

Investigators have also noted variability in responses to risk exposure and have sought to identify protective factors that enhance the resilience of those exposed to high levels of risk and protect them from undesirable outcomes. Three broad categories of protective factors against stress in children have been identified: (1) individual characteristics, including resilient temperament, positive social orientation, and intelligence (Radke-Yarrow & Sherman, 1990); (2) family cohesion and warmth or bonding during childhood; and (3) external social supports that reinforce the individual's competencies and commitments and provide a belief system by which to live (Garmezy, 1985; Werner, 1989). As distinct from risk factors, protective factors are hypothesized to operate indirectly through interaction with risk factors, mediating or moderating the effects of risk exposure (Hawkins et al., 1992b; Rutter, 1990).

The challenge for theory is to specify clearly the mechanisms by which identified risk and protective factors for drug abuse and crime interact in the etiology of these behaviors. Relationships across social structures and levels of analysis must be specified if community, family, school, peer, and individual effects are all to be considered in a general theory of antisocial behavior. As Bursik (this volume) points out, given the number of observed empirical predictors and the large number of possible functional alternatives for the relationships among these variables, specification of the relationships in a model must proceed theoretically. To some extent, risk and protective factors' developmental periods of salience and their covariation have been established, but theory specification forces a choice among a host of plausible rival hypotheses regarding the relationships among the factors. Further, as Thornberry (this volume) points out, citing evidence from several longitudinal investigations, antisocial behavior itself can affect levels of social bonding. Theories must take into account the possibility of reciprocal effects between prior behavior and subsequent levels of predictor variables (such as social bonding) in predicting any form or level of involvement in antisocial behavior beyond initiation.

In fields ranging from embryology to developmental psychopathology (Cicchetti, 1990), research has shown that contextual forces serve to organize individual development. Moreover, behavioral response to environment itself affects future development. Behavior is the dynamic result of and contributor to development.

The preceding evidence on risk and protective factors and development argues for theoretical specifications that account for the empirical evidence on risk and protective factors, including mechanisms for cross-level effects, period of salience, and effects of behavior on later levels of predictors as well as on later behaviors. These considerations suggest the importance of a developmental theory of delinquency and substance abuse that hypothesizes pathways to different forms of antisocial behavior and identifies causal mechanisms in etiological processes.

The Social Development Model

Key Features

The social development model incorporates these key features:

1. *Inclusion of both delinquency and drug use.* Both delinquency and drug abuse are predicted by the theory.
2. *Developmental perspective.* Four distinct, developmentally specific submodels incorporate notions of age-specific problem and prosocial behavior. The theory identifies salient socialization units and etiological processes for each of four phases of social development: preschool, elementary school, middle school, and high school. The phases are separated by major transitions in the environments in which children are socialized; they are not conceived as stages of cognitive or moral development (Kohlberg, 1969, 1976; Piaget, 1965). Transitions from the home environment to elementary school and from the relatively self-contained classrooms of elementary school to the modularized environments of middle school are nearly universally experienced transitions accompanied by shifts in the balance of influence among socializing units of families, schools, and peers. The four submodels delineate specific predictors for each developmental period. The theory describes reciprocal processes of causation between developmental periods in which behaviors at one period are expected to affect subsequent social development processes.
3. *Risk and protective factors.* The theory organizes the evidence regarding risk and protective factors for delinquency and substance use by hypothesizing the theoretical mechanisms through which these factors operate to increase or decrease the likelihood of antisocial behavior.

Theoretical Background

The social development model is consistent with a continuing tradition of integrated theory in the field of criminology (cf. Elliott et al., 1985; Hepburn, 1976; Messner, Krohn, & Liska, 1989). It seeks to synthesize into a coherent model those propositions from existing theories of deviance that have the strongest empirical support in order to achieve greater explanatory and predictive power than that of the separate theories from which the model is derived.

At present, no single theory of deviant behavior has survived an empirical test without disconfirmation of some hypothesized relationships between concepts. This has led to debate concerning the optimum path for future theoretical progress (Cressey, 1979; Elliott et al., 1985; Hirschi & Gottfredson, 1988; Matsueda, 1988; Messner et al., 1989). The theory outlined here is a synthesis of control theory (Briar & Piliavin, 1965; Hindelang, 1973; Hirschi, 1969; Kornhauser, 1978; Nye, 1958; Reiss, 1951), social learning theory (Akers, 1977; Akers, Krohn, Lanza-Kaduce, & Radosevich, 1979; Bandura, 1973, 1977; Burgess & Akers, 1966; Conger, 1976, 1980; Krohn, Lance-Kaduce, Radosevich, & Akers, 1980), and differential association theory (Cressey, 1953; Matsueda, 1982, 1988; Sutherland, 1973; Matza, 1969). Control theory is used to identify causal elements in the etiology of drug abuse and delinquency, as well as in the etiology of conforming behavior. Social learning theory is used to identify processes by which patterns of conforming and antisocial behavior are extinguished or maintained. Differential association theory is used to identify parallel but separate causal paths for prosocial and antisocial processes.

Assumptions

When integrative or synthetic theories are developed, careful attention must be paid to the underlying theoretical assumptions so that theoretical propositions are not based on conflicting assumptions. The first assumption of this theory is that human beings are satisfaction seekers and that human behavior depends upon acts of perceived self-interest. People engage in activities or interactions because of the satisfaction they expect to receive from them. This assumption is derived from social learning theory. Behavior in each immediate situation is expected to be conditioned by long- as well as short-term payoffs. It is recognized that the perception and exercise of self-interest are restrained or controlled by ability, opportunity, and experience. One's skills and opportunities largely determine one's capability of achieving or even perceiving self-interest. In addition, experience provides empirical information on which to judge the likely impact of one's contemplated next action (Tallman & Ihinger-Tallman, 1979). Together these three elements tend to set limits on and direct the exercise of "pure" self-interest in the Hobbesian sense. Like differential association theory, the social development model assumes that this process of constrained self-interest operates in both prosocial and antisocial encounters.

Second, it is assumed that a normative consensus exists in society to the extent that everyone knows the "rules of the game." This level of agreement on rules makes group life possible, yet does not "preclude conflicts of value or interest" (Kornhauser, 1978, p. 41). Matsueda (1988) points out that this assumption is also incorporated in differential association theory. However, despite shared understanding of the rules of the game, there is "variation in the strength and content of both prosocial and antisocial motives, beliefs and justifications. . . . Variations in these applications, and not necessarily an oppositional normative system, give rise to normative conflict and constitute the crucial elements of definitions favorable to law violations" (Sutherland, 1973, p. 125). In the social development model there is room for agreement about society's basic rules as well as for shifts in the strength of individuals' normative beliefs.

Overview of the Theory

It is hypothesized that children must learn patterns of behavior, whether prosocial or antisocial. They learn these patterns of behavior from socializing units of family, school, religious and other community institutions, and peers. It is hypothesized that the underlying socialization follows the same processes of social learning whether it produces prosocial or problem behavior. Children are socialized through processes involving four constructs: (1) perceived opportunities for involvement in activities and interactions with others, (2) the degree of involvement and interaction, (3) the skills to participate in these involvements and interactions, and (4) the reinforcement they perceive as forthcoming from performance in activities and interactions. When these socializing processes are consistent, a social bond develops between the individual and the socializing unit. Once strongly established, this social bond has power to affect behavior independently of the four social learning processes, by creating an informal control on future behavior. This control inhibits deviant behaviors through the establishment of an individual's stake in conforming to the norms and values of the socializing unit.

Following control theory, the social bond consists of attachment to others in the social unit, commitment to or investment in lines of action consistent with the socializing unit, and belief in the values of the unit. The deletion of involvement from Hirshi's original four elements of the bond is supported both empirically (Elliott, Huizinga, & Ageton, 1982; Kempf, 1993; Thornberry, 1987) and theoretically as discussed below. Bonding is expected to influence individuals' behavior choices by entering into their calculation of the costs and benefits of any particular behavior to self-interest. If individuals engage in behavior that is inconsistent with the standards and norms of those to whom they are bonded, the bond may be threatened if the behavior is exposed. Research on prosocial bonds has demonstrated an inhibitory effect on antisocial behavior (cf. Brook, Brook, Gordon, Whiteman, & Cohen, 1990; Brook, Gordon, Whiteman, & Cohen, 1986; Kempf, 1993; Krohn & Massey, 1980; Marcos, Bahr, & Johnson, 1986; Newcomb & Bentler, 1988).

It is hypothesized that the behavior of the individual will be prosocial or antisocial depending on the predominant behaviors, norms, and values held by those to whom the individual is bonded. This approach departs from the traditional control theory perspective, which asserts no causal role of bonding to antisocial others in the etiology of delinquency, characterizing relationships among delinquents as cold and brittle (Hirschi, 1969). However, much evidence suggests that the relationships among delinquents and drug-involved youth are not always characterized by negative affect (Agnew, 1991; Cairns, Cairns, Neckerman, Gest, & Gariepy, 1988; Gillmore, Hawkins, Day, & Catalano, 1992; Giordano, Cernkovich, & Pugh, 1986). Moreover, recent evidence on adolescent use of tobacco and alcohol indicates that attachment to parents interacts with parents' own use of alcohol and tobacco in predicting adolescents' use of these drugs. High attachment to parents who use alcohol or tobacco legally leads to drug use behavior consistent with parents' use, not necessarily to the legal alternative of no use by the adolescent (Foshee & Bauman, 1992). This indicates that bonding to a family involved in drug use can be positively associated with drug-using behavior.

The assumption of a normative consensus in society implies that prosocial modes of action will ordinarily be preferable to illicit ones. However, the theory hypothesizes that social learning processes can produce bonds of attachment, commitment, and belief in illicit action and that such action can provide a valued alternative to prosocial action. Although the theory assumes normative societal consensus, following Sutherland, it allows for variation in the strength of the individual's beliefs. Antisocial behavior can develop in three ways despite normative consensus.

1. Antisocial behavior results when prosocial socialization breaks down, that is, when people are denied the opportunities to participate in prosocial life or their skills are inadequate for prosocial performance to produce reinforcement, or when the environment fails to reinforce them consistently for effective prosocial performance. This conforms to Hirschi's (1969) theory of social control. Antisocial behavior results when low levels of prosocial bonding develop, providing few internal constraints against antisocial behavior.

2. Antisocial behavior results, even in the presence of prosocial bonding, when the individual's calculation of costs and benefits, under the assumption of constrained self-interest, shows a profit for the illicit action. Even individuals who are bonded to prosocial norms may be exposed to situational inducements to commit crime or use drugs (Matza, 1964). Even one bonded to society may engage in deviant behavior if the potential cost seems low (if, for example, the risk of detection by valued prosocial others is perceived as low) and the benefit seems high.

3. Finally, antisocial behavior results when a child is bonded to immediate socializing units of family, school, community, or peers who hold antisocial beliefs or values. When youth are bonded to parents who use drugs or are engaged in crime, to schools or communities that tolerate drug use and dealing, or to peer groups that have antisocial practices, it is likely that they will behave in a manner consistent with the norms and values of these groups. Thus, antisocial bonding provides a third direct path to antisocial behavior. This is consistent with differential association theory.

As shown in Figure 4.1, two general pathways are hypothesized in the model: a prosocial pathway and an antisocial pathway. Identical processes are hypothesized to operate on these paths. We believe this conception better represents the differential association mechanism (Agnew, 1991; Matsueda, 1982; Sutherland, 1973). Rather than define a ratio concept (the ratio of prosocial to antisocial definitions or behaviors), we have opted to measure both pro- and antisocial elements. This conception may better reflect the reality of the social encounters of developing children, which may include both pro- and antisocial influences. The social development model suggests how these encounters lead to bonds that have an inhibitory or promotional effect on antisocial behavior. When the preponderance of influences are prosocial, prosocial behavior results. When the preponderance of influence are antisocial, antisocial behavior results. Many youth experience both pro- and antisocial influences and engage in both types of

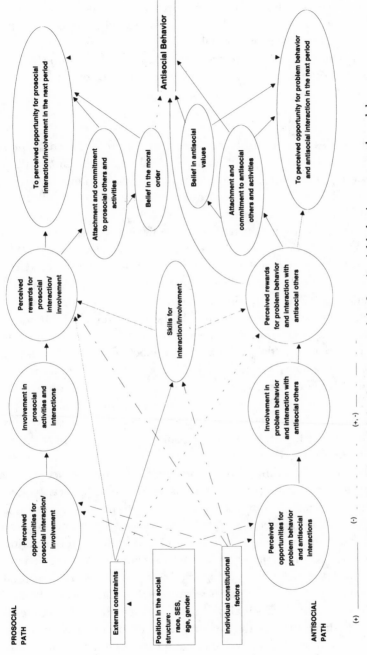

Figure 4.1. The social development model of antisocial behavior – general model.

behavior. For example, currently most youth use alcohol before they are legally permitted to do so, and most youth engage in minor delinquency. The social development model allows for this variation in experience by including separate paths whose processes of reinforcement, learning, and bonding are independent but influence one another over time.

The General Model

Three variables exogenous to the theory proper are included in the social development model: (1) position in the social structure, (2) constitutional or physiological factors, and (3) external constraints. The effects of these three variables on antisocial behavior are hypothesized to be fully mediated by other social development model constructs.

The first exogenous construct is an individual's position in the social structure defined by socioeconomic status, race, gender, and age. Whereas age and gender appear to have consistent relationships to crime (Gottfredson & Hirschi, 1990), studies linking socioeconomic status (Tittle & Meier, 1990) and race (Elliott, Huizinga, & Menard, 1989) to drug use and crime have produced contradictory results. The social development model hypothesizes that there is no direct effect of position in the social structure on antisocial behavior. Rather, the theoretical mechanism is indirect, through its impact on perceived opportunities for prosocial and antisocial involvements and interactions, as well as through the external constraints construct. Depending on the measure, one's position in the social structure is expected to increase or decrease the perceived opportunities variables. For example, coming from a low socioeconomic background is hypothesized to increase one's opportunities for antisocial involvement due to the higher prevalence of visible crime in low-income neighborhoods. Since more males commit delinquent acts, being male is expected to increase one's opportunities to engage in antisocial interactions and involvements. Being African-American may be associated with increased perception of opportunity for delinquent involvement due to higher rates of reported involvement in serious crime, but it may also be associated with decreased perception of opportunity for interaction with drug users due to lower rates of substance use compared to European-Americans (Elliott et al., 1989). Position in the social structure is also expected to increase or decrease external constraints, depending on the measure. For instance, socioeconomic status has been found to have a positive effect on parental management as measured by positive discipline and monitoring (Larzelere & Patterson, 1990). Several studies have found that girls are more strictly supervised than boys

(Hill & Atkinson, 1988; Singer & Levine, 1988). Younger children are less likely to be arrested by police, and there is some indirect evidence that sanctions increase with age in the deterrence literature, since fear of the legal risks of crime and certainty of punishment increase with age (Cusson & Pinsonneault, 1986; Grasmick & Bursik, 1990). Finally, there is also evidence that African-American families are more likely to provide positive, proactive management techniques than European-American families (Catalano et al., 1992).

The second exogenous construct comprises the individual's constitutional or physiological traits, which are hypothesized to be mediated by the constructs of prosocial and antisocial opportunities and skills, and prosocial reinforcement. Cognitive ability influences the development and acquisition of reading and math skills as well as verbal skills. Children with low cognitive ability may find alternative methods of obtaining reinforcement, such as resorting to aggressive behavior, instead of using skilled prosocial interpersonal interaction (Moffit, 1983). Similarly, individuals with low central and autonomic nervous system arousal levels may not perceive or recognize as significant rewards the routine positive responses that accompany prosocial interaction and involvement. Smiles, thank-you's, pats on the back, or good grades may not be perceived as rewarding when individuals have low arousal levels. Rather, sensational and other peak arousal experiences such as thrill seeking may be required for these individuals to perceive rewards because of their lowered physiological responsiveness to stimuli. Another example is the individual with Attention Deficit Disorder (ADD), who may not recognize opportunities for prosocial interaction and involvement. If an individual cannot perceive a friendly smile as an invitation to talk or the presence of the teacher in the classroom before school as an opportunity to get help to improve academic skills, he or she is less able to take advantage of existing opportunities. Individual constitutional factors are thus included in the model as exogenous factors whose effect on the etiology of conforming and deviant behavior is mediated through prosocial and antisocial perceived opportunities and skills, and prosocial perceived reinforcements.

The third exogenous concept involves the clarity, consistency, and immediacy of external constraints. External constraints are formal and informal social reactions to behavior (Nye, 1958) that affect the degree of reinforcement one perceives for involvement in behavior. Formal external constraints are exercised by police or other officials, while informal external constraints include "disapproval, ridicule, ostracism, banishment, the supernatural, and similar techniques used by informal groups or by the society as a whole" (Nye, 1958, p. 7). These external constraints are not the punishments or rewards one receives but, rather, the explicit clarity of rules, laws, and norms, and the degree of consistency and immediacy of the sanctions imposed. External constraints are hypothesized to affect perceived reinforcement for both prosocial and antisocial behavior. The formal and informal constraints to which children are exposed vary with developmental period. For example, early in life family management practices represent the dominant external constraints. These include normative regulation (rules made by parents), supervision or monitoring, and discipline or punishment. The clearer the family rules are, the more consistent the monitoring, and the higher the likelihood of positive or negative consequences for behavior that follows or violates the rules, the more reinforcement will be perceived as likely for involvement in prosocial behavior, and as less likely for involvement in problem behavior. In addition, the clearer and more consistent the external constraints, the more likely they are to lead to skill development. This later effect is derived from social learning theory (Akers et al., 1979). The same principles apply to the exercise of external constraints in other socializing institutions encountered as young people mature, including schools and communities.

It is likely that other relationships exist among the exogenous variables beyond that between external constraints and position in the social structure. However, with this exception, relationships among the model's exogenous variables are not specified here.

One path in the model specifies the processes that encourage prosocial behavior and one path specifies processes that encourage antisocial behavior. Each path is characterized by similar causal processes. In each path two dimensions of each variable are included: participation or involvement in activities and social interaction with others. Both dimensions are considered in the definition of the general constructs of the model along its two paths. The prosocial path is described first.

The first endogenous construct on the prosocial path consists of perceived opportunities to participate in the prosocial order. As noted, perceived opportunity is expected to be influenced by the exogenous factors of position in the social structure and individual constitutional factors. Inclusion of opportunities in the model does not presume the means/ends discontinuity hypothesis of strain theory (Merton, 1957). Rather, it is simply hypothesized that for prosocial involvements to occur, youth must perceive opportunities for such involvements. Perceived opportunity is hypothesized to be of causal importance, distinct from the actual number of different activities or interactions in which it is possible to participate. For example, some high schools may offer intramural sports activities, clubs in chess, fencing, and debate in addition to varsity athletics, while others offer only varsity athletics. The presence of such opportunities to participate in prosocial activities is a necessary condition for participation, but it is not sufficient to engage individuals, for they must know the opportunity is available and must also know how the opportunity satisfies their personal interests. In the absence of this knowledge and experience, the opportunity is powerless itself to influence behavior. Rather than expand the model to include mechanisms specifying relationships between "actual" and "perceived" opportunities, "perceived opportunities for involvement and interaction in prosocial activities" is specified as the causal factor. This avoids the problem of cross-level analysis and specifies how the context is important in influencing the behavior of the individual (Bursik, this volume).

Perceived opportunities for prosocial interaction and involvement affect the level of prosocial interaction and involvement. This causal ordering differs from the ordering of variables in Hirschi's control theory in which attachment predicts commitment and commitment, in turn, predicts involvement. In the present synthesis, prosocial interaction and involvement is viewed as a necessary, though insufficient, precondition to development of prosocial bonding. Involvement was not empirically supported in Hirschi's (1969) nor more recent research (Kempf, 1993) as an element of the social bond that prevents antisocial behavior. The present theory asserts that involvement and interaction precede the formation of attachments and commitments. This alteration in the causal paths appears consistent with the empirical work of behavioral researchers (Bandura, 1977; Bem, 1972; Festinger, 1964) who argue that behavior change (in this case involvement and interaction) precedes attitude change (such as attachment and commitment). In summary, prosocial interaction and involvement is viewed as a behavioral variable that is antecedent to and predicts the development of the social bond of attachment and commitment.

The development of attachments and commitments to the prosocial world depends on the extent to which prosocial involvements and interactions are positively reinforced. It is hypothesized that attachment to prosocial others and commitment to prosocial lines of action result only when prosocial interactions and involvements provide, in sum, positive reinforcement to individuals (Conger, 1976, 1980; Hundleby, 1986). This is hypothesized to be true whether the rewards are social or nonsocial. Thus, perceived rewards (positive reinforcements and punishments) have been added to the interaction and involvement path as intervening variables between involvement/interaction and attachment/commitment. As with perceived opportunities, we focus on the perception of rewards. What is actually rewarding varies with individual preferences, and the perception of an activity or interaction as rewarding involves assessment of several dimensions of the involvement. For example, a youth employed at a low-skilled food service job may dislike the job, hate having peers see him there, and think the wages are too low. Measurement of perceived rewards includes multiple sources of possible reinforcements beyond wages alone. Perception of rewards also incorporates experience over multiple encounters.

If attachment and commitment depend on the level of perceived rein-forcement for involvement, then factors that enhance reinforcement and perception of reinforcement should indirectly affect the development of attachment and commitment. Emotional, cognitive, and behavioral skills, including the ability to identify, express, and manage feelings, as well as skills to control impulses, cope with stress, read and interpret social cues, solve problems and make decisions, understand behavioral norms, per-form tasks such as academic work, and communicate verbally (W. T. Grant Consortium on the Promotion of Social Competence, 1992) all should increase the probability that one will experience rewards for prosocial involvement and interaction. Therefore, the individual's skills for prosocial interaction and involvement affect the level of reinforcement perceived as forthcoming from prosocial interaction and involvement. This may be a direct relationship with perceived reinforcements or may moderate the relationship between involvement and rewards. The actual form of the relationship is an empirical question; we have chosen to model it as a direct effect as shown in Figure 4.1.

Commitment and attachment to prosocial activities and people directly affect the development of belief in the moral validity of society's rules of conduct (the law and prosocial norms). Belief in the moral validity of society's rules of conduct is viewed as internalization of the standards for behavior of persons and institutions to which one is bonded. Once inter-nalized, these standards become part of the individual's value system and help determine which activities the individual views as morally acceptable. Belief is thus an internal constraint that is directly affected by attachment to prosocial others and commitment to prosocial activities. Belief is hypo-thesized to directly decrease the probability of antisocial behavior.

The social development model hypothesizes recursive relationships within developmental periods, but provides a mechanism for reciprocal relationships among constructs across developmental periods. These relationships will be mentioned here since they are part of Figure 4.1, but they will be more fully described after presentation of the developmentally specific models. On the prosocial path, perceived rewards for prosocial interaction and involvement, attachment and commitment to prosocial others and activities, and belief in the moral order are all hypothesized to affect one's perception of opportunities for prosocial interaction and involvement in the next developmental period. On the antisocial path, perceived rewards for problem behavior and interaction with antisocial others, attachment and commitment to antisocial others and activities, belief in antisocial values, and antisocial behavior itself are hypothesized to have a direct positive effect on perceived opportunity for problem behavior and antisocial interactions. Antisocial behavior is expected to have a direct negative effect on perceived opportunity for prosocial interaction and involvement, and a direct positive effect on perceived opportunity for antisocial interaction and involvement in the next developmental period.

The prosocial path inhibits deviance through strengthening bonds to prosocial others and activities. However, as shown in Figure 4.1, the model predicts the promotion of antisocial behavior as well as its inhibition. Therefore, the model includes a pathway of processes leading to the initiation, escalation, and maintenance of drug use and crime. Specification of this additional path makes this theoretical model less elegant than pure formulations of control theory, which assert that nonconformity is a natural state that need not be learned. However, research has indicated that control theory's assertion of "natural" motivation to deviance is empirically inadequate (Hirschi, 1969, p. 230). An adequate theory of deviant behavior must explain how deviant behavior emerges and is maintained. Crime and drug use are, to some degree social behaviors; that is, they are behaviors learned from others (Elliott & Menard, this volume). The principles of reinforcement hypothesized by social learning theorists are hypothesized in the social development model to be important in the process of learning deviant behaviors (Akers et al., 1979), just as they are in the process of developing prosocial behaviors. The path to drug use and criminal behaviors includes the same social processes as those inhibiting these behaviors.

The existence of prosocial and antisocial paths with similar social processes operating to produce bonding requires that careful distinction be made between interactions and involvements on the two paths. If an individual is employed as a counter employee at a fast food restaurant, this may be initially classified as prosocial involvement. However, if that individual finds ways to provide friends with free food from the restaurant, or encounters opportunities to buy drugs from other employees, the involvement may contribute to the antisocial path. It is therefore important to measure the extent to which both prosocial and antisocial opportunities are available to the individual, even in the same social unit.

The first endogenous concept on the antisocial path consists of perceived opportunities for antisocial involvement and interaction. If an individual does not perceive opportunities to interact with drug users and delinquents or to become involved in problem behaviors, actual interaction and involvement are not possible. The greater the perceived opportunities, the more actual interaction and involvement are expected.

As with the prosocial pathway, at this point we have combined into a single construct the two concepts of interaction with others engaged in antisocial behaviors and prior involvement in problem behavior. These are both types of behavior themselves. Both are expected to have similar effects in the model. Problem behavior as defined here is continuing involvement in the specific antisocial behavior measured in the prior developmental period. The specific behavior included is distinct from the antisocial behavior predicted in the current developmental period. As explicated in more depth in the specific submodel descriptions to follow, it is recognized that in some individuals, antisocial behaviors build along a traceable trajectory (see Loeber, this volume; Loeber & Le Blanc, 1990). Difficult early temperament predicts behavior problems, including aggressive behavior in early childhood, and aggressive behavior predicts the early initiation of both drug use and delinquent behavior. Early initiation is itself a predictor of more frequent and unspecialized involvement in later delinquent and drug-using behaviors. In late adolescence and early adulthood, more frequent involvement in a wide range of drug-using and criminal behaviors predicts more negative outcomes, such as alcoholism or drug abuse or other problems (arrests, DUI citations), associated with drug-using or criminal behavior. Importantly, however, significant numbers of children do not pass through these stages of development of antisocial behavior. For example, only about 40% of primary school children identified as aggressive became involved in frequent criminal or drug-using behavior (Loeber, 1991; Kellam, Ensminger, & Simon, 1980).

The challenge for theory is to explain both the development of antisocial behaviors over time and the desistance from such behaviors. Viewing prior antisocial behavior as problem behavior in the model allows inclusion of the empirically supported phenomenon of behavioral continuity, while avoiding the tautological and theoretically trivial claim that antisocial behavior predicts later involvement in the same antisocial behavior. At the same time, it allows specification of the mechanisms by which problem behaviors in one developmental period fail to escalate into antisocial behaviors in another. In sum, the empirically observed links among antisocial behaviors at different developmental periods are included in the model through the concept of involvement in problem behavior, which indicates behaviors distinct from and thought to be developmentally prior to the antisocial behaviors predicted in each subsequent developmental period.

Interaction with others involved in the antisocial behavior predicted during the period is included at the same point in the model as prior problem behavior. Research on predictors of drug use and crime has consistently found strong correlations between association with others engaged in antisocial behaviors and involvement in crime and drug abuse (Brook et al., 1990; Dembo, Farrow, Schmeidler, & Burgos, 1979; Elliott et al., 1985). Elliott and Menard's (this volume) data indicate that in the preponderance of cases in which temporal ordering can be established, interaction with others engaged in delinquent behaviors predicts delinquent behavior. Initial illicit interactions and involvements in problem behavior are hypothesized to increase the likelihood that an individual will perceive these interactions and involvements as rewarding. Perception of rewards is conditioned by the costs of legal and other sanctions as well as by benefits resulting from the behavior itself. Direct paths are hypothesized from perceived rewards for illicit interactions and involvements to attachment and commitment to antisocial others and activities. As discussed earlier, a direct path is also hypothesized to involvement in antisocial behavior.

Again, skills for interaction/involvement are hypothesized to directly affect perceived rewards for problem behavior and interaction with antisocial others. Thus, social and cognitive skills can be useful in enhancing reinforcement for involvement in both prosocial and antisocial groups and activities.

If one perceives that interactions with drug users and delinquents and involvement in problem behavior are rewarding, attachments to these individuals and commitments to these behaviors are predicted to develop. These attachments and commitments are hypothesized to directly positively affect involvement in drug use and crime. Further, attachment and commitment to antisocial others and activities are hypothesized to lead to internalized normative approval of antisocial behavior. As with belief in the prosocial moral order, belief in illicit lines of action can develop. Clearly, individuals can generate behavior norms that advocate antisocial behaviors as when those engaged in revolutionary actions advocate violence. Similarly, in the autobiography of one organized crime figure, there is evidence of an understanding of societal rules and norms, but these are perceived as superseded by "the rules of war," which condone the use of violence among "soldiers" (Bonanno, 1983). The development of belief in antisocial values provides another path to antisocial behavior. This path is hypothesized to be associated with frequent and prolonged involvement in antisocial behavior. The extent of such belief is variable in individuals and society.

Although bonds to prosocial others are generally preferred, bonds are hypothesized to develop among those engaged in antisocial behaviors (Colvin & Pauly, 1983). Thus, it is not bonding per se that inhibits deviance, but rather the norms, values, and beliefs of those to whom one is bonded that either inhibit or increase deviance.

As indicated in Figure 4.1, the social development model hypothesizes three direct predictors of antisocial behavior from the antisocial path. The direct link from each predictor indicates a different etiological path to antisocial behavior. Drug use and delinquency are hypothesized to be directly caused by perceived rewards for antisocial interaction and involvement in problem behavior, attachment and commitment to antisocial others or lines of action, and belief in antisocial values.

The first path to antisocial behavior is chosen simply for the rewards an individual perceives as forthcoming from the behavior. The personal calculation of reward is sufficient to produce antisocial behavior when low bonding to prosocial others results in low perceived costs of antisocial behavior (Hirschi, 1969) or in the presence of high bonding, when the perceptions of risks of detection, and thus, costs of antisocial behavior are perceived as low.

Attachment to those engaged in antisocial behavior and commitment to antisocial lines of action also directly increase antisocial behavior. Bonds of attachment and commitment may form among those engaged in antisocial behaviors and these attachments and commitments contribute to delinquent and drug involvement. These hypotheses are supported by Agnew's findings that delinquent friends have "the greatest effect on delinquency when the adolescent is attached to these friends, spends much time with them, feels they approve of his or her delinquency and feels pressure from them to engage in delinquency" (1991, p. 64). Further, commitment to a deviant line of action is hypothesized to develop when deviant involvement and interaction consistently produce profit of rewards over costs, such that one decides to forego prosocial involvements for antisocial ones. This type of commitment does not imply value reversal in Kornhauser's sense; rather, it may imply rationalizations or acceptance of deviance when "preferred alternatives are out of reach" (Kornhauser, 1978, p. 243).

Finally, antisocial behavior is encouraged by the internalization of a set of norms favorable to criminal involvement as illustrated by the belief structure advanced by those engaged in organized crime (Bonanno, 1983).

Developmentally Specific Models

Specific models for four developmental periods from birth through high school are presented in Figures 4.2–4.5. While the general model identifies the processes hypothesized to operate across developmental periods, the developmentally specific models specify the social units that are involved in the processes of each developmental period.

During the preschool period (Figure 4.2), position in the social structure is indicated by education and socioeconomic status of the child's household(s), together with the family's and child's race and the child's gender. In this period, low interpersonal, educational, and financial resources of caretakers increase risk for delays in development of cognitive skills, for school failure, and for child psychopathology (Barnard, 1992). Constitutional biological factors, such as preterm birth, small birth weight for age, or prenatal alcohol or drug exposure, negatively affect cognitive skill development (Barnard, 1992; Chasnoff, 1991; Howard, Beckwith, Rodning, & Kropenske, 1989; Rutter, 1985). Constitutional psychological factors, such as positive temperament and positive social orientation, are expected to have their greatest effects during this period (Werner & Smith, 1992) through their influence on enhancing early skill development. The preschool child's opportunity for prosocial involvement is indicated by degree of access to prosocial adult careproviders. For example, a family with four or fewer children spaced at least 2 years apart has been shown to predict resilience in at-risk children (Werner & Smith, 1992). These are indicators of greater opportunity for access to adult careproviders during the preschool period. As reflected in Figure 4.2, during this developmental period the use of such indicators may be preferable to seeking measures of the child's perception of opportunities. Prosocial involvements include the nature and extent of interaction with prosocial family members and child care providers. The child's nonverbal cue-giving skills, responses to social interactions with caregivers, and subsequently locomotion, verbal communication, and self-help skills appear important during this period (Barnard et al., 1989; Chasnoff, Griffith, MacGregor, Dirkes, & Burns, 1989; Werner

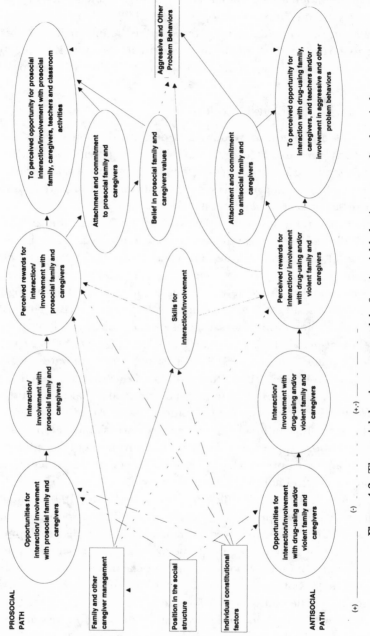

Figure 4.2. The social development model of antisocial behavior – preschool period.

& Smith, 1992) As the social development processes unfold in the preschool period, the family is of primary importance as a socializing unit (Egeland & Farber, 1984; Loeber & Dishion, 1983; McCord, 1979; Rutter, 1987; Sameroff & Seifer, 1990). In addition, the day care, preschool or alternative care environment can also affect social development if the child is involved in these settings (Berrueta-Clement, Schweinhart, Barnett, Epstein, & Weikart, 1984; Johnson, 1988; Ramey, Bryant, Campbell, Sparling, & Wasik, 1988) During this period, external constraints consist of family management practices and the child management practices of child care providers. The clearer, more consistent, and more immediate the positive reinforcement and moderate negative consequences are, the more likely children are to develop prosocial skills, and the more likely they are to perceive reinforcement for prosocial involvement and interaction. Further, as shown in the cross-path link, it is hypothesized that parental monitoring and discipline decrease the likelihood that children perceive positive reinforcement from involvement in problem behaviors during early childhood.

The social development process begins during this period when the mother picks up the infant and holds it in her arms, creating an involvement or interaction. Even at this early point developmentally, the child's skills in social interaction influence the reinforcement he or she will receive from this encounter. If the child attends to the mother, returns the mother's gaze, and responds with indications of pleasure, this is a skilled performance in the interaction. If the child stiffens, cries, or fails to attend to the mother, this is a less skilled performance. This response is less likely to be reinforced by the mother, and the interaction is less likely to be perceived as reinforcing by the child. The mother's own response also affects the child's perception of reinforcement from the interaction. If the mother's affect is flat or her response is otherwise disturbed (perhaps as a result of a mental disorder, Sameroff & Seifer, 1990), or if she is unable to attend to or recognize the child's performance as a result of drug abuse, even skilled performances by the child may not be reinforced. However, if the mother enjoys the child's attention or expression and responds in a nurturing manner, reinforcement is more likely to be perceived by the infant. It is through these numerous transactional interactions that feelings of attachment to mother begin to develop and grow in the infant (Ainsworth, Behar, Water, & Wall, 1978; Morisset, Barnard, Greenberg, Booth, & Spieker, 1990). The social units in which these processes occur on the prosocial path include non–drug using, noncriminally involved household members; members of extended support systems that participate in the child's socialization; and other caretakers. The antisocial path includes drug-using, criminally involved, and violent family and other caretakers. It is hypothesized that drug use in the home or child care setting and interpersonal conflict/violence are the most salient environmental factors in this period, predisposing an individual toward antisocial behavior, especially when children are attached to these people. The *belief in antisocial values* construct is not included in this period since it is not likely to develop during this period. The antisocial behavior predicted in the preschool period includes aggressive behavior and other conduct disorders.

Figure 4.3 presents the model for the elementary school period. During this period, the school joins the family as an important socializing environment. Teachers and classroom peers join parents, siblings, and other adult caretakers as important agents of socialization. Thus, external constraints in the school environment, specifically classroom management practices and school policies, join family management practices as important indicators of this exogenous variable. Again the clearer, more consistent, and more immediate the reinforcement and consequences, the more rewards are perceived for involvement, the more prosocial skills are learned, and the fewer the perceived positive rewards for interacting with drug users and delinquents.

During this period in the family, children can be provided opportunities to contribute to the family's maintenance and governance systems. For instance, children can be provided with opportunities to care for younger siblings. Werner and Smith (1992) found that involving older siblings in caring for younger siblings was a protective factor in inhibiting problem behavior of the older sibling. The greater these opportunities, the greater the family involvement. If parents teach children skills to perform effectively, the children will be more likely to perceive the experience as rewarding. Further, researchers have demonstrated that greater time spent on academic tasks due, in part, to effective classroom management has been associated with greater gains in achievement (skill) and higher grades (a reward for skillful academic performance) (Brophy & Good, 1986). Again, as in the previous period, this is a transactional process between caregivers and children in which mutual skills and reinforcement are important in shaping behavior.

The social development process at school is influenced by the ways schools and teachers structure opportunities for children to be involved in school. These include opportunities to be involved in academic tasks as well as in organizational maintenance, governance, nonacademic activities, and in interaction with classmates. The more schools and classrooms provide such opportunities, the greater the likelihood that children will be-

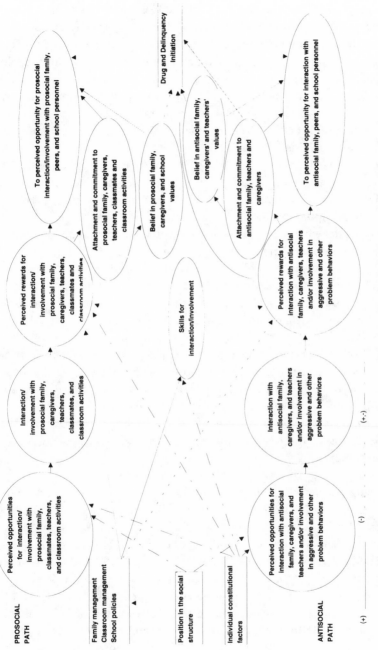

Figure 4.3. The social development model of antisocial behavior – elementary school period.

come involved. Active participation in the classroom has been associated with protection from involvement in problem behavior (Dryfoos, 1990). Perceived rewards include grades, the manner in which teachers provide both reinforcement and punishment, and perceived support and rejection by peers. Academic failure and peer rejection – costs of prosocial involvement – have been found to predict later involvement in antisocial behavior (Hawkins et al., 1992b). Supportive teachers who reinforce effort have been found to protect children from later involvement in problem behavior (e.g., see Hawkins & Lam, 1987).

Involvement with non–drug using and nondelinquent peers is hypothesized to increase in importance toward the end of elementary school, although parents and teachers remain the most significant influences on behavior during this period.

On the antisocial path, interaction may be with drug-using or criminally involved family members, school personnel, or, toward the end of this period, peers. Aggressive behaviors and other conduct or behavior problems at home or school are indicators of involvement in problem behaviors during this period. These appear to be nonspecific predictors of both delinquency and drug use initiation. The onset of drug use and delinquent behaviors are the antisocial behavioral outcomes predicted during the elementary school period. The relative weight of prosocial and antisocial influences will determine whether children begin to use drugs and engage in delinquent behavior during this period. It is hypothesized that prosocial bonding inhibits involvement with others who engage in drug use and / or delinquent behavior, as well as initiation of these behaviors, and that bonding to drug users and delinquents will increase the likelihood of drug use and delinquency initiation.

Figure 4.4 presents the model for the middle/junior high school period. During this period, peers increase in importance as a socialization force (Elliott et al., 1985). External constraints during this period include peer norms and behaviors, school policy and classroom management practices, family management practices, and, for the first time, the legal codes and police and court enforcement of these codes. As youth mature and initiate delinquent and drug-using behaviors, the response of the legal system becomes a potentially more important external constraint. Smith and Gartin (1989) found that arrest encourages the termination of criminal behavior for novice offenders and reduces future rates of offending for experienced offenders, suggesting that the external constraint of arrest may operate to reduce perceived rewards for criminal involvement and inhibit criminal behavior as hypothesized. On the prosocial path, prosocial others

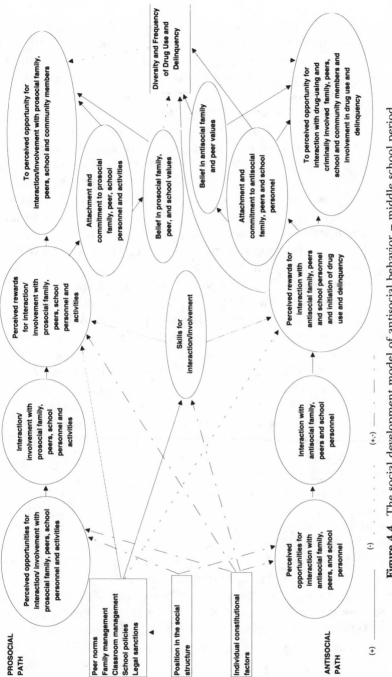

Figure 4.4. The social development model of antisocial behavior – middle school period.

PROSOCIAL PATH

Perceived opportunities for interaction/involvement with prosocial family, peers, school personnel and activities

Interaction/involvement with prosocial family, peers, school personnel and activities

Perceived rewards for interaction/involvement with prosocial family, peers, school personnel and activities

Attachment and commitment to prosocial family, peer, school personnel and activities

Belief in prosocial family, peer, and school values

To perceived opportunity for interaction/involvement with prosocial family, peers, school and community members

Diversity and Frequency of Drug Use and Delinquency

Belief in antisocial family and peer values

Attachment and commitment to antisocial family, peers and school personnel

To perceived opportunity for interaction with drug-using and criminally involved family, peers, school and community members and involvement in drug use and delinquency

Perceived rewards for interaction with antisocial family, peers and school personnel and initiation of drug use and delinquency

Skills for interaction/involvement

Interaction with antisocial family, peers and school personnel

Perceived opportunities for interaction with antisocial family, peers, and school personnel

ANTISOCIAL PATH

Peer norms
Family management
Classroom management
School policies
Legal sanctions

Position in the social structure

Individual constitutional factors

(+) (-) (+,-)

include non–drug using or noncriminally involved family members and school personnel as before. However, during this period non–drug using and noncriminal peers have an increased influence. Interaction with drug users and delinquents is indicated by the extent of interaction with drug-using or criminal family members as well as other children and adults engaged in criminal or drug-using behaviors.

The increase in peer influences during the middle school period has important implications for both prosocial and antisocial behavior. As children begin the process of individuation from family, peer interaction becomes an important socializing force. Middle school children are exposed to a variety of peers with both prosocial and antisocial behavior patterns. The norms and values of peers with whom one associates have a large impact on behavior that persists through young adulthood. During this period, peer bonding increases in importance and can have a positive or negative impact on behavior depending on the preponderance of prosocial or antisocial influence represented by a child's peer network. On the antisocial path, the predictive power of antisocial peer bonding increases during this period.

During this period, perceptions of rewards for antisocial involvement include those associated with drug and delinquency initiation. These perceptions of rewards include not only the results of applications of legal sanctions and other informal external constraints, but also the direct rewards and risks perceived as forthcoming from the behaviors themselves. Perceived physical and psychological effects of drugs following drug use initiation have been shown to be important determinants of the maintenance of drug use (Bailey, Flewelling, & Rachal, 1992). The antisocial outcomes predicted during this developmental period are the diversity and frequency of drug use and delinquent behaviors.

Figure 4.5 presents the model for the high school period. By the time youth enter this period, many of the risk and protective factors for drug use and delinquency have been established. For example, early and persistent antisocial behaviors (Blumstein, Farrington, & Moitra, 1985; Ensminger, Kellam, & Rubin, 1983; Farrington, 1978, 1985; Loeber & Dishion, 1983; Robins, 1979), poor parental child management techniques (Farrington, 1979a; Loeber & Dishion, 1983; Robins, 1979; West & Farrington, 1973), and poor educational attainment (Blumstein et al., 1985; Farrington, 1979b; Loeber & Dishion, 1983; Polk et al., 1981; Wolfgang, Figlio, & Sellin, 1972) are all evident before high school. During the high school period the model is characterized by factors relevant to the maintenance of prosocial or antisocial behaviors.

The external constraints construct is characterized by peers, school, the

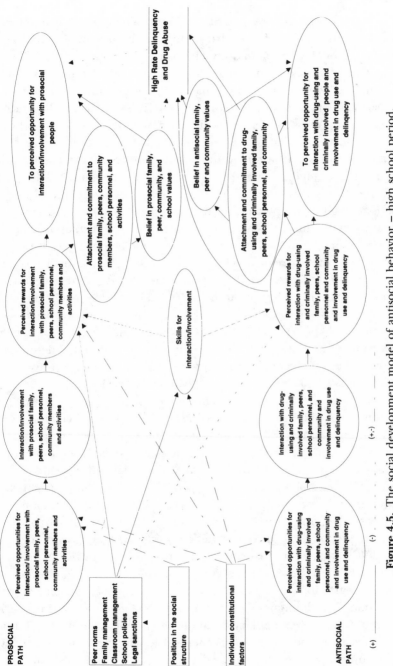

PROSOCIAL PATH

Perceived opportunities for interaction/involvement with prosocial family, peers, school personnel, community members and activities

Interaction/involvement with prosocial family, peers, school personnel, community members and activities

Perceived rewards for interaction/involvement with prosocial family, peers, school personnel, community members and activities

To perceived opportunity for interaction/involvement with prosocial people

Attachment and commitment to prosocial family, peers, community members, school personnel, and activities

Belief in prosocial family, peer, community, and school values

High Rate Delinquency and Drug Abuse

Peer norms
Family management
Classroom management
School policies
Legal sanctions

Position in the social structure

Individual constitutional factors

Skills for interaction/involvement

Belief in antisocial family, peer and community values

Attachment and commitment to drug-using and criminally involved family, peers, school personnel, and community

Perceived rewards for interaction with drug-using and criminally involved family, peers, school personnel and community and involvement in drug use and delinquency

To perceived opportunity for interaction with drug-using and criminally involved people and involvement in drug use and delinquency

Interaction with drug-using and criminally involved family, peers, school personnel, and community and involvement in drug use and delinquency

Perceived opportunities for interaction with drug-using and criminally involved family, peers, school personnel, and community and involvement in drug use and delinquency

ANTISOCIAL PATH

(+)

(-)

(+,-)

Figure 4.5. The social development model of antisocial behavior – high school period.

legal system, and, to a lesser extent, the family. The referent group for the prosocial path consists of non–drug using and noncriminal family, peers, school personnel, and community members. Although peers are increasing in importance, evidence suggests that parents remain an important force in socialization throughout high school especially concerning decisions such as drug use, sex, and contraceptive use (Munsch & Blyth, 1993). The referent groups for the antisocial path include drug users and those criminally involved. The actual and perceived rewards and costs of prosocial and antisocial involvement and interaction determine the behaviors that are maintained during this period. For some youths, delinquency decreases during this time (Elliott et al., 1985). It is hypothesized that the rewards for delinquency decrease for adolescents who are experimenting with antisocial behavior as a means of adolescent individuation, and who have not been exposed to high levels of early risk factors. In contrast, those who experience few rewards for prosocial interaction and involvement, have high levels of early risk factors, and are involved with drug use and delinquency are hypothesized to be more likely to become chronic delinquents. Poor grades, low social status, and lack of access to prosocial leadership roles are likely to characterize their background. The antisocial behavior outcomes in the high school period include a high rate of delinquency and drug abuse indicated by the frequency and persistence of these behaviors as well as by problems associated with the behaviors.

These four submodels of preschool, elementary, middle school, and high school social development have been constructed as recursive models. However, the social development model hypothesizes reciprocal relationships among constructs across developmental periods. If the four models are laid out end to end, prosocial and antisocial influences from one period affect variables at the beginning of the causal chain in the next. In this sense, each submodel is a phase or period, whose outcomes affect the levels of the beginning variables in the next phase or period. This notion of recurring phases allows the construction of models that account for reciprocal effects, that is, mutual causal influences among antisocial behaviors and hypothesized causes (Thornberry, 1987, this volume). To illustrate, the effects of early initiation of delinquency on prosocial bonding and on interaction with delinquent peers are both included in the cross-period transition from the elementary period to the middle school period. Initiation of antisocial behavior is hypothesized to directly increase perceived opportunities for interaction with drug-using and criminal family, peers, and school personnel, and to directly decrease perceived opportunities for prosocial interactions and involvements. In this way, the process of prosocial interaction and bonding is affected by prior antisocial behavior through this indirect path. This use of recurring model phases has the advantage over instantaneous reciprocal models of maintaining the ability to make assertions about the temporal priority of predictor variables and to specify mechanisms by which behaviors affect bonding. This is important, if theory is to meet the basic criterion for asserting causality, that is, if one wishes to claim that the predictor variable could have caused the particular outcome of interest. Models that solve the problem of mutual causal influences through the specification of instantaneous reciprocal effects do not appear to us to meet the test of temporal priority of the causal variable.

Transitions are times of change. They present opportunities to change behavior as old conditions of social life are replaced by new ones. These are times when the new conditions, rules, and structures are not yet clear, and the applicability of the old conditions, rules, and structures is diminished (Smelser, 1962). It is hypothesized that three factors determine the impact of the transition itself: (1) the level of prosocial and antisocial bonding to social units established during the previous period, (2) the rewards for prosocial and antisocial behaviors that the child perceives as a result of experiences in the prior period, and (3) the level of antisocial behavior manifested in the prior period.

Considering the transition from preschool to the elementary school period, it is hypothesized that the stronger the previous levels of prosocial bonding to the family (attachment, commitment, and belief), the greater the number of prosocial opportunities children will perceive in the new environment. In addition, it is expected that the greater the perceived rewards from interaction and involvement with prosocial family and caregivers, the more likely the child will be to perceive opportunities to interact and become involved with prosocial others in the elementary school setting as well as in other prosocial units during this period. Conversely, the greater the bonds to drug users and family members involved in violence or conflict, and the greater the perceived rewards from interaction and involvement with antisocial family members during the preschool period, the more likely children will be to perceive opportunities to interact with antisocial peers, family members, and other adults during the elementary school period. Moreover, if children have engaged in aggressive behavior in the preschool period, they will be less likely to perceive new encounters as opportunities for prosocial involvement in the elementary period. This in turn should predict lower levels of prosocial involvement, with these children finding opportunities to engage in aggressive and other problem behaviors and failing to perceive opportunities to engage in prosocial behaviors in the classroom or on the playground. Through this process, antisocial behavior diminishes prosocial bonds of attachment, commitment, and, ultimately, belief. The transitions from elementary to middle school and from middle to high school are expected to reflect similar dynamic relationships across periods. Note that across each transition antisocial involvement is expected to have a negative indirect effect on prosocial involvements and interactions, prosocial reinforcement, prosocial bonds of attachment and commitment, and belief in the legitimacy of laws and norms.

These four developmental models have been presented to demonstrate the utility of the social development model in summarizing cumulative processes during periods in which there is a degree of continuity in the constellation of socializing units affecting the child. Major changes in the amount of time spent in different units of socialization occur following entry to elementary school, middle or junior high school, and high school. These are predictable transitions between periods of somewhat greater stability.

However, it is also possible to conceptualize other transitions in the socialization environment as points at which a new phase of the model is begun. The factors affecting the outcomes of transition from one developmental period to another can also be expected to follow other transitions or life changes such as a residential move, school transfer, or separation from parents. It is hypothesized that the outcomes of these additional transitions within a developmental period will be affected by the same factors that affect the outcomes of transitions between periods. Prior levels of bonding, the rewards the child perceives for prosocial and antisocial involvement and interaction as a result of experiences in the previous environments, and the extent of prior antisocial behavior will influence the extent to which the child becomes involved in prosocial or antisocial activities and interactions in the new environments following the transition.

We have suggested that each phase or period of the social development model is a causal process that recurs following transitions, with beginning variables affected by factors from the prior period. It is possible that phases endure for much shorter time periods and recur across much more frequent transitions than those discussed so far. For example, opportunities for involvement are experienced daily in the classroom. Opportunities for involvement in classroom activities are differentially provided by teachers moment by moment. Teachers wait longer for children who they believe to be intelligent (skilled) to answer questions than they do for children who they believe are less skilled. As experienced by elementary children, these are likely to be perceived as differences in opportunities. Children not afforded opportunities for involvement in the classroom are not likely to perceive the classroom experience as rewarding. Opportunities and rewards are experienced in many such interactions each day. They are experienced in real time. The perceived opportunities and rewards for each incident of interaction or involvement should affect the developing child's degree of commitment and attachment to the social units in which the child is involved. Over the course of a day, the cumulative result of many rewarded interactions in the classroom should be to increase attachment and commitment to school among those with low attachment and commitment and to maintain high attachment and commitment to school among those with high attachment and commitment.

Commitment and attachment are more stable qualities than rewards. They are emotional and personal investments in social units themselves. The concept of investment implies a degree of stability and a future orientation, that is, the promise of future involvement in the same lines of action in which one has previously been involved. Such investments are built up through each day's involvements and rewards, but the cumulative weight of the investment is more than the sum of that day's rewards. Prosocial attachments and commitments are attitudes. They change more slowly than daily experience. Temporally, opportunities and rewards are experienced moment by moment, while social bonds of attachments, commitments, and beliefs are built up over time from these momentary interactions. These social bonds themselves influence future perceptions of opportunities for both prosocial and antisocial involvement.

There is a need for explicit consideration of the time frame or duration of effects expected for specific constructs as well as the time frames over which constructs are measured in testing theory. This is an issue with which we are only beginning to wrestle. In addition to etiological studies with annual or semiannual measurements in which we and many of our colleagues engage, useful tests of the social development model could also be undertaken in short-term studies seeking to investigate the effects of single events, cumulative daily experiences, and involvements and rewards measured over longer time frames in predicting levels and changes in attachment and commitment over shorter and longer intervals.

Implications for Developmentally Specific Intervention Design

Theory provides a basis for the design of approaches for preventing and reducing delinquent behavior and drug abuse. When the etiological pathways to antisocial behavior are specified, it is possible to identify intervention points to interrupt the causal process. Interventions to prevent or reduce antisocial behavior, most basically conceived, seek to interrupt the causal processes that lead to antisocial outcomes and strengthen the processes that lead to prosocial outcomes. This conception of intervention has several implications:

1. Each of the causal elements in the social development model is a potential focus of intervention.
2. Multiple interventions may be required because there are multiple direct and indirect paths to antisocial behavior.
3. Interventions to interrupt the causal processes in the development of antisocial behavior should include components seeking to promote processes that encourage prosocial behavior as well as to interrupt causal processes that encourage antisocial behavior.
4. The influence of prior bonding and behavior on future behavior suggests the importance of intervening early in development.
5. Interventions should be developmentally appropriate. They should affect the primary socializing units operative in the particular period targeted.
6. Transitions hold potential for interrupting causal pathways.

Using the social development model, interventions can be conceptualized in terms of their hypothesized effects on constructs and processes of the model. Specification of the model provides a set of guides for exploring the effects of intervention by examining effects on each construct along the hypothesized causal pathway to antisocial behavior. In the following pages, illustrative interventions at each of the four developmental periods are described from this perspective.

Early in the preschool period when children are infants, interventions that promote close physical proximity of mother and child should promote interaction and the development of bonding. Anisfeld and her colleagues (Anisfeld, Casper, Nozyce, & Cunningham, 1990) tested the use of infant carriers (the Snugli) in an experimental study with low-income inner-city mothers. In social development terms, this intervention increased opportunities for parent–child interaction when compared with an alternative intervention (the provision of an infant seat where the baby could be safely put down). By increasing time spent in close proximity, both the mother's monitoring of the baby and her responsiveness to the baby's cues also should have been enhanced, potentially strengthening external constraints and reinforcements for interaction. The social development model hypothesizes that rewarded interaction should increase bonding (attachment during this period). The infant carrier intervention produced higher rates of secure attachment when compared with the infant seat (Anisfeld et al., 1990).

High-quality early childhood education provides a second illustration of intervention consistent with the social development model during the preschool period. Early childhood education programs seek to enhance the cognitive and social skills of young children and often to teach parents effective methods for child management and for reinforcement of their children's learning. From a social development perspective, early childhood education intervenes by enhancing children's skills for prosocial interaction and involvement and parents' understanding and use of external constraints and reinforcements appropriate to the developmental level of the child. Early childhood education for low-income urban children has resulted in higher levels of cognitive skill development, enhanced school achievement, increased rates of high school graduation, and less involvement in delinquency (Berrueta-Clement et al., 1984), suggesting consequences of the intervention on constructs all along the social development pathways.

In the elementary period, as the school classroom emerges as an important domain of social development, the use of effective methods of management and teaching in the classroom becomes important in determining the extent to which opportunities and rewards for interaction and involvement are provided and for determining the degree to which cognitive, interpersonal, and self-management skills are learned by the developing child. Thus, teacher training in effective management and instruction techniques such as proactive classroom management (Doyle, 1986; Hawkins, Catalano, & Associates, 1992a), effective teaching strategies (Brophy & Good, 1986; Walberg, 1986), and cooperative learning (Slavin, 1990) is an intervention consistent with social development hypotheses. In field experimental studies based on the model, use of these methods by elementary teachers in a multiethnic urban school district revealed positive effects on constructs along the social development pathways. Students in intervention classrooms in grades 1 to 4 perceived more opportunities for prosocial involvement and interaction and were more attached and committed to school and less likely to have initiated alcohol use or delinquency by fifth grade than their counterparts in control classrooms (Hawkins et al., 1992c).

A brief discussion of proactive classroom management techniques illustrates how an intervention to train teachers in methods consistent with the social development model is viewed from the perspective of the theory. In this intervention, teachers are trained to teach students the rules and expectations for the classroom in the first few weeks of the school year. These rules and routines provide efficient methods of handling necessary but nonacademic tasks. The result of this explicit intervention to set clear expectations for classroom behavior is that more time is spent on academic tasks, providing more opportunities for active involvement with academic materials. Teaching these routines proactively results in clear and explicit external constraints. In this intervention, teachers also learn to use the method least disruptive to the flow of instruction to maintain control in the classroom when behavior problems begin. For example, instead of calling attention to disruptive behavior as a first response, teachers use techniques such as moving toward students who are disruptive while continuing to teach. This response often extinguishes the behavior without calling attention to the perpetrator or singling out that individual for stronger discipline and without cost to the class in academic work time. In social development terms, this component of proactive management minimizes the costs of classroom participation and increases proactive involvement in the classroom.

During the elementary period, parents and adult caretakers remain important in social development. Thus, developmentally appropriate parent training is another intervention consistent with the model during this period (Fraser, Hawkins, & Howard, 1988). An example of a parent-training curriculum designed to address the constructs in the social development model during the late elementary years is *Preparing for the Drug (Free) Years* (Hawkins et al., 1988). This curriculum trains parents in methods to increase children's opportunities for involvement in the family through holding regular family discussions of family management, health, maintenance, and financial issues. It teaches parents to involve children actively in contributing roles in the family in these areas, thereby increasing proactive involvement in the family. It also teaches parents skills for responding to unwanted behaviors from children in ways that express affect appropriately and are behaviorally specific. The curriculum emphasizes the importance of establishing clear and explicit family policies on drug use as a means of establishing clear external constraints. In this intervention, children and parents also learn to resist antisocial influences by assertively refusing opportunities for involvement in antisocial behavior. The curriculum also provides information to parents regarding evidence that involving children in their own alcohol or other drug use increases the children's risk for early initiation of alcohol and other drugs (Ahmed,

Bush, Davidson, & Iannotti, 1984) and encourages them to minimize involvement of children in their own alcohol or other drug-using behaviors. In sum, in social development terms, *Preparing for the Drug (Free) Years* is designed to enhance opportunities for prosocial involvement by expanding family roles and holding family meetings; reduce perceived costs of family involvement due to anger and conflict; set external constraints on drug use; enhance skills to minimize involvement with drug-using peers; and decrease children's interaction with family members when the family members are using alcohol or other drugs (Hawkins, Catalano, & Kent, 1991).

Middle school entry is a transition to an environment characterized by increased levels of drug use, school misbehavior, and delinquency. The structure of involvement with peers and teachers changes from a self-contained classroom with a single group of 25 to 35 classmates to modularized subject-oriented classes and daily exposure to an increased number and variety of students. During this period, a primary focus of preventive interventions with school, peers, and family should be to increase opportunities for interaction with prosocial peers and involvement in prosocial activities. Prosocial involvement is viewed as important during this period because youth without such involvement may seek alternative activities and groups for status attainment and social rewards. Children who become involved with peers engaged in delinquency and substance use are more likely to initiate substance use and illegal behavior.

The School Transitional Environment Program (Felner & Adan, 1988) is an example of a middle school intervention consistent with the social development model. This intervention seeks to ease the transition from elementary to middle school for children who are marginally bonded to school at the end of the elementary period. This intervention has been associated with increases in academic performance and decreases in absenteeism and dropout (Felner, Weissberg, & Adan, 1987). Replication studies have found less depression, substance abuse, and delinquency among program students than control students (Felner & Adan, 1988). The program makes structural changes in middle schools by keeping students in homerooms and core classes as a group during their first year of middle school. This provides increased opportunities for interaction with a limited number of students and reduces students' exposure to older students, whose behavioral norms are expected to be more favorable toward antisocial behavior. Homeroom teachers contact parents to explain the nature of the program and to encourage parents to contact their students' teachers. This increases home–school interaction and enhances the potential for external constraints, since home and school are linked in monitoring students' behavior. Further, homeroom teachers provide a single source of contact for guidance and administrative activities, increasing interaction and consistency of interaction. In theoretical terms, external constraints are strengthened as well as prosocial interaction and potential rewards for interaction. Increased interaction with a limited set of teachers and students has the potential to enhance bonding. Enhanced external constraints have the potential to increase perceived rewards for prosocial and decrease perceived rewards for antisocial behavior.

During the middle school period, the indicidence and prevalence of drug use and delinquency increase as do opportunities for interaction with others engaged in antisocial behavior (Elliott & Huizinga, 1989; Johnston, O'Malley, & Bachman, 1991). Therefore, from a social development perspective, interventions that seek to decrease interactions with others engaged in drug use or delinquency, interventions that seek to enhance perceptions of the salient costs associated with antisocial behavior, and interventions that enhance external constraints against antisocial behavior all appear warranted. A number of drug abuse prevention interventions have focused on goals consistent with these theoretically derived foci. In these classroom-based interventions, students have been trained to identify and resist influences to use drugs (Botvin, 1986) and have been encouraged, through various efforts to portray social, health, and other costs of drug use, to view drug use as costly and socially unacceptable (Hansen, Johnson, Flay, Graham, & Sobel, 1988; Perry, 1986). The Midwestern Prevention Project included these elements and has shown reductions in tobacco and alcohol use among middle school students (Pentz et al., 1989a, 1989b). The program consisted of a school component to teach social influence resistance skills and to examine the prevalence of use and risks associated with use, a parent component to support school activities and inform parents about substance abuse, and a mass media component to publicize the program and its message on the prevalence and risks associated with substance use. In social development terms, the program sought to enhance skills, reduce interaction with drug users, and enhance external constraints through peer, parent, school, and community messages regarding the risk of substance abuse.

During the high school period, delinquent behavior peaks and begins to decline for most individuals, while rates of substance use, school dropout, and pregnancy increase (Elliott, in press; Johnston et al., 1991). Providing the skills to successfully negotiate the proliferating behavioral choices while avoiding antisocial behavior is an appropriate intervention goal during this period. Social competence promotion is an intervention that addresses this goal. Using skills-training techniques, students of all racial/ethnic backgrounds and socioeconomic and risk statuses have been successfully trained to develop skills that are hypothesized to promote prosocial involvement (Elias & Weissberg, 1990; Jones, 1988; Presseisen, 1988). The W. T. Grant Consortium on the School-Based Promotion of Social Competence (1992) recommends that social competence promotion interventions during the high school period include training in recognizing the consequences of risky behaviors, protecting self from negative outcomes, planning a career, initiating and maintaining cross-gender friends and romantic relationships, making a realistic academic plan, being responsible at social events and parties, and understanding the importance of government and community service. In social development terms, these skills are hypothesized to directly enhance the probability of successful performance in prosocial settings, decrease antisocial interactions, and indirectly increase the development of prosocial commitment and attachment through the promotion of skillful performance in prosocial relationships at school and in the community.

As briefly illustrated here, the social development model provides a theoretical foundation for the design of diverse interventions at different developmental stages to promote prosocial bonding and reduce antisocial behavior. The theory provides guidelines for intervention by specifying constructs that serve as intervention targets and by ensuring that interventions focused on different constructs and interventions in different domains work compatibly toward consistent, theoretically specified goals.

Summary

This chapter has presented a theoretical statement of the social development model. The model is grounded in empirically supported theories of deviance. It is a general theory of human behavior that recognizes the importance of development by specifying submodels for different developmental periods during childhood and adolescence. Further, the model uses empirical evidence on risk and protective factors in its construction, employing a path that encourages antisocial behavior and a path that inhibits antisocial behavior. The authors are currently engaged in a series of theory-driven etiological studies and field experiments to explore the model's empirical adequacy and power (Catalano & Hawkins, 1985; Hawkins et al., 1992c; Hawkins & Lam, 1987; Hawkins, Catalano, & Wells, 1986;

Hawkins, Catalano, Gillmore, & Wells, 1989; Gillmore, Hawkins, Catalano, & Abbott, 1991; Farrington & Hawkins, 1991; Hawkins, Von Cleve, & Catalano, 1991).

REFERENCES

Agnew, R. (1985). Social control theory and delinquency: A longitudinal test. *Criminology, 23,* 47–61.

Agnew, R. (1991). The interactive effects of peer variables on delinquency. *Criminology, 29,* 47–72.

Ahmed, S. W., Bush, P. J., Davidson, F. R., & Iannotti, R. J. (1984, November). *Predicting children's use and intentions to use abusable substances.* Paper presented at the annual meeting of the American Public Health Association, Anaheim, CA.

Ainsworth, M. D. S., Behar, M. C., Water, E., & Wall, S. (1978). *Patterns of attachment: A psychological study of the strange situation.* Hillsdale, NJ: Erlbaum.

Akers, R. L. (1977). *Deviant behavior: A social learning approach* (2nd ed.). Belmont, CA: Wadsworth.

Akers, R. L., Krohn, M. D., Lanza-Kaduce, L., & Radosevich, M. (1979). Social learning and deviant behavior: A specific test of a general theory. *American Sociological Review, 44,* 636–655.

Anisfeld, E., Casper, V., Nozyce, M. & Cunningham, N. (1990). Does infant carrying promote attachment? An experimental study of the effects of increased physical contact on the development of attachment. *Child Development, 61,* 1617–1627.

Anthony, E. J., & Cohler, B. J. (1987). *The invulnerable child.* New York: Guilford.

Bailey, S. L., Flewelling, R. L., & Rachal, J. V. (1992). Predicting continued use of marijuana among adolescents: The relative influence of drug-specific and social context factors. *Journal of Health and Social Behavior, 1,* 51–65.

Bandura, A. (1973). *Aggression: A social learning analysis.* Englewood Cliffs, NJ: Prentice-Hall.

Bandura, A. (1977). Self-efficacy: Toward a unifying theory of behavioral change. *Psychological Review, 84,* 191–215.

Barnard, K. E. (1992). Prenatal and infancy programs. In J. D. Hawkins, R. F. Catalano, & Associates (Eds.), *Communities that care: Action for drug abuse prevention.* San Francisco: Jossey-Bass.

Barnard, K. E., Hammond, M., Booth, C. L., Bee, H. L., Mitchell, S. K., & Spieker, S. J. (1989). Measurement and meaning of parent-child interaction. In F. J. Morrison, C. E. Lord, & D. P. Keating (Eds.), *Applied developmental psychology* (Vol. 3, pp. 39–80). New York: Academic Press.

Bem, D. J. (1972). Self-perception theory. In L. Berkowitz (Ed.), *Advances in experimental social psychology* (Vol. 6, pp. 2–62). New York: Academic Press.

Berrueta-Clement, J., Schweinhart, L., Barnett, W., Epstein, A., & Weikert, D.

(1984). Changed lives: The effects of the Perry Preschool Program on youths through age 19. *Monographs of the High/Scope Educational Research Foundation, 8.*

Blumstein, A., Farrington, D. P., & Moitra, S. (1985). Delinquency careers: Innocents, desisters, and persisters. In M. Tonry & N. Morris (Eds.), *Crime and justice: An annual review of research* (Vol. 6, pp. 187–219). Chicago: University of Chicago Press.

Bonanno, J. (1983). *A man of honor.* New York: Simon & Schuster.

Botvin, G. J. (1986). Substance abuse prevention research: Recent developments and future directions. *Journal of School Health, 56,* 369–374.

Briar, S., & Piliavin, I. (1965). Delinquency, situational inducements and commitment to conformity. *Social Problems, 13,* 25–45.

Brook, J. S., Brook, D. W., Gordon, A. S., Whiteman, M., & Cohen, P. (1990). The psychosocial etiology of adolescent drug use: A family interactional approach. *Genetic, Social, and General Psychology Monographs, 116* (Whole No. 2).

Brook, J. S., Gordon, A. S., Whiteman, M., & Cohen, P. (1986). Some models and mechanisms for explaining the impact of maternal and adolescent characteristics on adolescent stage of drug use. *Developmental Psychology, 22,* 460–467.

Brophy, J., & Good, T. L. (1986). Teacher behavior and student achievement. In M. C. Wittrock (Ed.), *Handbook of research on training* (3rd ed., pp. 328–375). New York: Macmillan.

Burgess, R. L., & Akers, R. L. (1966). A differential association-reinforcement theory of criminal behavior. *Social Problems, 4,* 128–147.

Cairns, R. B., Cairns, B. D., Neckerman, H. J., Gest, S. D., & Gariepy, J-L. (1988). Social networks and aggressive behavior: Peer support or peer rejection? *Developmental Psychology, 24,* 815–823.

Catalano, R. F., & Hawkins, J. D. (1985). Project Skills: Preliminary results from a theoretically based aftercare experiment. In R. S. Ashery (Ed.), *Progress in the development of cost-effective treatment for drug abusers.* Washington, DC: U.S. Government Printing Office.

Catalano, R. F., Morrison, D. M., Wells, E. A., Gillmore, M. R., Iritani, B., & Hawkins, J. D. (1992). Ethnic differences in family factors related to early drug initiation. *Journal of Studies on Alcohol, 53,* 208–217.

Chasnoff, I. J. (1991). *The perinatal influences of cocaine in the term newborn infant: A current look.* Report of the 100th Ross Conference on Pediatric Research. Columbus, OH: Ross Laboratories.

Chasnoff, I. J., Griffith, D. R., MacGregor, S., Dirkes, K., & Burns, K. A. (1989). Temporal patterns of cocaine use in pregnancy: Perinatal outcome. *Journal of the American Medical Association, 261,* 1741.

Cicchetti, D. (1990). A historical perspective on the discipline of developmental psychopathology. In J. Rolf, A. S. Masten, D. Cicchetti, K. H. Nuechterlein, & S. Weintraub (Eds.), *Risk and protective factors in the development of psychopathology* (pp. 2–28). Cambridge: Cambridge University Press.

Colvin, M., & Pauly, J. (1983). A critique of criminology: Toward an integrated structural-Marxist theory of delinquency production. *American Journal of Sociology, 89,* 513–551.

Conger, R. D. (1976). Social control and social learning models of delinquent behavior: A synthesis. *Criminology, 14,* 17–40.

Conger, R. D. (1980). Juvenile delinquency: Behavior restraint for behavior facilitation. In T. Hirschi and M. Gottfredson (Eds.), *Understanding crime* (pp. 131–142). Beverly Hills, CA: Sage.

Conger, R. D., Conger, K. J., Elder, G. H., Lorenz, F. O., Simons, R. L., & Whitbeck, L. B. (1991) *A family process model of economic hardship and adjustment of early adolescent boys.* Paper presented at Society for Research on Child Development, Seattle, April.

Cressey, D. R. (1953). *Other people's money.* New York: Free Press.

Cressey, D. R. (1979). Fifty years of criminology: From sociological theory to political control. *Pacific Sociological Review, 22,* 451–480.

Cusson, M., & Pinsonneault, P. (1986). The decision to give up crime. In D. B. Cornish & R. V. Clarke (Eds.), *The reasoning criminal: Rational choice perspectives on offending* (pp. 72–82). New York: Springer-Verlag.

Dembo, R., Farrow, D., Schmeidler, J., & Burgos, W. (1979). Testing a causal model of environmental influences on early drug involvement of inner city junior high school youths. *American Journal of Drug and Alcohol Abuse, 6,* 313–336.

Dishion, T. J., Patterson, G. R., Stoolmiller, M., & Skinner, M. L. (1991). Family, school, and behavioral antecedents to early adolescent involvement with antisocial peers. *Developmental Psychology, 27,* 172–180.

Doyle, W. (1986). Classroom organization and management. In M. E. Wittrock (Ed.), *Handbook of research on teaching* (3rd ed., pp. 392–431). New York: Macmillan.

Dryfoos, J. G. (1990). *Adolescents at risk: Prevalence and prevention.* New York: Oxford University Press.

Egeland, B., & Farber, E. A. (1984). Infant-mother attachment: Factors related to its development and changes over time. *Child Development, 55,* 753–771.

Elias, M. J., & Weissberg, R. P. (1990). School-based social competence promotion as a primary prevention strategy: A tale of two projects. In R. P. Lorion (Ed.), *Protecting the children: Strategies for optimizing emotional and behavioral development* (pp. 177–200). New York: Haworth.

Elliott, D. S. (in press). Health enhancing and health compromising lifestyles. In S. G. Milstein, A. C. Peterson, & E. O. Nightingale (Eds.), *Adolescent health promotion.* New York: Oxford University Press.

Elliott, D. S., & Huizinga, D. (1989). The relationship between delinquent behavior and ADM problems. In C. Hampton (Ed.), *Juvenile offenders with serious drug, alcohol and mental health problems.* Washington, DC: U.S. Government Printing Office.

Elliott, D. S., Huizinga, D., & Ageton, S. S. (1982). *Explaining delinquency and drug use.* The National Youth Survey Project (Report No. 21). Boulder, CO: Behavioral Research Institute.

Elliott, D. S., Huizinga, D., & Ageton, S. S. (1985). *Explaining delinquency and drug use.* Beverly Hills, CA: Sage.

Elliott, D. S., Huizinga, D., & Menard, S. (1989). *Multiple problem youth: Delinquency, substance use and mental health problems.* New York: Springer-Verlag.

Ensminger, M. E., Kellam, S., & Rubin, B. R. (1983). School and family origins of delinquency. In K. Van Dusen & S. Mednick (Eds.), *Prospective studies of crime and delinquency.* Boston: Kluwer-Nijohoff.

Farrington, D. P. (1978). The family backgrounds of aggressive youths. In L. Hersov, M. Berger, & D. Shaffer (Eds.), *Aggression and antisocial behavior in childhood and adolescence* (pp. 73–93). Oxford: Pergamon.

Farrington, D. P. (1979a). Environment stress, delinquent behavior, and convictions. In I. G. Sarason & C. D. Spielberger (Eds.), *Stress and anxiety* (Vol. 6, pp. 93–107). Washington, DC: Hemisphere.

Farrington, D. P. (1979b). Longitudinal research on crime and delinquency. In N. Morris & M. Tonry (Eds.), *Crime and justice* (Vol. 1, pp. 289–348). Chicago: University of Chicago Press.

Farrington, D. P. (1985). Stepping stones to adult criminal careers. In D. Olweus, J. Block, & M. Yarrow, (Eds.), *Development of antisocial and prosocial behavior* (pp. 359–384). New York: Academic Press.

Farrington, D. P., & Hawkins, J. D. (1991). Predicting participation, early onset, and later persistence in officially recorded offending. *Criminal Behavior and Mental Health, 1,* 1–33.

Felner, R. D., & Adan, A. M. (1988). The school transitional environment project: An ecological intervention and evaluation. In R. H. Price, E. L. Cowen, R. P. Lorion, & J. Ramos-McKay (Eds.), *14 ounces of prevention: A casebook for practitioners* (pp. 111–122). Washington, DC: American Psychological Association.

Felner, R. D., Weissberg, R. P., & Adan, A. M. (1987). *Long-term follow-up of a school transition program.* Unpublished manuscript.

Festinger, L. (1964). Behavioral support for opinion change. *Public Opinion Quarterly, 28,* 404–417.

Foshee, V., & Bauman, K. E. (1992). Parental and peer characteristics as modifiers of the bond-behavior relationship: An elaboration of control theory. *Journal of Health and Social Behavior, 33,* 66–76.

Fraser, N. W., Hawkins, J. D., & Howard, M. O. (1988). Measuring effects of a skills training intervention for drug abusers. *Journal of Consulting and Clinical Psychology, 54,* 661–664.

Garmezy, N. (1985). Stress resistant children: The search for protective factors.

In J. Stevenson (Ed.), *Recent research in developmental psychopathology* (pp. 213–233). Oxford: Pergamon (a book supplement to the *Journal of Child Psychology and Psychiatry, 4*).

Gillmore, M. R., Hawkins, J. D., Catalano, R. F., & Abbott, R. D. (1991). *The dimensions of bonding: A confirmatory factor analysis.* Unpublished manuscript, School of Social Work, Social Development Research Group, University of Washington, Seattle.

Gillmore, M. R., Hawkins, J. D., Day, L. E., & Catalano, R. F. (1992). Friendship and deviance: New evidence on an old controversy. *Journal of Early Adolescence, 12,* 80–95.

Giordano, P. C., Cernkovich, S. A., & Pugh, M. D. (1986). Friendships and delinquency. *American Journal of Sociology, 91,* 1170–1202.

Gottfredson, M. R., & Hirschi, T. (1990). *A general theory of crime.* Stanford, CA: Stanford University Press.

Grant, W. T., Consortium on the School-Based Promotion of Social Competence. (1992). Drug and alcohol prevention curricula. In J. D. Hawkins, R. F. Catalano, & Associates, *Communities That Care: Action for drug abuse prevention.* San Francisco: Jossey-Bass.

Grasmick, H. G., & Bursik, R. J. (1990). Conscience, significant others, and rational choice: Extending the deterrence model. *Law and Society Review, 24,* 837–861.

Hansen, W. B., Johnson, C. A., Flay, B. R., Graham, J. W., & Sobel, J. (1988). Affective and social influences approaches to the prevention of multiple substance abuse among seventh-grade students: Results from Project SMART. *Preventative Medicine, 17,* 135–154.

Hawkins, J. D., Catalano, R. F., & Associates. (1992a). *Communities That Care: Action for drug abuse prevention.* San Francisco: Jossey-Bass.

Hawkins, J. D., Catalano, R. F., Brown, E. O., Vadasy, P. F., Roberts, C., Fitzmahan, D., Starkman, N., & Ransdell, M. (1988). *Preparing for the Drug (Free) Years: A family activity book.* Seattle, WA: Comprehensive Health Education Foundation.

Hawkins, J. D., Catalano, R. F., Gillmore, M. R., & Wells, E. A. (1989). Skills training for drug abusers: Generalization, maintenance and effects on drug use. *Journal of Consulting and Clinical Psychology, 57,* 559–563.

Hawkins, J. D., Catalano, R. F., & Kent, L. A. (1991). Combining broadcast media and parent education to prevent teenage drug abuse. In L. Donohew, H. E. Sypher, & W. J. Bukoski (Eds.), *Persuasive communication and drug abuse prevention.* Hillsdale, NJ: Erlbaum.

Hawkins, J. D., Catalano, R. F., & Miller, J. Y. (1992b). Risk and protective factors for alcohol and other drug problems in adolescence and early adulthood: Implications for substance abuse prevention. *Psychological Bulletin, 112,* 64–105.

Hawkins, J. D., Catalano, R. F., Morrison, D. M., O'Donnell, J., Abbott, R. D., &

Day, L. E. (1992c). The Seattle Social Development Project: Effects of the first four years on protective factors and problem behaviors. In J. McCord & R. Tremblay (Eds.), *The prevention of antisocial behavior in children* (pp. 139–161). New York: Guilford.

Hawkins, J. D., Catalano, R. F., & Wells, E. A. (1986). Measuring effects of a skills training intervention for drug abusers. *Journal of Consulting and Clinical Psychology, 54,* 661–664.

Hawkins, J. D., & Lam, T. (1987). Teacher practices, social development and delinquency. In J. D. Burchard & S. N. Burchard (Eds.), *The prevention of delinquent behavior.* Newbury Park, CA: Sage.

Hawkins, J. D., Von Cleve, E., & Catalano, R. F. (1991). Reducing early childhood aggression: Results of a primary prevention. *Journal of the American Academy of Child and Adolescent Psychiatry, 30,* 208–217.

Hepburn, J. R. (1976). Listing alternative models of delinquency causation. *Journal of Criminal Law and Criminology, 67,* 4–17.

Hill, G. D., & Atkinson, M. P. (1988). Gender, familial control, and delinquency. *Criminology, 26,* 127–149.

Hindelang, M. J. (1973). Causes of delinquency: A partial replication and extension. *Social Problems, 20,* 471–487.

Hirschi, T. (1969). *Causes of delinquency.* Berkeley, CA: University of California Press.

Hirschi, T., & Gottfredson, M. (1988). Toward a general theory of crime. In W. Buikhuisen & S. A. Mednick (Eds.), *Explaining criminal behavior* (pp. 8–26). Leiden: E. J. Brill.

Howard, J., Beckwith, L., Rodning, C., & Kropenske, V. (1989). The development of young children of substance-abusing parents: Insights from seven years of intervention and research. *Zero to Three, 9*(5), 8–12.

Hundleby, J. D. (1986). Drug usage and outstanding performance among young adolescents. *Addictive Behaviors, 10,* 419–423.

Johnson, D. L. (1988). Primary prevention of behavior problems in young children: The Houston Parent-Child Development Center. In R. H. Price, E. L. Cowen, R. P. Lorion, & J. Ramos-McKay (Eds.), *14 ounces of prevention* (pp. 44–52). Washington, DC: American Psychological Association.

Johnston, L. D., O'Malley, P. M., & Bachman, J. G. (1991). *Drug use among American high school seniors, college students, and young adults, 1975–1990: Vol. 1. High school seniors.* Washington, DC: National Institute on Drug Abuse.

Jones, B. (1988). Toward redefining models of curriculum and instruction for students at risk. In B. Presseisen (Ed.), *At-risk students and thinking: Perspectives from research* (pp. 76–103). Washington, DC: National Education Association/Research for Better Schools.

Kandel, D. B. (1982). Epidemiological and psychosocial perspectives on adolescent drug use. *Journal of American Academic Clinical Psychiatry, 21,* 328–347.

Kandel, D. B., Simcha-Fagan, O. & Davies, M. (1986). Risk factors for delinquency and illicit drug use from adolescence to young adulthood. *Journal of Drug Issues, 60,* 67–90.

Kaplan, H. B., Martin, S. S., Johnson, R. J., & Robbins, C. A. (1986, March). Escalation of marijuana use: Application of a general theory of deviant behavior. *Journal of Health and Social Behavior, 27,* 44–61.

Kellam, S. G., Ensminger, M. E., & Simon, M. B. (1980). Mental health in first grade and teenage drug, alcohol, and cigarette use. *Drug and Alcohol Dependence, 5,* 273–304.

Kempf, K. (1993). The empirical status of Hirschi's control theory. In F. Adler & W. S. Laufer (Eds.), *New directions in criminological theory: Vol. 4. Advances in criminological theory* (pp. 143–185). New Brunswick: Transaction.

Kohlberg, L. (1969). Stage and sequence: The cognitive-developmental approach. In D. A. Goslin (Ed.), *Handbook of socialization theory and research* (pp. 347–480). Chicago: Rand McNally.

Kohlberg, L. (1976). Moral stages and moralization: The cognitive-developmental approach. In T. Likona (Ed.), *Moral development and behavior: Theory, research, and social issues* (pp. 31–53). New York: Holt.

Kornhauser, R. R. (1978). *Social sources of delinquency: An appraisal of analytic models.* Chicago: University of Chicago Press.

Krohn, M. D., Lanza-Kaduce, L., Radosevich, M. & Akers, R. L. (1980). *Cessation of alcohol and drug use among adolescents: A social learning model.* Paper presented at the annual meeting of the Society of Social Problems, New York.

Krohn, M. D., & Massey, J. L. (1980). Social control and delinquent behavior: An examination of the elements of the social bond. *Sociological Quarterly, 21,* 529–544.

Larzelere, R. E., & Patterson, G. R. (1990). Parental management: Mediator of the effect of socioeconomic status on early delinquency. *Criminology, 28,* 301–324.

Loeber, R. (1991). Antisocial behavior: More enduring than changeable? *Journal of the American Academy of Child and Adolescent Psychiatry, 30,* 393–397.

Loeber, R., & Dishion, T. (1983). Early predictors of male delinquency: A review. *Psychological Bulletin, 93,* 68–99.

Loeber, R., & Le Blanc, M. (1990). Toward a developmental criminology. In M. Tonry & N. Morris (Eds.), *Crime and justice: An annual review* (pp. 373–473). Chicago: University of Chicago Press.

Loeber, R., Stouthamer-Loeber, M. S., Von Kammen, W., & Farrington, D. P. (1991). Initiation, escalation, and desistance in juvenile offending and their correlates. *Journal of Criminal Law and Criminology, 82,* 36–82.

Marcos, A. C., Bahr, S. J., & Johnson, R. E. (1986). Test of a bonding/ association theory of adolescent drug use. *Social Forces, 65,* 135–161.

Matsueda, R. L. (1982). Testing control theory and differential association: A causal modeling approach. *American Sociological Review, 47,* 489–504.

Matsueda, R. L. (1988). The current state of differential association theory. *Crime & Delinquency, 34,* 277–306.

Matza, D. (1964). *Delinquency and drift.* New York: Wiley.

Matza, D. (1969). *Becoming deviant.* Englewood Cliffs, NJ: Prentice-Hall.

McCord, J. (1979). Some child-rearing antecedents of criminal behavior in adult men. *Journal of Personality and Social Psychology, 37,* 1477–1486.

Menard, S., & Huizinga, D. (1990). The temporal priority of belief and delinquent behavior in adolescence. Unpublished manuscript, Institute of Behavioral Science, University of Colorado–Boulder.

Merton, R. K. (1957). *Social theory and social structure.* New York: Free Press.

Messner, S. F., Krohn, M. D., & Liska, A. E. (1989). *Theoretical integration in the study of deviance and crime: Problems and prospects.* Albany: State University of New York Press.

Moffit, T. E. (1983). The learning theory model of punishment: Implications for delinquency deterrence. *Criminal Justice and Behavior, 10,* 131–158.

Morisset, C. E., Barnard, K. E., Greenberg, M. T., Booth, C. L., & Spieker, S. J. (1990). Environmental influences on early language development: The context of social risk. *Development and Psychopathology, 2,* 127–149.

Munsch, J., & Blyth, D. A. (1993). An analysis of the functional nature of adolescents' supportive relationships. *Journal of Early Adolescence, 13,* 132–153.

Newcomb, M. D., & Bentler, P. M. (1988). Impact of adolescent drug use and social support on problems of young adults: A longitudinal study. *Journal of Abnormal Psychology, 97,* 64–75.

Nye, F. I. (1958). *Family relationships and delinquent behavior.* New York: Wiley.

Pentz, M. A., Dwyer, J. H., MacKinnon, D. P., Flay, B. R., Hansen, W. B., Wang, E. Y. I., & Johnson, C. A. (1989a). A multicommunity trial for primary prevention of adolescent drug abuse. *Journal of the American Medical Association, 261,* 3259–3266.

Pentz, M. A., MacKinnon, D. P., Flay, B. R., Hansen, W. B., Johnson, C. A., & Dwyer, J. H. (1989b). Primary prevention of chronic diseases in adolescence: Effects of the Midwestern Prevention Project on tobacco use. *American Journal of Epidemiology, 130,* 713–724.

Perry, C. L. (1986). Community-wide health promotion and drug abuse prevention. *Journal of School Health, 56,* 359–363.

Piaget, J. (1965). *The moral judgment of the child.* New York: Free Press.

Polk, K., Adler, C., Bazemore, G., Blake, G., Cordray, S., Coventry, G., Galvin, J., & Temple, M. (1981). *Becoming adult.* Final report to the National Institute of Mental Health.

Presseisen, B. Z. (1988). Teaching thinking and at-risk students: Defining a population. In B. Z. Presseisen (Ed.), *At-risk students and thinking: Perspectives from research* (pp. 19–37). Washington, DC: National Educational Association/Research for Better Schools.

Radke-Yarrow, M., & Sherman, T. (1990). Children born at medical risk: Factors affecting vulnerability and resilience. In J. Rolf, A. S. Masten, D. Cicchetti, K. H. Nuechterlein, & S. Weintraub (Eds.), *Risk and protective factors in the development of psychopathology.* Cambridge: Cambridge University Press.

Ramey, C. T., Bryant, D. M., Campbell, F. A., Sparling, J. J., & Wasik, B. H. (1988). Early intervention for high-risk children: The Carolina Early Intervention Program. In R. H. Price, E. L. Cowen, R. P. Lorion, & J. Ramos-McKay (Eds.), *14 ounces of prevention* (pp. 32–43). Washington, DC: American Psychological Association.

Reiss, A. J. (1951). Delinquency as the failure of personal and social controls. *American Sociological Review, 16,* 196–207.

Robins, L. N. (1979). Longitudinal methods in the study of normal and pathological development. In K. P. Kisker, J. E. Meyer, C. Muller, E. Stromgren (Eds.), *Psychiatrie der Gegenwart: Vol. 1. Grundlagen und Methoden der Psychiatrie* (2nd ed., pp. 627–684). Heidelberg, Springer-Verlag.

Robins, L. N., & Przybeck, T. R. (1985). *Age of onset of drug use as a factor in drug use and other disorders* (NIDA Research Monograph No. 56, U.S. Department of Health and Human Services Publication No. 1415). Washington, DC: U.S. Government Printing Office.

Rutter, M. (1985). Resilience in the face of adversity: Protective factors and resistance to psychiatric disturbance. *British Journal of Psychiatry, 147,* 598–611.

Rutter, M. (1987). Temperament, personality, and personality disorder. *British Journal of Psychiatry, 150,* 443–458.

Rutter, M. (1990). Psychosocial resilience and protective mechanisms. In J. Rolf, A. S. Masten, D. Cicchetti, K. H. Nuechterlein, & S. Weintraub (Eds.), *Risk and protective factors in the development of psychopathology.* Cambridge: Cambridge University Press.

Sameroff, A. J. (1990). *Prevention of developmental psychopathology using the transactional model: Perspectives on host, risk agent, and environment interactions.* Paper presented at the Conference on the Present Status and Future Needs of Research on Prevention of Mental Disorders, Washington, DC.

Sameroff, A. J., & Seifer, R. (1990). Early contributors to developmental risk. In J. Rolf, A. S. Masten, D. Cicchetti, K. H. Nuechterlein, & S. Weintraub (Eds.), *Risk and protective factors in the development of psychopathology* (pp. 52–66). New York: Cambridge University Press.

Shaw, D. S., & Bell, R. Q. (1992, May). *Developmental theories of parental contributors to antisocial behavior.* Unpublished manuscript, Department of Psychology, Clinical Psychology Center, University of Pittsburgh, Pittsburgh, PA.

Shedler, J., & Block, J. (1990). Adolescent drug use and psychological health: A longitudinal inquiry. *American Psychologist, 45,* 612–630.

Simcha-Fagan, O., Gersten, J. C., & Langner, T. S. (1986). Early precursors and concurrent correlates of patterns of illicit drug use in adolescents. *Journal of Drug Issues, 16,* 7–28.

Singer, S. I., & Levine, M. (1988). Power-control theory, gender, and delinquency: A partial replication with additional evidence on the effects of peers. *Criminology, 26,* 627–647.

Slavin, R. E. (1990). *Cooperative learning theory, research, and practice.* Englewood Cliffs, NJ: Prentice-Hall.

Smelser, N. J. (1962). *Theory of collective behavior.* New York: Free Press.

Smith, D. A., & Gartin, P. R. (1989). Specifying specific deterrence: The influence of arrest on future criminal activity. *American Sociological Review, 54,* 94–105.

Sutherland, E. H. (1973). Development of the theory [Private paper published posthumously]. In K. Schuessler (Ed.), *Edwin Sutherland on analyzing crime.* Chicago: University of Chicago Press.

Tallman, I., & Ihinga-Tallman, M. (1979). Values, distributive justice and social change. *American Sociological Review, 44,* 216–235.

Thornberry, T. P. (1987). Toward an interactional theory of delinquency. *Criminology, 25,* 863–891.

Tittle, C. R., & Meier, R. F. (1990). Specifying the SES/delinquency relationship. *Criminology, 28,* 271–299.

Walberg, H. J. (1986). Synthesis of research on teaching. In M. C. Wittrock (Ed.), *Handbook of research on teaching* (3rd ed., pp. 214–229). New York: Macmillan.

Werner, E. E. (1989). High risk children in young adulthood. *American Journal of Orthopsychiatry, 59,* 72–81.

Werner, E. E., & Smith, R. S. (1992). *Overcoming the odds: High risk children from birth to adulthood.* Ithaca, NY: Cornell University Press.

West, D. J., & Farrington, D. P. (1973). *Who becomes delinquent?* London: Heinemann.

Wolfgang, M. E., Figlio, R. M., & Sellin, T. (1972). *Delinquency in a birth cohort.* Chicago: University of Chicago Press.

Wolfgang, M. E., Thornberry, T. P., & Figlio, R. M. (1987). *From boy to man – from delinquency to crime: Follow-up to the Philadelphia birth cohort of 1945.* Chicago: University of Chicago Press.

CHAPTER FIVE

Empirical Support for Interactional Theory:

A REVIEW OF THE LITERATURE

TERENCE P. THORNBERRY

ABSTRACT: Interactional theory proposes that delinquent behavior develops in a dynamic fashion over the life course. Rather than seeing delinquency as a simple consequence of a set of social processes, an interactional perspective sees delinquency as both cause and consequence, involved in a variety of reciprocal relationships over time. This chapter summarizes this theoretical perspective and reviews empirical studies related to its major propositions.

Introduction

In the past 20 years criminological research has increasingly relied on longitudinal designs to better understand the dynamics of delinquent and criminal careers. Early longitudinal studies (e.g., Wolfgang, Figlio, & Sellin, 1972; Shannon, 1988; Blumstein, Cohen, Roth, & Visher, 1986) were primarily descriptive, tracing the development of delinquency over the life course. They suggest that while the prevalence of delinquency is rather high, only a small proportion of the population have extensive or chronic criminal careers. In the Philadelphia cohort of 1945, for example, 50% of the males had a delinquent or criminal career, but only 14% were chronic offenders by age 30 (Wolfgang, Thornberry, & Figlio, 1987). These studies, which relied primarily on official data, also found that persistent offenders are quite versatile, committing a wide range of offenses during their careers.

While these early studies provide rich descriptions of delinquent careers, they do not provide equally rich explanatory models of delinquency,

I would like to thank Marvin D. Krohn and Carolyn Smith for helpful comments on earlier drafts of this chapter. Prepared under grant no. 86-NJ-CX-0007 (S-3) from the Office of Juvenile Justice and Delinquency Prevention, Office of Justice Programs, U.S. Department of Justice. Points of view or opinions in this document are those of the author and do not necessarily represent the official position or policies of the funding agency.

in large part because of their reliance on official data. Recent studies based on panel models (e.g., Elliott, Huizinga, & Ageton, 1985a; Farrington & West, 1981) have moved research in this area to a more analytic level. Collecting interview data on the same subjects over time has allowed them to address important questions about the causes and correlates of delinquency and to assess proper temporal and causal sequences among variables. Their findings indicate that the explanation of delinquency is more complex than results of earlier cross-sectional research suggest. For example, it appears that factors associated with initiation are not necessarily the same as those associated with maintenance or with termination of careers.

Although criminological research has become increasingly dynamic over the past 20 years, criminological theories by and large have not; they tend to retain the recursive and static perspective that has always characterized theoretical criminology. Only very recently have more dynamic models been proposed. These models (e.g., Patterson, 1982; Hawkins & Weis, 1985; Catalano & Hawkins, 1986; Loeber & Le Blanc, 1990; Thornberry, 1987) suggest that developmental change and reciprocal causal relationships ought to be an important part of any effort to understand the causes of delinquent and criminal behavior.

This chapter further explores one of those theoretical perspectives – interactional theory – originally proposed by Thornberry (1987). The chapter begins with an overview of the basic claims of interactional theory and then assesses the support that this theory receives from longitudinal research.

Interactional Theory

Interactional theory attempts to provide a more dynamic explanation of delinquency than is found in social control theory (Hirschi, 1969), social learning theory (Akers, 1977), or integrated theory (Elliott, Ageton, & Canter, 1979; Elliott et al., 1985a). Interactional theory is more dynamic in two respects: (1) it explicitly recognizes the importance of developmental change in accounting for delinquency, and (2) it views human behavior, including delinquent behavior, as a result of interactive and reciprocal causal influences that develop over time.[1]

---

[1] In addition, interactional theory also focuses attention on the role of structural variables in the genesis of delinquency (Thornberry, 1987, pp. 884–885). Since that aspect of the model is not directly related to the topic of this chapter, it is not examined further here.

Developmental Perspective

The importance of development change can be seen in an examination of the age distribution of delinquent and criminal careers.[2] Crime does not appear to be a permanent trait of the individual. While criminal behavior demonstrates considerable stability during the adolescent years, it is, in the general life course, rather specific to the adolescent and very early adult ages. Most offenders initiate delinquent conduct around ages 12 or 13, rapidly increase their involvement to a peak around ages 16 or 17, and then terminate this behavior by the mid-20s (Wolfgang et al., 1987, pp. 37–44). Viewed in the 70-plus years of life expectancy, criminal careers occupy a rather small age span and even within that there appear to be three rather clearly delimited phases: initiation, maintenance, and termination. This general description of criminal careers derived from the Philadelphia data is robust and has been observed in a number of other studies (see Blumstein et al., 1986).

Given this general shape of the dependent variable, a complete theory of delinquency needs to respond to a number of somewhat different causal questions. For example, why do some people initiate delinquent conduct while others do not? Of those who do, why do some offenders maintain delinquent behavior over long periods of time while others do not? Why do some offenders terminate their involvement relatively early while others persist well into the adult years?

In responding to these questions, it is important to allow for the possibility that different causal factors may be at play at the different phases of delinquent careers. For example, the social and psychological variables that influence initiation may differ substantially from those that influence maintenance, precisely because the offender population has already been selected from the general population. Also, even within phases of delinquent careers, especially the maintenance phase, causal influences may differ substantially because of the age or developmental stage of the person. For example, among persistent offenders, the impact of family variables in maintaining behavior may be much greater for 14-year-olds than for 20-year-olds, while the impact of unemployment may be much greater for 20-year-olds than for 14-year-olds.

In general, it would seem that a theory that relies entirely on a single set of causal factors (see, e.g., Hirschi, 1969) may not be able to account for the diversity of behavior encompassed within the realm of delinquency and

---

[2] Throughout this chapter the terms *delinquency* and *crime* are used interchangeably unless the specific context requires their separation.

crime. First, there are rather distinct phases of delinquent careers, each of which poses somewhat different etiological questions. Second, some delinquent careers, especially those of chronic offenders, extend over long periods of time and different developmental stages, suggesting the importance of varying causal influences. Interactional theory begins to account for this by presenting different causal models for three general developmental stages – early, middle, and late adolescence. Rather than presenting a single model that presumably applies to offenders of all ages, an explicit attempt is made to account for the changing saliencies of causal variables as the subject passes through different developmental stages. A similar approach is found in the social development model of Hawkins and his colleagues (Hawkins & Weis, 1985; Catalano & Hawkins, 1986).

The recognition of developmental change in these theories is more than a theoretical nicety; it has both empirical and practical importance. For example, assume that the specification offered by interactional theory – that the causal influence of family factors decreases as adolescents age, while the influence of peer factors increases – is correct.[3] Then the empirical finding that parental attachment is relatively unimportant in explaining delinquency once association with delinquent peers is added to the causal model (Johnson, 1979; Elliott et al., 1985a) is equivocal. It may be, as those authors interpret their results (Johnson, 1979, p. 40; Elliott et al., 1985a, p. 118), that parental influences are, in general, relatively weak causes of delinquency, or it may be that the empirical data are drawn from too late a developmental phase to reflect accurately the causal impact of the family. These varying interpretations are important for drawing correct policy implications. In one case family interventions would be highlighted, especially at earlier ages, while in the other case they would be deemphasized. The decision to emphasize or deemphasize family intervention is a crucial one in generating successful efforts to reduce delinquency, and it should be informed by accurate theoretical and empirical evidence.

Reciprocal Effects

The second sense in which interactional theory is more dynamic concerns the causal structure of the theory. Contemporary theories of delinquency are overwhelmingly recursive or unidirectional, treating delinquency as an outcome variable produced by a variety of social and psychological forces. Reasonable representations of these recursive models can be seen in Fig-

---

[3] The theoretical rationale for this specification is presented in Thornberry (1987, pp. 877–879).

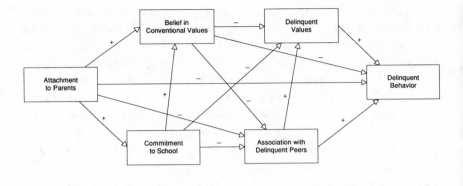

Source: Figure 1, Thornberry 1987: 868.

Figure 5.1. A typical recursive causal model of delinquency.

ures 4.1 and 6.1 of Elliott et al. (1985a) and Figure 1 of Thornberry (1987); the latter is reproduced here as Figure 5.1. In those models, there is little or no consideration of mutual causal influences among the explanatory variables (e.g., between parental attachment and commitment to school) or among delinquency and its presumed causes (e.g., between delinquent behavior and associations with delinquent peers). All concepts are arrayed in the lock-step of recursive systems with delinquent behavior the end result. Presumably, no matter how prolonged or serious the person's delinquent behavior, it has no causal impact on relationships within the family, selection of peers, success in school or work, and so forth. As implausible as

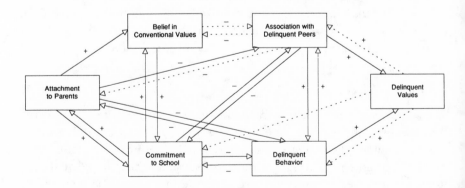

[a]Solid lines represent stronger effects; dashed lines represent weaker effects.

Source: Figure 2, Thornberry 1987: 871.

Figure 5.2. A reciprocal model of delinquent involvement at early adolescence.

this view of the development of human behavior over the life course may be, it is precisely the view represented in most theoretical examinations of delinquency and crime.

Because of the implausibility of this approach, interactional theory systematically considers the possibility of reciprocal causality among the major explanatory factors associated with delinquency. The theoretical model for early adolescence, originally presented in Thornberry (1987, p. 871), is reproduced here to summarize the basic claims of the theory (see Figure 5.2).

The fundamental cause of delinquency is the weakening of bonds to conventional society. Adolescents who are closely attached to their parents, who believe strongly in conventional values, and who are highly committed to school and other conventional activities are unlikely candidates for serious involvement in delinquency. Indeed, they are likely to be enmeshed in conventional social networks (Krohn, 1986) that further reduce the chances of delinquency. On the other hand, if conventional bonding is weak or absent, social controls over behavior are attenuated and the chances of delinquency escalate considerably. For the behavioral freedom caused by weakened bonds to lead to stable patterns of delinquency, however, a social environment in which delinquency is learned and reinforced is required. In this model such a setting is represented by associations with delinquent peers and delinquent values.

In interactional theory the causal relationships among these concepts are dynamic rather than static. A variety of reciprocal or bidirectional effects are hypothesized, precisely because behavior develops as people interact with others over time and as the consequences of their own past behavior impinge upon their future behavior. For example, belief in conventional values and commitment to school are thought to be reciprocally related, as are delinquent values and delinquent behavior (see Figure 5.2). The underlying explanation for both causal loops centers on the consistency of attitudes and behavior expected to develop over time, in one case in the conventional realm and in the other case in the deviant realm. Also, some reciprocal relationships between the bonding and learning variables are expected. For example, while attachment to parents reduces delinquent behavior, prolonged involvement in delinquency is apt to weaken attachment to parents.

The complete specification of this model, as well as the ones for middle and late adolescence, can be found in Thornberry (1987) and need not be repeated here. For purposes of the present essay the central point does not concern the detailed specification of interactional theory, but its basic claim that human behavior, including delinquent behavior, develops in a dynamic, interactive process over time. Causal models, therefore, have to represent those more complex reciprocal relationships. Hawkins and Catalano's social development model adopts a similar stance, especially across developmental phases (this volume). For example, Farrington and Hawkins hypothesize that "the level of antisocial behaviour in one developmental phase influences the social development process in subsequent phases" (1991, p. 7).

Again, the recognition of this issue is more than a theoretical nicety; it, too, has empirical and practical importance. Empirically, the insistence that delinquent behavior is an outcome of a recursive causal process runs the risk of misspecifying the model and substantially biasing the results. The observed covariance between delinquent behavior and other variables, say delinquent beliefs, can be produced by one of three underlying causal models:[4] either beliefs cause behavior, behavior causes beliefs, or they mutually cause one another over time. If either one of the last two models is in fact correct, it is likely that the typically imposed causal direction, from beliefs to behavior, would falsely receive empirical support because, under all three scenarios, these two concepts covary. Thus, an accurate interpretation requires an explicit consideration of these three competing models and, when bidirectional effects are plausible, an explicit empirical test of the direction of the relationship. If that is not done, it is likely that the causes and effects of delinquency will continue to be confused. Moreover, a misrepresentation for any one relationship distorts empirical estimates of indirect effects operating through it and, therefore, has ripple effects throughout the causal system.

The impact of this misspecification on forming correct policies can be quite severe. The misleading empirical results would focus prevention and treatment efforts on the *effects* of delinquency rather than its *causes*. For example, a variety of programs designed to prevent delinquency and drug use assume that attitudes of acceptance or toleration cause the behavior. This assumption is based in part on the empirically supported correlation between these variables and the typical causal interpretation that attitudes cause behavior. Thus, the reasoning goes, if attitudes can be changed (e.g., "just say no to drugs"), the behavior will follow suit. If, however, the causal direction between these variables is reversed, such that behavior drives the attitudes, then these programs would be quite ineffective since the other, real causes of drug use would continue to produce the behavior. The program may or may not alter the person's attitudinal set but that would

---

[4] It can also be produced by other effects, e.g., a spurious relationship or a common latent construct. Because this discussion assumes some causal relationship, these other types of effects are not discussed.

have no real impact on the objective of the program – reducing drug use – because the attitudes have no causal impact on use.

Summary

Criminology's almost total reliance on static models of delinquency has important theoretical, empirical, and policy implications. If a complete understanding of delinquent behavior requires the inclusion of developmental perspectives and reciprocal causal influences, then static models are seriously misspecified. Moreover, to the extent that they are misspecified they generate empirical results and policy implications that are misleading. Because of these possible consequences it is important to examine in detail the appropriateness of dynamic explanations of delinquency and crime.

Interactional theory offers a theoretical model incorporating both developmental and reciprocal effects. It is a more complex and somewhat less parsimonious explanation than is found in recursive models (cf. Johnson, 1979; Elliott et al., 1985a). Thus, it is important to evaluate the necessity of this theoretical complexity and the added burden it places on empirical tests. The present chapter does so by reviewing the results of empirical studies that examine these dynamic issues. It focuses particularly on reciprocal causal influences and only secondarily on developmental change, in large part because there are still very few criminological studies that trace subjects over major stages of the life course. Thus, the central question of this analysis is the following: Is there substantial empirical support for interactional theory's central contention that delinquent behavior is embedded in a set of mutually reinforcing causal relationships?

Available Literature

There are few studies that provide empirical evidence bearing on this issue since the empirical requirements for accurately testing reciprocal models are stringent. First, panel data that follow the same subjects across time using repeated measures are needed.[5] Second, statistical routines to estimate reciprocal effects are complex and cumbersome. Moreover, they have only recently been introduced into the criminological research.

Despite these limitations, 17 studies that examine bidirectional causal relationships concerning delinquency were identified at the time this paper was prepared. The studies, along with some of their basic design characteristics, are listed in Table 5.1. Only studies that employ structural equa-

---

[5] Instrumental variables can also be used to identify these models, but that option has not been used frequently in this research area.

Table 5.1. *Studies examining reciprocal causal effects involving delinquent behavior*

Author	Data set	Age/grade	Sex	Waves/lag	Delinquency variable	Other variables
Agnew (1985)	Youth in Transition	10th to 11th grades	Males	2/18 months	Total delinquency Serious delinquency	Parental attachment Grades Dating index School attachment Involvement Commitment Peer attachment Belief
Agnew (1989)	Youth in Transition	10th to 11th grades	Males	2/18 months	Agression Theft/vandalism Escape from school	Negative school attitudes Mean teachers Parental punitiveness
Agnew (1991)	National Youth Survey	Ages 11–17 to 12–18	Males/ females	2/12 months	Minor delinquency General delinquency Serious delinquency	Parental attachment School attachment Commitment Deviant beliefs Delinquent peers
Burkett & Warren (1987)	Pacific northwest city	10th to 12 grades	Males/ females	3/12 months	Marijuana use	Religious commitment Belief/sin Peer associations

Elliott, Huizinga, & Morse (1985b)	National Youth Survey	Ages 11–17 to 15–21	Males/ females	5/12 months	General delinquency	Normlessness Prosocial roles Involvement Strain Delinquent peers Deviant bonding Family sanctions
Elliott & Menard (1992)	National Youth Survey	Ages 11–17 to 18–24	Males/ females	1–5/12 months 6/36 months	General delinquency Minor delinquency Index delinquency	Delinquent peers
Ginsberg & Greenley (1978)	University of Wisconsin students	Freshman/ sophomore to junior/ senior	Males/ females	2/26 months	Marijuana use	Commitment Involvement Psychological stress Peer use
Kandel (1978)	New York State	9th to 12 grades	Males/ females	2/8 months	Marijuana use	Peer associations
Liska & Reed (1985)	Youth in Transition	10th to 11th grades	Males	2/18 months	Interpersonal violence Theft/vandalism	Attachment to parents School attachment

(*Continued*)

Table 5.1. (*Continued*)

Author	Data set	Age/grade	Sex	Waves/lag	Delinquency variable	Other variables
Matsueda (1989)	Youth in Transition	10th to 13th grades	Males	1–2/18 months 2–4/12 months	Minor deviance	Belief in conventional morality
Meier, Burkett & Hickman (1984)	Pacific Northwest city	10th to 12th grades	Males/ females	3/12 months	Marijuana use	Peer associations Perceived certainty of punishment
Menard & Huizinga (1990)	National Youth Survey	Ages 11–17 to 18–24	Males/ females	1–5/12 months 6/36 months	General delinquency Minor delinquency Index delinquency	Delinquent beliefs
Minor (1984)	College students	Median ages 18 to 18.3	Males/ females	2/3 months	Marijuana use Cocaine use Fighting Drunk & disorderly Shoplifting Variety index	Moral evaluations Excuse acceptance

Paternoster (1988)	Southeastern city	10th to 12th grades	Males/ females	3/12 months	Marijuana use Petty theft	Parental supervision Perceived certainty Deviant beliefs Peer attitudes Peer behavior
Reed & Rose (1991)	National Youth Survey	Ages 11–17 to 13–19	Males/ females	3/12 months	Serious delinquency	Delinquent peers Delinquent attitudes
Rosenberg, Schooler, & Schoenbach (1989)	Youth in Transition	10th to 11th grades	Males	2/18 months	General delinquency	Self-esteem
Thornberry & Christenson (1984)	Philadelphia birth cohort	Ages 21 to 24	Males	4/12 months	Official arrests	Unemployment

tion modeling or some other formal assessment of reciprocal effects are included. Studies that report only cross-lagged correlations (see Thornberry, 1987, p. 877 for a discussion) are not included because the correlations among these variables are not at stake; the direction of the causal effect given the correlation is at stake.

The paucity of panel designs in criminology can be seen clearly in Table 5.1. Of the 17 empirical investigations, five rely on the Youth in Transition study (Bachman, O'Malley, & Johnston, 1978), five use the National Youth Survey (Elliott et al., 1985a), two use data from a study conducted at Washington State University (Meier, Burkett, & Hickman, 1984), and five use other data sets. Also, some of the studies that use the same data set include the same or very similar measures in the analyses. Thus, these studies do not represent "independent observations."[6]

A few methodological notes should be mentioned. First, the review of the findings to be presented is limited to an examination of reciprocal causal influences between delinquent behavior and its presumed causes. While reciprocal effects among the presumed causes (e.g., between attachment to parents and commitment to school) are included in interactional theory and in many of these empirical studies (e.g., Agnew, 1991; Paternoster, 1988), they are not considered here. They are excluded because a full discussion of them would cloud an already complex picture, and the more central point of interactional theory concerns the dynamic relationships in which delinquent behavior is embedded.[7] Second, for the same reasons, stability effects for these variables are not discussed in this chapter. Almost universally the stability effects reported are positive and significant, as expected. Third, while some of these studies estimate the models for major demographic subgroups they are not, with one exception, reviewed here. They will be the subject of a separate analysis that attempts to link the effects of these social processes to the person's structural position.

As can be seen from the last column in Table 5.1 these 17 studies cover a relatively wide array of causal variables. While some of them focus on only one explanatory variable (e.g., Matsueda's [1989] investigation of belief in conventional morality or Elliott and Menard's [this volume] investigation of delinquent peers), others focus on the impact of a number of bonding

---

[6] I would like to thank Delbert Elliott, David Huizinga, Scott Menard, and Mark Reed for making forthcoming manuscripts available for this review.

[7] The complete results, including the impact of indirect effects, can be seen in the original articles, such as those by Agnew (1991), Paternoster (1988), and Elliott, Huizinga, and Morse (1985b).

and learning variables (e.g., the studies by Agnew [1991] and Paternoster [1988]). Also some of the studies only examine social bonding variables, others examine only social learning variables, while still others examine both. In this review the studies will be discussed in three broad clusters: those concerned with bonding variables, those concerned with learning variables, and the more comprehensive studies that include both sets. This organizational schema is employed since it is reasonably consistent with the model specification for interactional theory presented by Thornberry (1987).

Bonding Variables

In interactional theory the basic cause of delinquent activity is the weakening of bonds to conventional society. The bond to conventional society is represented by three broad constructs: attachment to parents, commitment to school, and belief in conventional values (see Thornberry, 1987, pp. 866–867 for definitions). Individuals who are tightly bonded to society are unlikely candidates for delinquency while individuals who are only weakly bonded are far more likely to be delinquent. On the other hand, involvement in delinquency, especially over prolonged periods of time, is apt to feed back and further attenuate the person's link to conventional society.

Seven of the studies listed in Table 5.1 focus attention on these or related variables: Agnew (1985), Agnew (1989), Liska and Reed (1985), Matsueda (1989), Minor (1984), Rosenberg, Schooler, and Schoenbach (1989), and Thornberry and Christenson (1984). The studies by Agnew (1989) and Rosenberg et al. (1989) do not include variables that are explicitly incorporated in interactional theory since they deal with perceptions of environmental adversity and self-esteem, respectively. In light of the paucity of panel studies of delinquency, however, they are included in this review, and these variables appear closer to this general cluster than the others.

Liska and Reed (1985), relying on the first two waves of the Youth in Transition study, examine parental attachment (PA) and school attachment (SA), two central concepts in social control theory and in interactional theory. Delinquency was measured by self-reports of violence (V) and theft (T). Liska and Reed estimated both lagged and simultaneous causal models and, since these different specifications produce similar patterns, discuss the simultaneous models that had substantially larger effects.

When self-reports of violent behavior are examined they report the following results.[8] Parental attachment has a significant negative effect on violence (PA → V = −0.28)[9] but violence does not have a significant effect on attachment to parents. On the other hand, violence does have a significant effect on school attachment (V → SA = −0.28) but attachment to school does not affect violence. In other words, these relationships are unidirectional, but in one case (parents) the direction is from the bonding variable to delinquency while in the other (school) it is from delinquency to the bonding variable.

When theft behavior is considered, the results are somewhat complicated for parental attachment. Liska and Reed estimated two simultaneous models, one with instrumental variables and the other without them. In the former, theft significantly influences parental attachment (T → PA = −0.13) but not vice versa. In the latter, parental attachment influences theft (PA → T = −0.13) but not vice versa. The results for school attachment and theft are more consistent; these variables appear in a reasonably strong causal loop; theft reduces attachment to school (T → SA = −0.25) and school attachment reduces theft (SA → T = −0.10).[10]

Overall, these results suggest that parental attachment affects delinquency but delinquency does not affect parental attachment. School attachment and delinquency, however, appear to be embedded in a causal loop, with the effect from delinquency to school attachment being somewhat stronger than the more typical specification of school attachment to delinquency.

Agnew's investigation (1985) also uses the Youth in Transition data, but expands the measurement space to include eight variables derived from Hirschi's original work (1969) and especially from Wiatrowski, Griswold, and Roberts' cross-sectional test of control theory (1981). These variables are: parental attachment (PaA), grades (G), dating index (DI), school

---

[8] All these results are reported in Table 5.2 (Liska & Reed, 1985, p. 554). With one noted exception the results reported here are from their model "1c," which includes instrumental variables.

[9] Unless otherwise noted, all coefficients reported in this chapter are standardized. In this notational scheme the first variable is treated as the cause and the second as the effect. In this case it can be read as: the causal effect of parental attachment on violence is estimated to be −0.28.

[10] Liska and Reed focus their attention on the stronger of the two causal effects in each of the reciprocal relations rather than discussing all significant effects. Since the issue here concerns reciprocity, discussion focuses on the significant effects reported in the table.

attachment (SA), involvement (I), commitment (C), peer attachment (PeA), and belief (B). Delinquency is represented by total delinquency and serious delinquency scales (Agnew, 1985, pp. 49–51). The results reported here are taken from Tables 3 and 4 of Agnew (1985) and because the pattern of results are the same for the two delinquency measures refer only to the total delinquency (D) scale.

The results reported by Agnew are from two separate regression analyses. First, time 2 delinquency was regressed on time 1 delinquency and the eight bonding variables. This provides the estimate of the effect of the bonding variables on delinquency $(X_i \rightarrow D)$. Then each time 2 social bonding variable was regressed on time 1 delinquency and all the time 1 bonding variables, providing the delinquency to bonding variables estimates $(D \rightarrow X_i)$.

Agnew reports that neither parental attachment nor commitment is involved in any significant relationships with delinquency. Three of the control variables have significant unidirectional effects on delinquency.[11] They are: grades $(G \rightarrow D = -0.09)$, involvement $(I \rightarrow D = -0.03)$, and peer attachment $(PeA \rightarrow D = 0.05)$. On the other hand, delinquency has significant unidirectional effects on the dating index $(D \rightarrow DI = 0.15)$ and school attachment $(D \rightarrow SA = -0.08)$. Finally, belief and delinquency are reciprocally related $(B \rightarrow D = -0.07; D \rightarrow B = -0.09)$.

The results reported by Liska and Reed (1985) and by Agnew (1985), using the same data set, are somewhat inconsistent. Parental attachment is only significant in the Liska and Reed study $(PA \rightarrow D)$; school attachment has a bidirectional relationship in Liska and Reed $(SA \rightarrow D)$ but a "reversed effect"[12] in Agnew $(D \rightarrow SA)$. This may be due in part to the inclusion of other variables in the model estimated by Agnew or by the use of a full-information statistical model by Liska and Reed. The overall impact of the bonding variables will be discussed in the concluding section of this chapter.

The other five studies in this section examine the reciprocal relationship between a single explanatory variable and delinquency. Agnew (1989) em-

---

[11] Some effects are significant but with the wrong sign, e.g., school attachment has a positive impact on delinquency. Since interactional theory offers clear directional hypotheses these coefficients are treated as not significant in this review. Across all the studies discussed there are very few of these anomalous findings.

[12] The term *reversed effect* is used to indicate a unidirectional effect that is the reverse of the traditional specification. That is, a reverse effect is from delinquency to the other variable.

ploys the Youth in Transition study to test a central hypothesis from his revised version of strain theory. He examines simultaneous relationships between two latent constructs: environmental adversity (measured by negative school attitudes, perceptions of mean teachers, and parental punitiveness) and delinquency (measured by aggression, theft, and escape from school) (pp. 378–380).

Using the structural equation modeling provided by EQS (Bentler, 1985), Agnew finds that environmental adversity has a significant effect on delinquency (A → D = 0.26) but that delinquency has no significant effect on adversity. The interpretation of this finding in the present context is somewhat ambiguous. First, it is the only study reviewed here that reports no significant effects from delinquency to at least one other variable. Second, the explanatory concept, environmental adversity, is derived from a strain perspective and of all the concepts examined here has the least direct link to interactional theory. Nevertheless, Agnew's study demonstrates a unidirectional effect from environmental adversity to delinquency.

The study by Thornberry and Christenson (1984) differs from the others reviewed in this chapter in two respects: it is the only one to deal exclusively with the adult years, ages 21 to 24, and to use official data to indicate criminal involvement. Based on the follow-up study of the 1945 Philadelphia birth cohort (Wolfgang et al., 1987), it examines the link between the bonding variable of commitment to conventional activity (measured [in reverse] by the proportion of time in the past 12 months the person was unemployed) and crime (measured by the number of arrests in the past 12 months). Using LISREL to estimate the model, instantaneous effects from unemployment to crime (U → C), and instantaneous and 1- and 2-year lagged effects from crime to unemployment (C → U), were examined.

All the instantaneous effects from unemployment to crime are significant (U2 → C2 = 0.13; U3 → C3 = 0.35; U4 → C4 = 0.48)[13] and increase substantially with age. This is reasonable because, developmentally, success in the conventional activity of work takes on increasing importance at these ages. The effect from crime to unemployment is primarily evident in the lagged coefficients. All five are significant, ranging from C2 → U3 = 0.10 to C1 → U3 = 0.18. The first two instantaneous effects from crime to unemployment are negligible but the last one is sizable (C4 → U4 = 0.36). Overall, it appears that unemployment does increase the chances of criminal behavior and that criminal behavior in turn increases the chances of

[13] The U2 → C2 coefficient is significant at $p < 0.10$.

unemployment. Stated in terms of the theoretical constructs, commitment to conventional activity and criminal behavior appear to be reciprocally related.

Rosenberg et al. (1989) examine the link between self-esteem and delinquency. They point out that causal loops need not be amplifying (i.e., have the same signs) as all the other ones examined in this chapter are. Indeed, they suggest that self-esteem and delinquency may have a "countervailing" relationship (Rosenberg et al., 1989, pp. 1005–1007). That is, self-esteem may be negatively related to delinquency, but delinquency, "if it improves reflected appraisals, social comparisons, and self-attributions" (Rosenberg et al., 1989, pp. 1006), may have a positive effect on self-esteem.

Rosenberg et al. use data from the first two waves of the Youth in Transition study to test this hypothesis. Estimates of instantaneous effects at wave 2 were generated by LISREL, using a large number of instrumental variables to identify the model. The results are intriguing. First, self-esteem was found to have a significant negative effect on delinquency (SE2 → D2 = −0.19) while delinquency has a positive, albeit not quite significant (t = 1.82) effect on self-esteem (D2 → SE2 = 0.08).

Rosenberg et al. (1989) next examine these relationships within categories of SES since deviance may be more accepted or normative in lower SES groups and, therefore, the self-esteem–delinquency relationship could vary by SES. In particular, "one expectation would be that lower-class delinquency would be more a product of normative influences whereas higher-class delinquency would be more a product of personality influences" (Rosenberg et al., 1989, p. 1011). If that is the case then the self-esteem to delinquency path would increase in magnitude as one moved from lower to higher SES while the reciprocal path, from delinquency to self-esteem, would decrease in magnitude as one moved from lower to higher SES. The data bearing on this relationship (Table 2 in Rosenberg et al., 1989, p. 1011) are reproduced here as Table 5.2. The results clearly support this specification. All the delinquency to self-esteem effects (SE → D) are significant and increase from −0.17 to −0.24 across SES groups. On the other hand, the effect from delinquency to self-esteem is positive, but it is significant only for the lower SES subjects (D → SE = 0.14). This finding is intuitively appealing since delinquent conduct, or any conduct for that matter, should enhance self-esteem only if it is normatively approved.

Rosenberg et al.'s (1989) results are important for three reasons. First, they show a strong reciprocal relationship for a variable – self-esteem – not yet incorporated into interactional theory. Second, they demonstrate the theoretical and empirical plausibility of countervailing causal loops. Third,

Table 5.2. *Reciprocal causal effects of self-esteem and delinquency, by SES*

| | Effects of | | |
	Self-esteem on delinquency	Delinquency on self-esteem	X^2 / df ratio
Total sample	−.19*	+.08	3.64
Low SES	−.17*	+.14*	2.63
Medium SES	−.22*	+.05	1.69
High SES	−.24*	+.0.1*	2.51

Source: Rosenberg et al. (1989); p. 1011, Table 2.
*Significant at the .05 level.

they point to the importance of linking social structural variables, here SES background, to causal loops involving delinquency. There is no a priori reason to assume that causal effects will always be of the same magnitude, or even sign, for different structural groups, an outcome demonstrated by Rosenberg et al.

The final two studies examined in this section are concerned with moral beliefs and delinquency. Matsueda (1989) investigates the relationship between belief in conventional morality (B) and minor deviance (D). This examination relies on the Youth in Transition data set but extends the analysis to the first four waves of data, beginning when the subjects were in the 10th grade. The first two waves are separated by 18 months, the remainder by 12 months.

The model, estimated by LISREL, specifies contemporaneous and 1-year lagged effects from deviance to beliefs (D → B) and only 1-year lagged effects from beliefs to deviance (B → D). Results suggest a very modest negative effect of beliefs on deviance. Only the first effect (B1 → D2 = −0.22) is significant. Examining the effect of deviance on beliefs (D → B), the lagged effects from deviance to belief are not significant; indeed, the first lagged effect is implausibly positive. The contemporaneous effects, however, are reasonably strong although they diminish with age (D2 → B2 = −0.62; D3 → B3 = −0.53; D4 → B4 = −0.14).[14] It would appear that engaging in delinquency has a consistent feedback effect on beliefs, especially at middle, rather than later, adolescence.

Minor (1984) examines the relationship between two aspects of moral

---

[14] The last effect, D4 → B4, is significant at $p < 0.10$.

beliefs – moral evaluations of specific forms of delinquency (M) and the acceptance of excuses for committing these acts (E) – and engaging in these delinquent behaviors (D). The forms of delinquency are: marijuana use, cocaine use, fighting, being drunk and disorderly, shoplifting, and a variety index.[15] The sample used in Minor's analysis is composed of 478 college students, with a median age of 18, enrolled in introductory criminology classes. Students responded to questionnaires at the beginning of the semester and once more, 3 months later; the attrition rate (40%) is high.

Although Minor analyzes a number of models with somewhat different specifications, only the lagged endogenous model (Table 4 in Minor, 1984) is discussed here because "a more accurate explanation of change over time [is obtained] when autoregressive effects are considered" (1984, p. 1016). The particular model discussed here estimates lagged, but not instantaneous, effects of behavior on moral beliefs and of moral beliefs on behavior.

Results indicate that, depending on the type of delinquency examined, either moral evaluations or excuse acceptance measured at time 1 has an effect on behavior at time 2. For three delinquency measures – the variety index, fighting, and marijuana use – moral beliefs at time 1 impact delinquent behavior at time 2 (M1 → D2), while for shoplifting, being drunk and disorderly, and cocaine use, excuse acceptance at time 1 impacts delinquent behavior at time 2 (E1 → D2). As Minor notes, however, none of these coefficients are large (1984, p. 1006). The lagged effect of delinquent behavior on either moral evaluations (D → M) or on excuse acceptance (D → E) is somewhat less pronounced. Behavior affects moral evaluations only for fighting, marijuana use, and cocaine use, and behavior affects excuse acceptance only for marijuana use. Again, as Minor notes, these coefficients are modest in magnitude.

In sum, Minor's analysis of college students suggests that moral beliefs and relatively minor forms of delinquency are embedded in a modest reciprocal relationship. Either moral evaluations or excuse acceptance, but not both, affect delinquent behavior for each of the types of delinquency examined. On the other hand, delinquency influences moral evaluations

---

[15] Minor also examines two forms of deviance: cheating on exams and nonmarital sex. However, since they are not technically acts of delinquency for a college-aged sample, however, they are not discussed in this review, except insofar as they influence the variety index. In any event, results for these forms of deviance are quite similar to those reported here for the other forms of behavior.

for only three of the behaviors and excuse acceptance for only one of them.

Summary

Overall, the relationship between bonding variables and delinquency appears to be more complex than traditional theories anticipate. In his classic formulation of control theory, Hirschi predicted strong unidirectional effects from the four elements of the bond to delinquent behavior. There is little support evident for that contention. Only Liska and Reed (1985) report an effect from parental attachment to delinquency, and Agnew (1985) reports unidirectional effects from grades, involvement in school, and peer attachment to delinquency. All other relationships are either from delinquency to the bonding variable or bidirectional, a situation not generally anticipated by social control theory.

Interactional theory, on the other hand, anticipates a number of reciprocal relationships, especially between parental attachment and delinquency at early adolescence and between commitment to conventional activity and delinquency, at all stages.[16] It does not anticipate any direct effects between conventional beliefs and delinquency, however.

The findings for parental attachment are somewhat hard to assess because none of these studies deal with early adolescence when family effects are predicted to be strongest. Nevertheless, the reverse effect from delinquency to parental attachment expected by interactional theory during middle adolescence is not evident. Indeed, the overall family effect appears quite weak, a finding not anticipated by any control-based theory.

The studies by Agnew (1985), Minor (1984), and Matsueda (1989) suggest that the role of conventional belief has been underestimated in interactional theory, which viewed it as having only an indirect relationship with delinquent conduct. Agnew reports a reciprocal relationship between these variables, Minor reports a reciprocal relationship between them with a stronger impact of beliefs on delinquency than vice versa, and Matsueda reports an effect from delinquency to conventional beliefs.

On the other hand, the anticipated reciprocal relationship between commitment and delinquency is strongly supported. Agnew (1985) presents multiple indicators of this concept: grades and school involvement affect delinquency while delinquency affects school attachment. Liska and Reed (1985) report a reciprocal relationship between school attach-

---

[16] In adolescence the commitment variable is primarily measured in the educational realm and, after the transition to adulthood, in the occupational realm.

ment and delinquency for middle adolescence, and Thornberry and Christenson (1984) report a strong reciprocal relationship between unemployment and crime for the early adult years.

In general, these findings suggest that delinquency and crime are embedded in rather complex causal networks. While some bonding variables appear to have unidirectional effects on delinquency, others appear to be effects of delinquency and still others are involved in bidirectional relationships. Whether these relationships are maintained after social learning theory variables are added to the equation is discussed in the final section of this chapter. The next section discusses studies that include only social learning variables.

Learning Variables

Interactional theory argues that the freedom created by weakened conventional bonds requires an appropriate learning environment before it is likely to lead to prolonged delinquent behavior. That environment is represented by two concepts derived primarily from the differential association and social learning theory traditions: associations with delinquent peers and delinquent beliefs. The latter refers to beliefs that tolerate or accept delinquent conduct. In interactional theory both these concepts exert a causal influence on delinquency and, reciprocally, are influenced by delinquent conduct. The bidirectional relationship between peers and behavior is thought to be quite strong at all developmental stages, but the link between beliefs and behavior is thought to emerge over time, especially as delinquent behaviors and associations become entrenched.

Elliott and Menard (1992) examine the causal order between associations with delinquent peers and delinquent behavior using the first six waves of the National Youth Survey. The NYS is based on a nationally representative sample of youth selected in 1976 when they were ages 11 through 17. The sixth wave was conducted when the subjects were 18 to 24 years of age. The first five waves were separated by 12 months and the last wave by 36 months; all have excellent retention rates.

Two variables are included in the analysis: delinquent peers and delinquent behavior. The former is based on the subject's report of the proportion of his or her friends who are involved in delinquency. Since Elliott and Menard use a stage–state method of analysis,[17] five peer group types were

---

[17] This technique traces the probability of moving from one state, e.g., nondelinquent, to another state, e.g., delinquent, as a function of some other variable, such as associating with delinquent peers.

created. They are: isolates, saints, prosocial, mixed, and delinquent. Three self-reported delinquency scales are used: general, minor, and index delinquency (Elliott & Menard, 1992, pp. 7–8). Since results are virtually identical for the general and minor delinquency scales, however, only the latter is discussed here. Also, since the NYS had a relatively wide age range at wave 1 (11- to 17-year-olds) results are presented for all cohorts, and then separately for the 11- and 12-year-old and the 15- and 16-year-old cohorts.

For both minor and index offending there is a strong initial tendency for exposure to delinquent peers to precede delinquent behavior. This is especially so for index offending: in 71% of the cases the direction of causality is from peers to delinquency and in only 1% is it from delinquency to peers.[18] Results for the minor offense scale are in the same direction but the differences are less dramatic. In 24% of the cases the causal direction is from peers to delinquency and in 8% of the cases from delinquency to peers. The same magnitudes of effect are observed for the younger and older cohorts analyzed separately.

In addition, Elliott and Menard report rather clear developmental patterns for each of these variables. Minor delinquency is initiated before index delinquency and associations with less delinquent peers occur before associations with more delinquent peers (Elliott & Menard, 1992, pp. 19–22). These findings suggest that the relationship between peer associations and delinquent behavior may vary across different phases of delinquent careers. Indeed, Elliott and Menard report a rather complex, dynamic relationship between these two variables over time: "The typical progression for those who are non-delinquent and in non-delinquent peer groups is (1) movement into a slightly more delinquent peer group, (2) onset of Minor delinquency, (3) movement into a more delinquent peer group, (4) onset of Index delinquency, and (5) movement into a predominantly delinquent peer group" (Elliott & Menard, 1992, pp. 25–26). In other words, the influence of associations on behavior is much more pronounced at the initiation or onset stage. After that, the relationship between associations and behavior is more reciprocal, with each variable tending to amplify the other as the delinquent career is maintained. As Elliott and Menard state: "we believe the data are most consistent with [an] explanation, which combines learning and control theories and argues for bidirectional causation after onset" (1992, p. 27).

---

[18] For the other 28% the causal direction could not be determined, primarily because of left-hand censoring. This is even more problematic for minor offending, where directionality could not be determined in 68% of the cases. See Elliott and Menard (1992) for a discussion of censoring.

Kandel (1978) examines the impact of peer networks on drug use. Unlike other studies, however, she collects data from best friend dyads so that the measures of peer drug use are not filtered through the focal subject's perceptions. The subjects were drawn from nine high schools in New York State during the 1971–72 academic year. A total of 957 dyads were identified and the members were interviewed near the beginning and end of the school year.

Kandel was particularly interested in separating the selection process, in which similar people form friendship networks, from the socialization process, in which friends "irrespective of their prior similarity, influence one another" (Kandel, 1978, p. 428). In the selection process the direction of causality is from behavior to peer associations; in the socialization process it is from associations to behavior.

Using panel data on these friendship dyads Kandel reports that dyadic similarity is quite high for marijuana use. Moreover, the selection and socialization processes appear to be of equal importance. This suggests a reciprocal relationship between these variables: "adolescents who share certain prior attributes in common tend to associate with each other and tend to influence each other as the result of continued association" (Kandel, 1978, p. 435). Kandel's study is quite important because it validates the other studies of peer associations, all of which rely on the subject's reports of peer delinquency and drug use.

Meier et al. (1984), in a study that focuses on the deterrent effect of the perceived certainty of punishment on marijuana use, examine the relationship between marijuana use and peer use of marijuana. The study is based on a 3-wave panel study conducted in a Pacific Northwest high school. The students were in the 10th grade at wave 1; the waves are separated by 12-month intervals.

Meier et al. report a strong reciprocal relationship between peer use of marijuana (P) and subject's self-report of marijuana use (M). There are contemporaneous effects from peers to marijuana (P2 $\rightarrow$ M2 = 0.57 and P3 $\rightarrow$ M3 = 0.49), and there are 1-year lagged effects from marijuana use to peers (M1 $\rightarrow$ P2 = 0.47 and M2 $\rightarrow$ P3 = 0.16).

Unlike the previous studies in this section that focused on delinquent peers, Menard and Huizinga (1990) use the first six waves of the National Youth Survey to examine the relationship between delinquent beliefs and delinquent behavior. Behavior is measured by self-report scales of general, minor, and index delinquency. Only the latter two are discussed here.

While Menard and Huizinga present the belief measure as an indicator of "conventional beliefs," it is treated here as an indicator of delinquent beliefs for a number of reasons. First, the scale asks respondents "how wrong it is" to engage in a variety of illegal behaviors, with responses ranging from "very wrong" to "not wrong at all." This measure, which assesses acceptance or tolerance of delinquent behaviors, is consistent with interactional theory's definition of delinquent beliefs (Thornberry, 1987, p. 866). Second, this scale was originally intended to measure attitudes toward deviance in the NYS (Menard & Huizinga, 1990, p. 8) and it is not clear why its theoretical meaning was reversed in this analysis. Third, this scale does not measure conventional beliefs as defined in interactional theory: "Belief in conventional values represents the granting of legitimacy to such middle-class values as education, personal industry, financial success, deferral of gratification, and the like" (Thornberry, 1987, p. 866). For these reasons it seems more appropriate to treat this measure as an indicator of delinquent beliefs in the context of this review.

Using the same stage–state model approach as Elliott and Menard (1992), Menard and Huizinga (1990) report a general tendency for beliefs to precede behavior. This is particularly noticeable for index offenses, where 72% report delinquent beliefs prior to delinquent behavior and only 3% report index offenses before adopting delinquent beliefs. The differences are much less sizable for minor offenses. Here, 28% report beliefs prior to behavior and 12% report behavior prior to beliefs.

After examining the developmental patterns of each of these variables separately, Menard and Huizinga conclude that the same type of intricate developmental relationships observed for peer associations and delinquency appear to be at play here as well. The results of their analyses "suggest that the relationship between . . . beliefs and illegal behavior may be a relationship of mutual influence rather than one-way causation. Some minimal weakening of Belief usually appears to precede illegal behavior for those cases in which the temporal order is ascertainable, and some illegal behavior appears to precede any really substantial weakening of Belief, again for those cases in which temporal order is ascertainable" (Menard & Huizinga, 1990, p. 24).

The final study reviewed in this section, Reed and Rose (1991), includes both delinquent peers and delinquent beliefs, as well as delinquency. Data are once again drawn from the National Youth Survey, this time covering the first three waves of data collection, from ages 11–17 to 13–19. Reed and Rose focus on serious delinquency (D), measured by theft of more than $50, motor vehicle theft, and serious assault. The items measuring delinquent peers (P) and delinquent attitudes (A) were selected to match the behavioral domain of the serious delinquency scale. Using the measurement model of LISREL, Reed and Rose create a latent construct for each of these concepts.

The structural equation model they estimate only allows for lagged effects among the three endogenous variables; instantaneous effects are not estimated. Delinquent behavior has substantial lagged effects on delinquent peer associations (D1 → P2 = 0.49; D2 → P3 = 0.22), but peer associations has only one significant effect on delinquent behavior (P2 → D3 = 0.06). In this model it would appear that the effect of behavior on associations is substantially stronger than the effect of associations on behavior.

Turning to the relationship between delinquent behavior and delinquent attitudes, we see a reciprocal relation but only at the first time period. Delinquent behavior at time 1 increases delinquent attitudes at time 2 (D1 → A2 = 0.24), and delinquent attitudes at time 1 increase delinquent behavior at time 2 (A1 → D2 = 0.09). Neither of these effects is significant at the second observation point.

Summary

These investigations offer strong support for reciprocal causal effects between learning variables and delinquent behavior. The simple, recursive model leading from differential associations through delinquent beliefs to delinquent conduct typically present in learning and integrated theories is simply not consistent with these results. The five studies discussed in this section are quite consistent with the bidirectional relationships suggested by interactional theory.

Moreover, the stage–state analyses based on the NYS data suggest that these relationships are developmentally complex and vary across phases of the delinquent career. For the explanation of onset or initiation a unidirectional effect from delinquent peers and from delinquent beliefs to delinquent behavior appears appropriate. For the explanation of maintenance, however, these relationships are reciprocal and amplifying. Just as Rosenberg et al. (1989) demonstrate how structural position can specify reciprocal relationships involving delinquency, the work of Elliott, Menard, and Huizinga shows how developmental stages can also specify reciprocal relationships.

Bonding and Learning Variables

The last set of studies includes variables derived from both bonding and learning perspectives. These studies, therefore, provide more complete information with respect to interactional theory, which argues that weakened bonds to conventional society set the stage for delinquency but that an appropriate learning environment is needed before that freedom is translated into prolonged and serious delinquency. For reasons discussed in the two previous sections, reciprocal effects are expected between delinquent behavior and many bonding and learning variables[19] (see Figure 5.2). The question now is whether the types of reciprocal effects found in the previous sections are also observed in studies that simultaneously examine both sets of variables. The studies included here are: Agnew (1991), Burkett and Warren (1987), Elliott et al. (1985b), Ginsberg and Greenley (1978), and Paternoster (1988). These studies are briefly described in Table 5.1.

The first two studies reviewed here – Agnew (1991) and Elliott et al. (1985b) – are based on the National Youth Survey and include similar variables in the analyses. Agnew measures delinquency with three scales – general, minor, and serious delinquency – but focuses on the minor delinquency scale, while Elliott et al. use the general delinquency scale. To indicate ties to conventional society, Agnew uses scales to measure parental attachment, school attachment, and commitment (1991, pp. 134–136); Elliott et al. use scales to measure family sanctions, aspirations for prosocial roles, involvement in prosocial contexts, normlessness, and strain (1985b, p. 2).[20] To measure the learning variables Agnew uses scales to measure deviant beliefs and delinquent peer associations (1991, pp. 136–137), and Elliott et al. use scales to measure internal deviant bonding (a measure similar to delinquent beliefs) and exposure to delinquent peers (1985b, p. 2). The Elliott et al. study is based on the first five waves of the NYS, while the Agnew study is based on only the first two.

Elliott et al. use a path model that insures correct temporal orderings; each equation includes the prior level (1-year lag) of the dependent variable. They report that none of the bonding variables has a direct effect on delinquency nor does delinquency have a direct effect on any of the bonding variables. Moreover, delinquency and internal deviant bonding are not directly related to each other. The only variables that are directly associated are delinquent peers and delinquent behavior, and these variables are involved in a rather strong causal loop. The effects from peers to delinquen-

---

[19] Reciprocal effects are also expected among bonding variables and learning variables, and many of these are in fact tested in the studies reviewed in this section. Since this review is limited to relationships involving delinquency, however, they are not discussed here.

[20] The normlessness and strain scales derive more from a strain theory perspective but, given a generous definition of bonding, more or less fit in this category.

cy are: P2 → D2 = 0.42; P3 → D3 = 0.26; P4 → D4 = 0.30; P5 → D5 = 0.32. The effects from delinquency to peers are: D1 → P2 = 0.14; D2 → P3 = 0.16; D3 → P4 = 0.21; D4 → P5 = 0.10 (Elliott et al., 1985b, p. 4).

Using only the first two waves of the NYS and a structural equation model that allows for contemporaneous but not lagged effects, Agnew (1991) reports strikingly similar results. The bonding variables and delinquency are not directly related to each other nor are deviant beliefs and delinquent behavior. On the other hand, delinquent peers (P) and delinquency (D) are involved in a bidirectional relationship: P2 → D2 = 0.26 and D2 → P2 = 0.38.

In combination, these results raise serious questions about the anticipated importance of the bonding variables. These variables neither impact delinquency nor are they impacted by delinquency in a direct and substantial manner once delinquent peers and prior delinquency are added to the equations. On the other hand, delinquent peers and delinquent behavior continue to mutually reinforce one another over time even when the impact of the bonding variables is held constant.

Ginsberg and Greenley (1978) studied marijuana use among University of Wisconsin students. The first data collection occurred when the students were freshmen or sophomores and the second occurred 26 months later when they were juniors and seniors. Five variables are included: involvement in school, commitment, psychological stress, peer marijuana use, and respondent's marijuana use (Ginsberg & Greeley, 1978, pp. 25–26). Involvement and commitment are not directly related to marijuana use but it should be noted that the sample – University of Wisconsin students – is highly selected on these variables. Stress at time 1 is not related to later marijuana use, but marijuana use (M) at time 1 tends to *decrease* stress (S) at time 2: M1 → S2 = − 0.16. On the other hand, peers and behavior once again seem to be mutually reinforcing: P1 → M2 = 0.29; M1 → P2 = 0.24.

Burkett and Warren (1987) examine marijuana use in a 3-wave panel study conducted in a Pacific Northwest city. The waves were separated by 12 months and began when the students were 10th-graders. This is the same data set used by Meier et al. (1984). Two bonding variables are used in the analysis: religious commitment and belief in the sinfulness of marijuana use. In addition, associations with peers who use marijuana and marijuana use are included (Burkett & Warren, 1987, pp. 118–119). Models with both lagged and instantaneous effects were estimated by LISREL.

Marijuana use (M) is involved in direct relationships with two variables: belief (B) and peer associations (P). The relationship between belief and marijuana use is rather weak. Marijuana use has a negative, lagged effect on belief, but only from waves 1 to 2 (M1 → B2 = −0.14). On the other hand, there is a contemporaneous effect from belief to marijuana use, but only at the third wave (B3 → M3 = −0.20). The relationship between peers and marijuana use is more consistent and exhibits an interesting pattern. Marijuana use has lagged effects on peer associations (M1 → P2 = 0.34; M2 → P3 = 0.13), but not contemporaneous effects. On the other hand, peer associations have contemporaneous effects on use (P2 → M2 = 0.56; P3 → M3 = 0.52), but not lagged effects. From these data it would appear that marijuana use leads to peer associations and, in turn, associations intensify use. This is similar to the pattern described by Kandel (1978).

The final study reviewed in this chapter is Paternoster's (1988) examination of marijuana use and petty theft. Although his investigation focused on the deterrent role of perceived certainty of sanctions, which is not of central interest to interactional theory, the analytic model included a number of variables that are important to interactional theory: parental supervision, deviant beliefs,[21] peer deviant behavior, and peer attitudes toward deviance. Since Paternoster's theoretical interests lie in the study of deterrence, he only discusses these interactional theory variables from a unidirectional perspective (1988, pp. 167–168, 173). Their bidirectional relationships are quite informative, however, and a portion of his results are presented in graphic form here and discussed in some detail.

Paternoster's analysis is based on a 3-wave panel study of high school students selected from nine schools in and around a midsize Southeastern city (1988, pp. 140–143). The first wave took place during the students' 10th grade. Although the retention rate is low (46% of the wave 1 respondents completed all three waves), the remaining sample is sizable (1244 respondents). Also, Paternoster reports that a comparison of subjects who remained in the study with those who dropped out showed, in general, no substantial differences between them (1988, p. 142).

Using structural equation models, Paternoster examined mutual lagged effects between deviance and the explanatory variables. Since the results for marijuana use and petty theft are substantially the same, only the former are discussed here. The significant lagged effects for marijuana use are

---

[21] Paternoster refers to this scale as measuring moral beliefs. It was measured in the same way – how wrong is it to engage in various deviant behaviors – as the belief scale used by Menard and Huizinga (1990). For the same reasons presented in the discussion of Menard and Huizinga's study, the scale is referred to as *deviant beliefs* in this chapter.

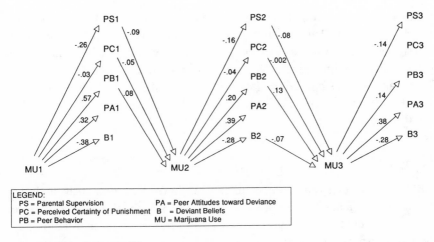

Source: Table 3, Paternoster 1988: 165.

Figure 5.3. Direct effects (standardized) between bonding/learning variables and marijuana use.

presented in Figure 5.3. Recall that only relationships involving delinquency (here marijuana use) are discussed in this review; stability effects and effects among the explanatory variables are excluded here but are presented in Tables 3 through 6 of Paternoster (1988, pp. 165ff.).

Of the results presented in Figure 5.3, the most striking overall finding is the number of lagged reciprocal effects in which marijuana use is involved. Unlike the other studies in this section, the effect of the bonding variable of parental supervision (PS) is significant even after the learning variables are included in the model. Indeed, it has a rather consistent lagged reciprocal relationship with marijuana use (MU). The effects from parental supervision to marijuana use are: PS1 → MU2 = −0.09; PS2 → MU3 = −0.08; the effects from marijuana use to parental supervision are: MU1 → PS1 = −0.26; MU2 → PS2 = −0.16 and MU3 → PS3 = −0.14.

The perceived certainty of punishment (PC) variable, the central focus of Paternoster's analysis, is seen to have few strong relationships with marijuana use. The effects from perceived certainty to marijuana use (PC → MU) range from −0.002 to −0.05 while the effects from use to perceived certainty (MU → PC) range from −0.03 to −0.04.

Turning to the learning-based variables, a number of reciprocal relationships are seen. Marijuana use has strong effects on peer behavior (PB), but these effects diminish over time, (MU1 → PB1 = 0.57; MU2 → PB2 = 0.20; MU3 → PB3 = 0.14). On the other hand, peer behavior has much smaller, but increasing effects on marijuana use (PB1 → MU2 = 0.08; PB2 → MU3 = 0.13). Peer attitudes toward deviance (PA) have no significant impact on marijuana use, but marijuana use has sizable and rather stable effects on peer attitudes (MU → PA ranges from 0.32 to 0.39). Finally, marijuana use has no strong effects on beliefs (MU → B range from −0.28 to −0.38), but beliefs have only one small effect on use (B2 → MU3 = −0.07).

Summary

This section reviewed panel studies that have simultaneously included bonding and learning variables in analysis. Using National Youth Survey data, Elliott et al. (1985b) and Agnew (1991) report no direct relationships between various bonding variables and delinquency. Thus, neither the unidirectional effects expected by control theory (Hirschi, 1969) nor the bidirectional effects expected by interactional theory are evident in these studies. Also, Ginsberg and Greenley (1978) report no direct effects of commitment and school involvement on marijuana use, but it should be recalled that their sample – University of Wisconsin students – is highly selected on these variables.

On the other hand, the studies by Burkett and Warren (1987) and by Paternoster (1988) report relationships between some of the bonding variables and delinquency. Paternoster reports a consistent, but not very large, reciprocal relationship between parental supervision and delinquency for both marijuana use and petty theft. Burkett and Warren report somewhat inconsistent effects from conventional beliefs to marijuana use and marijuana use to conventional beliefs, but no direct effect involving religious commitment.

For the learning variables, however, reciprocal effects are consistently observed even after the bonding variables are held constant. In Paternoster's study delinquent behavior had a consistent and sizable impact on delinquent beliefs, while beliefs had some effects on delinquent behavior. In all the studies reviewed here, association with delinquent peers and delinquent behavior have been shown to be mutually reinforcing variables. As expected, association with delinquent peers increases delinquent conduct and delinquent conduct increases association with delinquent peers.

Conclusion

This review attempted to respond to the following question: Is there substantial empirical support for interactional theory's central contention that delinquent behavior is embedded in a set of mutually reinforcing causal networks? The general response to this question is clearly affirmative. Of the 17 panel studies reviewed, only one, Agnew (1989), found a purely unidirectional effect and that is for the variable (environmental adversity) that is most distant from interactional theory. In the 16 other studies, at least some of the relationships involving delinquency are bidirectional and, across all the studies, the overwhelming weight of the evidence suggests that many of the presumed unidirectional causes of delinquency are in fact either products of delinquent behavior or involved in mutually reinforcing causal relationships with delinquent behavior. The consistency of this finding suggests that recursive causal models of delinquency are seriously misspecified.

The remainder of this section summarizes the results of the literature review that underline the importance of including reciprocal causal effects and explicitly considering developmental change in the construction of theories of delinquency. Finally, some implications of these results are briefly discussed.

Bonding Variables

Interactional theory offers three general hypotheses about the direct relationships between bonding variables and delinquency. First, parental attachment and delinquency are thought to be mutually reinforcing, but only during early adolescence. Second, belief in conventional values has a weak and primarily indirect effect on delinquency. Third, commitment to conventional activities (school during early and middle adolescence and work after that) and delinquency are reciprocally related at all developmental stages.

It is difficult to evaluate fully the first of these expectations because in all these studies the subjects were already in the middle adolescent years or beyond at the first data collection point.[22] Nevertheless, there is little evidence of reciprocal (or unidirectional) effects between attachment to parents and delinquency. Unfortunately, this finding is subject to two interpretations. First, the absence of a strong reciprocal relationship between attachment to parents and delinquency may reflect the general independence of these variables, a conclusion not consistent with interactional theory. Second, these findings may be developmentally specific and, if data from earlier ages were available, the anticipated recipro-

---

[22] The exception is for the youngest cohorts of the National Youth Survey, but none of these studies examine the family variables separately for these cohorts.

cal influence of these variables would be seen. Perhaps the strength of the direct relationship[23] between parental attachment and delinquency anticipated by interactional theory, and most other theories of delinquency (e.g., Hirschi, 1969; Elliott et al., 1985a), is simply overestimated. Before that conclusion is accepted, however, additional data collected at earlier developmental stages are required.

The strength of the relationship between belief in conventional values and delinquency has been underestimated by interactional theory. Rather weak and indirect effects from conventional beliefs to delinquency were anticipated. Yet three of the four studies that examined this variable report direct effects. Agnew (1985) and Burkett and Warren (1987) report modest bidirectional relationships, and Matsueda (1989) reports a lagged effect from delinquency to beliefs. It would appear that belief in conventional values, at least during the midadolescent years, influences and is influenced by delinquent conduct. Acceptance of traditional values appears to reduce delinquency; delinquent behavior, however, appears to erode those moral beliefs.

The third relationship, which concerns commitment to conventional activities and delinquency, is expected to be mutually reinforcing at all developmental stages. Of all the hypotheses concerning the bonding variables this one received the strongest support. Agnew (1985) reports that grades and involvement in school reduce delinquency, but that delinquency reduces attachment to school. Liska and Reed (1985) and Thornberry and Christenson (1984) report reciprocal relationships between school attachment and delinquency and between unemployment and arrests, respectively. It would appear that the "rational" component of the bond works as expected: investments in conformity – school and employment – reduce delinquency and crime, but delinquent behavior feeds back upon and attenuates attachment to school and involvement in work.

The results concerning the relationship between bonding variables and delinquency are, in general, quite consistent with predictions offered by interactional theory. The importance of conventional beliefs appears to have been underestimated, but the weak effects for the family variables at midadolescence and the reciprocal effects of commitment and delinquency at all developmental stages are apparent.

---

[23] Recall that this review is only concerned with the direct relationships between these variables and delinquency and that indirect effects, in either direction, are not being considered. They are obviously of substantial theoretical importance and will be analyzed in future reviews.

Learning Variables

The role of the two learning variables in interactional theory – delinquent beliefs and associations with delinquent peers – is quite clear-cut. At mid-adolescence both are expected to be involved in mutually reinforcing relationships with delinquent behavior. At early adolescence the effect from beliefs to behavior is expected to be somewhat weaker than the effect from behavior to beliefs.

Four studies examined delinquent beliefs and delinquent conduct. Two of them, based on the National Youth Survey (Agnew, 1991; Elliott et al., 1985b), report no association between delinquent beliefs and behavior, when the peer association variable is also in the model. On the other hand, Menard and Huizinga (1990), also using the NYS, report effects from beliefs to behavior at onset and then bidirectional effects for the maintenance of delinquency. Paternoster (1988) reports consistent effects from behavior (both marijuana and petty theft) to beliefs and less consistent effects from beliefs to behavior.

The strongest and most consistent reciprocal relationship is observed for delinquent peers and delinquent behavior. Nine of the 17 studies examine this relationship and all report strong bidirectional relationships. Moreover, the relationships appear to be approximately equal in strength; in four studies the peers to behavior coefficients are higher, in three the behavior to peers coefficients are higher, and in two they are equal.

In combination, these results for the learning variables and for the bonding variables clearly show the general importance of reciprocal causal relationships in theories of delinquency. When nonrecursive models are tested, a number of relationships previously thought to be unidirectional are shown to be reciprocal.

Developmental Change

In addition to its concern with reciprocal relationships, interactional theory is also concerned with the importance of developmental change. While the present essay focuses on the former, a few comments about developmental issues can be offered.

Although it is hard to draw firm conclusions in this area since almost all of these analyses focused on midadolescence, there is some support for interactional theory's contention that causal effects vary over the life course. It is not clear, however, how large these differences may be. For example, Elliott et al. (1985b) report that the causal model they estimated at each of the first five waves of the NYS is quite stable. That is, the coefficients do not vary greatly as the panel ages from a median age of 15 to 18. This suggests few developmental differences.

On the other hand, a number of specific findings in the studies reviewed here suggest that causal effects do vary with age and with phases of the delinquent career. For example, also using the NYS, Elliott and Menard (1992) and Menard and Huizinga (1990) both report distinct findings for onset and maintenance. For onset, both delinquent peers and delinquent beliefs have unidirectional effects on delinquent behavior but, for maintenance, each of these variables and delinquency appear to have mutually reinforcing causal effects. Indeed, these analyses suggest an intricate pattern of amplification in which beliefs and behavior, and associations and behavior, tend to increase the intensity of the other in an alternating, or leap-frogging, fashion. This is precisely the developmental pattern of mutual causal effects suggested by the behavioral trajectories included in interactional theory (Thornberry, 1987, pp. 882–884).

One other example of the importance of developmental change can be discussed. Paternoster reports that "when these respondents first entered high school, parental influence was strong; peer influence was present, but weaker than parental factors; [and] moral beliefs were not related at all to marijuana use" (1988, p. 168). Over time, however, the peer influences became stronger and both use and associations with users had feedback effects to weaken the impact of parental supervision. These results suggest that "marijuana users become more immersed in a marijuana 'subculture' while their ties with parents were eroded" (Paternoster, 1988, p. 169). These findings are quite consistent with the general developmental thrust of interactional theory and point to the importance of examining different causal influences at different stages of development.

Implications

Overall, these findings support the importance of constructing dynamic theories of delinquency. Delinquent behavior is clearly not the simple product or outcome of a recursive social process. It is part and parcel of that process – influenced by but also influencing other variables. In addition, this process changes over time and does not maintain the same form at different developmental stages. Both causal factors and the direction of causal influences change systematically over the life course, and a complete explanation of the causes of delinquency requires an understanding of this complexity. For only by constructing accurate and precise models of delinquency, rather than oversimplified static models, can we begin to separate cause from effect and identify the proper temporal sequence of events. In the end, then, this review of the empirical literature offers evidence that is quite consistent with an interactional perspective on delinquency. And that knowledge is essential to the establishment of effective intervention strategies.

REFERENCES

Agnew, R. (1985). Social control theory and delinquency: A longitudinal test. *Criminology*, *23*, 47–62.

Agnew, R. (1989). A longitudinal test of the revised strain theory. *Journal of Quantitative Criminology*, *5*, 373–387.

Agnew, R. (1991). A longitudinal test of social control theory and delinquency. *Journal of Research on Crime and Delinquency*, *28*, 126–156.

Akers, R. L. (1977). *Deviant behavior: A social learning perspective*. Belmont: Wadsworth.

Bachman, J. G., O'Malley, P. M., & Johnston, J. (1978). *Youth in transition: Adolescence to adulthood – Change and stability in the lives of young men* (Vol. 6). Ann Arbor: Institute for Social Research.

Bentler, P. M. (1985). *Theory and implementation of EQS: A structural equations program*. BMDP Statistical Program, Los Angeles.

Blumstein, A., Cohen, J., Roth, J. A., & Visher, C. A. (1986). *Criminal careers and "career criminals."* Washington: National Academy Press.

Burkett, S. R., & Warren, B. O. (1987). Religiosity, peer influence, and adolescent marijuana use: A panel study of underlying causal structures. *Criminology*, *25*, 109–131.

Catalano, R. F., & Hawkins, J. D. (1986). The social development model: A theory of antisocial behavior. Safeco Lecture on Crime and Delinquency, School of Social Work, University of Washington.

Elliott, D. S., Ageton, S. S., & Canter, R. J. (1979). An integrated theoretical perspective on delinquent behavior. *Journal of Research in Crime and Delinquency*, *16*, 3–27.

Elliott, D. S., Huizinga, D., & Ageton, S. S. (1985a). *Explaining delinquency and drug use*. Beverly Hills, CA: Sage.

Elliott, D. S., Huizinga, D., & Morse, B. J. (1985b). *The dynamics of deviant behavior: A national survey*. Progress report submitted to the National Institute of Mental Health, Department of Health and Human Services.

Elliott, D. S., & Menard, S. (1992). *Delinquent friends and delinquent behavior: Temporal and developmental patterns*. Unpublished manuscript, Institute of Behavioral Science, University of Colorado–Boulder.

Farrington, D. P., & Hawkins, J. D. (1991). Predicting participation, early onset and later persistence in officially recorded offending. *Criminal Behavior and Mental Health*, *1*, 1–33.

Farrington, D. P. & West, D. J. (1981). The Cambridge study of delinquent development. In S. A. Mednick and A. E. Baert (Eds.), *Prospective longitudinal research* (pp. 137–145). Oxford: Oxford University Press.

Ginsberg, I. J., & Greenley, J. R. (1978). Competing theories of marijuana use: A longitudinal study. *Journal of Health and Social Behavior, 19,* 22–34.

Hawkins, J. D., & Weis, J. G. (1985). The social development model: An integrated approach to delinquency prevention. *Journal of Primary Prevention, 6,* 73–97.

Hirschi, T. (1969). *Causes of delinquency.* Berkeley: University of California Press.

Johnson, R. E. (1979). *Juvenile delinquency and its origins.* Cambridge: University of Cambridge Press.

Kandel, D. B. (1978). Homophily, selection, and socialization in adolescent friendships. *American Journal of Sociology, 84,* 427–436.

Krohn, M. D. (1986). The web of conformity: A social network approach to the explanation of delinquent behavior. *Social Problems, 33,* 601–613.

Liska, A. E., & Reed, M. D. (1985). Ties to conventional institutions and delinquency: Estimating reciprocal effects. *American Sociological Review, 50,* 547–560.

Loeber, R., & Le Blanc, M. (1990). Toward a developmental criminology. In M. Tonry and N. Morris (Eds.), *Crime and Justice* (Vol. 12, pp. 375–473). Chicago: University of Chicago Press.

Matsueda, R. L. (1989). The dynamics of moral beliefs and minor deviance. *Social Forces, 68,* 428–457.

Meier, R. F., Burkett, S. R., & Hickman, C. A. (1984). Sanctions, peers and deviance: Preliminary models of a social control process. *Sociological Quarterly, 25,* 67–82.

Menard, S., & Huizinga, D. (1990). The temporal priority of belief and delinquent behavior in adolescence. Unpublished manuscript, Institute of Behavioral Science, University of Colorado–Boulder.

Minor, W. W. (1984). Neutralization as a hardening process: Considerations in the modeling of change. *Social Forces, 62,* 995–1019.

Paternoster, R. (1988). Examining three-wave deterrence models: A question of temporal order and specification. *Journal of Criminal Law and Criminology, 79,* 135–179.

Patterson, G. R. (1982). *A social learning approach, Vol. 3: Coercive family processes.* Eugene, OR: Castalia.

Reed, M. D., & Rose, D. R. (1991). Modeling the reciprocal relations of delinquent peers, delinquent attitudes and serious delinquency: A covariance structure analysis. Unpublished manuscript, Department of Sociology, Duke University.

Rosenberg, M., Schooler, C., & Schoenbach, C. (1989). Self-esteem and adolescent problems: Modeling reciprocal effects. *American Sociological Review, 54,* 1004–1018.

Shannon, L. W. (1988). *Criminal career continuity: Its social context.* New York: Human Sciences Press.

Thornberry, T. P. (1987). Toward an interactional theory of delinquency. *Criminology, 25,* 863–891.

Thornberry, T. P., & Christenson, R. L. (1984). Unemployment and criminal involvement: An investigation of reciprocal causal structures. *American Sociological Review, 49,* 398–411.

Wiatrowski, M. D., Griswold, D. B., & Roberts, M. R. (1981). Social control theory and delinquency. *American Sociological Review, 46,* 525–541.

Wolfgang, M. E., Figlio, R. M., & Sellin, T. (1972). *Delinquency in a birth cohort.* Chicago: University of Chicago Press.

Wolfgang, M. E., Thornberry, T. P., & Figlio, R. M. (1987). *From boy to man – From delinquency to crime: Follow-up to the Philadelphia birth cohort of 1945.* Chicago: University of Chicago Press.

CHAPTER SIX

The Use of Contextual Analysis in Models of Criminal Behavior

ROBERT J. BURSIK, JR.

HAROLD G. GRASMICK

ABSTRACT: One of the central assumptions of most of the early classics of the criminological literature was that a full understanding of crime and delinquency is impossible without a joint consideration of the individual processes leading to illegal behavior and the social contexts that shape those processes and give them meaning. Shaw (1929), for example, argued that a comprehensive theory of delinquent and criminal behavior could be developed only through a simultaneous examination of the "inner personal world of the subject" (i.e., psychological and motivation processes) and the group contexts that defined the situations for that subject. Thus, as Morris points out (1957, p. 72), Shaw's life history and ecological work are complementary components of a single general orientation. Likewise, although Healy (1915, p. 283) developed an explicitly psychological/psychiatric model of delinquency, he also recognized that it can be "clearly appreciated that delinquency is a product of a personal reaction to a given environment." Unfortunately, the subsequent development of criminology generally did not maintain a balanced perspective on the dual roles of group and individual dynamics in the etiology of illegal behavior. As a result, the discipline traditionally has been characterized by alternating periods in which one of these dynamics is given theoretical primacy while the other is relatively neglected (see Stark, 1987; Bursik, 1988; Gottfredson & Hirschi, 1988).[1]

A number of criminologists have observed that such a focal limitation significantly impedes the growth of our understanding of criminal dynamics. Reiss (1986), for example, argues persuasively for the integration of the individual and group traditions into a single, more comprehensive theoretical framework. Despite such proposals, only a handful of truly contextual studies appeared in the literature prior to the mid-1980s, due in large part to the high costs involved in the design and implementation of such research. However, since that time, a growing (albeit still small) number of criminolo-

---

[1] Similar trends have characterized other disciplines in the social sciences. Coleman (1986, pp. 1316–1318) provides some interesting insights concerning these developments.

gists successfully have solicited the necessary funding to conduct such studies. As a result, the body of contextual research has developed to the point that efforts to construct multilevel theories validly can be considered to be a core component of contemporary criminology.[2]

The statistical techniques that have been used as the basis of such multilevel research are, for the most part, deceptively simple. Yet, since these models are grounded in a number of subtle theoretical and statistical assumptions, the findings of contextual analyses can be misleading if these assumptions are not carefully considered. In the first part of this chapter, we will examine the theoretical issues that must be resolved for a contextual model to be meaningful in criminology. The second section discusses the primary contemporary techniques of contextual analysis, with special attention paid to the inferential difficulties that may arise. The final section reviews the contextual studies that have appeared in criminology and evaluates them in terms of the issues raised in the first two parts of the chapter.

The Theoretical Issues of Contextual Analysis

The Problems of Specification Error

In its most general sense, specification error refers to two separate issues in the development of statistical models: the failure to include all relevant explanatory variables in an equation, and the failure to correctly identify the functional form of the equation (see the general discussion of Theil, 1971). Although tests exist that enable a researcher to compare the effects of alternative specifications of a model, these are extremely limited in the sense that a nearly infinite number of explanatory variables may potentially be included in a model; the analyst also may choose from an equally large set of potential functional forms. Therefore, the specification of a model only can be justified and evaluated on the basis of theoretical assumptions concerning the processes under examination.

At either the individual or group level of analysis, the specification of a particular model can be guided by a variety of theoretical perspectives, each of which is characterized by a set of assumptions concerning the appropriate explanatory variables and the causal dynamics that link the exogenous processes to criminal behavior. As Blalock has noted (1984,

---

[2] Criminology is certainly not alone in its renewed attempts to develop models incorporating both individual and group dynamics. For example, Ritzer (1988, p. 366) observes that there is a growing consensus that "the central problem in sociological theory is the study of the relationship between macroscopic and microscopic theories or levels of social reality."

p. 353), it is equally important for contextual analysis to be guided by a similar set of theoretically grounded assumptions concerning how group-level dynamics shape individual behavior. Unfortunately, these assumptions rarely are made explicit and, as Meier (1989) has argued, many efforts to integrate micro- and macrosociological theories of crime into a general model have not been successful because of a failure to fully specify the processes that operate within and between each level of analysis.

Erbring and Young (1980) nicely illustrate the implications of this failure in their critique of contextual models in which academic achievement is assumed to be a function of an individual's educational aspirations as well as the average aspiration level among the other students in the individual's classroom. If the mechanisms that link the group aspirations to individual performance are not specified, the effect of the group context on individual behavior appears to work through an almost magical form of "social telepathy" (p. 30). Erbring and Young argue that such models assume that group norms have an effect on individual behavior through structured patterns of social interaction and communication among members of a group, and propose a model of social contagion in which the social structure of the group becomes a central part of the model specification.

The problem of an assumed social telepathy also characterizes several of the central contextual models that have appeared in the criminological literature. Reiss and Rhodes (1961), for example, base the interpretation of their findings, in part, on the assumption that greater levels of interaction exist among members of different classes in neighborhoods with heterogeneous class structures than in homogeneous neighborhoods. A similar assumption characterizes Johnstone's (1978) contextual relative deprivation argument. Unfortunately, neither study incorporates this central causal mechanism in its model. In sum, it is impossible to evaluate the efficacy of a particular contextual model without an explicit theoretical specification of the mechanisms through which such contexts have an effect on individual behavior (Blalock, 1984) and the incorporation of indicators of these processes into one's model. However, the operationalization of these dynamics in a multilevel model can be extremely problematic. Two issues in particular deserve special consideration.

The Selection of an Appropriate Context

Munch and Smelser (1987, p. 357) provide a good working definition of group contexts as those structures in society that constitute both opportunities and constraints on individual behavior and interactions; a similar orientation is reflected in Coleman's (1986, p. 1310) emphasis on the institutional and structural settings that shape the incentives and actions of individuals. Unfortunately, an individual is a member of many different groups simultaneously: the family of procreation, the family of socialization, various peer groups, occupational groups, residential groups, status groups, and so forth. Often the incentives, opportunities, and constraints imposed by each of these groups are incompatible with one another, sometimes resulting in role strains and conflicts. In addition, many of these groups overlap or are nested within one another. Therefore, the selection of the appropriate group context for a particular individual behavior is not always straightforward.

For example, many criminologists assume that the etiology of juvenile delinquency cannot be fully understood without a consideration of the peer group context within which that behavior develops. As a result, a number of important studies of delinquency have included items pertaining to the illegal activities of the respondents' "close" friends (as in Elliott, Huizinga, & Ageton, 1985), "best" friends, friends with whom they associate most often, or friends whom they have known for the longest time (as in Akers, Krohn, Lanza-Kaduce, & Radosevich, 1979). However, Klein (1969) and Gold (1970) have presented evidence that delinquency is not necessarily committed in the company of one's best friends. Gold (1970, p. 91), for example, notes that only a third of the offenses reported by members of his sample were committed in the company of their most frequent companions. In addition, he finds that the most active delinquents had a more varied set of companions than the least delinquent youths. Thus, as Arnold and Brungardt (1983, pp. 179–184) argue, the peer group context is a particularly complex phenomenon in which small groups of friends form subsets of larger cliques of youth, which in turn may be characterized by transitory formal and informal alliances. Therefore, any analysis of the peer group context of individual delinquency requires a fairly sophisticated delineation of the nature of that context.

Similar problems also have characterized recent multilevel studies of criminal behavior, victimization, and recidivism that have been framed at the neighborhood level (see, e.g., Bursik, 1983; Gottfredson & Taylor, 1986; Gottfredson, McNeill, & Gottfredson, 1991; Kennedy & Forde, 1990; Miethe & McDowall, 1993; Simcha-Fagan & Schwartz, 1986; Smith & Jarjoura, 1989; Sampson & Groves, 1989; Sampson & Wooldredge, 1987). One longstanding criticism of such studies is that the boundaries used to operationalize the local community usually are defined by the Bureau of the Census or some other administrative agency. As Hunter (1974) notes, although such official definitions sometimes are congruent with the perceptions of local residents concerning the scope of the local community, this is not always the case. Rather, the concept of "the community" has a very symbolic dimension, representing a sense of "collective commonality" and shared physical space (p. 89). The degree to which the census tracts that often have been used in contextual studies are able to adequately represent the concept of the "neighborhood" is a question that has been largely unaddressed in such studies (see Bursik & Grasmick, 1993a, pp. 5–12).

Neighborhood-based contextual studies also have been plagued by inconsistencies in the size of the officially defined aggregations that have been used in the analyses. Gottfredson et al. (1991), for example, use census block groups that typically have a population of between 1,000 and 1,200 residents. In contrast, the research of Kennedy and Forde (1990) utilizes the census metropolitan areas of Canada to define the neighborhood contexts of individual behavior; these areas can range from 100,000 to over 2 million people. As a result, the contextual effects that have been estimated in such studies are affected to some unknown degree by aggregation bias, that is, the magnitudes and directions of the coefficients are partly dependent on the size of the contextual unit of analysis (see Moorman, 1980; Bailey, 1985). Therefore, it is possible that in some cases, the differences that have been found among contextual studies may simply represent the effects of the different definitions of the neighborhood contexts that have been utilized (see Farrington, 1993, p. 26).

There is a final, fairly subtle complication entailed in neighborhood-based contextual studies that is analogous to one that was noted for the peer group. Within most major urban areas, neighborhood boundaries typically overlap or are nested within the boundaries of other relevant geographic aggregations, such as school districts, political wards, and police precincts. Thus, a neighborhood-based contextual model may not represent the effects of local community dynamics per se but the effect of some other aggregate context that is partially coterminous with the neighborhood (Firebaugh, 1980, p. 19). In such situations, the attribution of a contextual effect to any particular characteristic of the local community and the interpretation of that effect is especially problematic.

The Selection of Appropriate Indicators of the Context

In one of the most influential methodological articles published during the 1970s, Robert Hauser (1970, p. 661) presented a strong criticism of the methods of contextual analysis that were dominant at that time within sociology. Recent developments in the nature of the statistical models used in contextual analysis have largely resolved many of the issues raised in his paper (see the second section of this chapter). Nevertheless, his comments concerning the choice of contextual indicators that are used in such research still are very pertinent.

The body of research examined by Hauser typically operationalized the group context by aggregating the individual characteristics of the members of the group. These *compositional* approaches to the creation of contextual indicators are reflected in such traditional variables as the median income and unemployment rate of a neighborhood, the socioeconomic composition of a school, and so forth. Hauser argues (1970, p. 659) that it is very dangerous to infer that the effects of such variables represent any kind of contextual dynamics since the differences among groups may simply reflect the differential distribution of individual characteristics within those groups.

In addition, as noted by Blalock (1984, p. 361), individuals with particular characteristics may locate themselves in those group contexts that are perceived as being supportive of such characteristics. Wilson and Herrnstein (1985, p. 291) argue, for example, that certain types of neighborhoods attract persons predisposed to criminality. Sampson (1987, p. 97) has referred to this phenomenon as "selective aggregation." Criticisms of contextual analysis on the basis of such selective processes are analogous to those made of differential association that argue that involvement in illegal activity precedes membership in delinquent groups. In such a situation, the group has no actual effect on individual behavior, although a poorly specified model may suggest incorrectly that such is the case (see Liska, 1973).

Situations exist, however, in which compositional indicators may provide important information concerning the normative or structural "climate" that group members experience (Blalock, 1984, p. 359). Simcha-Fagan and Schwartz (1986), for example, use compositional measures to draw conclusions concerning structural constraints on the development of social bonds and, in turn, delinquency. In these models, however, it is necessary to control for the individual-level characteristic represented in the compositional effect. Through such controls, Simcha-Fagan and Schwartz were able to determine that both the socioeconomic status of the respondent *and* the economic status of the community in which that respondent lives have independent and significant effects on the level of officially recorded delinquency. Similarly, Smith and Jarjoura (1989, p. 632) use a compositional approach to show that when controls are made for the racial composition of a neighborhood, there is no relationship between the race of the house-holder and victimization.

Although compositional variables are still the most common contextual indicators used in multilevel models, another class of group properties does not represent a simple aggregation of individual attributes. These characteristics are referred to by a variety of terms, such as systemic qualities (Eisenstadt & Helle, 1985; Coleman, 1987), macroproperties (Munch & Smelser, 1987), structural qualities (Blau, 1981), integral variables (Boyd & Iverson, 1979), or, more commonly, emergent properties (Harré, 1981). The concept of emergent properties assumes that there are characteristics of the whole that are not manifested by any of its parts when considered independently (Harré, 1981, p. 142), and can be traced to Durkheim's arguments concerning the existence of "social facts." For example, Blau (1964) and Schelling (1978) have developed fascinating arguments concerning the complex processes by which unforeseen social structures may develop when people are responding to an environment that consists of other people responding to their own environment (Schelling, 1978, p. 14).

Although most sociologists take the existence of emergent properties for granted, the concept has provoked some extremely heated debates within the social sciences. Cartwright and Zander (1968, p. 12) note that during the 1920s psychology was characterized by a conflict between the "institutionalists," who assumed that groups had a reality apart from the particular individuals who participated in them, and the "behavioral scientists," who assumed that groups were only "abstractions from collections of individual organisms." More recently, the same issues were raised in a series of articles in which Parsons (1964) and Homans (1971) debated the existence of emergent properties (see the discussion of Ritzer, 1988). As Cartwright and Zander note (1968, p. 12), this conflict involves a philosophical resolution of the nature of reality; thus, the "true" answer will always remain moot.

Nevertheless, many emergent contextual variables exist that are extremely promising for criminology, such as the communication structure and level of social cohesion in a group, the degree of normative and compositional heterogeneity in a group, and so forth. One of the finest illustrations of this potential is found in the classic study of Cloward and Ohlin (1960), which argues that the nature of the adolescent delinquency that occurs within a particular neighborhood will depend on the structures of legitimate and illegitimate opportunities that exist in that neighborhood, and the articulation between those opportunity structures.

Unfortunately, it is often difficult to collect data that facilitate the incorporation of indicators of emergent properties into contextual models. At times this is because the relevant individual-level data are not available. For example, the orientation of Messner and Tardiff's (1986) study of inequality and homicide is explicitly contextual, arguing that there is a "chain of postulated psychological processes which translate objective conditions of inequality into motivations for criminal attack" (p. 299). However, since individual-level data were not available, they were forced to utilize data collected at the neighborhood level. Thus, although the theoretical argument was contextual, the analysis was not.

More commonly, the measurement of the emergent properties presents the problem. For example, the theory of social disorganization is grounded in such emergent properties as the structure of interaction networks among the residents of a neighborhood, the viability of local neighborhood organizations as agencies of informal social control, the linkages among these organizations, the political power base of the neighborhood, and the relationship of the local community to the wider urban community. Although case studies of a small number of neighborhoods have successfully examined these emergent issues (such as Suttles, 1968), it is extremely costly to collect the relevant data at the individual and group level in a large number of contexts. Thus, those few studies that have attempted to measure these properties have been forced to rely on compositional approximations. Sampson and Groves (1989), for example, utilize the average number of friends living within a 15-minute walk of the respondents' homes as an estimate of the scope of the interaction network in each of the 238 areas used in their analysis. While this operationalization represents a major improvement over earlier studies in the social disorganization framework (which typically had no measures of this key structural feature at all), its compositional features make it at best an indirect indicator of a complex emergent contextual property (Bursik & Grasmick, 1993a).

The measurement of emergent properties has fared somewhat better in contextual research that has been grounded in the routine activities theory of victimization. Contextual effects, in fact, are intrinsically central to this framework, for the model proposes that crime is more likely when a motivated offender and a suitable target converge in a particular location in the absence of a capable guardian (Felson & Cohen, 1980, pp. 392–393). Therefore, as Miethe and McDowall (1993) have noted, the routine activities perspective suggests that victimization is a function of an interaction between individual and locational (i.e., contextual) variables. While a number of victimization studies have analyzed compositional variables similar in spirit to those noted for Sampson and Groves, Miethe and McDowall create a variable called "busy places" that reflects the number of places available for public activity within three blocks of the resident's home. This approach avoids the problems that have been noted concerning compositional variables and is one of the clearest direct measurements of an emergent property found in the neighborhood literature.

Nevertheless, due to the problems that have been noted, most contextual analyses have been forced to rely strictly on compositional indicators. While such measures provide a great deal of information, many of the contextual effects that are implicit to the major theories of criminology involve strictly emergent properties of groups. Until such properties can be measured with a satisfactory degree of validity and reliability, contextual models will be misspecified in a very important sense and seriously limited in the contributions they can make to the growth of existing criminological theory.

Estimating the Contextual Model

The earliest sociological attempts to separate statistically the effects of individual and group processes on a dependent variable generally are recognized to be those of Blau (1960) and Davis, Spaeth, and Huson (1961; see the discussion of Boyd & Iverson, 1979). Although the techniques that they proposed could examine only a limited number of variables, were primarily developed for the examination of dichotomous variables, and were characterized by the problems addressed by Hauser, they provided a major impetus for the general interest in contextual modeling. With the widespread availability of powerful mainframe and personal computer software, much more sophisticated models are available to contemporary researchers.

Covariance Analysis

The covariance contextual approaches are statistically identical to the widely used analysis of covariance models in which the variation of a dependent variable is decomposed simultaneously in terms of both discrete and continuous variables. In the general contextual application, a set of dummy variables is created to represent all but one of the group contexts in question, while the continuous variables represent measurements of the individual processes under examination, that is,[3]

$$Y_{ij} = \alpha + \beta_1 X_{1ij} + \ldots + \beta_n X_{nij} + \delta_1 D_{ij} + \ldots \delta_j D_{ij} + \epsilon_{ij}$$

[3] In the discussion to follow, it is assumed that all of the equations have been theoretically well specified.

where Y_{ij} is the level of the dependent variable for person i in context j, α is the traditional constant term, X_{nij} is the measure of individual-level variable n for person i in context j, β_n represents the individual-level regression coefficient, D_{ij} equals 1 if person i is a member of context j and is 0 otherwise, and δ_j represents the effect of membership in group j on the dependent variable.

For example, assume that we are trying to predict the level of an individual's delinquency from a control theory perspective, and reliable and valid indicators are available for each of the primary bonds implied by the theory. In a purely individual-level analysis we would simply regress the rate of delinquency on these variables. However, we might additionally hypothesize that after controlling for the level of these bonds, delinquency tends to be higher in certain schools than others. We would therefore create a dummy variable for each of these schools (except for a single reference school) and include these variables in the equation. If the beta weights for any of these dummies are significant, we could conclude that something about the context of those schools has an effect on individual rates of delinquency over and above what could be predicted from the respondent's bonds.

The covariance approach has an obvious, intuitive appeal and, as Firebaugh (1980) has noted, it has a greater predictive power than any other contextual model because the dummy operationalization represents a composite of all possible group-level effects (see also Boyd & Iverson, 1979, p. 11). However, this is also an important drawback of the covariance approach, for it simply enables one to determine that an effect exists without providing any specific information concerning the nature of that effect. For example, in the illustration presented in the preceding paragraph, a contextual effect could represent many possible aspects of the school environment (such as the pupil/teacher ratio, quality of curriculum, internal gang activity, and so forth) that each have significantly different theoretical implications. For this reason, Boyd and Iverson (1979, p. 11) suggest that the covariance approach is most useful at the earliest stages of theoretical development in which one simply may want to document the existence of a contextual effect without specifying its nature.

A second problem with the covariance approach is that it is extremely cumbersome when a large number of contextual groups are under consideration. For example, if our fictitious school study had been conducted in a large metropolitan area such as New York, Los Angeles, or Chicago, there literally might be hundreds of dummy variables incorporated into the model. Not only would this make the interpretation of the effect difficult, but one also would expect that many of the individual school coefficients would be significant simply on the basis of chance (about 5 per 100). One might consider summarizing the effects of all the dummy variables by means of a single sheaf coefficient (Heise, 1972), but this provides even less information to the researcher. Not only is the particular nature of the effect unclear, but one is no longer able to determine the specific group context(s) in which the effect occurs.

Overall, the covariance approach is extremely limited as a model of contextual effects, being most appropriate during the early stages of model building when there are relatively few contexts under consideration.

Contextual Analysis

Given its traditional dominance in the literature, the term *contextual analysis* generally is reserved for the second major multilevel model (Firebaugh, 1980). Like covariance analysis, it is also a regression-based approach to the problem, but it requires that the researcher make specific theoretically derived predictions concerning the nature of the contextual effect. That is, rather than using a set of dummy variables, a series of specific compositional or emergent variables that represent these substantive predictions is included in the model, that is,

$$Y_{ij} = \alpha + \beta_1 X_{1ij} + \ldots + \beta_n X_{nij} + \gamma_1 Z_{1j} + \ldots + \gamma_m Z_{mj} + \epsilon_{ij}$$

where Y_{ij} is the level of the dependent variable for person i in context j, α is the traditional constant term, X_{nij} is the measure of individual-level variable n for person i in context j, β_n represents the individual-level regression coefficient, Z_{mj} is the value of compositional or emergent variables m in context j, and γ_m is the effect of Z_m on the dependent variable.

Although the contextual approach also has an intuitive simplicity, some care must be taken when compositional variables are used as indicators of the context to avoid the problem of selective aggregation. In general, if a compositional variable is used, its individual-level counterpart must also be included in the equation. For example, if the racial composition of the neighborhood is included in the model, a variable pertaining to the race of the individual must also be included. This is not a consideration when the emergent properties of the group context are examined, for they do not represent a simple aggregation of individual characteristics.

Since this operationalization of the context is more limited than that used in the covariance approach, it always will explain less variation in the dependent variable than the series of dummy variables. However, the theoretical contributions of the approach greatly outweigh this drawback, for the substantive sources of that variation are explicit. Nevertheless, researchers should be aware that the dangers of misspecification are especially relevant when using this approach to contextual analysis, for if the variables selected to represent the context are relatively poor indicators of the underlying theory, the existence of a contextual effect may be rejected prematurely (see the criticism of Farrington, 1993).

Both of the models that we have discussed to this point assume that the effect of the group context on the dependent variable is independent of the individual-level variables that are included in the model. Drawing from the work of Olweus (1977), Gottfredson and Taylor (1986, p. 153) have called this the "unidirectional" perspective in which the group context neither constrains nor accentuates the explanatory power of the individual-level variables. However, Blau (1960) has argued that the effects of the individual-level variables on the dependent variable may systematically differ, depending on the nature of the group context. Although relatively little work in criminology has examined this possibility, the work of Johnstone (1978), Bursik (1983), Gottfredson and Taylor (1986) and Miethe and McDowall (1993) all provide support for the interactive effects of individual and group dynamics on criminally related activity.

Such conditional considerations are easily incorporated into the contextual analysis model by introducing product terms between individual- and group-level variables into the equations, that is,

$$Y_{ij} = \alpha + \beta_n X_{nij} + \gamma_m Z_{mj} + \lambda_{nm} X_{nij} Z_{mj} + \epsilon_{ij}$$

where X_{nij} and Z_{mj} are defined as before, and λ_{nm} is the regression coefficient for the interaction term. One danger in such a specification, however, is that the number of interaction terms can become huge very easily. Therefore, as noted by Miethe and McDowall (1993), some of the coefficients associated with the interaction terms can be expected to be significant simply by chance.

The Hierarchical Linear Model (HLM)

Mason, Wong, and Entwisle (1983) show that the simple interactive model discussed at the end of the preceding section is a special case of the situation in which regression coefficients from individual-level equations estimated within each group are used as the dependent variables in an equation using only group characteristics as independent variables. Such "regression with random coefficients," "covariance component," or "multilevel linear" models have been discussed widely in the statistical literature, and were developed in part to meet the needs of a contextual analysis (see, e.g., Mason et al., 1983). Although these models are extremely powerful and flexible, most discussions of the estimation techniques have been highly technical. In addition, since the software necessary for such estimation was not widely accessible, a criminologist interested in the use of the multilevel models needed to have some fairly sophisticated programming skills. For example, the model discussed by Mason et al. entails an iterative, restricted maximum likelihood/Bayesian estimation procedure. As a result, although these techniques had a great deal of potential within criminology, they were not practical for the majority of analysts.

This situation has changed within the past few years for two reasons. First, a number of clear expositions of the multilevel model appeared that were accessible to a much broader audience than had been the case previously (see, e.g., Bryk & Raudenbush, 1987, 1992; Goldstein, 1987; Raudenbush, 1993). Second, it became much easier to obtain software written expressly for such analyses (see Bryk, Seltzer, & Congdon, 1986; Prosser, Rasbash, & Goldstein, 1991) and at least one major software package (BMDP) has included subroutines that make such analyses possible (although with a little effort) through the decomposition of variance components. As a result, there has been a growing interest in these models. We will focus our discussion on the hierarchical linear model (HLM) of Bryk and Raudenbush, for a number of papers using some variant of this technique have already appeared in the criminological literature (see, e.g., Bursik & Grasmick, 1992, 1993b; Raudenbush, 1993).[4]

The technique is hierarchical in the sense that a number of nested regression equations are estimated. The first stage is very similar to a fairly standard specification of the process under consideration at the individual level, that is,

$$Y_{ij} = \pi_{0j} + \pi_{1j}X_{ij} + \epsilon_{ij}$$

where Y_{ij} is the observation on the dependent variable for person i in context j, the X_{ij} represents a vector of explanatory variables for that same person, and π_{0j} and π_{1j} represent the regression coefficients. The central difference from the traditional specification is that the equation is estimated separately within each of the j contexts, leading to j values of the regression coefficients for each of the explanatory variables.

---

[4] For the ease of presentation, we will restrict our attention in this chapter to a 2-level model that focuses on individuals and contexts; the full 3-level specification incorporates data collected from the i individuals in j contexts at k points in time.

In the second stage, these coefficients themselves become the dependent variables, that is,

$$\pi_{0j} = \beta_{00} + \gamma_0 Z_j + \mu_{0j}$$
$$\pi_{1j} = \beta_{10} + \gamma_1 Z_j + \mu_{1j}$$

where π_{0j} and π_{1j} represent the coefficients estimated for each of the j groups in stage 1, and Z_j represents the level of a series of compositional or emergent variables in group j. The intercept term in the first equation is equivalent to the grand mean of the original Y_{ij}, while the intercepts in the subsequent equations represent the grand means of the j regression coefficients. The γ coefficients, therefore, represent the effect of the contextual variables on the direction and magnitude of the first-stage regression coefficients.

Inferences concerning the existence of contextual effects are made on the basis of a decomposition of the variance into within-context and between-contexts components. For example, in an illustration of the model, Raudenbush (1993) shows how such an approach can lead one to the conclusion that while there is not a great deal of variation among school contexts in initial mathematics ability, over 80% of the variation in the learning rate of mathematics can be attributed to contextual differences.

It is tempting to use ordinary least squares (OLS) techniques to estimate these equations and, in fact, if the intraclass correlations among the variables in question are zero, OLS models can be used (see the discussion of Goldstein, 1987, pp. 18–19). In the general case, however, the standard errors will be underestimated and the coefficients will be biased; the severity of this bias increases with the size of the sample in each of the contexts (see Goldstein as well as Raudenbush, 1993). Therefore, the software programs that have been written for such purposes use some variant of generalized least squares and an iterative maximum (or quasi-maximum) likelihood estimation procedure.

Unfortunately, the full possibilities of the HLM approach have not yet been explored in criminology. However, Rountree, Land, and Miethe presented a paper at the 1993 meetings of the American Society of Criminology in which the model is used to find that neighborhood characteristics such as average family income and neighborhood deterioration are significantly related to the nature of the relationships between violent victimization and individual-level risk factors. In addition, there are several major studies that have been designed with just such models in mind, such as the Chicago Neighborhood Project (directed by William J. Wilson), the Denver Youth Study (directed by Delbert Elliott), and the Program on Human

Development and Criminal Behavior (directed by Felton Earls and Albert J. Reiss, Jr.; for a description of these three projects, see Sampson, 1993). Many in the criminological community are anxious to see the degree to which the HLM models live up to their high degree of promise.

Contextual Models of Criminal Behavior

Given the historical development of the dominant theories of criminology and the relative simplicity of the appropriate contextual models themselves, one would expect that multilevel studies would occupy a large, visible, and central position in criminological research. However, this definitely is not the case, for only a handful of truly contextual studies have been conducted since 1960 despite the availability of hardware and software that could make such analyses commonplace. This situation is easily explained: although the analyses themselves may be very straightforward, the collection of the appropriate data is not.

These complications arise because contextual studies necessitate a multistage sampling design, that is, groups and individuals within groups. The easiest solution is to rely on large files of officially collected data, such as those typically compiled by police departments or court systems. Many of these files assign each individual coming in contact with that agency a unique identification that remains constant over time. Through these numbers it is possible to derive individual-level measures of the total number of arrests, referrals, and so forth, that have occurred during a particular period of time. More important, when such files pertain to a large jurisdiction, these records often make it possible to classify the individuals into a large number of subunits that are relevant for contextual analysis. For example, the residential address is usually noted on each record, making it possible to group the observations into local communities. Thus, with a little bit of computer manipulation, the effects of many neighborhood contexts on the delinquent or criminal behavior of their residents can be easily examined.

Of course, the problematic nature of official records has been widely discussed in the literature. When used in a multilevel analysis, a further complication arises in that the discretionary behavior of agents of social control may depend systematically on the nature of the context. Smith (1986), for example, has presented evidence that all other factors being equal, police are more likely to make arrests in lower-class neighborhoods. Thus, what may appear to be a contextual effect in a model using such records may actually reflect the operation of an unmeasured variable (the use of police discretion) that is strongly correlated with the neighborhood context. Such possibilities must be considered carefully before contextual inferences can be made.

One obvious solution to this problem is to utilize an alternative source of crime/delinquency data such as self-reported approaches. This presents no special problems when only a limited number of contexts are under consideration. However, when the population of potential contexts is large (such as in the case of neighborhoods or schools), other very serious problems arise, for the researcher needs to sample both a representative sample of contexts and, within each context, a representative sample of respondents. For example, the data used in Johnstone's (1978) contextual analysis of 221 census tracts averaged just over five respondents per tract, which made it impossible to obtain reliable estimates of the patterns that existed within each tract. Conversely, Simcha-Fagan and Schwartz (1986) were able to collect data from a relatively large and representative sample within each of the neighborhoods included in their study, but had to restrict the number of neighborhoods to 12 census tracts, which is a relatively small percentage of the total number of tracts in New York City.

These problems arise because the collection of data from a large group of respondents within each of a large number of contexts can be extremely expensive and has complicated logistical problems. Perhaps the best sampling design in this respect is that found in Miethe and McDowall (1993), who analyze data collected from 5,302 adults living on 600 city blocks in 100 of the 121 census tracts of Seattle. In other studies, however, the generalizability of the findings is not clear. For example, while Smith and Jarjoura (1989) collected data from 9,006 households in 57 different neighborhoods located in three different standard metropolitan statistical areas (SMSAs), no information is provided concerning the representativeness of either the households or target neighborhoods.

In general, most studies have cautioned the reader that less than ideal sampling designs may jeopardize the representativeness of the data and findings (see the discussion of Gottfredson et al., 1991). Johnstone (1978), for example, reclassified his 221 census tracts into nine groups that had similar economic characteristics. Likewise, Simcha-Fagan and Schwartz (1986) developed measures of the neighborhood level of family disorganization and neighborhood social rank on the basis of all the census tracts in New York, cross-classified these dimensions, and selected communities from within each cell of the table. Nevertheless, the practical limitations of their budget made it necessary to eliminate census tracts in which Hispanics constituted over 20% of the population (a major limitation in New York City).

Thus, almost all of the studies that truly can be classified as having a contextual orientation have been forced to utilize study designs that are less than optimal. However, despite such limitations, these studies have provided some important insights into the processes through which a group context may constrain, accelerate, or modify individual-level processes related to crime and delinquency. In general, they may be classified into four general groups.

The Socioeconomic Context
of the Neighborhood and Delinquent Behavior

Many of the central theories of illegal behavior are grounded in a presumed relationship between social class and criminality. Thus, it is no surprise that two of the earliest and most widely cited contextual studies focused directly on this association.[5] The primary focus of the seminal study of Reiss and Rhodes (1961) is on the relative effects of "ascribed social status" (an individual-level indicator measured by the occupation of the head of the household) and the "social status structure" of that individual's school (a compositional contextual variable created by aggregating the ascribed social statuses of the pupils in that school) on the likelihood that male juveniles are referred to juvenile court in Davidson County (Nashville), Tennessee.[6]

Their analysis focuses on the range of delinquency rates associated with the individual and contextual indicators of socioeconomic status, and they

---

[5] See Braithwaite (1979) for a review of early analyses of the socioeconomic characteristics of neighborhood contexts.

[6] Reiss and Rhodes argue (pp. 722, 725) that this contextual indicator generally reflects the residential community in which that school is located, and their discussion of the findings is oriented along these lines. However, McDonald (1969, p. 37) notes that the school itself represents an important contextual factor in that the students are affected by the "prevailing attitudes and customs" of that social environment. Since the validity of the school-based measure as an indicator of neighborhood social status is not empirically examined by Reiss and Rhodes, it may have been more appropriate for them to frame their discussion along these lines.

In addition, Reiss and Rhodes examine the effect of the delinquency rate of the neighborhood of residence on individual levels of illegal behavior. However, this analysis is secondary to the primary orientation of this essay. It should also be noted that Reiss and Rhodes also collected self-reported data, although they are not used in the contextual analysis of this chapter.

conclude that the status structure of the school has a stronger effect on the likelihood of delinquency than the youth's ascribed social status. In addition, they present a very strong argument that the effect of the ascribed social status depends on this context, noting that "the occupational structure of the school 'virtually eliminates' the risk of being a delinquent of court record for low status boys in schools with a predominantly high status student body and substantially increases the risk of a low status boy in a predominantly low status school" (p. 725).

By modern analytic standards, the contextual model of Reiss and Rhodes is fairly crude in that no tests of significance or measures of association are presented. Therefore, their determination of the relative effects of ascribed status, contextual status, and their interaction is based on a nonstatistical (although persuasive) analysis of the data. Nevertheless, the Reiss and Rhodes piece has played a central role in the development of contextual models in criminology, for it is generally recognized as the first to suggest empicially that the group context provides a source of relevant information for the analysis of criminal behavior.

Shortly after the appearance of the Reiss and Rhodes paper, Clark and Wenninger (1962) published a related research note that examined the relative effects of individual and neighborhood socioeconomic status on delinquency in four communities in northern Illinois selected on the basis of their "unique social class structure" (p. 828). Clark and Wenninger then administered a self-reported instrument to 1,154 sixth- to 12th-grade students enrolled in the public school systems of these industrial, lower-class urban, upper-class urban, and rural farm areas.

Like the research of Reiss and Rhodes, the Clark and Wenninger analysis was limited by the available technology of the time: Wilcoxian matched-pairs signed ranks tests were used to examine interclass differences in delinquency rates within each of the communities (p. 832). Clark and Wenninger concluded that the social class of the individual is generally unrelated to delinquent behavior, arguing that "there are community-wide norms which are related to illegal behavior and to which juveniles adhere regardless of their social class origins" (p. 833).

Although the work of Clark and Wenninger suggests that the likelihood of juvenile delinquency is primarily a function of the socioeconomic context of the community and not the individual status of the adolescent, this finding must be considered with extreme caution. They note (footnote 24) that because of the small within-class sample sizes in three of the communities, certain categories of ascribed social status had to be either collapsed or ignored; these are the same three communities in which their statistical tests find no significant class-related differences in delinquent behavior. However, there was a sufficient number of respondents in each of the class categories within the industrial city, and two of the three interclass comparisons made in this community were significant.

Overall, therefore, it is difficult to reach any firm conclusions concerning the nature of contextual effects on the basis of the Clark and Wenninger study. Evidence is presented for at least one community that both the individual characteristics and the community context have independent effects on the likelihood of delinquency. The restrictions imposed by the small sample sizes within each class in the other three communities make it nearly impossible to evaluate the contextual hypothesis.

Since the Reiss and Rhodes and Clark and Wenninger papers appeared within one year of each other, it appeared as if contextual models were emerging as an important analytic approach within criminology. However, such a conclusion would have been very premature, for the next major contextual study did not appear until 16 years later. In 1978, Johnstone took an explicitly conditional approach to the contextual effect of socioeconomic status, arguing that "actors who share the same ascribed status may behave differently in different types of social environments" (p. 50). As noted earlier in this section, although he collected data from 221 census tracts, the average number of respondents in each community was very small. Therefore, he trichotomized the individual and community measures of status and cross-classified the variables to produce a 9-cell "property space."

Johnstone ranked these nine combinations of individual and areal socioeconomic status on the basis of the relative delinquency rates that were predicted by various theories, and computed the rank-order coefficients of these predicted rankings and the rankings empirically determined on the basis of data collected from 1,124 (weighted to 1,237) 14- to 18-year-olds residing in the Chicago SMSA. He concludes that for automobile-related, property, drug-related, and status offenses, additive models do not adequately predict the ranking of the individual and contextual combinations. However, conditional models fit the observed data well.

Both the Reiss and Rhodes and the Johnstone studies suggest that the likelihood of delinquency partially reflects an interaction of individual and contextual processes. However, these studies reach diametrically opposed conclusions concerning the nature of those effects. While Reiss and Rhodes argue that individual rates of delinquency are determined largely by the behavior of the dominant class of an area, Johnstone concludes that living in a middle-class area accelerates the rate of delinquency committed by lower-class individuals due to processes of relative deprivation. Unfortunately, the data analyzed in these two studies were collected in very different sections of the country during very different historical periods, the operationalizations of individual and contextual socioeconomic status are not consistent, and extremely different analytic techniques were used. Therefore, it is nearly impossible to evaluate the relative merits of these two positions on the basis of the studies that have been discussed in this section.

Other Neighborhood Contexts of Delinquent Behavior

As might be deduced from the preceding discussion, the examination of socioeconomic status has been a central theme of contextual models in criminology. However, community context is also a central component of other, not necessarily economic, theories of delinquent behavior. Earlier in this chapter, for example, we noted the explicitly contextual aspects of the Cloward and Ohlin thesis. Similarly, Kornhauser (1978, pp. 104–118) has noted that the community context is a central theme in Shaw and McKay's formulation of social disorganization. Likewise, the existence of community variation in normative standards of behavior is an assumption of most cultural theories of crime and delinquency. Recently, several important studies have incorporated the contextual assumptions implicit to these theories directly into multilevel models of juvenile delinquency.[7]

In her very ambitious dissertation, Marsden (1982) examined the contextual and individual-level causal processes implied by the social disorganization and cultural deviance models of crime and delinquency using data collected from a statewide survey of 3,098 adolescents aged 14 to 18 residing in 175 Illinois communities in 1972.[8] These self-reported data are supplemented by aggregate-level official delinquency data for each community obtained from the Illinois Bureau of Identification. In addition, census materials were used to obtain indicators of a wide variety of commu-

[7] In this section we will not consider the recent work of Shannon (1984, 1988) in which he examines the development of delinquent and criminal careers within neighborhood contexts since he does not simultaneously consider characteristics of the individual and the community. However, his description of the data suggests that such analyses would be possible.

[8] Marsden also examines social structural approaches to delinquency. However, since her explication of that theory focuses on perceptions of the social structure and not community contexts per se, that aspect of her work will not be discussed here. Johnstone's analysis of communities in the Chicago SMSA is based on a subset of this data set.

nity characteristics, such as size, density, racial/ethnic heterogeneity, socio-economic level, occupational structure, family structure, residential stability, quality of housing, and characteristics of the adolescent population.

The particular indicators used in Marsden's social disorganization and cultural deviance models were selected on the basis of the central theoretical themes of these two approaches. For example, the contextual variables for social disorganization reflect community differentiation and change in the community between 1960 and 1970, which are the basic components of the Shaw and McKay model (see Kornhauser, 1978). Her individual-level indicators pertain to the bonding of these youth to local social institutions such as the family, school, and religious organizations, which is congruent with the control theory of Hirschi (1969). Marsden presents evidence (pp. 77–87) that the community has a small but significant role in delinquency causation, and that this effect varies by gender and type of delinquency, concluding that "delinquent behavior is more highly associated with a youth's attachment to social institutions than it is to the community context."

Marsden's cultural deviance model examines two different aspects of the community context: the level of crime in the community and the structural characteristics of that community. The structural characteristics are assumed to have a direct effect on delinquency, and an indirect effect through the delinquency of the peer group, the individual's tolerance for deviance, and the community level of crime. Like the studies discussed in the preceding section, she finds evidence that the relation of social class to delinquency depends on the level of poverty in the community (p. 129). Overall, however, she concludes that the community context has a primarily indirect effect on delinquency through its association with the delinquency of the respondent's peers and the respondent's tolerance for deviance, and that the relationship of the community context to delinquency is "limited" (p. 143) and "far less important" than either model would predict (p. 144).

The contextual model of Simcha-Fagan and Schwartz (1986) also examines the viability of the social disorganization and cultural deviance theories. As previously noted, their study analyzes the self-reported and official levels of delinquency of 553 adolescents living in 12 New York City neighborhoods. Like Marsden, Simcha-Fagan and Schwartz utilize census materials to create a series of compositional contextual variables pertaining to the economic level and residential stability of the neighborhoods. However, they supplement their primary data collection efforts with a survey of the respondents' mothers that focused on the informal structure of the community (e.g., the extent of neighboring and the strength of personal ties to the neighbors), the existence of disorder and criminal subcultures in the neighborhood (e.g., the existence of illegal economies), and organization-al participation. Not only do these indicators provide an excellent source of information concerning dimensions of social disorganization and cultural deviance that are extremely difficult to address in traditional study designs, but they also enable Simcha-Fagan and Schwartz to examine characteristics of the neighborhoods that are similar in spirit to the concept of emergent properties.

Overall, Simcha-Fagan and Schwartz find that although the contextual characteristics are significantly related to self-reported, officially recorded, and severe self-reported delinquency, the amounts of variation uniquely associated with these variables range only from 2% to 4% after controlling for individual-level characteristics. Therefore, they conclude that the effect of the neighborhood context on delinquency is primarily indirect, being mediated through the socialization experiences within the community (p. 695).[9]

Similar conclusions are drawn by Gottfredson and her colleagues (1991) in their study of 3,729 students attending middle school or junior high in four different areas: five schools were in urban centers located in Charleston or Baltimore, three were in suburban areas of Charleston or Kalamazoo, one in a farming community outside Charleston, and one in Christiansted, St. Croix. The relevant contexts represented the 321 different block groups or enumeration districts in which the students resided. On the basis of a factor analysis of a number of indicators drawn from the census, Gottfred-son et al. create two contextual variables, one pertaining to the disorganiza-tion of the neighborhood (i.e., the percentage of female-headed house-holds, the percentage of welfare recipients, the unemployment rate, the divorce rate, and the percentage living below the poverty level) and the other pertaining to an affluence/education dimension.

The findings of Gottfredson et al. also provide very little support for the existence of independent neighborhood effects. For males, the level of disorganization is related to drug dealing and the affluence factor is re-lated to a measure of theft and vandalism. For females, the disorganization factor only was related to aggression. Yet, while all of these effects are extremely small, these findings must be considered with a great deal of

[9] Although Simcha-Fagan and Schwartz do not test for the presence of interaction effects between individual and community characteristics, they do note that such an effect is suggested by the social disorganization model.

caution (as noted by the authors). First, the ages of the typical respondents generally do not reflect the peak periods of adolescent offending, as is the case in most other studies. Second, the data appear to have been collected in a school setting, and such studies have often been criticized in that the most active delinquents also are most likely to be truant on the day of the data collection. Third, questions have been raised about the comparability of the causal processes that exist in these four general areas, although the authors report that they did not detect any significant heterogeneity in the regression equations. Finally, and most important, the authors make it clear that the analysis is grounded in a convenience sample that is representative neither of the schools nor school-aged population of the nation (p. 205). Therefore, while the empirical patterns are highly suggestive, they certainly cannot be considered definitive.

At least one study based on non-U.S. data also does not provide strong support for the contextual effects argument. Sampson and Groves (1989) analyze data drawn from the 1982 British Crime Survey, in which nearly 11,000 respondents residing in 238 electoral wards and polling districts were interviewed. They create all their contextual variables by aggregating the survey responses to the neighborhood level. Thus, in addition to such traditional considerations as the stability, socioeconomic composition, and the racial/ethnic heterogeneity of a neighborhood, they also are able to examine the effects of such key contextual considerations as the scope of local friendship relational networks, the degree of organizational participation in the neighborhood, and the supervisory capacity in the area.

Sampson and Groves find that the effects of the traditional ecological variables on crime are primarily indirect, being mediated primarily through the degree to which unsupervised peer groups exist in the area. In addition, relatively high rates of family disruptions make property crime (but not personal crime) more likely while extensive friendship networks decrease the rate of such behavior. Nevertheless, as in the case of the Simcha-Fagan and Schwartz and Gottfredson et al. studies, these effects are fairly small. In a later, more extended discussion of such findings, Sampson (1993) proposes that the effects of neighborhood dynamics on individual behavior may primarily be indirect, mediated by "the monitoring of youth activities and time spent with peers, networks between parents and their children's friends and parents, and the effective and consistent discipline of children" (p. 165).

While fairly minor direct effects have been found in the studies that have been discussed, Farrington (1993) cautions that the relevance of such effects should not be prematurely dismissed due to less than optimal definitions of the neighborhood, the relatively weak measurement of key contextual variables, and the lack of longitudinal and experimental studies. Farrington's point concerning the lack of longitudinal contextual research is a very important one, for Reiss (1993) has argued that such studies require an explicitly dynamic orientation at both the aggregate and individual level. This contention is underscored by some preliminary findings presented by Loeber and Wikstrom (1993), who provide evidence that the neighborhood contexts significantly shape the developmental patterns of illegality engaged in by local juveniles. Therefore, we find Farrington's assessment to be compelling, suggesting that we still know relatively little about the interplay of community dynamics and individual processes of illegal behavior.

Neighborhood Contexts
and the Likelihood of Victimization

While the estimated contextual effects associated with criminal behavior have tended to be fairly weak or nonexistent, this is not the case in the victimization literature. Perhaps this should not be surprising since most studies have been grounded in the routine activities/lifestyle framework, which is intrinsically multilevel in its theoretical specification (see Hindelang, Gottfredson, & Garafalo, 1978, pp. 270–271).

The first major study of victimization with an explicitly contextual statistical orientation is most likely that of Cohen, Kluegel, and Land (1981), who base their analyses on 1974 and 1977 LEAA National Crime Surveys. In addition to using individually based measures of income, race, age, and lifestyle, Cohen et al. operationalize proximity to motivated offenders by categorizing the respondents on the basis of the median incomes of their neighborhoods and the size of the urban areas in which they resided. While the estimated effects associated with these two contextual variables are fairly small, they did show that proximity to the central city and to low-income areas increases the risk of predatory victimization.

Contextual analyses appear to have become an essential component of victimization research by 1987, when one of the most influential studies in the area was published. In the first of a series of studies based on the 1982 British Crime Survey, Sampson and Wooldredge (1987) create a wide range of neighborhood contextual variables that they use to analyze the likelihood of household and individual victimization: the percentage of primary individual households, the percentage of households with children under 16 living with only one parent, the unemployment rate, the percentage of housing units in the area comprised of apartments, a neighborhood social cohesion scale, the percentage of households with a VCR, the percentage of households in the area that are empty for more than 6 hours during the daylight hours, the area cash flow, and the amount of street activity. One or more of these contextual variables was related to the four kinds of victimization considered in the study; the effects of neighborhood unemployment and housing density were especially strong (see also the related findings of Sampson & Groves, 1989; Sampson & Lauritsen, 1990).

Similar patterns were uncovered by Smith and Jarjoura (1989) on the basis of the same data set analyzed in their 1988 research. For example, they present evidence that after controlling for individual-level features of household, the risk of burglary victimization is strongly related to racial heterogeneity, residential instability, the age composition of the neighborhood, the percentage of single-parent households, the median community income, and the level of social cohesion. Further confirmation of contextual effects is provided by Kennedy and Forde's (1990) analysis of Canadian data.

While such accumulated evidence suggests that the incorporation of neighborhood characteristics into individual-level models of victimization significantly increases the explanatory power of such models, they are limited in the sense that there have been few attempts to explore the degree to which victimization is a function of an interaction between individual and community dynamics. Thus, they assume that the effect of certain lifestyle characteristics on the likelihood of victimization is not contingent on the nature of the area in which those characteristics are imbedded. One important study that has questioned this orientation is that of Miethe and McDowall (1993), who document that after controlling for individual-level factors, the risk of violent victimization is significantly higher in neighborhoods with relatively high numbers of places for public activity and poor socioeconomic conditions. Such poor conditions are also shown to be related to the risk of becoming a burglary victim.

In the second step of their analysis, Miethe and McDowall examine the degree to which such contextual factors interact with individual characteristics to further increase the likelihood of victimization. While they find that the effects of individual determinants of risk for violent crime were relatively constant across different neighborhood contexts, this was not the case with burglary. Rather, measures of target attractiveness and guardianship substantially altered the risks of victimization in more affluent and less busy neighborhoods, but had a minimal impact in more disorganized areas (pp. 752–754). Confirmation of conditional effects were observed in the HLM analyses conducted on these same data (Rountree et al., 1993).

Neighborhood Contexts
and the Likelihood of Recidivism

The final set of studies to be discussed in this chapter have a somewhat more specialized orientation than those that have been described in the two preceding sections. Rather than focusing on the likelihood of delinquent or criminal behavior in general, these studies examine the effect of the neighborhood context on the likelihood that sanctioned offenders will become recidivists. Bursik (1983, p. 169), for example, argues that while the perceived costs of potential future sanctions may be an important consideration in the decision to become a recidivist, the community may be used as a general referent in the calculation of the costs and benefits of engaging in further delinquency. Therefore, he argues that the effectiveness of official sanctions depends on the neighborhood context of the offender.

Bursik examines this proposition on the basis of the subsequent court referral histories of 938 juveniles who were referred to the Cook County Juvenile Court system for the first time in 1978. In addition to the ethnicity, gender, living situation, and age of the offender, Bursik considers the effects of two compositional dimensions of the neighborhood context. The first reflects the rate of police contacts and court referrals in the neighborhood. The second pertains to the community-specific probabilities that a police contact leads to an arrest and that a court referral results in a filed petition. Bursik's analysis indicates that the contextual probability of official action affects both the likelihood of recidivism and the length of time between the imposition of the initial sanction and the subsequent court referral. In addition, he finds that, in general, sanction effectiveness depends on this aspect of the neighborhood context.

A more recent examination of the recidivism issue conducted by Gottfredson and Taylor (1986) is one of the most conceptually and analytically sophisticated contextual approaches of all the studies that have been discussed in this chapter. Gottfredson and Taylor examine the offense histories of approximately 500 offenders who had been released from incarceration into one of 67 randomly selected neighborhoods in Baltimore. The subsequent behavior of these subjects was monitored for the occurrence of an arrest, the time elapsed until that arrest, and the nature of the illegal activity.

The primary consideration of Gottfredson and Taylor concerned those physical characteristics of the neighborhood environment that make recidivism most likely. In order to capture this information, they collected additional data pertaining to the structural aspects of the block on which the potential recidivist resided (e.g., the number of dwellings, percent residential versus commercial street frontage), the physical appearance of the block, the predominant type of land use, and the social climate (e.g., group size and sex of people hanging out); they refer to this cluster of variables as "social decay." However, they recognized that other aspects of the local environment might also be related to the likelihood of recidivism. To capture this variation, they also utilized a covariance approach to contextual analysis by regressing the various indicators of recidivism on 66 dummy variables, and constructing a sheaf coefficient to reflect the effects of these unmeasured contextual variables.

In general, although the main effects of the social decay variables were unrelated to any of the indicators of recidivism, significant interactions with the individual characteristics of the offender emerged for three of the four indicators of recidivism, resulting in R^2 increments ranging from 5% to 13%. In addition, the sheaf coefficient was significantly related to all four indicators and was associated with R^2 increments ranging from 4% to 12%.

Overall, the models of recidivism of Bursik and Gottfredson and Taylor indicate that a consideration of contextual effects leads to a significant increase in explanatory power. While both studies caution that a full understanding of the relationship will necessitate more sophisticated measures of the pertinent neighborhood dynamics, they both clearly underscore the pertinence of such dynamics to the evaluation of sanction effectiveness.

Summary

In this chapter we have tried to emphasize the relevance of contextual models to the growth of criminological theory. Such models present special problems of theoretical specification, measurement, and analysis that are not present in studies that focus on only a single level of analysis and, consequently, only a handful of studies have addressed the contextual effect issue. While the results that have emerged tend to support the contextual hypothesis, the magnitudes of some of these effects have been fairly weak. However, due to the sporadic nature of these studies and the variety of study designs and analytic techniques that have been used in such research, any general conclusions concerning the nature of contextual effects would be very premature. Nevertheless, most of the major contemporary criminological paradigms are at least implicitly contextual, and, as Reiss (1986) has argued, the development of a "full criminology" depends on the resolution of these problems. Until such analytic issues receive a wider degree of attention within the discipline, our understanding of the dynamics of criminal behavior may be significantly incomplete and potentially misleading.

REFERENCES

Akers, R. L., Krohn, M. K., Lanza-Kaduce, L., & Radosevich, M. (1979). Social learning and deviant behavior: A specific test of a general theory. *American Sociological Review, 44,* 636–655.

Arnold, W. R., & Brungardt, T. M. (1983). *Juvenile misconduct and delinquency.* Boston: Houghton Mifflin.

Bailey, W. C. (1985). Aggregation and disaggregation in cross-sectional analyses of crime rates: The case of states, SMSAs and cities. Paper presented at the annual meetings of the American Society of Criminology, San Diego.

Blalock, H. M. (1984). Contextual effects models: Theoretical and methodological issues. *Annual Review of Sociology, 10,* 353–372.

Blau, P. M. (1960). Structural effects. *American Sociological Review, 25,* 178–193.

Blau, P. M. (1964). *Exchange and power in everyday life.* New York: Wiley.

Blau, P. M. (1981). Behavioral *sociology* or *behavioral* sociology? *American Sociologist, 16,* 170–171.

Boyd, L. H., Jr., & Iverson, G. R. (1979). *Contextual analysis: Concepts and statistical techniques.* Belmont: Wadsworth.

Braithwaite, J. (1979). *Inequality, crime and public policy.* London: Routledge & Kegan Paul.

Bryk, A. S., & Raudenbush, S. W. (1987). Applications of hierarchical linear models to assessing change. *Psychological Bulletin, 101,* 147–158.

Bryk, A. S., & Raudenbush, S. W. (1992). *Hierarchical linear models.* Newbury Park: Sage.

Bryk, A. S., Seltzer, M., & Congdon, R. T. (1986). *An introduction to HLM: Computer program and user's guide.* University of Chicago.

Bursik, R. J., Jr. (1983). Community context and the deterrent effect of sanctions. In G. P. Whitaker & C. D. Phillips (Eds.), *Evaluating performance of criminal justice agencies.* Beverly Hills: Sage.

Bursik, R. J., Jr. (1988). Social disorganization and theories of crime and delinquency: Problems and prospects. *Criminology, 26,* 514–551.

Bursik, R. J., Jr., & Grasmick, H. G. (1992). Longitudinal neighborhood profiles in delinquency: The decomposition of change. *Journal of Quantitative Criminology, 8,* 247–263.

Bursik, R. J., Jr., & Grasmick, H. G. (1993a). *Neighborhoods and crime: The dimensions of effective community control.* New York: Lexington.

Bursik, R. J., Jr., & Grasmick, H. G. (1993b). Methods of studying community change in the rate and pattern of crime. In D. P. Farrington, R. J. Sampson, & P-O. H. Wikstrom (Eds.), *Integrating individual and ecological aspects of crime* (pp. 241–258). Stockholm: National Council for Crime Prevention.

Cartwright, D., & Zander, A. (1968). *Group dynamics: Research and theory* (3rd ed.). New York: Harper & Row.

Clark, J. P., & Wenninger, E. P. (1962). Socioeconomic class and area as correlates of illegal behavior among juveniles. *American Sociological Review, 27,* 826–834.

Cloward, R. A., & Ohlin, L. (1960). *Delinquency and opportunity.* New York: Free Press.

Cohen, L. E., Kluegel, J. R., & Land, K. C. (1981). Social inequality and predatory criminal victimization: An exposition and test of a formal theory. *American Sociological Review, 46,* 505–524.

Coleman, J. S. (1986). Social theory, social research and a theory of action. *American Journal of Sociology, 91,* 1309–1335.

Coleman, J. S. (1987). Microfoundations and macrosocial behavior. In J. C. Alexander, B. Giesen, R. Munch, & N. J. Smelser (Eds.), *The micro-macro link.* Berkeley: University of California Press.

Davis, J. A., Spaeth, J. L., & Huson, C. (1961). A technique for analyzing the effects of group composition. *American Sociological Review, 26,* 215–225.

Eisenstadt, S. N., & Helle, H. J. (Eds.). (1985). *Macro-sociological perspectives: Perspectives on sociological theory.* Vol. 1. Beverly Hills: Sage.

Elliott, D. S., Huizinga, D. & Ageton, S. S. (1985). *Explaining delinquency and drug use.* Beverly Hills: Sage.

Erbring, L. & Young, A. A. (1980). Individuals and social structure: Contextual effects as endogenous feedback. In E. F. Borgatta & D. J. Jackson (Eds.), *Aggregate data: Analysis and interpretation.* Beverly Hills: Sage.

Farrington, D. P. (1993). Have any individual, family or neighborhood influences on offending been demonstrated conclusively? In D. P. Farrington, R. J. Sampson, & P-O. H. Wikstrom (Eds.), *Integrating individual and ecological aspects of crime* (pp. 7–38). Stockholm: National Council for Crime Prevention.

Felson, M., & Cohen, L. E. (1980). Human ecology and crime: A routine activity approach. *Human Ecology, 8,* 389–406.

Firebaugh, G. (1980). Assessing group effects: A comparison of two methods. In E. F. Borgatta & D. J. Jackson (Eds.), *Aggregate data: Analysis and interpretation.* Beverly Hills: Sage.

Gold, M. (1970). *Delinquent behavior in an American city.* Belmont: Brooks/Cole.

Goldstein, H. (1987). *Multilevel models in educational and social research.* New York: Oxford University Press.

Gottfredson, D. C., McNeil, R. J., III, & Gottfredson, G. D. (1991). Social area influences in delinquency: A multilevel analysis. *Journal of Research in Crime and Delinquency, 28,* 197–226.

Gottfredson, M. R., & Hirschi, T. (1988). The positive tradition. In M. R. Gottfredson & T. Hirschi (Eds.), *Positive criminology.* Beverly Hills: Sage.

Gottfredson, S. D., & Taylor, R. B. (1986). Person-environment interactions in the prediction of recidivism. In J. M. Byrne and R. J. Sampson (Eds.), *The social ecology of crime.* New York: Springer-Verlag.

Harré, R. (1981). Philosophical aspects of the micro-macro problem. In K. Knorr-Cetina & A. V. Cicourel (Eds.), *Advances in social theory and methodology. Toward an integration of micro- and macro-sociologies.* Boston: Routledge & Kegan Paul.

Hauser, R. M. (1970). Context and consex: A cautionary tale. *American Journal of Sociology, 75,* 645–664.

Healy, W. (1915). *The individual delinquent.* Boston: Little, Brown.

Heise, D. R. (1972). Employing nominal variables, induced variables and block variables in path analysis. *Sociological Methods and Research, 1,* 147–173.

Hindelang, M. J., Gottfredson, M. R., & Garafalo, J. (1978). *Victims of personal crime.* Cambridge, MA: Ballinger.

Hirschi, T. (1969). *Causes of delinquency.* Berkeley: University of California Press.

Homans, G. C. (1971). Commentary. In H. Turk & R. Simpson (Eds.), *Institutions and social exchange.* Indianapolis: Bobbs-Merrill.

Hunter, A. (1974). *Symbolic communities.* Chicago: University of Chicago Press.

Johnstone, J. W. C. (1978). Social class, social areas and delinquency. *Sociology and Social Research, 63,* 49–72.

Kennedy, L. W., & Forde, D. R. (1990). Routine activities and crime: An analysis of victimization in Canada. *Criminology, 28,* 137–152.

Klein, M. W. (1969). On the group context of delinquency. *Sociology and Social Research, 54,* 63–71.

Kornhauser, R. R. (1978). *Social sources of delinquency.* Chicago: University of Chicago Press.

Liska, A. E. (1973). Causal structures underlying the relationship between delinquent involvement and delinquent friends. *Sociology and Social Research, 58,* 23–36.

Loeber, R. & Wikstrom, P-O. H. (1993). Individual pathways to crime in different types of neighborhoods. In D. P. Farrington, R. J. Sampson, and P-O. H. Wikstrom (Eds.), *Integrating individual and ecological aspects of crime* (pp. 169–204). Stockholm: National Council for Crime Prevention.

Marsden, M. W. (1982). *Community context, social structure, and delinquency: A test of three causal models.* Ph.D. diss., Department of Sociology, University of Chicago.

Mason, W. M., Wong, G. Y., & Entwisle, B. (1983). Contextual analysis through the multilevel linear model. In S. Leinhardt (Ed.), *Sociological methodology 1983–1984.* San Francisco: Jossey-Bass.

McDonald, L. (1969). *Social class and delinquency.* Hamden, CT: Archon.

Meier, R. F. (1989). Deviance and differentiation. In A. E. Liska, M. K. Krohn, & S. Messner (Eds.), *Theoretical integration in the study of deviance and crime.* Albany: State University of New York Press.

Messner, S. F., & Tardiff, K. (1986). Economic inequality and levels of homicide: An analysis of urban neighborhoods. *Criminology, 24,* 297–318.

Miethe, T., & McDowall, D. (1993). Contextual effects in models of criminal victimization. *Social Forces, 71,* 741–760.

Moorman, J. E. (1980). Aggregation bias: An empirical demonstration. In E. F. Borgatta & D. J. Jackson (Eds.), *Aggregate data: Analysis and interpretation* (pp. 131–156). Beverly Hills: Sage.

Morris, T. (1957). *The criminal area.* London: Routledge & Kegan Paul.

Munch, R., & Smelser, N. J. (1987). Relating the micro and macro. In J. Alexander, B. Giesen, R. Munch, & N. J. Smelser (Eds.), *The micro-macro link.* Berkeley: University of California Press.

Olweus, D. (1977). A critical analysis of the "modern" interactionist position. In D. Magnusson and N. S. Endler (Eds.), *Personality at the crossroads: Current issues in interactional psychology.* Hillsdale, NJ: Erlbaum.

Parsons, T. (1964). Levels of organization and the mediation of social interaction. *Sociological Inquiry, 34,* 207–220.

Prosser, R., Rasbash, J., & Goldstein, H. (1991). *ML3: Software for three-level analysis.* London: Institute of Education, University of London.

Raudenbush, S. W. (1993). Modeling individual and community effects on deviance over time: Multi-level statistical models. In D. P. Farrington, R. J. Sampson, & P-O. H. Wikstrom, (Eds.), *Integrating individual and ecological aspects of crime* (pp. 205–240). Stockholm: National Council for Crime Prevention.

Reiss, A. J., Jr. (1986). Why are communities important in understanding crime? In A. J. Reiss, Jr. & M. Tonry (Eds.), *Communities and crime.* Chicago: University of Chicago Press.

Reiss, A. J., Jr. (1993). Key issues in the integration of individual and community explanations of crime and criminality. In D. P. Farrington, R. J. Sampson, & P-O. H. Wikstrom, (Eds.), *Integrating individual and ecological aspects of crime* Stockholm: National Council for Crime Prevention.

Reiss, A. J., Jr., & Rhodes, A. L. (1961). Delinquency and social class structure. *American Sociological Review, 26,* 720–732.

Ritzer, G. (1988). *Contemporary sociological theory* (2nd ed.). New York: Knopf.

Rountree, P. W., Land, K. C., & Miethe, T. (1993). Macro-micro integration in the study of victimization: A hierarchical linear models analysis across Seattle neighborhoods. Paper presented at the annual meetings of the American Society of Criminology, Phoenix.

Sampson, R. J. (1987). Communities and crime. In M. R. Gottfredson & T. Hirschi (Eds.), *Positive criminology.* Beverly Hills: Sage.

Sampson, R. J. (1993). Family and community-level influences on crime: A contextual theory and strategies for research testing. In D. P. Farrington, R. J. Sampson, & P-O. H. Wikstrom (Eds.), *Integrating Individual and Ecological Aspects of Crime* (pp. 153–168). Stockholm: National Council for Crime Prevention.

Sampson, R. J., & Groves, W. B. (1989). Community structure and crime: Testing social disorganization theory. *American Journal of Sociology, 94,* 774–802.

Sampson, R. J., & Lauritsen, J. L. (1990). Deviant lifestyles, proximity to crime, and the offender-victim link in personal violence. *Journal of Research in Crime and Delinquency, 27,* 110–139.

Sampson, R. J., & Wooldredge, J. D. (1987). Linking the micro- and macro-level dimensions of lifestyle-routine activity and opportunity models of predatory victimization. *Journal of Quantitative Criminology, 3,* 371–393.

Schelling, T. C. (1978). *Micromotives and macrobehavior.* New York: Norton.

Shannon, L. W. (1984). *The development of serious criminal careers and the delinquent neighborhood.* Executive Report. Washington, DC: National Institute of Juvenile Justice and Delinquency Prevention.

Shannon, L. W. (1988). *Criminal career continuity: Its social context.* New York: Human Sciences Press.

Shaw, C. (1929). *Delinquency areas.* Chicago: University of Chicago Press.

Simcha-Fagan, O. & Schwartz, J. E. (1986). Neighborhood and delinquency: An assessment of contextual effects. *Criminology, 24,* 667–704.

Smith, D. A. (1986). The neighborhood context of police behavior. In A. J. Reiss, Jr. & M. Tonry (Eds.), *Communities and crime.* Chicago: University of Chicago Press.

Smith, D. A., & Jarjoura, G. R. (1988). Social structure and criminal victimization. *Journal of Research in Crime and Delinquency, 25,* 27–52.

Smith, D. A., & Jarjoura, G. R. (1989). Household characteristics, neighborhood composition, and victimization risk. *Social Forces, 68,* 621–640.

Stark, R. (1987). Deviant places: A theory of the ecology of crime. *Criminology, 25,* 893–909.

Suttles, G. D. (1968). *The social order of the slum.* Chicago: University of Chicago Press.

Theil, H. (1971). *Principles of econometrics.* New York: Wiley.

Wilson, J. Q., & Herrnstein, R. J. (1985). *Crime and human nature.* New York: Simon & Schuster.

CHAPTER SEVEN

An Adaptive Strategy Theory of Crime and Delinquency

DAVID C. ROWE

ABSTRACT: Crime and delinquency are persistent human problems. Throughout history, during both feast and famine, societies have recorded the depredations of one person against another, including theft of goods, destruction of property, murder, and rape. In the twentieth century in the United States, we live in a society of unparalleled material abundance, where few people suffer from the kinds of malnutrition and extreme hardship associated historically with poverty and with lower-class status. Yet crime persists. Indeed, in the postwar period, wealth grew in the United States to an unprecedented extent, yet crime rates soared until the mid-1970s. Although social class bears a statistical relationship with crime, it explains little of its variation. Many criminals were reared in the plain and ordinary surroundings of the suburb. How can we explain the historical endurance of crime? How do we account for its apparent normalcy as a part of the "human condition"?

In this chapter, I propose *adaptive strategy theory* to account for the development of criminal behavior tendencies in the individual and for the persistence of crime in society as a form of social behavior. In this theory, a diverse set of conceptual tools is applied to crime. The theory draws extensively upon concepts from the framework of evolutionary biology, such as strategies and adaptation. These concepts may account for the functional value of crime. I use conceptual models of genetic and cultural trait transmission to explain the acquisition of criminal behavior by learning. Other explanations of crime couched in terms of behavioral evolution have been presented (Cohen & Machalek, 1988; Harpending & Draper, 1988; Kenrick, Dantchik, & MacFarlane, 1983; Rushton, 1985).

Although I borrow some important ideas from these neighboring models, adaptive strategy theory is not identical with any one of them. It emphasizes biologically based dispositions more than Cohen and Machalek and social conditions in industrialized societies more than Harpending and Draper. Rushton based the empirical evaluation of his r/K theory partly on behav-

I wish to thank John Alcock, Michael Bailey, Carol Bender, Martin Daly, Patricia Draper, Alejandro Figueroa, David Hawkins, Barry Hewlett, Kevin MacDonald, Joan McCord, Joan Loehlin, Rolf Loeber, Dennison Smith, and James Q. Wilson for their comments and suggestions.

ioral differences among racial groups, whereas adaptive strategy theory is focused more on within-race genetic variation and on the behavioral choices made by individuals. Kenrick et al. identified possible "conditional" human adaptations, such as greater predatory crime against strangers than against familiar others. The chapter touches briefly on several possible adaptations, but focuses more on individual differences in criminal propensity and behavior. Although elegant evolutionary explanations have been proposed for specific crimes, such as homicide (Daly & Wilson, 1988) and rape (Thornhill & Thornhill, 1983), this chapter focuses more broadly on both common forms of theft and violent crimes. Criminals' lack of specialization in a single type of criminal activity encourages a theory of general criminal tendency (e.g., Wolfgang, Figlio, & Sellin, 1972; Wolfgang, Thornberry, & Figlio, 1987).

An Overview of the Theory

The use of a concept of *strategy* facilitates the analysis of behavioral evolution. A strategy is an organized set of behaviors evolved to maximize individual reproductive success over the life span. The piecemeal elements of a strategy are the particular behaviors required to complete it (i.e., tactics). Animals instinctively adopt different strategies to secure food, find mates, raise young, and defend themselves against predators. For example, male hamadryas baboons adopt a mating strategy of holding harems of females, whereas male *Papio anubis* baboons attempt to exclude rivals from receptive females but do not try to monopolize them completely (Wilson, 1975, pp. 531–535). Such alternative strategies can be used as a conceptual unit for an evolutionary analysis of behavior.

Evolved strategies may be of two general kinds. A pure evolved strategy is a genetically distinct phenotype. Each distinct phenotype would intently pursue a different behavioral strategy. For example, in bluegill fish, males pursuing a strategy of "sneak" mating with females are smaller in body size and have larger gonads than the more ostentatious "parental" males who mate with females they guard (Daly & Wilson, 1983, pp. 102–103). The males pursuing these two strategies possess genetically distinct morphologies. Another kind of evolved strategy is a conditional strategy. In this type, organisms possessing the capacity for the strategies are genetically identical for the *relevant* genes – that is, the genes "have gone to fixation," meaning that they are the same in all individuals. However, these genes may create neurological mechanisms for adaptive response to the environment. For example, a bird species might have the evolved strategies of aggressively defending a rich food source when food is scarce or not showing aggression when food is abundant. These conditional strategies may be biologically based – that is, they may appear without prior exposure or learning – and yet they would not represent genetic differences among organisms (Crawford & Anderson, 1989). The latter kind of hypothesis could apply to criminal behavior if people tend to resort to crime when environmental conditions are poor and to noncrime when they are good. Such a conditional strategy could depend on sensitivity to different environmental cues (e.g., food abundance), with all people having the same genetic constitution with regard to criminal behavior.

We acknowledge that conditional strategies may contribute to criminal motivations. For example, situations that trigger jealous rages may be the result of behavioral evolution (Daly & Wilson, 1988). We focus here, however, on the former type of pure evolved strategies: genetically based phenotypes contributing to crime.

Reproductive effort refers to all physical and mental effort devoted to successful reproduction. It is divisible into two conceptual components: *parenting effort* and *mating effort*. The former refers to the care invested in rearing young, including pregnancy and lactation. Mating effort refers to the time and energy devoted to finding a mate and protecting him or her from rivals. A major hypothesis of adaptive theory is that crime results from an evolved behavioral strategy that maximizes mating effort and minimizes parenting effort. (This hypothesis is not original – it was stated in related ways by Harpending and Draper [1988] and Rushton [1985].)

Crime and noncrime are not themselves evolved behavioral strategies. However, crime can be identified with the behaviors that tend to promote mating effort and noncrime with those that tend to promote parenting effort. One reason for this is that high levels of mating effort tend to conflict with noncriminal, productive activities. Moreover, the kinds of traits evolved to maximize mating effort – which constitute an interrelated cluster – also promote crime. These traits may include strong sexual drive and preference for sexual novelty, a lack of strong emotional attachments, dissimulation concerning one's true emotions, and the use of aggression to deter potential rivals. The opposite traits tend to promote parenting effort. On the other hand, even if crime is not itself an evolved behavioral strategy, it is still sometimes useful to treat crime and noncrime as behavioral strategies, partly because of crime's dependence on what is perhaps an evolved strategy (mating versus parenting effort), and partly for the conceptual power of treating behaviors as strategy alternatives even without recourse to assumptions about behavioral evolution. For example, the relative payoffs for a particular crime may depend on the relative proportions of individuals in the population choosing criminal strategies because of a purely social process.

It is hypothesized that mating effort and parenting effort are normal, behavioral alternatives. They will typically be maintained in some kind of equilibrium in human populations by the existence of normal genes tending to promote one strategy or the other, and by the existence of some kind of equilibrium of the social advantages and disadvantages of both strategies.[1]

In this respect, it is noteworthy that nonhuman animals routinely adopt behavioral strategies that, if they were consciously chosen courses of action, would qualify for labeling as "crimes." For example, a male langur monkey, once it removes a male previously dominating a troop, will attempt to kill the infants it may not have fathered (Hrdy, 1981). The cuckoo bird has evolved the adaptation of laying its egg surreptitiously in the nest of a bird of another species, which mistakenly raises it as its own young (Payne, 1977). Lions drive other animals off their kills and then take proceeds – theft of food is common, both within and across species, throughout the animal kingdom. Eagles lay two eggs, and the earlier hatching sibling habitually kills its less fortunate and unprotected brother or sister. All these diverse behavioral patterns, although they involve one animal exploiting another – even a member of its own species – can be interpreted as maximizing the reproductive success of the perpetrator: They are regarded by evolutionary biologists as the behavioral products of biological evolu-

---

[1] Treating criminal acts as partly a result of evolved strategies does not imply that crimes are always biologically adaptive. Long jail terms or injury may result in a crime being biologically maladaptive for a particular individual, as that person may fail to have children. At issue, however, is the *average* reproductive value of particular behavioral strategies over long periods.

The behavioral genetic notion of *phenocopy* is also relevant here. A phenocopy results from haphazard environmental or genetic effects that mimic a trait produced by the normally operative genetic and environmental influences. Phenocopy traits may be totally maladaptive. For example, injuries to the brain may cause a type of epilepsy that induces violent behavior, but this behavior is not expected to be biologically adaptive. Numerous other influences exist that are probably able to produce phenocopies of adaptive antisocial traits, including fetal alcohol syndrome, lead-induced brain injury, some perinatal traumas, and so on. The adaptive strategy theory is not an explanation for the antisocial behavior of these individuals.

tion. None is abnormal or in any way out of the ordinary for the species involved.[2]

important distinction in this chapter is that between *proximate* and *ultimate explanations*. Although I will not introduce these ideas again, it should be clear that my argument will shift between these levels of explanations: (1) Proximate explanations refer to the psychological processes shaping immediate behavioral response; (2) ultimate explanations refer to the evolutionary and social history and function of the proximate mechanisms as they have developed over time. For example, the pleasure that an illicit sexual affair gives can be experienced, without any thought that a desire for illicit sex may serve reproductive interests. Yet a process of biological evolution selecting particular genes may have produced the brain neurology responsible for sexual interest and may have endowed particular environmental stimuli, such as shapely legs and a pretty face, with the power to elicit this interest (see Langlois et al., 1987, for evidence of inborn discrimination of facial attractiveness). This ultimate level of explanation is often ignored in sociological or psychological accounts of behavior, but it is fundamentally important to evolutionary (or historical) analysis.

Another critical issue is whether people switch among behavioral strategies or retain one strategy for their lifetimes. There is truth to both positions. For example, most teenagers who commit crimes later desist. This may represent a shift of behavioral strategies for many individuals. Similarly, even a law-abiding person may react to some temptations by committing a crime. Surveys of male college students give the distressing result that a high proportion (about 40%) say they would commit a rape (thereby perhaps advancing their reproductive interests) if the probability of detection and capture were nil (Malamuth, Haber, & Feshbach, 1980).

On the other hand, criminal and related behaviors demonstrate considerable within-person stability across different life periods (Jessor & Jessor, 1977; Olweus, 1979; Farrington, 1988; Loeber & Dishion, 1983; Farrington, Ohlin, & Wilson, 1986, pp. 47–50). This lifetime stability is so impressive that many individuals may be regarded as fairly single-minded strategists who pursue one strategy (crime/mating effort) or the other (noncrime/

---

[2] These examples are not meant to imply that only injurious or deceptive behaviors evolve. Evolution also produces many behaviors that we would regard as prosocial, such a parental love and concern for offspring, altruism toward kin, and so on. It is the complex interaction among competing motives, and their compromise with one another, which make an evolutionary analysis of instinct quite distinct from the gross oversimplifications of Social Darwinism.

parenting effort) for most of their lifetimes. Note that changes in the level of criminal behavior may preserve rank-order individual differences – the 40-year-old is less criminal than the 20-year-old, but the most extreme individuals may hold their relative position. Thus, historical or lifetime changes do not negate the importance of accounting for individual differences in the selection of strategies.

Figure 7.1 presents one way of conceptualizing the relationship between

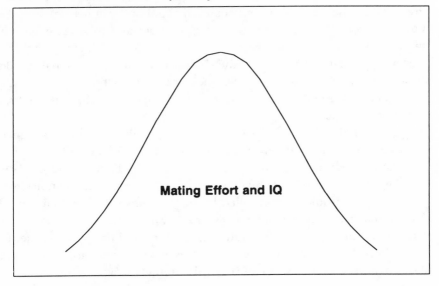

Normal Distribution of Propensity

Mating Effort and IQ

Offenses per Unit Time

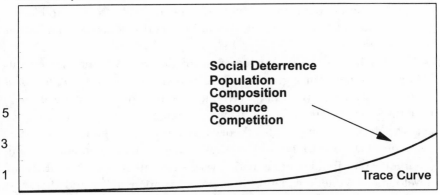

**Social Deterrence
Population
Composition
Resource
Competition**

5

3

1

Trace Curve

Figure 7.1. Individual propensities and crime rates.

individual differences and criminal behavior. Individual differences in propensity to crime appear on the x-axis. They are normally distributed along this dimension. We assume that this trait captures all relatively enduring aspects of personality that contribute to the tendency to engage in crime; thus, it is criminal propensity in the broadest sense. The trait may be composed of the combination of relatively independent traits, such as IQ and the mating effort trait. An hypothesized trace curve translates this trait disposition into a mean rate of offending (say, criminal acts per year) as shown along the y-axis. For example, in Figure 7.1, someone who scored 2.0 greater than the trait mean would commit about one criminal act per time unit. The general shape of the trace curve is important. We assume that it is highly nonlinear. Thus, it takes a strong trait disposition before someone has an appreciable rate of offending. Most low-scoring individuals would commit no criminal acts (because their rates would be well below one crime per year; see Rowe, Osgood, & Nicewander, 1990 for mathematical details of this model).

Figure 7.1 also serves to separate two conceptually distinct ways in which the total crime rate is determined. On the one hand, any change in the population mean on the crime-proneness trait would alter the crime rate. On the other hand, the rate may also be changed by moving the trace line. The trace line would be controlled by all those environmental and social factors that fail to affect individuals' trait dispositions but influence the likelihood that a person with a given disposition will engage in crime. In other words, crime depends on the *interaction* of a trait disposition and social conditions. The exact nature of this interaction, and the components of the crime-proneness trait, are discussed in later sections.

Another way to organize a model of criminal behavior is developmentally (see Figure 7.2). This model follows the development of individuals from childhood to maturity and ends with a concern for social and biological outcomes within a complete system loop and feedback on individual development.

It will help to organize our coverage of the theory to first review the major components of Figure 7.2. Development begins with *constitutional traits* that influence (in adulthood) the selection of the mating effort/parenting (M/P) effort strategies, and secondarily, committing criminal acts. We do not claim that this theory identifies all components of crime-proneness in Figure 7.1, but we hypothesize that two major component traits are intellectual abilities and a mating versus parenting effort trait. Early in development, genetic variation influences variation in IQ and the M/P trait, which is then manifest as temperamental differences among children.

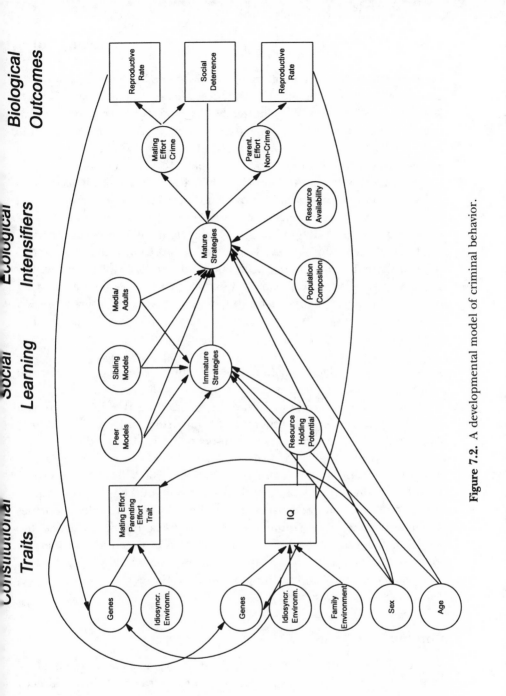

Figure 7.2. A developmental model of criminal behavior.

Idiosyncratic environment refers to environmental influences unique to each child; these environmental influences are not well understood (Rowe & Plomin, 1981). IQ is also influenced by family environment, but this influence may diminish with age (see Plomin, 1986). Note also that the effect of IQ on later crime-proneness is through *resource-holding power,* an evolutionary term for the competitive capacity of an individual.

Sex is another constitutional trait. Biological sex genetically moderates the expression of the mating effort strategies. Biological age also has a direct effect on strategy selection and learning.

During middle childhood and adolescence, many antisocial behaviors are learned. Learning processes depend on the reciprocal social interactions of the child and sibling, peer, and adult models. I place less importance on variables tied to the family environment (e.g., child-rearing styles or family income). Mating/parenting strategies are not fully expressed until the teenage years, when the individual is reproductively mature. The final adoption of one strategy or the other may depend on the existence of *ecological intensifiers.* Conceptually, these factors produce gene by environment interactions such that the genetic mating/parenting strategies are more fully activated under some ecological conditions than others (i.e., they move a trace line, as in Figure 7.1, connecting the disposition with behavioral outcomes). The list of possible intensifiers is large. This chapter covers population composition and resource availability factors.

The last part of the figure deals with social and biological consequences. The relative reproductive rates of individuals who adopt mating effort versus parenting effort strategies serves to maintain the genetic variation; hence, reproduction works backwards in the model to effect the genotypes of the next generation. Crime also produces social reactions. Hence, the model includes social deterrence, all the actions by which society attempts to reduce crime, acting backwards on teenage/adult strategy selection. This model is complex, but the phenomenon we seek to explain, crime, eludes any simple explanation.

Constitutional Traits

Figure 7.1's crime-proneness trait can be described as a latent trait because various indicators for it can be defined, but the trait itself is not directly observable. Because this trait is composed of numerous components, we cannot expect to refine our understanding of it without further empirical and conceptual work. Moreover, different components of the trait may be weighted differently in producing crime-proneness and may operate on that proneness through different processes. Tremendous complexity may underlie the apparent simplicity of Figure 7.1.

It is hypothesized that a mating effort versus parenting effort trait is a major component of crime-proneness (Figure 7.1). Mating effort versus parenting effort is, of course, a set of behaviors displayed during adulthood. The hypothesized parenting effort versus mating effort *trait* is a genetically based disposition to follow one strategy or the other. We expect this trait to be displayed in a variety of behaviors, not all of which are criminal.

The best method of establishing this trait would be to correlate a set of behavioral indicators with the outcome of parenting effort versus mating effort. Parenting effort could be measured using reports of long-term monogamy, emotional closeness to spouse and children, and heavy investment in child care; the opposite life history would assess mating effort. It is a prediction of this theory that certain behavioral combinations would be rare (e.g., a highly promiscuous lifestyle accompanied by devoted child care, or a criminal who takes his ill-gotten gains and lavishes them on his children).

I assert the following hypotheses about the mating effort trait (the term *mating effort* will be used interchangeably with *mating/parenting effort*):

1. This trait has evolved under balancing selection (both trait extremes can lead to having children) and is heritable.
2. As the best indicators of this trait should be influenced by these genes, different hypothesized indicators should be genetically as well as phenotypically correlated (i.e., they will correlate across relatives as well as within persons).
3. Mating effort is more evolutionarily favored in males than in females. Males should therefore have greater mean values on indicators of mating effort than females.
4. Those indicators producing the largest sex difference tend to be the best predictor of mating effort versus parenting effort within the sexes – that is, a factor-structure of delinquency correlates within a sex should mirror mean sex differences.

We lack extensive data on mating effort versus parenting effort in human populations. This dearth of evidence makes direct investigation of the indicators of mating effort versus parenting effort impossible at present. However, as we postulate that mating effort traits also tend to produce many kinds of criminal behavior, we can test some hypotheses about mating effort using criminal behavior as the outcome.

Figure 7.3 lists a set of traits that may be indicators of the hypothesized

Mating Effort/Parenting Effort

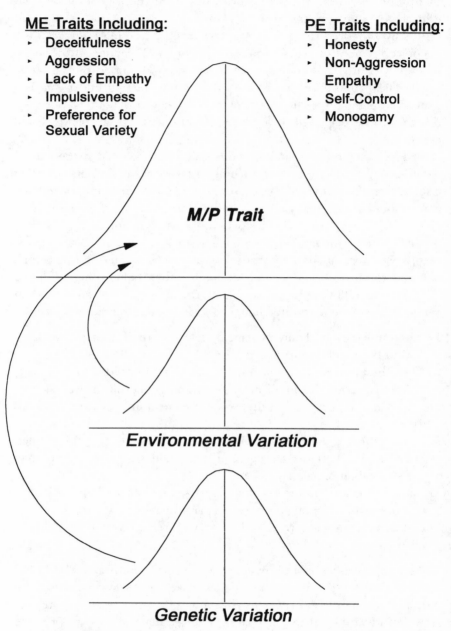

ME Traits Including:
- Deceitfulness
- Aggression
- Lack of Empathy
- Impulsiveness
- Preference for Sexual Variety

PE Traits Including:
- Honesty
- Non-Aggression
- Empathy
- Self-Control
- Monogamy

M/P Trait

Environmental Variation

Genetic Variation

Figure 7.3. Variation in mating effort/parenting effort traits.

mating versus parenting effort trait. The psychological traits consist of aggression, lack of empathy, deceitfulness, anger, impulsiveness, novelty preference, sexual drive, and onset of sexual motivation. Physical traits corresponding to these psychological traits should be present as well, mostly represented as differences in brain–nervous system functioning. However, at least one overt physical trait, Sheldon's mesomorphic body type, is reliably associated with crime in males and would possibly also be associated with mating effort (Wilson & Herrnstein, 1985). For three of the psychological traits listed – impulsivity, anger, and deceitfulness – a twin study has provided evidence of a genetic, intertrait correlation, because the monozygotic (MZ) twin (cross-trait) correlations were greater than the dizygotic (DZ) twin correlations (Rowe, 1986). However, for the other traits, this kind of evidence is unavailable.

Heritability. If variation in crime partly depends on variation in a heritable mating effort versus parenting effort trait, then twin and adoption studies of arrests or self-reports of offending should show genetic variation. Literature reviews of family, twin, and adoption studies confirm this conclusion (Rowe & Osgood, 1984; Rowe, 1990; Ellis, 1984). MZ twins are usually more concordant for crime than DZ twins. Crime appears in the adopted-away relatives of biological criminals, despite a lack of social contact between the adoptees and their biological parents.

Association with Sexual Life History. If mating effort is the central construct defining the latent trait, then a connection should exist between crime and sexual life histories indicating high mating effort (e.g., Ahlstrom & Havighurst, 1971; Glueck & Glueck, 1968; Jessor, Costa, Jessor, & Donovan, 1983; Reitsma-Street, Offord, & Finch, 1985). Criminals, as compared to others in the population, are likely to initiate sexual activity at a younger age, to be sexually promiscuous, and to be separated and divorced from their spouses. These correlates of crime are often found cross-culturally (Ellis, 1987).

The correlation between crime and the early initiation of sexuality may result partly from genetic variability. Rowe, Rodgers, Meseck-Bushey, and St. John (1989) analyzed the correlation between self-reported delinquency and the age of onset of sexual intercourse among teenagers and young adults in Florida and Oklahoma. Within persons, sexual intercourse onset and delinquency correlated (mean $r = 0.45$). In siblings, there was a cross-correlation of sexual onset in one sibling and the level of deviance in the other (mean $r = 0.19$). The mating effort trait, as indexed by delinquency and relatively early onset of sexual intercourse, yielded moderate sibling correlations (0.33 in brothers and 0.47 in sisters). Nonetheless, a sibling study cannot exclude a rival interpretation that familial effects are attributable to variation in family environments – but I will speak later to the frailty of this interpretation.

Sex Differences

Sex differences in criminal behavior are large and cross-culturally universal (Wilson & Herrnstein, 1985). It is therefore a weakness of some criminological theories that they focus on only the male gender.

Darwinian theories, however, provide an account of the adaptive value of sex differences. In particular, I will use *sexual selection theory* to explain the greater adaptive value of mating effort (and crime) for males than females that appears as an average sex difference in behavior. It is an extension of sexual selection theory to apply it to variation within the sexes (although within-sex genetic variation, at some historical point, must have been "fixed" to produce differential adaptations of males and females).

According to sexual selection theory, sex differences evolve in response to intrasexual competition for mates and intersex mate preferences. The general rule is that the sex that is least involved with parenting duties is most free to compete among itself for mating opportunities. In most other mammals, males compete for mating opportunities more than females. This choice of strategy is evolutionarily advantageous for males because it will result in more surviving offspring than a strategy of low mating effort and high parental effort. Females usually take the opposite strategy. In mammals, a major reason for the evolution of these different reproductive strategies is the constraints imposed by male and female reproductive biology. Females carry a fetus to term, and then provide all the early nutrition (milk). They unavoidably invest heavily in their offspring. If ecological conditions demand paternal care of the young, then the sexes' allocation of mating versus parental effort will be more balanced. However, in many mammals, young can be raised without substantial paternal help. Hence, male mammals will gain more biological fitness by competing among themselves for mates than by devoting attention to a single female and her offspring. Hence, in a given breeding period, most nonhuman females will reproduce roughly at their biological limit, whereas males will vary widely in reproductive success, depending on how successfully they have competed with one another for mates (if a male chooses not to compete, then its genes will be absent in later generations).

Humans, although they fit the mammalian pattern of greater female than male investment in offspring, are not nearly as extreme in this respect as most mammals. In many societies, men make substantial economic, physical, and emotional investments in the rearing of their children. Nonetheless, a sexual selection process does appear to exist in humans such that men tend to devote more of their total reproductive effort to mating effort than do women. For example, these consequences of sexual selection have been observed: men's greater size and strength, men's greater aggressiveness, greater variability of men's than women's reproductive success, and delay of puberty in boys (Daly & Wilson, 1983). The latter may not be self-evident: a later puberty may be favored for males evolutionarily because of the greater risks males face in the competition with older males. It is noteworthy, however, that spermatogenesis appears early in the sequence of male pubertal development. This developmental sequence permits reproductive success to "immature" males, if they get "lucky."

If we hypothesize a link between crime and mating effort, then genetic thresholds for crime should differ in males and females. Two studies using samples that were large and fairly representative of their populations support this hypothesis. In the Swedish Adoption Study, this kind of pattern was found for crime (Sigvardsson, Cloninger, Bohman, & Von Knorring, 1982). The researchers found that the risk of criminality in the biological parents of (adopted-away) criminal women was double that in the biological parents of (adopted-away) criminal men (50% versus 21%), indicating that affected females may carry the greater gene "dosage."

Cloninger, Christiansen, Reich, and Gottesman (1978) reanalyzed Christiansen's (1970) study of the incidence of crime in Danish twins. Using data on the population prevalences of crime in men and women, the twin concordances were converted into correlation coefficients. For example, the concordance for MZ twin males (51.5%) was considerably greater than that for MZ twin females (35.3%), but the twin correlations were nearly the same (r MZ males $= 0.70$; r MZ females $= 0.72$). The opposite-sex twin correlation was somewhat smaller than the same-sex DZ twin correlation. However, their ratio suggests that about 61% of the genetic factors contributing to crime are common to the two sexes. Together, the twin correlations yielded an excellent fit to a statistical model, indicating that the criminal convictions of males and females have roots in the same latent trait but that this trait is more readily exhibited in males.

The mating effort trait may take an alternative manifestation in females. Harpending and Sobus (1987) argued that the female form of criminality consists of a set of "hysterial traits," including the display of strong but insincere emotions. Such emotional displays may elicit male investment and so they may correspond to mating effort (e.g., abandonment of one sexual partner for another because a real emotional attachment was lacking). As supporting evidence, an excessive prevalence of hysterical behaviors has been reported in the female, biological relatives of male criminals (Cloninger & Guze, 1970, 1973).

Age Differences

Even in an alleyway, the shuffling gait of an elderly man does not scare us. We know, intuitively, that the incidence of crime declines dramatically with age. The per capita arrest rate of 15- to 19-year-olds is about 4 times the population average, whereas that of 50- to 54-year-olds is about one-fourth the population average. Individuals older than 40 years seem to have lost their motivation for all types of crime: their per capita arrest rates are far below those of younger men (Wilson & Herrnstein, 1985).

Hirschi and Gottfredson (1987) ignited a lively controversy in criminology with their assertion that this age decline was so regular as to stump the most determined criminological theorist. The favored variables of criminology, they announced, cannot account for the spontaneous reform out-of-crime. That is, regardless of how one subdivides a population, age declines in crime will occur at equal rates within categories as well as across them: It is present in the lower and upper classes; in males and females; and in different marital and labor force participation statuses. Hence, the categorizations we anticipate can explain age trends may fail to do so.

Adaptive theory offers a new explanation of age effects in terms of the life-span balance between mating and parenting effort strategies. Evolution should prompt humans to adopt the lifetime mix of these two strategies that results in the overall maximization of fitness. In adolescence, reproductive maturity is achieved, but the individual does not yet possess children in which to invest parenting effort. To achieve the result of mating, mating effort strategies must dominate early in the life span. Crime prevalences – the proportion of adolescents involved in crime – peak around 16 to 19 years of age, immediately after most males have completed pubertal development and are sexually fully mature.

To some extent, the intensity of adolescent rebellion may reflect a difference in perceived reproductive interests in parents and children. Parents, who are fully cognizant of the mature skills required to rear children (something like the patience of Job and the moral authority of Moses), may wish to delay their children's reproduction until they are married and self-supporting. However, because adolescents are fertile, early intercourse may produce a child. Given that the offspring of unwed couples have survived in the past – although they may be at greater risk than the children of stable, married couples – evolution may have predisposed children to seek sexual opportunities before their parents consider this to be wise. The adolescent's defiance of parental wishes, therefore, may be an evolved response promoting his or her reproductive interests. Early reproduction may benefit the adolescent more than the parents because illegitimate grandchildren may require considerably more of the grandparents' own resources (time and money), detracting from resources that could be spent on other children and grandchildren. Conversely, the adolescent immediately gains in units of his or her biological fitness.

As implied by this thesis, pubertal development is closely linked to the onset of sexual and mildly deviant behaviors (smoking, drinking). It is perhaps fair to say that hormones rage in the bloodstreams of adolescent boys – their levels jump more than 10-fold in just a few years' time. The shot of testosterone received by adolescent males may directly determine the onset of sexual and mildly deviant behaviors. Udry, Billy, Morris, Groff, and Raj (1985) found that 16% of the males with low testosterone levels reported they had had sex, versus 69% with high levels so reported. Udry et al. drew the conclusion that hormones directly affected sexual behavior. A competing model, that adolescents became sexually active because of social reactions to changes in their physical appearance, was ruled out by statistical analyses controlling for appearance. Adolescent hormone levels also correlate with general delinquency and with aggression, especially in reaction to social provocations (Olweus, 1986). In these examples, hormones may activate evolved behavioral responses.

The most rapid increase in the rate of all kinds of crimes occurs early in adolescence (10 to 17 years of age). Hence, the idea that puberty and crime rise together is uncontroversial. It is much more difficult to explain the distribution after the peak, because physiological capabilities probably do not decline as rapidly as crime.

As individuals have children, reproductive success will benefit more from parental investment in existing offspring than in further mating effort. As noted earlier in the discussion of sex differences, in general, parenting effort strategies would be more evolutionarily beneficial for females than males. This relative asymmetry probably increases with age, because postmenarchal women can no longer reproduce, whereas older men's reproductive capability is lost more gradually. There is a corresponding asymmetry in sexual drive and interest. Middle-aged women, especially post-40 years, report much less pleasure derived from sexual intercourse than do men in the same age range. For instance, 40- to 55-year-old women rated sexual intercourse as less pleasurable than watching TV, doing housework, or sleeping (Mellen, 1981, pp. 178–80). In contrast, men of the same age rated sex as the second most pleasurable activity in the list of 22 behavioral alternatives ("the family" was first). Moreover, divorced women older than 40 years rarely remarry. It would be interesting to determine whether remarriage rates for older women differ depending on the presence of children (a higher remarriage rate would be predicted for women without children).

Nevertheless, the effectiveness of the two reproductive strategies varies with age for men. Older men, like older women, are less fecund because of the deteriorative process of aging. More crucially, older men must compete against younger men for access to women in the reproductively desirable 20- to 40-year-old age range. At some age, the likelihood of succeeding in this competition against younger men will be reduced to the point that further reproductive success will be better insured by investing in existing children – or in the existing children of biological relatives. At this point, criminal activities should largely cease, partly as a result of biological programming of behavioral inclinations.

Another explanation leads to a similar conclusion, but from a different assumption about human evolution. Adult males may have monopolized the market on wives, forcing younger men into riskier and more dangerous tactics as they competed with one another for access to wives in a society dominated by these older males (older, in this context, meaning 40 years of age). The proximal mechanism of testosterone effects may be attuned to motivate the riskiest tactics in adolescence or early adulthood, when this competition among the numerous males without wives was most intense. Older males would be more inclined to take charge of their current wives, and be relatively unconcerned about younger competitors whom they dominated.

The validity of a biological basis to the age–crime relationship may be investigated in research seeking biological markers with which to replace chronological age as the correlate of crime rates. Using a within-individual analysis, crime rates should decline more with measures of physical fitness (vital capacity, visual acuity, maximum heart rate, testosterone concentrations) than with chronological age. Prediction may be further improved by combining information on physical status with information on existing offspring. The crossover point from a largely crime to a noncrime strategy should occur as criminals have more opportunities to invest in children and as their future reproductive potential becomes greater by parenting effort than mating effort. Anecdotally, one reason middle-aged male criminals often give for ceasing criminal activities is strong love for a particular woman – they may have unconsciously switched strategies.

Intelligence. Inherited genes partly determine nervous system functioning, which in turn affects learning and behavioral preferences. Genes do not code themselves for jimmying a lock or stealing a car – criminal acts must be acquired by socialization and learning because the genome does not waste precious DNA encoding the specifics. The mating/parenting trait represents only one way in which the nervous system affects learning. Independently, another genetically based trait, intellectual ability (IQ), can influence the competence to acquire and perform a wide range of learned behaviors. Because crime and noncrime behaviors must be learned, IQ also may affect the development of criminal strategies.

Even at a young age, the difficulty of learning the two strategies is asymmetric: In general, criminal behaviors are rather simple to learn; noncriminal behaviors are more difficult to learn. The skilled car thief has to learn how to hot wire a car. The skilled safe cracker has to learn how to break into a safe with special tools. While such learning is in the more difficult range of criminal behavior, it is still probably well within the capacity of even an individual with a low IQ – it hardly compares to the ability level required to master academic subjects such as calculus. Other criminal behaviors, like shoplifting or hitting, are elementary to learn. Indeed, even without exposure to individuals who may act as social models, many children may invent spontaneously "taking a toy by grabbing it" or other basic, exploitive acts. One does not need to be Holmes' rival Moriarty to think like a criminal: Most children, and adolescents, possess the intellectual capacity to exploit others.

In contrast, noncriminal behaviors are more difficult to acquire by learning. Consider the example of a child who wants another child's toy. Taking the toy by force requires little thought. Persuading the other child to give up the toy by offering another toy or by phrasing a request is a more intellectually demanding approach involving a sequence of behavioral acts. This example, of course, understates the difference in cognitive demands between lifetime use of crime and noncrime. Most occupations in the United States today require at least a high school education. Thus, 12 years of mastering basic academic subjects is a necessary condition before entry into the workforce. Mastering academic subject matter is more cognitively demanding than learning common crime. The occupational hierarchy is also roughly a hierarchy of level of cognitive ability needed to complete the tasks in a particular occupation, with lower-status occupations requiring lower levels of cognitive ability.[3]

By this line of argument, we would expect a correlation to exist between cognitive ability (e.g., IQ test scores) and crime. Such an expectation is amply confirmed in the literature. Hirschi and Hindelang (1977), in their review of the delinquency–IQ association, estimated that delinquents had on average an IQ 8 points lower than nondelinquents. They also found evidence for this relationship in both self-report and official data on crime. For example, the percentage of blacks admitting to delinquent acts increased 1½ times from the highest IQ category to the lowest. In the same range of categories, the percentage of whites doubled (12% versus 24%).

Low IQ may result in the adoption of criminal behaviors because of failure to learn the alternatives. I assume low IQ is not intrinsically antisocial. This interpretation can explain the existence of an IQ–conduct disorder relationship as early as preschool, before experiences of school failure may become critical (McMichael, 1979).

In evolutionary biology terms, strategy selection depends on *resource-holding power*, the competitive capacity of an individual. In competition for valued resources, low IQ children may face continual disadvantage compared to high IQ children. Hence, they may resort to using criminal tactics, despite the greater social costs those tactics may impose in comparison to noncriminal ones. Interestingly, relative IQ differences may be more important than the absolute IQ. In a group of children with high IQs, a child of moderate IQ may be disadvantaged in learning the more subtle and indirect strategies of behavioral manipulation employed by his or her brighter peers. Thus, this child, in the context of this group, may be at risk for adopting aggressive or direct manipulative behaviors. The same child, in a group in which he or she was of average IQ, may be at less risk because his or her social competencies would be more advanced than children whose IQs are lower (see Simonton, 1985 for an analogous argument that groups favor as leaders someone moderately brighter than the average member).

---

[3] Not all individuals with high levels of cognitive ability, of course, hold high-status occupational positions. For many reasons, individuals may fail to reach their occupational potential. Rather, in general, high levels of cognitive ability are a *necessary* but not sufficient condition for attaining prestigious professional and managerial occupations.

IQ and the hypothesized mating/parenting effort trait probably relate interactively. High IQ and high mating effort individuals will continue to exploit others, but their behaviors may be less overtly criminal and hence less subject to prosecution. The street criminal, and, for the most part, the white-collar criminal as well (see Hirschi & Gottfredson, 1987), commit crimes of low complexity, with little planning or forethought, because they are low in IQ but high in mating effort.

Given that genetic variation underlies both IQ variation and hypothesized M/P variation, one can ask whether the same set of genes underlies the expression of both. Probably not. The two traits appear to encounter different selective pressures. Nearly any measure of crime will yield a relatively large sex difference. By comparison, sex differences in intellectual abilities are slight. An evolutionary process of *directional selection* is suggested for IQ, because this trait contains a component of genetic dominance variation (see, e.g., studies of inbreeding depression and IQ, Afzal, 1988; Schull & Neel, 1965, p. 419). Directional selection occurs when reproductive success has been positively correlated with high trait values.

Social Learning Processes

How does a child learn criminal strategies? What environmental factors may modify this learning? Many standard theories of crime – such as social control theory and social learning theory – refer to upbringing in the family as the main causal factor in crime.

More generally, cultural transmission theories distinguish three ways in which behaviors may be transmitted by learning (Boyd & Richerson, 1985; Cavalli-Sforza & Feldman, 1981). *Vertical transmission* refers to transmission in the family from parent to child, a learning mechanism often emphasized for crime. *Horizontal transmission* refers to learning from same-generation peers. *Oblique transmission* refers to learning from adults other than the parents; like vertical transmission, it is intergenerational. In contrast to genetic transmission, cultural transmission can proceed in three directions: (1) adults → children, (2) children → children, and (3) children → adults.

In this theory of crime, I must distinguish between transmission of the underlying disposition toward crime (which involves heritable factors) and the acquisition of specific criminal behaviors that are learned (e.g., those not spontaneously invented by the criminal). I regard most family influence on crime as arising indirectly through the transmission of genetic traits. In contrast, I believe that family environments play a minor role in development of criminogenic traits. Rather, I surmise that the acquisition of specific criminal behaviors (and not personality dispositions) may occur most frequently in peer groups, with perhaps some oblique transmission (unrelated adult to child) as well. Interacting peer groups also create the social context in which most criminal acts occur, especially in adolescence.

Vertical Transmission: Family Environmental Effects?

Environmental theories posit a variety of family-influence mechanisms, including parental discipline styles (whether parents monitor their children's whereabouts, show them love and acceptance, etc.), parental modeling (e.g., aggression against a spouse may legitimize a child's aggression against an outsider), and specific sequences of rewards and punishments (e.g., children may learn that punching a sibling gains them the toys they want). There is abundant evidence that features of the family environment, such as parental rejection and inconsistent discipline, are statistically associated with outcomes such as children's delinquency (Maccoby & Martin, 1983). At issue here is whether these family environment–child outcome associations reflect the postulated environmental causal processes, or whether they merely represent the accidental by-products of genetic traits possessed by both child and parent. Popular psychology lays instant claim to all kinds of parental treatment effects – and children sometimes look and act like their parents – without reflection that the causality may not be due to direct environmental influence.

To begin, a basic premise of family theories is that harmful treatments cause poor outcomes and vice versa. The premise is an emotionally appealing one because we wish to hold power over our children's fates. Like most people, I admit to this emotional tug, but I recognize that as a basis of scientific theory, we cannot trust it (Rowe, 1994). In the animal kingdom normal development can lead to displays of the most crudely self-interested, and hurtful, behavior in adult organisms. Do humans hold a "favored species" status as a rare exception? It's doubtful. Mating effort traits may be adaptive in humans as in other species. If so, why must we resort to any assumption of family pathology? As would be expected for normal traits, the traits conducive to crime should be able to arise in families not experiencing the litany of stresses, such as single parenthood, poor parental supervision, and unkind parents, repeated frequently in many criminological theories.

Second, human evolution has probably produced general learning mechanisms that can lead to the acquisition of new behaviors from any source. Hence, acquisition of specific criminal skills by learning should be *equally* effective whether the behavioral model is a parent, another adult, or a peer. It is probably the case that most children know how to commit crimes, but don't display those behaviors (e.g., the well-worn distinction between competence and performance in social learning theory). In this context, early family experiences should lack particular primacy. Indeed, there is overlooked evidence against the idea that parents are particularly potent behavioral models: the learning of sex-stereotyped behavior proceeds quickly, regardless of whether the parents conform to sex role stereotypes (Maccoby & Jacklin, 1974).

Using a game theory analysis, one might imagine a child who is biologically programmed to learn only from her parents. To the extent that successful behavioral innovations arise that are first displayed by another peer or adult, such a child would be adaptively disadvantaged. Genes leading to a flexible phenotype, able to learn from any source, should quickly be able to replace those that restrict learning only to parents. Some general learning rules may exist – for example, a bias to model a behavior that is frequently displayed in a population (Boyd & Richerson, 1985) – but learning, in general, is unlikely to be tied solely to the parent as source.

This abstract argument may not convince many. However, the evidentiary basis of popular theories of family effects is very weak. Consider Patterson's (1982, 1986a, 1986b) view that coercive interactions in the family are responsible for aggression and delinquency. Coercive interactions occur when one child uses force to get what he or she wants from a sibling (or parent), which may produce a forceful counteract from the target, until eventually the target yields and the child receives as a Skinnerian reward the cessation of opposition to his or her wishes. The social learning model is that such sequences gradually lead to habitual patterns of aggressive behavior.

But are these the important causes? Friendly critics have noted anomalous findings in Patterson's behavioral studies. In Patterson's excellent observational data, most strings of coercive interactions end *positively* in both the families of aggressive boys and in control families (Robinson & Jacobson, 1987, pp. 133–134). The frequency of negative outcomes was also about equal in the two types of families. This lack of differentiation in the microarchitecture of behavior was especially striking in view of the enormous differences in rates of coercion (lesser in controls). How can different contingencies, then, account for aggressive behavior?

More to the point of our critique, none of Patterson's work controls directly for children's genetic traits. The temperamental traits described earlier (lower threshold for anger, impulsiveness, lack of empathy) would foster coercive social interactions in a family. The fact that siblings would tend to share these traits genetically would only intensify the resulting family interactions – each child would have a partner who tends to respond in kind. Coercive interaction, therefore, may be an outcome of inherited temperamental traits, rather than a behavioral pattern fostered mainly by its psychological outcomes (which is not to say that the outcomes do not help maintain the behaviors). In his work, Patterson acknowledges that children's temperamental traits play some role in increasing the risk for antisocial behavior (1986b). I regard these individual differences in temperament as primary causal factors, rather than merely as secondary ones.

A weakness in this argument may be that family interventions are sometimes effective (Dumas, 1989). The aggressive and oppositional behavior of children can be reduced in some families through training parents in parenting skills. I expect, however, that such interventions will be most effective with children who are least extreme in temperamental traits. Moreover, controlling behavior in the family context may not alter a child's preferences (e.g., for novelty seeking, sexual variety, or aggression). Behavioral therapies for delinquents have been effective in group home settings as well, but little generalization may exist from the settings in which strong social control applies to other social settings. Individuals may rightly perceive that their interests in particular settings are best served by overt conformity. When they have the opportunity to select their own behavioral settings, however, they pursue the behaviors that may best satisfy their personality dispositions.

Adoption and Crime. Probably the research design most revealing of family environmental effects is the adoption design (Rowe, 1994). In recent years, as the number of families wishing to adopt started to exceed the ever dwindling supply of potential adoptive children, private and public adoption agencies have become quite selective about who is permitted to adopt. They attempt to screen out unstable and conflictful marriages, abusers of drugs and alcohol, and parents with psychopathology. Adoption represents more than just a possible change in parenting styles. Because adoptive families tend to have high incomes, adoptive placement can take children who may have been provided with poorer quality schools and place them in communities with better school systems; and it can take them from communities with higher rates in crime and place them in ones with lower crime rates. Of course, not all adoptive families are good ones. Relative to the conditions under which the adoptee would have been reared, however, adoption is a massive social intervention removing many of the social conditions statistically associated with crime.

Environmentally, then, adoptive placement should sharply lower the prevalence of antisocial traits among adoptees. Genetically, however, the effect of adoption will depend on the average of the biological parents' traits. Given that a major genetic correlate of crime may be early and more impulsive sexual behavior, I predict that biological parents' traits would deviate positively from the population mean. However, the effect of this deviation on the offspring mean may be a small one. Suppose the average of the parental trait scores is a full half standard deviation above the population mean. Suppose further a realistic heritability of 30%. The genetically expected mean of the children is then only 0.15 standard deviation above the population mean – not a great distance, but an outcome opposite in direction to that predicted under an environmental model. We would therefore anticipate that, in actual data, adoptees will be equally as antisocial as the population as a whole, or more so, although detecting the latter effect may require large samples.

One of the best-designed adoption studies looking at crime, the Danish Adoption Study, found that the prevalence of crime was higher in biological parents and their relinquished children than in the general population (Mednick, Gabrielli, & Hutchings, 1984). Figure 7.4 displays these results. Biological fathers were more antisocial than adoptive fathers (28.6% versus 6.2%), yet the latter's adoptive sons had a *higher* rate of property criminality than either their adoptive fathers or the general population (15.9%). A similar pattern held for mothers and adoptive daughters. Exposure of the adoptive child to the natural parents cannot account for this pattern. One-quarter of the adoptees were placed with the adoptive families immediately after birth; the remainder were placed temporarily in orphanages. The latter infants were usually adopted as infants (under 2 years). Statistical analyses indicated that age of placement did not affect the relationship of criminality in the biological parent to criminal outcome (Mednick et al., 1984).

Other adoptive studies have found an excess rate of behavior problems among male adoptees, even when adopted during infancy. Brodzinsky (1987, pp. 394–396) reviewed adoption outcomes from methodologically sound studies of nonclinical populations and from studies of clinical groups. The adoptee's problems often were in the conduct disorder domain (e.g., hyperactivity, attention span deficits, impulsivity, behavior prob-

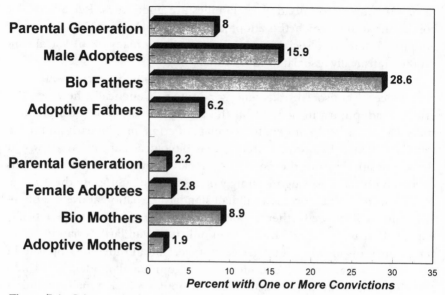

Figure 7.4. Crime prevalences among the population, adoptive offspring, and adoptive and biological parents.

lems at school). For example, Deutsch et al. (1982) discovered an eightfold increase in attention deficit disorder (a consistent correlate of aggression) among nonrelative, adoptees 6 to 13 years old, who were compared to the general population.

The Texas adoption study also strengthens the hypothesis of genetically mediated effects (Horn, Green, Carney, & Erickson, 1975; Loehlin, Willerman, & Horn, 1987). Horn et al. (1975) found that unwed mothers had substantial elevations on Minnesota Multiphasic Personality Inventory scales indicative of antisocial tendencies. In two cohorts, unwed mothers had about a one standard deviation elevation on the Psychopathic Deviation (PD) scale, and 16% of these mothers had clinically abnormal scores (2 SDs above the mean). A control group of pregnant mothers demonstrated that pregnancy itself did not influence antisocial traits (pregnant women did get more anxious, however).

The adoptive children were tested when they were about the ages at which their unwed mothers had been when tested *before* their births. The adoptive children were less well socialized (according to their adoptive mothers' ratings) and scored higher on the assertiveness and impulsivity scales of Cattell's 16PF test than the biological children in the same families. "Psychopathic" tendencies were transmitted genetically – the unwed mothers' PD scores correlated ($r = 0.27$) with those of their adopted-away children. (However, the results mentioned here should not mislead one into concluding that most adoptive children were maladjusted. Most had normal social traits in this and in the other studies mentioned.)

Parental treatment theories fare no better when applied to childhood conduct disorder. Jary and Stewart (1985) compared rates of psychopathology in the adoptive versus biological fathers and mothers of children diagnosed as conduct-disordered. As expected by a biological model, the rates were higher among the biological relatives. The study sounds one note deserving of special attention: the absence of a diagnosis of antisocial personality in the adoptive fathers. Jary and Stewart fairly concluded that a diagnosis of the adoptive father was not necessarily a precondition for the appearance of conduct problems: "If it is true that these disorders in fathers are largely responsible for the factors known to be associated with aggressive conduct disorder, such as broken homes, wife and child abuse, and inconsistent discipline, then our findings suggest that these social factors are not necessary to the origin of the disorder" (p. 10).

In summary, the adoption results upset a prevailing assumption of child-rearing effects on the development of antisocial traits.

Horizontal Transmission

The preceding section delved into the development of personality traits. I assume that such traits will develop, constrained only by environmental *extremes* outside the normal range of experience for humans (for elaboration, see Rowe, 1987). Specific environmental conditions, however, are more important for the learning of specific behaviors. A person cannot program a computer in Basic unless he or she is given the manual and instructions on how to use it. Complex behaviors may be formally taught, but most criminal behaviors may be acquired by simple observation. Thus, another transmission process involves observational learning by observing peers or adults.

Groups, however, are important for crime in more ways than merely transmitting discrete bits of knowledge about crime. The next section covers all these processes of social group influence. Social groups affect criminal behaviors in many operant ways, namely, by affecting the potential rewards for and risks of different behaviors.

It should be made abundantly clear, however, that the present model of behavioral motivation is conceptually distinct from that of social learning theories of crime. The model of the psyche in these theories is of a person who strives to maximize the balance between pain and pleasure. Even more complex learning models maintain this central assumption and assume that a pleasure–pain calculus is what motivates behavior – with pleasure always preferred to pain. Wilson and Herrnstein (1985) introduce a psychological time horizon into a learning theory model. Their noncriminal individual, looking more into the future, weighs the deferred costs of crime more than the criminal; and he or she has greater self-control to wait for deferred positive outcomes of noncrime. Despite these different time horizons, the underlying model of humankind is no more differentiated than the popular one of a "me generation" of pleasure seekers.

By contrast, the adaptive approach shares with other evolutionary theories the idea that motivations are not externally imposed, but depend instead on one's interests, broadly defined to refer to the degree perceived options for behavior satisfy a cognitively and emotionally structured psyche seeking to realize biological fitness. People are self-interested in the sense that they act in fitness-maximizing ways (or ways serving the proximate motives evolved to this end). An automatic evaluation of behavioral options occurs through different emotional responses, which are assumed to contain a large unlearned component. These responses are *not* equivalent to the simple-minded pursuit of pleasure or reward.

For example, an adolescent girl suffers discomfort while dieting, but she does not give up because she wants to make herself more attractive to boys. She may be biologically prepared to experience this goal positively, and to weigh it more heavily than the temporary discomforts imposed by her diet. In other words, the primary motives in the brain are evolved, psychological motives (e.g., a motive to control sexual partners), and people will put up with pain, even death, to achieve them.

Peer Groups. Scholars have argued whether association with delinquent peers causes crime ("bad apples will spoil a good one"), or whether crime-prone peers find one anoth   ("birds of a feather will flock together"). The interpretation to be placed on this statistical association is a vexing problem, because the finding itself is one of the most reliable in the delinquency literature with many implications for delinquency theory and public policy.

Elliott and Menard (this volume) have provided evidence that peer groups are causally most important. Although peers may have some causal impact (e.g., someone can be coerced into committing criminal acts), directionality is probably not as strong as they suggest. Their analytic procedure may not control for the possible size of acquaintanceship networks.

For instance, if the network includes everyone in a school class, then most individuals' delinquency would necessarily follow that of a peer. The report that someone in a peer network has done the act first, an ordering of events suggestive of peer group effects, may not imply causality.

Why not allow the relationship to be a bidirectional one (Thornberry, 1987; and this volume)? The peer group may foster crime in a number of ways, but at the same time males who may wish to avoid the risks associated with crime will avoid association with delinquent peers. Rowe and Osgood (1984) interpret twin data on this association (delinquency of self to that of friends) as showing a genetic component. In other words, individuals with a genetic tendency toward crime may befriend one another.

In terms of mating effort, the interests of these individuals may be better served by belonging to such a delinquent peer group. Delinquent groups demand little in the way of strong emotional attachments (Yablonsky, 1959). Group membership changes often. Gold (1970) observed that delinquent groups were like "pick-up" games in that the "delinquent group" consisted of casually acquainted individuals temporarily joined together for the sake of delinquent activity. Similarly, Farrington and Reiss (1988), in a study of co-offending using the London Youth Cohort, found that criminal companions associated with one another for only a short time. As with Gold's study, an implication is that criminal associations may be highly opportunistic. Delinquent groups permit impulsive acts, that is, the group is watchful for opportunities to pursue pleasure hedonistically. They provide an opportunity to dominate other individuals (who are not necessarily group members) by force and intimidation. Cairns, Neckerman, and Cairns (1989) traced the development of group structure in elementary school. Even prior to adolescence, more aggressive youths chose other aggressive youths as friends and reinforced one another's behaviors. That is, although these youths were rejected by the broader peer society, they belonged to friendship networks that may have encouraged their antisocial behavior.

The peer context is also an important one for learning delinquent and criminal behaviors. Peers who are familiar with a type of delinquent activity can demonstrate that activity to a nondelinquent peer. Because deviant behaviors are usually not complex, they may be readily learned by observing such behavioral models. Rowe and Rodgers (1991) modeled mathematically the spread of mildly deviant behaviors (e.g., the initiation of drinking alcohol and smoking) among teenagers. With increasing age, more and more teenagers in a generation try each behavior. The growth in the proportions of a generation who have tried the behavior follows a logistic curve. A mechanism that can explain this growth curve is epidemic spread, where most learning of the behaviors occurs in a face-to-face contact of one youth with another, where the naive youth adopts the behavior after exposure to the non-naive youth. Some use of alcoholic drinks was adopted by nearly everyone. About one-third of the teenagers became smokers. For more serious deviancy, the population at risk of adopting deviant acts would be smaller, and more a function of the mating/parenting effort trait. Nonetheless, the basic "epidemic" form of the spread of novel, serious deviant behaviors may be quite similar to that of these mildly deviant ones.

Peer groups may increase crime in other ways. For example, they can provide for temporary coalitions among men interested in criminal activity. Some crimes are more costly or more risky when committed alone than when committed with others. For example, it is less risky to rob someone if two people are present than one because the victim is less likely to put up resistance against such overwhelming odds. Or, breaking into a house may have a lower risk if one group member acts as a lookout. A group, by making the risk/benefit ratio of a delinquent act more favorable, will increase the likelihood of crime.

Peer groups unavoidably increase crime by fostering male–male competition for social status. The fruits of criminal activity – money, cars, good clothes, as well as crime itself – are sometimes rewarded with social status among delinquent peers. (Of course, noncriminal traits, such as a sense of humor, may also enhance status.) Social status can be viewed as something like a zero sum game – high status for one individual implies relatively lower status for others. This means that as males compete among themselves, one by-product may be increasing numbers of delinquent and criminal acts. Reproductively, social status is probably not a minor issue. Issues of face and status among peers may be a critical component of sex appeal. Given these kinds of evolutionary stakes, it is not surprising that seemingly trivial quarrels among men are a principal cause of homicide (Daly & Wilson, 1988).

Siblings. Siblings provide another potential route for the horizontal transmission of crime knowledge. Like peers, siblings are usually close in age and interact with one another intensely. One sibling can learn a criminal act from another. Moreover, if both siblings have some personality trait inclination to crime, they may serve as actual partners. In the Cambridge study (Farrington & Reiss, 1988), 9% of brothers co-offended. Co-offending rates were greater for brothers close in age than for brothers more removed in age, indicating the importance of interaction frequency among siblings. Twin and nontwin siblings also report committing acts together on self-report delinquency inventories (Rowe & Rodgers, 1989). The main determinant of the prevalence of co-offending was the prevalence of an act itself: The greater the proportion of siblings committing an act, the more likely they committed it with a sibling. Twins and siblings who have more frequent social contact with one another were also more likely to co-offend.

The exact process by which siblings influence one another is unknown. Patterson (1986) suggests a mutually coercive process, whereby siblings fight with one another, and this fighting increases their level of antisocial behavior. On the other hand, Rowe and Gulley's (1992) evidence, from teenage rather than preteen children, is more consistent with some kind of mutual imitation process. Two facts fit with this interpretation. One is that a mathematical model of imitation effects, genetic effects, and idiosyncratic environment effects best reproduced twin and nontwin sibling correlations for delinquency. Second, siblings who co-offend enjoy spending time together, indicative of a positive kind of social influence process. Whatever the process, a sibling can be another source contributing to the learning and maintenance of antisocial behaviors.

Oblique Transmission

Adults and symbolic media (television, newspapers) can also serve to teach and reinforce criminal behaviors. In some communities, young adults, other than immediate peers, may encourage crime. For example, stolen goods must be fenced, and the presence of an adult ready to pay for stolen goods may encourage theft for profit. Juveniles who serve time in correctional institutions are said to learn the details of criminal activities from other incarcerated youth. Many gangs in large cities contain members in their early 20s – older individuals who can socialize younger recruits into the ways of criminal activities. Despite these possible sources of criminal learning and socialization, the role of oblique transmission in crime has been underemphasized.

Another possible source of criminal teachings is the media. Contrary to media critics, I doubt that fictional television programs contribute to crime rates except in the most minor way (see Freedman, 1986). Rather than fictional programs, I believe that nonfiction local and national news programs affect the crime rate to some extent. These programs lead to the rapid spread of innovative crimes among the nation's population of criminal individuals. For example, media reports spread car jacking – stealing cars at gunpoint from their owners – nationwide. The crimes portrayed in nonfiction programs are real ones, so that imitation of them is practical, and the models of real crimes are people with characteristics similar to those of other criminals. In summary, nonfictional media crime reports may increase the peer-to-peer transmission of crimes in local social networks.

Ecological Conditions

Ecological conditions may produce increased crime rates. We are interested in ecological conditions that would tip a person with a given personality disposition into greater or lesser rates of criminal behavior (see Figure 7.1). That is, ecological intensifiers do not change immediately the underlying trait disposition. Rather, they affect its degree of expression as particular behaviors and impact more strongly on those individuals predisposed to crime.

Ecological conditions probably vary most cross-culturally. For instance, in some Middle Eastern countries, adolescents may confront more obstacles to translating mating effort dispositions into related problems like teenage pregnancy. In these societies, teenage girls are physically sequestered until marriage and teenage boys are under the constant watchfulness of adult eyes. Thus, the expression of mating effort is strongly inhibited.

The ecological intensifiers reviewed here are interactive effects of population composition, the sex ratio, the availability of resources needed to achieve social prestige, and the predictability of reproductive success.

Population Composition

Population composition refers to the distribution of the crime-proneness trait in a population. In our analysis, this refers primarily to the population distribution of the mating effort versus parenting effort trait. Any given population would possess a mean and variance on this trait. Greater mating effort, and probably greater criminal behavior, would be expected in local populations with the greater M/P trait mean.

A number of processes could change the mating effort distribution in a community, but probably the most important is the rate of in- and out-migration of families high and low in the trait. Individuals interested in criminal activity, of course, may be attracted to neighborhoods with high crime rates because they can find criminal companions there. Crime-prone families may congregate in some neighborhoods for socioeconomic reasons. Criminals, compared to their natal families of origin, may fall in social class because they do not hold steady, well-paying jobs (but see Tittle & Villemez, 1977 for a positive association between minor crime and upward social mobility). Their legitimate, and illegitimate children, are likely to be reared in poor neighborhoods. Thus, the average phenotype will vary from one neighborhood to another, accounting for some neighborhood variation in crime rates.

Other forces will tend to reduce intercommunity variation. First, as with any multigene trait, parents with only average trait values can give birth to children with extreme ones. Second, mating effort is probably less important for social mobility than other intellectual and academic traits with which its correlation is modest (e.g., IQ and years of education). Wealth, too, can be socially inherited by anyone. Hence, children in neighborhoods varying widely in socioeconomic status will nonetheless be more likely to commit crimes because they inherit a bias toward mating effort.

A more interesting phenomenon is the possibility of *interactive* effects resulting from differences in population composition. As many teachers know, a single difficult child in a classroom can be quelled. Having three such children, who can feed off one another, can present an insurmountable problem. Similarly, small changes in population composition may result in effects beyond the mere head count of the increasing number of at-risk individuals.

For example, if there are more young males in a given geographic area, the opportunities for crime-prone ones to find each other and to spend more time together may be greater. They also may have more easy contact with potential victims. Youth gang formation may be encouraged, because youth may organize in loose coalitions to protect themselves against other aggressive groups. Self-identified youth gangs may operate as a threshold effect, coming into existence only when a high level of competition exists among a high density of crime-prone individuals. Yet, once in existence, they may rapidly increase the overall crime rate, which now consists of gang-related crimes as well as other crimes. Moreover, neutral youths will have more difficulty avoiding involvement with the gangs. For self-protection, they may be forced to affiliate with one or another group of antisocial youths. The "socialized" delinquent may be coerced into crime by social circumstances and neither morally approve of crime nor find it intrinsically rewarding. The type of community processes described here may account for an effect of adoptive family social class on criminal behavior (Mednick et al., 1984). Independently of genetic risk, adoptees in more middle-class communities had fewer property crime convictions, suggesting that improved social conditions can lead to some reduction of crime (although not necessarily of mating effort).

Sex Ratio

The sex ratio may be another ecological intensifier. If females are fewer in number, or if some men can monopolize a disproportionate number of women through legal marriage practices such as polygamy, then intermale competition will intensify. Thus, greater crime is to be predicted under either condition. We know of no particular evidence on this hypothesis in industrial societies. However, the trends are in the correct direction in the United States. In the pre–World War II period (1900–1945) there were proportionately more marriage-eligible females 15 to 24 years of age than marriage-eligible males 20 to 29 years of age (Pitcher & Hamblin, 1982). From the male's perspective, but perhaps not from the female's, this ratio has worsened during the postwar period due to lowered male mortality, for now there are fewer marriage-eligible females per male. This change has accompanied postwar crime rate increases. Even if changing these sex ratios exerted some effect on crime and were not merely coincidental, they cannot be the main cause of crime rate trends, because the very rapid crime rate increase from 1958 to 1974 cannot be explained solely in these terms (see Noble, 1977 for an explanation in terms of the spread of drug use). Nonetheless, the hypothesis is an intriguing one.

Group Norms

A third intensifier may be prevailing group norms that determine what level of acquired resources confer social prestige. If low levels are required, they may be obtained more easily through both legitimate and illegitimate means. A requirement of higher levels would tend to increase the amount of criminal activity. Speculatively, the high crime rates now associated with widespread drug sales may reflect this kind of process. With the large amount of cash obtained from drug sales, it is possible to buy expensive cars, boats, and other goods once beyond the economic means of most criminals. Group norms may specify that to achieve high social status, expensive items must be displayed. This process could intensify competition, because each person would be trying to accumulate through legal and illegal means goods with a greater total dollar value than before.

Reproductive Success

Daly and Wilson (1988) propose another possible ecological factor: the relative certainty of reproductive success. Using computer simulation models, they demonstrated how high-"risk" (of mortality) behavioral strategies – if they lead occasionally to high reproductive success – can be favored evolutionarily, despite frequent mortality among risk takers. In conditions of reproductive uncertainty – as in poor, inner-city neighborhoods in which individuals possess few resources and lack the kinds of skills needed to obtain resources with certainty – pursuit of a high-risk reproductive strategy may be adaptive. Daly and Wilson comment: "Natural selection will especially tend to favor risk-proneness in circumstances where one's anticipated life trajectory, in the absence of risk, is so poor that one has little or no expected fitness to lose. . . . Dangerous competitive tactics are predicted to be especially prevalent within those demographic categories in which the probability of reproductive failure is high" (p. 168).

Biological and Social Consequences

As shown in Figure 7.2, ultimately reproductive and social consequences will determine the frequencies of different types of behavioral strategies in later generations. We can think of two forces as being at work. One is the relative rates of reproduction of individuals adopting mating effort/crime versus parenting effort/noncrime strategies. These relative rates of reproduction will determine the frequencies of the genes determining the mating effort trait, and hence, its mean and variance in the next generation. The other force is the pressure of social deterrence on crime/noncrime strategies themselves. As the pressure of social deterrence increases, crime strategies become more risky and are less likely to be adopted. This interpretation, of course, implies a degree of conscious response to social coercion in making one's behavioral choices. Social deterrence could possibly have eugenic consequences as well. It is unlikely, however, that such consequences would be felt over the short run of a few generations.

Biological Equilibrium

It is extremely difficult to gather the kind of empirical evidence that would allow one to determine the nature of the overall selective process. A number of alternatives have been proposed by others. For example, Rushton's r/K theory attributes the within- and between-population distribution of

M/P traits to a process of r/K selection: r selection refers to ecological conditions that confer greater fitness on high reproductive rates, short life spans, short birth intervals, large number of offspring, and other related traits; K selection confers fitness on the opposite suite of traits. Compared to other animals, all humans are at the K end of the reproductive continuum. Rushton (1989) has attempted to specify the ecological conditions responsible for genetic variability in r/K traits in human populations. His theory requires a fairly speculative reconstruction of humankind's evolutionary past. Furthermore, it emphasizes population (racial and ethnic) differences, whereas the adoptive strategy theory is mainly concerned with individual differences.

In another explanation, Harpending and Draper (1988) attribute M/P genetic variation to intercultural variation among human societies. They argue that in some societies high mating effort is reproductively favored, whereas in others high parenting effort is favored.

I conceptualize the maintenance of genetic variability in terms of *frequency dependent selection*. An advantage of this conceptualization is that it can explain the heritability of mating-crime/parenting-noncrime strategies in almost any society. Nontechnological societies, with very different ecological conditions, may come to be dominated by one type of individual or the other. In large and complex societies, however, individuals who adopt both strategies probably have about equal rates of reproductive success. Another advantage is that a completely analogous process may occur with respect to social reactions and counterreactions to criminal activity.

Frequency dependent selection corresponds to Dawkin's (1976) familiar "hawks versus doves" mixed motive game. That is, when hawks meet hawks, both lose. When doves meet doves, both win. However, when a hawk meets a dove, the hawk obtains the larger payoff. Given specific values of costs and rewards, a mathematical equilibrium exists such that payoffs to the hawks and doves are equal when a certain proportion of the population consists of hawks and doves (e.g., a 70%, 30% split). Departures from this equilibrium tend to restore population structure because the decreasing group gains in payoff whereas the increasing group loses in payoff. The equilibrium is the same if members of the population switch between strategies (say, hawk 70% of the time; dove 30% of the time), but we have already established that rapid switching among criminal strategies is uncharacteristic of people under modern ecological conditions. Thus, mating effort/crime and parenting effort/noncrime strategies may coexist in some kind of frequency dependent equilibrium such that, given the population composition, reproductive rates for people pursuing either strategy would be about equal.[4] A possible quantitative model of frequency dependent selection for human mating strategies was presented by Gangestad & Simpson (1989).[5]

Social Equilibrium

A comparable process may apply to social reactions and counterreactions to crime. If an imaginary population had no criminal behavior, then probably few sanctions would be imposed against it. Even if such sanctions existed on the books, their infrequent use may over time erode society's vigilance. If people are habitually trusting, individuals who do adopt the exploitive strategy would find easy pickings and the reward/cost ratio of the strategy would be highly favorable. The rich products of a society of nonexploitive producers would also invite exploitation, just as Genghis Khan's followers decided to take for themselves the wealth of the productive, non-nomadic societies. The number of individuals selecting this strategy would then increase.

[4] A prisoner's dilemma contest between hawk and dove strategies has as a stable equilibrium the tit-for-tat strategy of first cooperating and then exploiting, if one's partner exploits. That the theoretical game has this stable strategy, however, does not mean that criminal individuals will first attempt cooperation. For a number of reasons, such strategies may not be stable in natural populations. For example, the game assumes perfect memory of previous partners. In the natural world, however, perfect memory may be absent or criminal individuals may move into new communities where they are unknown. The costs of learning noncriminal versus criminal strategies may differ. A variety of factors could make the tit-for-tat strategy unattainable.

[5] Gangestad and Simpson's model makes many of the same assumptions as the present adaptive strategy theory, including the idea of an underlying trait dimension favoring commitment in sexual relationship and investment in offspring versus noncommitment and sexual promiscuity. Gangestad and Simpson's derivation of their evolutionary model, however, focuses on the potential benefits and costs to *females* pursuing what we have labeled mating effort versus parenting (in Gangestad's terms, "unrestricted" and "restricted" strategies). Females may gain from the unrestricted strategy by producing reproductively more successful sons. They propose several empirical tests of their model, including the prediction that unrestricted females will produce more sons than daughters in comparison to restricted females.

Of course, as society bore the increasing costs of criminal activity, adverse social reaction would be to increase penalties against criminals, the number of police, and the use of other tactics to underscore crime's costs. These increased costs should lead to the abandonment of the strategy, or at least its reduction. The most likely result is an oscillation around the equilibrium point, as society adopts greater vigilance, finds it effective but costly, relaxes vigilance, and then experiences an increase in crime, until the cycle repeats. Moreover, external factors, such as plague, war, and weather conditions, may produce temporary tears in the social fabric that raise and lower the costs imposed on criminal behavior, again encouraging shifts in the relative frequency of the dual strategies.

Although unlikely except by hypothesis, a society starting from the other extreme – composed entirely of criminal strategists – would bear the high costs of interpersonal conflict and the inability of groups to carry out their long-term activities. Such a society would be open to an increase in the numbers of noncriminal strategists, as people who cooperate with one another and fulfill social obligations obtain more material and psychological rewards than others. Alternatively, populations composed of pure criminal strategists may go extinct, and their ecological niches may be filled by societies of strategists of both types. As expressed by Cohen and Machelek (1988, p. 481), "Because pure strategy systems invite invasions by opportunistic alternative strategists, behavioral diversity in the form of populations composed of both producer and expropriator [equivalent to our crime] strategists should be the expected rule, not the exception. In this way, crime can be said to be 'normal' in populations."

Relationship to Other Theories

Adaptive strategy theory (AST) is clearly distinct from the mainstream criminological theories of crime, yet areas of agreement do exist. Social control theory (Hirschi, 1969) postulates that delinquent and criminal individuals possess weaker attachments to parents and other significant individuals and have less stake in conformity. Low attachment to others is one indicator of AST's postulated mating effort/parenting effort trait. Lack of investment in school may be partly a result of low IQ. Thus, both theories agree on a set of attitudinal or personality correlates of delinquency. However, the theories differ in their interpretations of these surface traits. AST assumes the existence of genetic variation underlying the traits and deemphasizes family-environmental influences, whereas social control theory attributes variation in these traits to, among other factors, variation in family environments.

Subcultural theory (Cohen, 1955) assumes that the existence of different norms in some groups promotes delinquent behavior, along with the inability of lower-class children to compete in middle-class school environments. The short-run, shared hedonism of delinquents coincides with indicators of the mating/parenting trait. On the other hand, subcultural theory does not identify reproductive fitness as the ultimate source of trait variability or as the ultimate end of delinquent-type behaviors. The theories generally agree on the difficulty delinquents have competing against others, in school and in the occupational arena, although only AST theory emphasizes the genetic component in IQ trait variation.

Strain theory (Cloward & Ohlin, 1960) attributes delinquent behaviors to the frustration lower-class youth experience when they are unable to meet middle-class expectations for material success. Unable to achieve their aspirations, delinquents may turn to deviant behaviors as alternative routes for attaining money, goods, and social prestige. In AST theory, youth are not assumed to compare themselves with distant middle-class standards. Instead, the main source of strain is the attempt by males to win in male–male encounters a high level of social prestige in local peer groups. Conditions that intensify male–male competition, such as resource uncertainty, population composition, and so on, would lead to higher rates of delinquent behavior.

Miller (1958), in another type of subcultural theory, associated crime with female-headed households and with serial monogamy mating patterns, in which desertion by males was common. Boys growing up such households were thought to assert their masculinity against their subordination to their mothers and other women as they sought a masculine identity in delinquent activities outside of the family. AST theory regards this pattern as indicating high mating effort. That these families produce more criminal and delinquent youth than others reflects the genetic transmission of the mating effort trait from antisocial fathers to their sons. That these boys often live in mother-headed families is seen as unrelated to their eventual personality development (e.g., as noted earlier, similar traits may develop when children are adopted by two-parent families). Again, the theories agree about the description of the delinquent and his or her family context, but differ when deeper issues of underlying determination are considered.

Like social control theory, AST theory views crime as essentially a normal behavioral alternative. Social control theory assumes that criminal acts were so attractive to youth – because of their inherent pleasure-giving properties – that no special conceptual apparatus was necessary to explain delinquency, once conventional attachments, involvements, and commitments were weakened. AST theory, however, finds positive motivation for crime and delinquency that is stronger for individuals who fall on the mating effort side of the M/P trait. Unlike earlier biological theories of crime (Lombroso, 1911), though, AST theory postulates that the genes underlying this trait variation are normal genetic alternatives rather than some type of defective genetic material. Nor are criminals assumed to be in any way more biologically primitive than noncriminals. AST theory goes further than social control theory, nonetheless, by asserting that, because criminal tendencies are essentially normal traits, they may arise when parental psychopathology is absent. Indeed, the more society tends to a homogeneous, noncriminal way of life, the more it opens itself up to the risk of invasion by criminal strategists.

Social Policy Implications

This relatively new theory is not ready to meet the needs of social policy makers. Social policy makers are concerned with interventions involving manipulable variables; AST theory focuses on an evolutionary and social explanation of crime designed to increase the understanding of criminal behavior and to direct research efforts.

The variables identified in AST theory may affect crime but not be particularly amenable to interventions. The theory clearly places a great emphasis on individual differences in personality dispositions. The existence of a mating effort trait is hypothesized. Whether the hypothesized trait serves a mating effort function or not, the particular temperaments increasing the risk of later crime are of interest to policy makers. We need better measures of temperament in childhood and further predictive studies relating these traits to later outcomes.

Better identification of the trait, however, may not easily solve policy makers' problems. As summarized earlier, the data from adoptions both in the United States and abroad support a hypothesis that mating effort traits are *normally* occurring ones. Although these traits usually arise in families typified by psychopathology and behavioral problems, they may arise equally in families with good parenting styles and with access to the many valued resources afforded by high incomes. Indeed, it is difficult to believe that social interventions aimed at altering family conditions so that most families exhibit the discipline practices of intelligent, middle-class parents would greatly reduce the mating effort traits of children who are at the trait extreme. Whether preadolescent interventions would decrease the tendency of high mating effort children to commit crimes later should be evaluated using experimental research designs.

A biologically based trait, of course, raises the possibility of using biological as opposed to social interventions. Biological interventions could take two forms. First, eugenic interventions would involve adopting public policies that control human reproduction. Most Americans would find this policy direction morally abhorrent. Moreover, given that genetic selection against a trait is a slow process, it would take several generations to reduce crime through changing inherited behavioral traits. Because state-enforced eugenic methods are both impractical and violate the fundamental right of every person to have a family, they would fail to serve as policy alternatives.

Therapeutic interventions could involve administering drugs to alter nervous system functioning (Cloninger, 1987). The use of drug interventions is not an impossibility, but too little is known about the physiological bases of most behavioral traits and the effectiveness of drug treatments to recommend this approach at present. AST theory's focus on nervous system functioning will further encourage the ongoing search for drug-therapeutic interventions. This should be an area of active research, because we cannot really anticipate what we might learn from a better understanding of the neurological bases of traits predisposing individuals to crime. Whether drug therapies for criminality would be compatible with the values of a democratic society is an issue that deserves further study and debate. It is hardly automatic that effective drugs should be used, even if they were found.

Ecological intensifiers could be another target of intervention efforts, but they are not manipulatable in our social context. For example, if threshold effects are associated with population composition, one could plan communities to keep the at-risk population below the threshold level – an intervention contravening our most fundamental democratic values favoring freedom of association and movement. The control of crime is not worth tearing up the U.S. Constitution. Similarly, it would be morally abhorrent to take steps to increase the female:male sex ratio as a crime control strategy, assuming the sex ratio has some influence on mating effort and crime.

Given that the theory offers no immediate handle on crime control, we believe that the best intervention strategy is that of an *experimenting society*. That is, evaluation research designs should be applied to different crime control strategies, both punitive (e.g., imprisonment) and therapeutic (e.g., job training during parole), and those methods found to be most effective should be disseminated and applied. In the crime control field, there is currently an attitude that "nothing works." This pessimism has arisen because few evaluations of programs for criminals have produced strikingly positive results. Given the limitations of much evaluation research (Sechrest, West, Phillips, Redner, & Yeaton, 1979), however, accepting these negative results may be overly pessimistic. It is probable that we could do worse than we are doing now, and we could do better. New social interventions may yield incremental improvements that make a dent in America's pressing crime problem.

Conclusions

This chapter has presented a new theory of crime and delinquency: adaptive strategy theory. The components of the theory consist of constitutional factors (mating effort/parenting effort trait, IQ, sex, age); social learning influences (peers, siblings, unrelated adults); ecological intensifiers (population composition and resource availability); and social and biological outcomes. These components explain the prevalence of crime and noncrime in the population and its maintenance over generations. The constitutional factors account for broad individual differences in rates of criminal behavior.

This theory assumes that crime and delinquency are *normal* behavioral alternatives, ultimately supported in the population by genetic variation and by the constant competition among alternative behavioral strategies. Crime is conceptualized as a behavioral strategy partly resulting from the evolutionary strategy of mating effort, by which reproductive success is maximized through multiple matings. This strategy is assumed to compete in the population against a strategy of parenting effort, whereby parental investment in children maximizes fitness. A mating effort/parenting effort (M/P) trait biases toward the selection of one strategy or the other. Possible indicators of the trait include aggression, sensation seeking, and strong sexual drive. Variation in the indicators results from genetic variation with pleiotropic effects. Another trait, intelligence, is also related to crime. However, the M/P trait and IQ are hypothesized to be genetically independent. IQ affects the capacity to compete successfully in the social hierarchies of modern, industrial societies.

The constitutional factors of age and sex are also related to crime through their association with the selection of mating effort versus parenting effort strategies. In general, mating effort increases more the fitness of males, relative to females, and of young individuals, relative to old. Criminal behaviors are acquired by a process of socialization and learning. The theory emphasizes horizontal (peer) and oblique (unrelated adult-child) transmission of these behaviors, rather than family-environmental factors.

Crime rates can be affected by ecological conditions, namely, population composition factors and resource availability factors. In general, conditions that intensify male–male competition will increase crime rates.

Finally, criminal strategies are maintained in the population by both biological and social outcomes. The relative reproductive rates of criminals and noncriminals maintain genetic variability in the mating effort trait. Under a process of frequency dependent selection, increases in mating effort may be self-limiting, as the strategy loses its reproductive advantage if genes supporting it become too frequent in the population. Similarly, social deterrence acts against the adoption of criminal behaviors. Social responses to crime, like the genetic variation itself, may exist in some kind of oscillating, frequency dependent equilibrium.

The idea that human behavior evolves toward a morally neutral goal, the maximization of biological fitness, is not a particularly appealing one. The mere production of offspring favors this goal in a biological sense, regardless of whether behaviors so evolved would justify moral indignation in us. This chapter has been about "what is" – a explanation of crime and noncrime behavioral variation in the United States and other societies. It is not a prescription about "what ought to be." Cognitive abilities allow humans to imagine social arrangements that do not now exist; they allow us to search for alternative, sometimes utopian societies. By describing crime in these biological terms, we do not mean to discourage the search for better social conditions – although we probably will not find them without first comprehending both the biological and social bases of crime and the real difficulties that they present.

REFERENCES

Afzal, M. (1988). Consequences of consanguinity on cognitive behavior. *Behavior Genetics, 18,* 583–594.

Ahlstrom, W. M., & Havighurst, R. J. (1971). *400 losers.* San Francisco: Jossey-Bass.

Boyd, R., & Richerson, P. J. (1985). *Culture and the evolutionary process.* Chicago: University of Chicago Press.

Brodzinsky, D. M. (1987). Looking at adoption through rose-colored glasses: A critique of Marquis and Detweiler's "Does adoption mean different? An attributional analysis." *Journal of Personality and Social Psychology, 52,* 394–398.

Cairns, R. B., Neckerman, H. J., & Cairns, B. D. (1989). Social networks and the shadows of synchrony. In G. R. Adams, R. Montemayor, & T. P. Gullotta (Eds.), *Biology of adolescent development and behavior* (pp. 275–305). Newbury Park, CA: Sage.

Cavalli-Sforza, L. L., & Feldman, M. W. (1981). *Cultural transmission and evolution: A quantitative approach.* Princeton, NJ: Princeton University Press.

Christiansen, K. O. (1970). Crime in a Danish twin population. *Acta Geneticae Medicae et Gemellologiae, 19,* 323–326.

Cloninger, C. R. (1987). Pharmacological approaches to the treatment of antisocial behavior. In S. A. Mednick, T. E. Moffitt, & S. A. Stack (Eds.), *The causes of crime: New biological approaches* (pp. 329–350). Cambridge: Cambridge University Press.

Cloninger, C. R., Christiansen, K. O., Reich, T., & Gottesman, I. I. (1978). Implications of sex differences in the prevalences of antisocial personality, alcoholism, and criminality for familial transmission. *Archives of General Psychiatry, 35,* 941–951.

Cloninger, C. R., & Guze, S. B. (1970). Psychiatric illness and female criminality: The role of sociopathy and hysteria in the antisocial women. *American Journal of Psychiatry, 127,* 303–311.

Cloninger, C. R., & Guze, S. B. (1973). Psychiatric illness in the families of female criminals: A study of 288 first-degree relatives. *British Journal of Psychiatry, 122,* 697–703.

Cloward, R. A., & Ohlin, L. E. (1960). *Delinquency and opportunity.* New York: Free Press.

Cohen, A. K. (1955). *Delinquent boys.* Glencoe, IL: Free Press.

Cohen, L. E., & Machalek, R. (1988). A general theory of expropriative crime: An evolutionary ecological approach. *American Journal of Sociology, 94,* 465–501.

Crawford, C. B., & Anderson, J. L. (1989). Sociobiology: An environmentalist discipline? *American Psychology, 44,* 1449–1459.

Daly, M., & Wilson, M. (1983). *Sex, evolution, and behavior* (2nd ed.). Boston: PWS Publishers.

Daly, M., & Wilson, M. (1988). *Homicide.* New York: Aldine de Gruyter.

Dawkins, R. (1976). *The selfish gene.* Oxford: Oxford University Press.

Deutsch, C. K., Swanson, J. M., Bruell, J. H., Cantwell, D. P., Weinberg, F., & Baren, M. (1982). Overrepresentation of adoptees in children with the attention deficit disorder. *Behavior Genetics, 12,* 231–238.

Dumas, J. E. (1989). Treating antisocial behavior in children: Child and family approaches. *Clinical Psychology Review, 9,* 197–222.

Ellis, L. (1984). Genetics and criminal behavior. *Criminology, 20,* 43–66.

Ellis, L. (1987). Criminal behavior and r/K selection: An extension of gene-based evolutionary theory. *Deviant Behavior, 8,* 149–176.

Farrington, D. P. (1988). Long-term prediction of offending and other life outcomes. In H. Wegener, F. Losel, & J. Haisch (Eds.), *Criminal behavior and the justice system: Psychological perspectives.* New York: Springer-Verlag.

Farrington, D. P., Ohlin, L. E., & Wilson, J. Q. (1986). *Understanding and controlling crime: Toward a new research strategy.* New York: Springer-Verlag.

Farrington, D. P., & Reiss, A. J. (1988). Co-offending in a prospective longitudinal survey of London males. Manuscript under review.

Freedman, J. L. (1986). Television violence and aggression: A rejoinder. *Psychological Bulletin, 100,* 372–378.

Gangestad, S. W., & Simpson, J. A. (1989). On human sociosexual variation: An evolutionary model of mating propensities. Unpublished manuscript.

Glueck, S., & Glueck, E. (1968). *Delinquents and nondelinquents in perspective.* Cambridge, MA: Harvard University Press.

Gold, M. (1970). *Delinquent behavior in an American city.* Belmont, CA: Wadsworth.

Harpending, H. C., & Draper, P. (1988). Antisocial behavior and the other side of cultural evolution. In T. E. Moffitt & S. A. Mednick (Eds.), *Biological Contributions to Crime Causation* (pp. 293–307). Boston: NATO ASI Series D: Behavioral and Social Sciences – No. 40, Martinus Nijhoff.

Harpending, H. C., & Sobus, J. (1987). Sociopathy and adaptation. *Ethology and Sociobiology, 8,* 63S–72S.

Hirschi, T. (1969). *Causes of delinquency.* Berkeley: University of California Press.

Hirschi, T., & Gottfredson, M. (1983). Age and the explanation of crime. *American Journal of Sociology, 89,* 552–584.

Hirschi, T., & Gottfredson, M. (1987). Causes of white collar crime. *Criminology, 25,* 949–974.

Hirschi, T., & Hindelang, M. J. (1977). Intelligence and delinquency: A revisionist review. *American Sociological Review, 42,* 571–587.

Horn, J. M., Green, M., Carney, R., & Erickson, M. T. (1975). Bias against genetic hypotheses in adoption studies. *Archives of General Psychiatry, 32,* 1365–1367.

Hrdy, S. B. (1981). *The women that never evolved.* Cambridge, MA: Harvard University Press.

Jary, M. L., & Stewart, M. A. (1985). Psychiatric disorder in parents of adopted children with aggressive conduct disorder. *Neuropsychobiology, 13,* 7–11.

Jessor, R., Costa, F., Jessor, L., & Donovan, J. E. (1983). Time of first intercourse: A prospective study. *Journal of Personality and Social Psychology, 44,* 608–626.

Jessor, R., & Jessor, S. (1977). *Problem behavior and psychological development: A longitudinal study.* New York: Academic Press.

Kenrick, D. T., Dantchik, A., & MacFarlane, S. (1983). Personality, environment, and criminal behavior: An evolutionary perspective. In W. S. Laufer

& J. M. Day (Eds.), *Theory, moral development, and criminal behavior* (pp. 217–241). Lexington, MA: Lexington Books.

Langlois, J. H., Roggman, L. A., Casey, R. J., Ritter, J. M., Rieser-Danner, L. A., & Jenkins, V. Y. (1987). Infants' preferences for attractive faces: Rudiments of a stereotype? *Developmental Psychology, 23,* 363–369.

Loeber, R., & Dishion, T. (1983). Early predictors of male delinquency: A review. *Psychological Bulletin, 94,* 68–99.

Loehlin, J. C., Willerman, L., & Horn, J. M. (1987). Personality resemblance in adoptive families: A 10-year follow-up. *Journal of Personality and Social Psychology, 53,* 961–969.

Lombroso, C. (1911). *Crime, its causes and remedies.* Boston: Little, Brown.

Maccoby, E. E., & Jacklin, E. N. (1974). *The psychology of sex differences.* Stanford: Stanford University Press.

Maccoby, E. E., & Martin, J. A. (1983). Socialization in the context of the family: Parent-child interaction. In E. M. Hetherington (Ed.) & P. H. Mussen (Series Ed.), *Handbook of child psychology: Vol. 4. Socialization, personality, and social development* (pp. 1–101). New York: Wiley.

Malamuth, N., Haber, S., & Feshbach, S. (1980). Testing hypotheses regarding rape: Exposure to sexual violence, sex differences, and the normality of rapists. *Journal of Research in Personality, 14,* 121–137.

McMichael, P. (1979). The hen or the egg? Which comes first – antisocial emotional disorders or reading disability? *British Journal of Educational Psychology, 49,* 226–238.

Mednick, S. A., Gabrielli, W. F., & Hutchings, B. (1984). Genetic influences in criminal convictions: Evidence from an adoption cohort. *Science, 224,* 891–894.

Mednick, S. A., Gabrielli, W. F., & Hutchings, B. (1985). Criminality and adoption. *Science, 227,* 984–989.

Mellen, S. L. W. (1981). *The evolution of love.* Oxford: W. H. Freeman.

Miller, W. B. (1958). Lower-class culture as a generating milieu of gang delinquency. *Journal of Social Issues, 14,* 5–19.

Noble, J. V. (1977). Feedback, instability and crime waves. *Journal of Research in Crime and Delinquency, 14,* 107–128.

Olweus, D. (1979). Stability of aggressive reaction patterns in males: A review. *Psychological Bulletin, 86,* 852–875.

Olweus, D. (1986). Aggression and hormones: Relationship with testosterone and adrenaline. In D. Olweus, J. Block, & M. Radke-Yarrow (Eds.), *Development of antisocial and prosocial behavior: Research, theories, and issues* (pp. 51–72). Orlando, FL: Academic Press.

Patterson, G. R. (1982). *Coercive family process.* Eugene, OR: Castalia.

Patterson, G. R. (1986a). The contribution of siblings to training for fighting: A microsocial analysis. In D. Olweus, J. Block, & M. Radke-Yarrow (Eds.),

Development of antisocial and prosocial behavior: Research, theories, and issues (pp. 235–261). Orlando, FL: Academic Press.

Patterson, G. R. (1986b). Performance models for antisocial boys. *American Psychologist, 41,* 432–444.

Payne, R. B. (1977). The ecology of brood parasitism in birds. *Annual Review of Ecology and Systematics, 8,* 1–28.

Pitcher, B. L., & Hamblin, R. L. (1982). Collective learning in ongoing political conflicts. *International Political Science Review, 3,* 71–90.

Plomin, R. (1986). *Development, genetics, and psychology.* Hillsdale, NJ: Erlbaum.

Reitsma-Street, M., Offord, D. R., & Finch, T. (1985). Pairs of same-sexed siblings discordant for antisocial behavior. *British Journal of Psychiatry, 146,* 415–423.

Robinson, E. A., & Jacobson, N. S. (1987). Social learning theory and family psychopathology: A Kantian model in behaviorism? In T. Jacob (Ed.), *Family interaction and psychopathology: Theories, methods, and findings* (pp. 117–162). New York: Plenum.

Rowe, D. C. (1983). A biometrical analysis of perceptions of family environment: A study of twin and singleton sibling kinships. *Child Development, 54,* 416–423.

Rowe, D. C. (1986). Genetic and environmental components of antisocial behavior: A study of 265 twin pairs. *Criminology, 24,* 513–532.

Rowe, D. C. (1987). Resolving the person-situation debate: Invitation to an interdisciplinary dialogue. *American Psychologist, 42,* 218–227.

Rowe, D. C. (1990). Inherited dispositions for learning delinquent behavior: New evidence. In L. Ellis & H. Hoffman (Eds.), *Evolution, the brain, and criminal behavior: A reader in biosocial criminology* (pp. 197–218). New York: Praeger.

Rowe, D. C. (1994). *The limits of family influence: Genes, experience, and behavior.* New York: Guilford.

Rowe, D. C., & Gulley, B. (1992). Sibling effects on substance use and delinquency. *Criminology, 30,* 217–233.

Rowe, D. C., & Osgood, D. W. (1984). Sociological theories of delinquency and heredity: A reconsideration. *American Sociological Review, 49,* 526–540.

Rowe, D. C., Osgood, D. W., & Nicewander, A. (1990). A latent trait approach to unifying criminal careers. *Criminology, 28,* 237–270.

Rowe, D. C., & Plomin, R. (1981). The importance of nonshared (E_1) environmental influences in behavioral development. *Developmental Psychology, 17,* 517–531.

Rowe, D. C., & Rodgers, J. L. (1989). Behavioral genetics, adolescent deviance, and "d": Contributions and issues. In G. Adams, R. Montemayor, & T. P. Gullotta (Eds.), *Biology of adolescent behavior and development* (pp. 38–67). Newbury Park, CA: Sage.

Rowe, D. C., & Rodgers, J. L. (1991). Smoking and drinking: Are they epidemics? *Journal of Studies on Alcohol, 52,* 110–117.

Rowe, D. C., Rodgers, J. L., Meseck-Bushey, S., & St. John, C. (1989). Sexual behavior and nonsexual deviance: A sibling study of their relationship. *Developmental Psychology, 25,* 61–69.

Rushton, J. P. (1985). Differential K theory: The sociobiology of individual and group differences. *Personality and Individual Differences, 6,* 441–452.

Rushton, J. P. (1989). The evolution of racial differences: A response to M. Lynn. *Journal of Research in Personality, 23,* 7–20.

Schull, W. J., & Neel, J. V. (1965). *The effects of inbreeding on Japanese children.* New York: Harper & Row.

Sechrest, L., West, S. G., Phillips, M. A., Redner, R., & Yeaton, W. (1979). Some neglected problems in evaluation research: Strength and integrity of treatments. In L. Sechrest et al. (Eds.), *Evaluation studies review annual* (Vol. 4, pp. 15–35). Beverly Hills, CA: Sage.

Sigvardsson, S., Cloninger, C. R., Bohman, M., & Von Knorring, A. L. (1982). Predisposition to petty criminality in Swedish adoptees. III. Sex differences and validation of the male typology. *Archives of General Psychiatry, 39,* 1248–1253.

Simonton, D. K. (1985). Intelligence and personal influence in groups: Four nonlinear models. *Psychological Review, 92,* 532–547.

Stark, R. (1987). Deviant places: A theory of the ecology of crime. *Criminology, 25,* 893–909.

Thornberry, T. P. (1987). Toward an interactional theory of delinquency. *Criminology, 25,* 863–891.

Thornhill, R., & Thornhill, N. W. (1983). Human rape: An evolutionary analysis. *Ethology and Sociobiology, 4,* 137–173.

Tittle, C. R., & Villemez, W. J. (1977). Social class and criminality. *Social Forces, 56,* 474–502.

Udry, J. R., Billy, J. O. G., Morris, N. M., Groff, T. R., & Raj, M. H. (1985). Serum androgenic hormones motivate sexual behavior in adolescent boys. *Fertility and Sterility, 43,* 90–94.

Wilson, E. O. (1975). *Sociobiology: The new synthesis.* Cambridge, MA: Belknap.

Wilson, J. Q., & Herrnstein, R. J. (1985). *Crime and human nature.* New York: Simon & Schuster.

Wolfgang, M. E., Figlio, R. M., & Sellin, T. (1972). *Delinquency in a birth cohort.* Chicago: University of Chicago Press.

Wolfgang, M. E., Thornberry, T. P., & Figlio, R. M. (1987). *From boy to man, from delinquency to crime.* Chicago: University of Chicago Press.

Yablonsky, L. (1959). The delinquent gang as a near-group. *Social Problems, 7,* 108–117.

Author Index

Abbott, R. D., 124, 183, 187, 188
Abrams, N., 8, 97
Achenbach, T. M., 76
Adams, M., 94
Adan, A. M., 185
Adler, C., 176
Afzal, M., 287
Ageton, S. S., xv, 29, 33, 55, 57, 58, 62, 98, 108, 152, 155, 157, 167, 174, 178, 198, 199, 201, 205, 210, 230, 239
Agnew, R., 151, 157, 158, 168, 206, 210, 211, 212, 213, 214, 218, 224, 225, 228, 229, 230, 231
Ahlstrom, W. M., 279
Ahmed, S. W., 185
Ainsworth, M. D. S., 171
Akers, R. L., 29, 55, 155, 162, 165, 199, 239
Alder, C., 87
Alderson, M. R., 98
Alexander, J. F., 121
Allen, L., 84
Allen, N., 8
Althaus, M., 76
Amdur, R. L., 82
American Psychiatric Association, 12, 69
Anderson, J. L., 270
Andrews, D. A., 115
Andry, R. G., 90
Anisfeld, E., 182, 183
Anthony, E. J., 150, 151
Applegate, B., 7
Arbuthnot, J., 112
Arnold, W. R., 239

Atkinson, M. P., 161
August, G. J., 8
Bachman, J. G., 94, 186, 210
Bahr, S. J., 157
Bailey, S. L., 176
Bailey, W. C., 240
Baker, E., 124
Baker, R. L., 84, 85, 124
Baldwin, J., 101, 102
Ball, J. C., 10
Bandura, A., 29, 55, 107, 155, 163
Barclay, G. C., 74
Baren, M., 292
Barnard, K. E., 169, 171
Barnes, H. V., 87, 120
Barnett, W. S., 120, 171, 183
Baron, G. D., 76
Barton, C., 121
Bass, D., 112, 121
Bates, J. E., xiii, 78
Bates, M. E., 86
Bauman, K. E., 157
Bayles, K., 78
Bazemore, G., 87, 176
Beauchesne, H., 147
Beckwith, L., 169
Bee, H. L., 169
Behar, M. C., 171
Bell, R. M., 125
Bell, R. Q., 151
Bem, D. J., 163
Benn, R. T., 101
Bennett, D. S., 78
Bentler, P. M., 151, 157, 214

315

Berg, I., 112
Berger, M., 101
Bergman, L. R., 76
Berk, R. A., 123, 127
Berrueta-Clement, J. R., 120, 171, 183
Berry, W. D., 37
Bertrand, L., 122
Bessler, A., 9
Beyer, J. A., 87
Billy, J. O. G., 283
Birch, H. G., 4, 11
Blackburn, R., 68
Blake, G., 87, 176
Blalock, H. M., 237, 238, 241
Blau, P. M., 242, 244, 247
Block, J., 89, 151
Blouin, A. G., 86
Blouin, J., 86
Blum, H. M., 92
Blumstein, A., 12, 70, 71, 113, 176, 198, 200
Blyth, D. A., 178
Bohman, M., 281
Boileau, H., 122
Bonagura, N., 8
Bonanno, J., 168, 169
Bonta, J., 115
Booth, C. L., 169, 171
Bottoms, A. E., 102
Botvin, E. M., 124
Botvin, G. J., 123, 124, 186
Bowen, S., 126
Bowlby, J., 90
Boyd, L. H., 242, 244, 245
Boyd, R., 287, 289
Boyle, M. H., 92, 96
Braithwaite, J., 252
Brakke, N. P., 11
Brasswell, M., 121
Breaux, A. M., 11
Brennan, P. A., 85
Breslau, N., 84
Briar, S., 155
Bright, J., 89
Brody, S. R., 114
Brodzinsky, D. M., 291
Brook, D. W., 157, 167
Brook, J. S., 157, 167
Brooks-Gunn, J., 83, 116, 117
Brophy, J., 172, 183
Brown, E. D., 114
Brown, E. O., 184
Brown, M. M., 78
Bruell, J. H., 292
Brungardt, T. M., 239
Bryant, D. M., 171
Bryk, A. S., 248

Buckle, A., 126
Buikhuisen, W., 127
Burgess, R. L., 29, 155
Burgos, W., 36, 167
Burkett, S. R., 206, 208, 210, 221, 224, 225, 228, 230
Burns, K. A., 169
Burns-Howell, T., 126
Burrows, J., 74, 126
Bursik, R. J., 100, 101, 161, 163, 236, 239, 240, 243, 247, 248, 261–2
Bush, P. J., 185
Byrne, D., 116

Cadoret, R. J., 9
Cairns, B. D., 157, 295
Cairns, R. B., 157, 295
Camasso, M. J., 115
Campbell, F. A., 120, 171
Campbell, J. T., 127
Campbell, S. B., 7, 11
Canter, R. J., 29, 34, 55, 57, 58, 62, 199
Cantwell, D. P., 292
Caplinger, T. E., 123
Carey, M. B., 8
Carney, R., 292
Cartwright, D., 242
Casey, R. J., 272
Casper, V., 182, 183
Catalano, R. F., 123, 124, 125, 150, 152, 157, 161, 174, 183, 184, 185, 187, 188, 199, 201
Cavalli-Sforza, L. L., 287
Cernkovich, S. A., 157
Chamberlain, P., 121
Chamberlain, R., 117
Chamberlin, R. W., 7
Chambliss, W. J., 35
Chandler, M. J., 107
Chandola, C. A., 85
Charlebois, P., 11, 122
Chasnoff, I. J., 169
Chess, S., 4, 11
Christ, M. A. G., 2, 3, 12
Christenson, R. L., 209, 211, 214, 219, 230
Christiansen, K. O., 281
Cicchetti, D., 150, 153
Clark, J. P., 100, 253–4
Clarke, R. V., 103, 126, 127
Cloninger, C. R., 281, 282, 307
Cloward, R. A., 95, 105, 242, 305
Cohen, A. K., 88, 95, 105, 305
Cohen, J., 12, 70, 71, 198, 200
Cohen, L. E., 103, 243, 259, 268, 304
Cohen, P., 157, 167
Cohler, B. J., 150, 151
Coie, J. D., 11

Coleman, J. S., 236, 239, 241
Colvin, M., 168
Congdon, R. T., 248
Conger, K. J., 162
Conger, R. D., 155, 162, 163
Conners, C. K., 86
Consortium for Longitudinal Studies, 120
Cordray, S., 87, 176
Cornish, D. B., 103, 127
Costa, F. M., 76, 279
Coventry, G., 87, 176
Cox, A., 101
Crawford, C. B., 270
Cressey, D. R., 105, 155
Cromwell, R. E., 121
Cullen, F. T., 115
Cunningham, N., 182, 183
Cusson, M., 161

Dalphin, J. R., 32
Daly, M., 269, 270, 281, 296, 301
Dantchik, A., 268-9
David, L., 122
Davidson, F. R., 185
Davidson, W. S., 115, 116
Davies, M., 151
Davis, J. A., 244
Dawkins, R., 302
Day, L. E., 124, 157, 183, 187
DeBarysh, B. D., xiii
Dembo, R., 36, 167
Denno, D. W., 84
Deutsch, C. K., 292
DiLalla, L. F., 90
Dill, C. A., 123
Dirkes, K., 169
Dishion, T. J., 13, 83, 107, 121, 152, 171, 176, 272
Dodge, K. A., xiii, 11
Donovan, J. E., 76, 279
Doueck, H. J., 124
Douglas, E., 78
Douglas, J. W. B., 96
Doyle, W., 183
Draper, P., 268, 270, 302
Dryfoos, J. G., 174
Dumas, J. E., 290
Dunford, F. W., 35
Dwyer, J. H., 186

Earls, F., 78
Egeland, B., 91, 171
Eisenberg, J. G., 6, 7
Eisenstadt, S. N., 242
Elder, G. H., 162
Elias, M. J., 187
Ellickson, P. L., 125

Elliott, D. S., xv, 29, 33, 34, 35, 37, 40, 44, 45, 48, 53, 55, 57, 58, 62, 73, 74, 98, 108, 151, 152, 155, 157, 160, 165, 167, 174, 178, 186, 198, 199, 201, 205, 206, 210, 219, 220, 222, 224, 225, 228, 230, 231, 232, 239, 294
Ellis, L., 86, 279
Empey, L. T., 29
Eng, A., 123
Ensminger, M. E., 77, 92, 166, 176
Entwisle, B., 247, 248
Epstein, A. S., 120, 171, 183
Erbring, L., 238
Erickson, M. F., 91
Erickson, M. L., 29, 30, 104
Erickson, M. T., 292
Eron, L. D., 11, 80
Esveldt-Dawson, K., 112
Evans, R. I., 123
Ewing, L. W., 11
Ewles, C. D., 119
Eysenck, H. J., 106

Fabiano, E. A., 119
Fagot, B. I., 11
Farber, E. A., 171
Farley, F. H., 86
Farnworth, M., 57, 96
Farrington, D. P., 9, 11, 18, 29, 48, 61, 68, 69, 70, 71, 73, 74, 75, 76, 77, 78, 79, 80, 81, 82, 85, 86, 87, 89, 90, 92, 93, 94, 95, 96, 97, 98, 99, 102, 103, 104, 105, 108, 112, 113, 115, 126, 150, 152, 153, 176, 188, 198, 203, 240, 247, 258-9, 272, 295, 296
Farrow, D., 167
Faust, R., 18
Feldman, J. F., 78
Feldman, M. W., 287
Feldman, R. A., 123
Feldman, S., 37
Felner, R. D., 185
Felson, M., 103, 243
Ferguson, T., 95
Feshbach, S., 272
Festinger, L., 163
Figlio, R. M., 74, 76, 77, 87, 151, 176, 198, 200, 214, 269
Filazzola, A. D., 124
Finch, T., 279
Finckenauer, J. O., 127
Finnegan, T. A., 75
Firebaugh, G., 240, 245, 246
Fischer, D. G., 94
Fisher, W. A., 116
Fitzmahan, D., 184
Flay, B. R., 186

Fleeting, M., 69, 83, 84, 91, 94
Fletcher, R. H., 120
Flewelling, R. L., 176
Forde, D. R., 239, 240, 260
Foshee, V., 157
Foster, J., 126
Fraser, N. W., 184
Frechette, M., 103, 116
Freedman, J. L., 297
French, N. H., 112
Frick, P. J., 2, 3, 7, 12
Frum, H. S., 14
Furstenberg, F. F., 83

Gabrielli, W. F., 94, 291, 299
Gagnon, C., 11, 122
Gallagher, B., 79, 82, 86, 97, 113
Galvin, J., 87, 176
Gangestad, S. W., 303
Garafalo, J., 259
Gariepy, J-L., 157
Garmezy, N., 153
Garrett, C. J., 115
Gartin, P. R., 174
Gatzanis, S. R. M., 69, 83, 84
Gendreau, P., 114, 115, 119
Gensheimer, L. K., 115, 116
Gersten, J. C., 6, 7, 151, 153
Gest, S. D., 157
Ghodsian, M., 80
Giampino, T., 9
Gibbs, J. P., 104
Giller, H., 68
Gillmore, M. R., 157, 161, 188
Ginsberg, I. J., 207, 224, 225, 228
Giordano, P. C., 157
Giroux, B., 16, 18
Gittelman, R., 8
Glass, G. V., 127
Glow, P. H., 1
Glow, R. A., 1
Glueck, E., 29, 61, 279
Glueck, S., 29, 61, 279
Gold, M., 100, 101, 239, 295
Golden, M. M., 11
Goldstein, H., 248, 249
Good, T. L., 172, 183
Gordon, A. S., 157, 167
Gordon, D. A., 112
Gottesmann, I. I., 90, 281
Gottfredson, D. C., 124, 239, 240, 251,
     257–8
Gottfredson, G. D., 239, 240, 251, 257–8
Gottfredson, M. R., xiii, 29, 30, 32, 61, 79,
     108, 149, 155, 160, 236, 259, 282, 287
Gottfredson, S. D., 239, 247, 261–2
Gottschalk, R., 115, 116

Graham, J. W., 186
Graham, P. J., 5, 7, 8, 78
Grandon, G., 36
Grant, W. T., Consortium on the School-
     Based Promotion of Social Compe-
     tence, 164, 187
Grasmick, H. G., 161, 163, 240, 243, 248
Gray, P. S., 32
Green, M., 292
Green, S. M., 7, 9
Greenburg, M. T., 171
Greenley, J. R., 207, 224, 225, 228
Griffith D. R., 169
Griswald, D. B., 212
Groeneveld, L. P., 123
Groff, T. R., 283
Groves, W. B., 239, 243, 258, 260
Guerra, N., 107
Gulley, B., 297
Guthrie, T. J., 123
Guze, S. B., 282

Haber, S., 272
Halper, A., 123
Hamblin, R. L., 300
Hammond, M., 169
Hammond, W. A., 96
Hanley, J. H., 122
Hansen, W. B., 186
Hanson, K., 2, 3, 12
Harbin, H. T., 20
Hardt, R. H., 29
Harpending, H. C., 268, 270, 281, 302
Harr, R., 242
Hart, E. A., 2, 3, 12
Hart, E. L., 7
Hauser, R. M., 240, 241
Havighurst, R. J., 279
Hawkins, J. D., 71, 81, 105, 108, 123, 124,
     125, 150, 152, 153, 157, 161, 174,
     183, 184, 185, 187, 199, 201, 203
Hayes, C. D., 116
Healy, W., 236
Hedges, L. V., 114
Heimer, K., 29
Heise, D. R., 246
Helle, H. J., 242
Henderson, A. H., 123
Henderson, C. R., 117
Henggeler, S. W., 122
Henker, B., 118
Henricson, C., 89
Henry, B., 88
Hepburn, J. R., 32, 155
Herjanic, B. L., 92
Herrnstein, R. J., 68, 87, 107, 241, 279,
     280, 282, 294

Hickman, C. A., 208, 210, 221, 225
Hill, G. D., 161
Hill, P. C., 123
Hill, S. Y., 87
Hindelang, M. J., 73, 83, 86, 87, 96, 155, 259, 286
Hinshaw, S. P., 8
Hirschi, T., xiii, 29, 30, 32, 61, 73, 79, 86, 87, 96, 108, 149, 155, 157, 160, 163, 165, 168, 199, 200, 212, 228, 230, 236, 256, 282, 286, 287, 304
Hoffman, K. P., 120
Hoge, R. D., 115
Hollin, C. R., 68, 107
Homans, G. C., 242
Honig, A. S., 118
Hope, T., 126
Horacek, H. J., 120
Horn, J. M., 292
Howard, J., 169
Howard, M. O., 184
Hrdy, S. B., 271
Huesmann, L. R., 11, 80
Huizinga, D., xv, 14, 29, 32, 34, 35, 39, 53, 55, 57, 73, 74, 98, 108, 152, 155, 157, 160, 167, 174, 178, 186, 198, 199, 201, 205, 206, 208, 210, 221, 222, 224, 225, 226, 228, 230, 231, 232, 239
Hullin, R., 112
Hundleby, J. D., 163
Hunter, A., 239, 240
Huson, C., 244
Hutchings, B., 87, 94, 291, 299

Iannotti, R. J., 185
Ihinga-Tallman, M., 156
Inui, T. S., 78
Iritani, B., 161
Iverson, G. R., 242, 244, 245

Jacklin, E. N., 289
Jacobson, N. S., 289
Jang, S. J., 57
Jarjoura, G. R., 239, 241, 251, 260
Jary, M. L., 293
Jenkins, V. Y., 272
Jensen, G. F., 29, 30, 104
Jessor, L., 279
Jessor, R., 76, 272, 279
Jessor, S. L., 76, 272
Johnson, C. A., 123, 186
Johnson, D. L., 118, 171
Johnson, R. E., 157, 201, 205
Johnson, R. J., 151
Johnston, C., 11
Johnston, J., 94, 210
Johnston, L. D., 186

Johnstone, J. W. C., 238, 247, 251, 254–5
Jonassen, C. T., 100, 101
Jones, B., 187
Jones, M. B., 97, 112
Jöreskog, K. G., 58

Kagan, J., 86
Kandel, D. B., 18, 20, 29, 40, 151, 207, 221, 226
Kandel, E., 85, 87
Kaplan, H. B., 151
Karp, D. A., 32
Kavanagh, K. A., 121
Kazdin, A. E., 112, 116, 121
Keenan, K., 9, 16, 18
Kellam, S. G., 77, 92, 166, 176
Kelley, K., 116
Kempf, K., 157, 163
Kennedy, L. W., 239, 240, 260
Kenrick, D. T., 268–9
Kent, L. A., 185
Kercher, K., 29
Killen, J. D., 123, 124
Kinlock, T. W., 10
Kirkegaard-Sorenson, L., 87
Kitzman, H., 118
Klackenberg-Larsson, I., 87
Klebanov, P. K., 117
Klein, M. W., 12, 75, 239
Klein, N. C., 84, 121
Klein, R. G., 9
Klepp, K-I., 123
Kluegel, J. R., 259
Knight, B. J., 104
Knop, J., 87
Knowles, B. A., 34
Kohlberg, L., 5, 154
Kolvin, I., 69, 83, 84, 91, 94
Kolvin, P. A., 69, 91, 94
Konig, P. H., 3
Kornhauser, R. R., 155, 156, 169, 255, 256
Krohn, M. D., xiv, 29, 57, 155, 157, 162, 165, 203
Krohn, M. K., 29, 239
Kropenske, V., 169
Kulik, J. A., 85
Kupersmidt, J. B., 11

Lab, S. P., 115
Labouvie, E. W., 86
La Greca, A. M., 7
Lahey, B. B., 2, 3, 7, 9, 12
Lally, J. R., 118
Lam, T., 174, 187
Land, K. C., 259, 261
Langlois, J. H., 272
Langner, T. S., 6, 7, 151, 153

Lanza-Kaduce, L., 29, 155, 162, 165, 239
LaPadula, M., 9
Larive, S., 11, 122
Larson, C., 117
Larzelere, R. E., 160
Laub, J. H., 36
Lauritsen, J. L., 260
LaVoie, L., 36
Le Blanc, M., 11, 22, 71, 77, 78, 103, 116,
    122, 150, 166, 199
Ledingham, J. E., 7
Lefkowitz, M. M., 11
Lenihan, K. J., 123
Lerner, J. A., 78
Levine, M., 161
Lewis, R. V., 127
Liaw, F., 117
Lipsey, M. W., 115
Lipton, D., 114
Lishner, D. M., 124
Liska, A. E., xiv, 155, 207, 211, 212, 213,
    218, 230, 241
Lizotte, A. J., 57
Loeber, R., 1, 2, 3, 5, 7, 9, 10, 11, 12, 13,
    14, 15, 16, 17, 18, 20, 21, 22, 29, 61,
    71, 77, 83, 85, 88, 107, 115, 150, 153,
    166, 171, 176, 199, 259, 272
Loehlin, J. C., 292
Lombroso, C., 306
Lorenz, F. O., 162
Luepker, R. V., 123
Lynam, D., 87

McAlister, A. L., 123-4
McCarthy, E. D., 6, 7
McCord, J., 69, 77, 89, 90, 91, 92, 112,
    121, 171
McDevitt, S. C., 8
McDonald, L., 252
McDowall, D., 239, 243, 247, 251, 260
MacFarlane, S., 268-9
McGee, R., 84
MacGregor, S., 169
McGuffin, P., 85
McGuigan, K., 125
McGuire, R., 112
McKay, H. D., 100, 105, 125, 256
MacKinnon, D. P., 186
McMichael, P., 286
McNeil, R. J., 239, 240, 251
Maccoby, E. E., 288, 289
Maccoby, N., 123, 124
Machalek, R., 268, 304
Madden, D. J., 20
Magnusson, D., 8, 11, 76, 77
Malamuth, N., 272
Maliphant, R., 101

Malloy, P., 9
Mangione, P. L., 118
Mannuzza, S., 8, 9
Marcos, A. C., 157
Marcus, J., 77
Markus, G. B., 48
Marsden, M. W., 255-6
Martin, J. A., 288
Martin, S. S., 151
Martinson, R. M., 114
Mason, W. M., 247, 248
Massey, J. L., 157
Massimo, J. L., 112
Matheny, A. P., 11
Matsueda, R. L., 29, 32, 37, 155, 156, 158,
    208, 210, 211, 218, 230
Matza, D., 155, 158
Maughan, B., 99
Mawson, A. R., 86
Maxwell, S. E., 123
Mayer, J. P., 115, 116
Mednick, B. R., 84, 85
Mednick, S. A., 85, 87, 94, 291, 299
Meier, R. F., 160, 208, 210, 221, 225, 238
Mellen, S. L. W., 284
Melton, G. B., 122
Melville-Thomas, G., 85
Menard, S., 29, 34, 35, 37, 40, 44, 45, 48,
    53, 55, 57, 74, 152, 160, 165, 167,
    207, 208, 210, 219, 220, 221, 222,
    226, 231, 232, 294
Merton, R. K., 162
Meseck-Bushey, S., 279
Messner, S. F., xiv, 155, 243
Michelson, L., 118
Miethe, T., 239, 243, 247, 251, 260, 261
Miller, F. J. W., 69, 83, 84, 91, 94
Miller, J. Y., 123, 153, 174
Miller, W. B., 29, 305
Minor, W. W., 208, 211, 215, 218
Mischel, W., 85
Mitchell, S. K., 11, 169
Mittelmark, M. B., 123
Moffitt, T. E., 69, 78, 85, 87, 88, 161
Moitra, S., 113, 176
Moorman, J. E., 240
Morash, M., 83, 85, 92
Morgan, S. P., 83
Morisset, C. E., 171
Morley, L., 79, 82, 86, 97, 113
Morris, J. N., 98, 101
Morris, N. M., 283
Morris, T., 236
Morrison, D. M., 124, 161, 183, 187
Morse, B. J., 29, 207, 210, 224, 225, 228,
    231
Mortimore, P., 99

Moskowitz, D. S., 7
Mueller, C. W., 95
Mulligan, D. G., 96
Munch, R., 238, 242
Munsch, J., 178
Murray, D. M., 123

Neckerman, H. J., 157, 295
Neel, I. V., 287
Newcomb, M. D., 151, 157
Newell, C., 48
Newson, E., 89, 94
Newson, J., 89, 94
Nicewander, A., 274
Nietzel, M. T., 107
Noble, J. V., 300
Nozyce, M., 182, 183
Nurco, D. N., 10
Nye, F. I., 96, 155, 161, 162

O'Donnell, J. A., 20, 124, 183, 187
Offord, D. R., 8, 84, 92, 96, 97, 112, 279
Ohlin, L. E., 95, 105, 112, 242, 272, 305
Olds, D. L., 116–7, 118
Olkin, I., 114
Olweus, D., 5, 7, 247, 272, 283
O'Malley, P. M., 94, 186, 210
Osborn, S. G., 81, 102
Osgood, D. W., 274, 279, 295
O'Tuama, L., 7
Ouston, J., 94, 99

Paikoff, R. L., 116
Parcel, T. L., 95
Parsons, B. V., 121
Parsons, T., 242
Paternoster, R., 209, 210, 211, 224, 226,
    227, 228, 231, 232
Patterson, G. R., xiii, 20, 89, 107, 121,
    122, 152, 160, 199, 289–90, 297
Pauly, J., 168
Payne, R. B., 271
Pearson, F. S., 108
Pelham, W. E., 11
Pentz, M. A., 186
Perry, C. L., 123, 124, 186
Petee, T. A., 87
Peters, T. J., 85
Peterson, P. L., 125
Peterson, S. J., 29
Pettit, G., xiii
Phillips, M. A., 308
Phillipson, C. M., 98
Piaget, J., 154
Pickles, A., 79
Piliavin, I., 155
Pinsonneault, P., 161

Pitcher, B. L., 300
Platt, J. R., 37
Plomin, R., 276
Polk, K., 87, 176
Power, C., 80
Power, M. J., 98, 101
Presseisen, B. Z., 187
Prosser, R., 248
Przybeck, T. R., 151
Pugh, M. D., 157
Pulkkinen, L., 69, 76, 85

Quay, H. C., 7
Quinton, D., 79, 101

Rachal, J. V., 176
Racine, Y., 96
Radke-Yarrow, M., 153
Radosevich, M., 29, 155, 162, 165, 239
Raine, A., 86
Raines, B. E., 123
Raj, M. H., 283
Ramey, C. T., 120, 171
Ramsey, E., xiii
Rankin, J. H., 92
Ransdell, M., 184
Rasbash, J., 248
Ratcliff, K. S., 70, 76
Raudenbush, S. W., 248, 249
Redner, R., 308
Reed, M. D., 207, 209, 211, 212, 213, 218,
    222, 230
Reich, T., 281
Reid, J. B., 20, 121
Reimer, D. J., 100
Reiss, A. J., Jr., 29, 30, 93, 97, 102, 155,
    236, 238, 252–5, 259, 263, 295, 296
Reitsma-Street, M., 84, 279
Renick, N. L., 124
Reznick, J. S., 86
Rhodes, A. L., 29, 238, 252–5
Richerson, P. J., 287, 289
Richman, N., 5, 7, 8, 78
Ricks, D., 5
Ridge, B., 78
Rieser-Danner, L. A., 272
Riley, D., 89
Ritter, J. M., 272
Ritzer, G., 237, 242
Rivara, F. P., 85
Robbins, C. A., 151
Roberts, A. R., 115
Roberts, C., 184
Roberts, M. R., 212
Robins, L. N., 18, 19, 69, 70, 76, 78, 87,
    89, 92, 151, 176
Robinson, E. A., 289

Robling, M. R., 85
Rodgers, J. L., 279, 295, 297
Rodning, C., 169
Rodriguez, M. L., 85
Roff, J. D., 11
Roff, M., 11
Roggman, L. A., 272
Rosa, P., 11
Rose, D. R., 209, 222
Rose, S. A., 78
Rose, S. L., 78
Rosenberg, M., 209, 211, 215, 216, 223
Rosenberg, R., 87
Ross, B. D., 107, 119
Ross, H. L., 127
Ross, J. M., 96
Ross, R. R., 107, 114, 119
Rossi, P. H., 123
Roth, J. A., 12, 70, 71, 198, 200
Rountree, P. W., 261
Routh, D. K., 7
Rowe, D. C., 274, 276, 279, 288, 290, 293, 295, 297
Rowlands, O., 101
Rozelle, R. M., 123
Rubin, B. R., 77, 92, 176
Rucker, L., 83, 85, 92
Rump, E. E., 7
Rushton, J. P., 268, 270, 301–2
Rutter, M., 5, 8, 68, 79, 90, 94, 99, 100, 101–2, 153, 169, 171

St. John, C., 279
St. Lawrence, J. S., 107
St. Ledger, R. J., 79, 82, 86, 97, 113
Sameroff, A. J., 151, 171
Sampson, R. J., 36, 239, 241, 243, 250, 258, 259, 260
Sarason, I. G., 107, 119
Sarbin, T. R., 85
Savage, L. J., 10
Schachar, R., 8, 86
Schelling, T. C., 242
Schiavo, R. S., 121
Schleifer, M., 7
Schlossman, S., 125
Schmaling, K. B., 2, 13
Schmeidler, J., 36, 167
Schoenbach, C., 209, 211, 215, 216, 223
Schoenwald, S. K., 122
Schooler, C., 209, 211, 215, 216, 223
Schroeder, C. S., 7
Schull, W. J., 287
Schulsinger, F., 87
Schwartz, J. E., 101, 239, 241, 251, 256–8
Schwartzman, A. E., 7, 78

Schweinhart, L. J., 87, 120, 171, 183
Scott, D. M., 69, 83, 84
Sechrest, L., 114, 308
Sedlak, M., 125
Seidel, W. T., 86
Seifer, R., 171
Sellin, T., 87, 176, 198, 269
Sells, S. B., 11
Seltzer, M., 248
Sewell, T., 86
Shaffer, J. W., 10
Shannon, L. W., 100, 198, 255
Shaw, C. R., 100, 105, 125, 236, 256
Shaw, D. S., 151
Shaw, M., 89, 126
Shedler, J., 89, 151
Shenker, R., 8
Sherman, L. W., 127
Sherman, T., 153
Shoda, Y., 85
Shoenberg, E., 98
Shore, M. F., 112
Short, J. F., 29, 96, 101, 121, 125
Shover, N., 81
Shryock, H. S., 48
Sieck, W., 16
Siegel, J. S., 48
Siegel, T. C., 112, 121
Sigvardsson, S., 281
Silva, P. A., 69, 78, 84, 87, 88
Simcha-Fagan, O., 6, 7, 101, 151, 153, 239, 241, 251, 256–8
Simon, M. B., 166
Simons, R. L., 162
Simonton, D. K., 286
Simpson, D. D., 10
Simpson, J. A., 303
Singer, S. I., 161
Skinner, M. L., 152
Skogan, W. G., 34
Slavin, R. E., 183
Slinkard, L. A., 124
Smelser, N. J., 179, 238, 242
Smith, A., 8
Smith, D. A., 174, 239, 241, 250, 251, 260
Smith, L. A., 122
Smith, R. S., 169, 171, 172
Snarey, J., 5
Snidman, N., 86
Snyder, H. N., 75
Snyder, J., 89
Sobel, J., 186
Sobus, J., 281
Sörbom, D., 58
Spaeth, J. L., 244
Sparling, J. J., 171

Speed, M., 126
Spieker, S. J., 169, 171
Spiker, D., 117
Spivack, G., 11, 77
Spohr, H-L., 84
Sroufe, L. A., 2, 91
Stark, R., 236
Starkman, N., 184
Stattin, H., 77, 87
Stein, K. B., 85
Steinhausen, H-C., 84
Stevenson, J., 5, 7, 8, 78
Stewart, M. A., 8, 9, 293
Stoolmiller, M., 152
Stouthamer-Loeber, M., 11, 13, 16, 18, 71,
    83, 87, 88, 107, 153
Streissguth, A. P., 84
Sullivan, K., 8
Sutherland, E. H., 29, 55, 105, 155, 156,
    158
Suttles, G. D., 243
Swanson, I. M., 292
Swift, M., 77
Szatmari, P., 84
Szumowski, E. K., 11

Tallman, I., 156
Tannenbaum, L., 2, 3, 12
Tardiff, K., 243
Tatelbaum, R., 117
Taylor, E. A., 85, 86
Taylor, R. B., 239, 247, 261–2
Telch, M. J., 123
Temple, M., 87, 176
Theil, H., 237
Thoits, P., 123
Thomas, A., 4, 11
Thomas, C. W., 14, 112
Thorley, G., 86
Thornberry, T. P., xvi, 32, 40, 57, 58, 60,
    74, 76, 77, 96, 150, 157, 178, 198,
    199, 200, 201, 202, 203, 209, 210,
    211, 214, 219, 222, 230, 232, 269, 295
Thornhill, N. W., 269
Thornhill, R., 269
Thornton, D. M., 114
Tisdelle, D. A., 107
Tittle, C. R., 160, 299
Tobler, N. S., 124
Tolan, P. H., 121
Trad, P. V., 84
Trasler, G. B., 106
Tremblay, R. E., 11, 77–8, 112, 122
Trupin, E. W., 78
Tupling, C., 101
Turner, C. W., 121

Udry, J. R., 283
Unis, A. S., 112
Utting, D., 89

Vadasy, P. F., 184
Van Horn, Y., 2, 3, 12
Van Kammen, W. B., 9, 10, 16, 18, 71,
    85
Venables, P. H., 86
Verhulst, F. C., 76
Vigil, J. D., 36
Villemez, W. J., 299
Visher, C. A., 12, 70, 71, 198, 200
Vitaro, F., 122
Von Cleve, E., 124, 125, 188
Von Kammen, W., 153
Von Knorring, A., 281
Voss, H. L., 29

Wadsworth, M., 91, 94
Walberg, H. J., 183
Walder, L. O., 11
Waldron, H., 121
Walker, T., 118
Wall, S., 171
Wallis, C. P., 101
Walsh, A., 87
Walters, R., 29, 55
Wang, E. Y. I., 186
Warburton, J., 121
Warren, B. O., 206, 224, 225, 228, 230
Wasik, B. H., 171
Water, E., 171
Webb, J., 101
Weikart, D. P., 87, 120, 171, 183
Weinberg, F., 292
Weiner, N. A., 108
Weis, J. G., 73, 96, 108, 199, 201
Weismann, W., 20
Weiss, G., 7
Weissberg, R. P., 185, 187
Wells, E. A., 161, 187, 188
Wells, L. E., 92
Wenniger, E. P., 100, 253–4
Werner, E. E., 11, 84, 153, 169, 172
Werry, J. S., 7
West, D. J., 11, 29, 61, 69, 73, 75, 76, 79,
    81, 82, 86, 87, 89, 90, 92, 93, 94, 95,
    96, 98, 113, 176, 198
West, P. J., 92
West, S. G., 308
Whalen, C. K., 118
Whitbeck, L. B., 162
White, H. R., 86
White, J. L., 78, 87
White, S. O., 114

Whitehead, J. T., 115
Whiteman, M., 157, 167
Wiatrowski, M. D., 212
Widom, C. S., 36, 90, 117
Wieselberg, M., 86
Wikstrom, P. O., 69, 77, 259
Wilks, J., 114
Willerman, L., 292
Williams, S., 84
Williamson, J. B., 32
Willms, J., 84
Wilson, E. O., 269
Wilson, H., 89, 93
Wilson, J. Q., 68, 87, 107, 112, 241, 272, 279, 280, 282, 294
Wilson, M., 269, 270, 281, 296, 301
Wish, E., 70
Wodarski, J. S., 123

Wolfgang, M. E., 74, 76, 77, 87, 151, 176, 198, 200, 214, 269
Wong, G. Y., 247, 248
Wooldredge, J. D., 239, 259
Wung, P., 16, 18

Yablonsky, L., 295
Yamaguchi, K., 40
Yeaton, W., 308
Young, A. A., 238
Yule, B., 101
Yule, W., 101

Zander, A., 242
Zhang, Q., 16
Zimring, E. E., 97
Zinger, I., 115
Zoccolillo, M., 79

Subject Index

academic performance (*see* school
  factors)
adaptive strategy theory (AST), 268–309
  and age effects, 282–7
  biological and social consequences,
    301–4
  definitions, 268–9
  and intervention, 306
  and other theories, 294, 304–6
  overview, 269–76
  social policy implications, 306–8
  summary, 308–9
  types of strategy, 269–70
adoption (*see* family and parenting
  factors)
age and problem behavior, 45–8, 74, 151,
  160, 161, 199–20, 261, 276, 282–5
aggressive behavior, 4–7, 8, 9, 10, 11,13,
  17–18, 20, 34, 78, 80, 85, 166, 174,
  217, 270, 278–9, 290, 295
  intergenerational transmission, 90
  atransactional effects, 19
alcohol consumption, 109
  underage, 20
animal behavior, 271–2, 288
antisocial behavior, definition of, 150
antisocial personality/tendency, 71–3,
  75–9, 82, 109–10, 111, 276, 291, 292,
  295, 296
  antisocial personality disorder, 9, 69,
    76
  classifications of, 13
  continuity, 78–80, 112–13, 166–7, 176
  versatility, 75
  (*see also* child problem behaviors; crimi-

nal potential; individual difference
  factors)
arousal, low/high, 86, 161
attachment (*see* bonding)
attention problems, 4, 7, 8, 9, 17, 291
  attention deficit disorder (ADD), 8,
    161, 292
  attention-deficit hyperactivity disorder
    (ADHD), 9
  (*see also* hyperactivity)
authority conflict, 15

belief
  in conventional values, 36–37, 109, 151,
    164, 211–19, 222, 229–30
  in antisocial values, 167, 204, 219–23
biological factors (*see* individual difference factors)
bonding, 156–7, 181
  to antisocial others, 28, 35, 158, 168–9,
    174
  to conventional society, 163–4, 203,
    211, 219, 223–4
  mother/child, 151, 171
  to prosocial others, 158, 163–5
  variables, 211–19, 223–30
  (*see also* family and parenting factors)
British Crime Survey, 258, 259
bullying (*see* aggressive behavior)

Cambridge-Somerville Youth Study, 92
Cambridge Study in Delinquent Development, 69, 296
  desistance, 81, 94

Cambridge Study in Delinquent Development (*cont.*)
developmental continuity, 78, 80, 112–13
measuring offending, 73–4, 93
risk factors, 85–6, 87, 89, 92, 94–5, 96, 97–8, 99, 102, 103, 105
versatility of offending, 75–6
Carolina Abecedarian Project, 120
Catch 'Em Being Good, 124–5
causes/causal factors (*see* risk factors; protective factors)
censoring bias, 38–9, 61
Chicago Area Project, 125
Chicago Neighborhood Project, 249
child management (*see* family and parenting factors)
child problem behaviors
classification of, 1, 10–16
confrontational, overt behaviors, 3, 14
covert/concealing behaviors, 5, 11, 15, 20
dimensions of, 2–3
classification schemes, 10–11, 12, 13, 14
"dynamic" classification, 1, 14–16
cognitive deficit, 88, 107, 119
commitment (*see* bonding; school factors)
community factors, 81, 100–3, 152, 239–40, 243, 250, 252–62, 298–300
interventions, 125–6
population composition, 298–9
Communities That Care, 125
conditioning theories, 106–7 (*see also* social learning theory)
conduct problems, 9, 11, 77–8, 174
conduct disorder, 8, 9, 12, 79, 86, 291, 293
conscience, definition of 107
Consortium for Longitudinal Studies, 120
constitutional traits (*see* criminal potential; individual difference factors)
contextual analysis, 236–63
compositional approach, 241–3, 256
emergent properties, 242–3
estimating the contextual model, 244–50
group contexts, definition of, 238–9
models of criminal behavior, 250–62
as a multilevel model, 246–7
and neighborhood contexts, 252–62
selective aggregation, 241, 246
theoretical issues, 237–44
continuity (*see* antisocial personality, continuity; maintenance of problem behaviors; offending, developmental continuity)
control theory (*see* social control theory)

costs/benefits of behaviors, 157, 178
antisocial/criminal, 103–4, 107, 110–12, 158, 168, 271, 293, 303–4
interventions, 126–7
prosocial, 174
covariance analysis, 244–6
criminal career, definition of, 70–2
criminal potential, 29, 72, 107, 126, 269, 273–4, 276–7, 298 (*see also* antisocial personality)
cultural deviance theory, 256–7
cultural transmission theory
definition of, 287
horizontal transmission, 287, 288, 293–7, 309
oblique transmission, 287, 288, 297–8, 309
vertical transmission, 287, 288–93

Danish Adoption Study, 291
delinquency, definitions of, 30, 149–50
as a group behavior, 31, 97, 296
Denver Youth Study, 249
desistance, 18, 71, 81, 94, 111–2, 152, 166, 198, 200, 201, 272
developmental sequences, 3–5, 9, 28, 33, 35–6, 44–57, 60–63, 71–2, 74–5, 112, 150–2, 231–2, 274–6, 280–2
pathways, 14–16, 21, 158–88
(*see also* social development model)
differential association theory, 155, 156, 158, 219, 241
discipline (*see* family and parenting factors, child management)
disobedience, 9
diversification of problem behavior, 1, 17–21, 22 (*see also* offending, versatility)
drug use (*see* substance use)
DSM-III-R, 12
DSM-IV, 69

ecological conditions (*see* environmental/external influences)
educational performance (*see* school factors)
empirical variables vs. theoretical constructs, 72
environmental/external influences, 158, 160–2, 214, 269–70, 276, 293, 298–301 (*see also* community factors; family and parenting factors; peer influences; school factors; sibling relations; social influences; socioeconomic status)
equivalence hypothesis, 42–4, 60
evolution (*see* adaptive strategy theory)

equilibrium, biological and social, 301–4, 309

family and parenting factors, 69, 74, 81, 109–12, 152, 153, 157, 171, 178, 200–1, 232, 276, 279–80, 287–90, 304–5
 adoption, 290–93, 299
 aggressive parents, 89
 antisocial/criminal parents, 83, 92–4, 110, 291, 293, 305
 bonding, 151, 211–19, 224, 229–30
 broken homes, 85, 90–2, 110, 111, 293, 305
 child management, 82, 83, 88–90, 106–7, 108, 111, 113, 121, 160–2, 171, 174, 176, 288, 293
 conflict, 7, 89, 111, 172, 293
 vs. community factors, 102–3
 family size, 94–5, 169
 genetic traits, 288
 interventions, 121–2, 184–5, 290–91
 modeling, 288
 vs. peer influences, 152
 (see also bonding; cultural transmission theory; sibling relations; socioeconomic status)
Farrington theory, 108–12
fetal alcohol syndrome, 84
fighting (see aggressive behavior)

gender, 68, 82, 160, 169, 261, 276, 277, 280–2, 287, 300
A General Theory of Crime, 149–50

Head Start, 120
heritability, 277, 279, 287, 291, 302
hierarchical linear model (HLM), 247–50, 261
hyperactivity, 4, 7, 8–9, 11, 17, 69, 71, 86, 118–19
 hyperactivity-impulsivity-attention deficit syndrome (HIA), 85–6
 (see also attention problems)

impulsivity, 4, 7, 8, 9, 10, 69, 76, 81, 85–6, 107–8, 109–10, 118–9, 278–9, 290, 291, 292
individual difference factors, 81, 82, 106–7, 153, 160–1, 169, 260, 269, 273–9, 306
 person- vs. variable-oriented approach, 76–7
 trait transmission, cultural vs. genetic, 268
 (see also antisocial personality; criminal potential; intelligence)

individual vs. group effects (see contextual analysis)
infancy (see prenatal/perinatal)
Infant Health and Development Program, 117
influences (see risk factors)
initiation (see onset of problem behaviors)
integral variables (see contextual analysis, emergent properties)
integrated theory, 199
intelligence, 81, 83, 86–8, 107, 109–10, 111, 113, 153, 161, 274–6, 285–7, 299, 304
 (see also individual difference factors)
interaction, pro- vs. antisocial, 163–88
interactional theory, 28, 32, 42, 58, 60–63, 198–233, 295
 aims, 199
 developmental perspective, 199–201, 231–2
 literature review, 205–11
 vs. other theories, 199, 205
 policy implications, 204
 and reciprocal effects, 201–11
 (see also reciprocal effects; transactional effects among problem behaviors)
intervention
 biological, 307
 developmentally specific, 21–2, 112–13, 181–7
 effectiveness, 114–16
 elementary school, 183–5
 ethical issues, 113–14
 high school, 186–7
 middle school, 185–6
 preschool, 182–3
 and risk factors, 116–27
 treatment, 22–3, 112–4, 307
involvement, pro- vs. antisocial, 163–88, 174

LEAA National Crime Surveys, 259
learning theory and variables (see social learning theory)
legal codes, influence of, 174–5, 176
London Youth Cohort, 295
longitudinal vs. cross-sectional designs, 82, 198
lying, transactional effects, 20

maintenance of problem behaviors, 5–7, 16, 71, 81, 111–2, 152, 198, 200, 201, 232 (see also antisocial personality; continuity; offending, developmental continuity)

mating/parenting effort as adaptive
    strategy
  and age, 282–3
  biological/social consequences, 301
  crime/crime proneness, 270–2, 277–9,
    282–3
  constitutional traits, 274–6
  and intelligence, 287
  intercultural variation, 302
  peer context, 295–6
  population composition, 298–300
  sexual selection theory, 280–1
  (see also adaptive strategy theory)
maturational reform hypothesis, 48
media, influence of, 297–8
meta-analysis, definition of 114–15
Midwestern Prevention Project, 186
Minnesota Multiphasic Personality Inven-
    tory, 292
multilevel modeling (see contextual
    analysis)
multisystemic therapy, 122

National Youth Survey (NYS), 33, 44–57,
    33–57, 74, 98, 210, 219–20, 222–3,
    224–5, 228, 231, 232
Newcastle Thousand Family Study, 91
norms, 156–7, 162, 169, 238, 253, 300
  (see also belief)
Nottingham Study, 94

offender, typical, 69
offending
  classification, 33–4
  definitions of, 70, 71, 72, 73–4
  developmental continuity, 77–80, 150,
    199–201
  duration, 71, 81 (see also desistance; main-
    tenance of problem behaviors)
  escalation, 71
  frequency, 48, 71, 81
  measurement, 73–4
  natural history, 74–5 (see also develop-
    mental sequences; onset of problem
    behaviors)
  versatility, 75–7
offence types, 33–4
  and age, 47–8
  transitions among, 51–6
  official records vs. self-reports, 250–52
onset of problem behaviors, 9–10, 28, 37–
    44, 71, 81, 111–2, 152, 166, 174, 198,
    200, 232
Ontario Child Health Study, 92, 96
opportunities for involvement/ interac-
    tion, 156, 160–5, 172, 180
  antisocial, 72, 103, 110

interventions, 126–7
  prosocial, 158, 162–3, 169
oppositional behavior, 17, 290
oppositional defiant disorder, 9, 12

parental factors (see family and parenting
    factors)
parenting effort as adaptive strategy (see
    mating/parenting effort)
pathways (see developmental sequences)
peer group types, 35–6
  and age, 45–8
  transitions among, 48–51, 53–6, 62, 220
peer influences, 5, 10, 28–64, 69, 81, 97–
    8, 110, 152, 153, 172, 174, 176, 178,
    201, 219–23, 227–8, 231–2, 239, 256,
    276, 294–6, 298, 299
  interventions, 123–4
  measuring, 30, 33–4
  (see also bonding; cultural transmission
    theory, horizontal)
peer relations, 11, 18, 74–5, 81, 97–8,
    300, 305
Perry Preschool Program, 81, 120
persistence of problem behaviors (see
    maintenance of problem behaviors)
policy implications
  adaptive strategy theory, 306–8
  behavioral development, 21–2
  interactional theory, 201–4
  offending, prevention and treatment,
    112–27
  social development model, 181–7
Positive Action Through Holistic Educa-
    tion (PATHE) program, 124
poverty (see socioeconomic status)
predictors (see risk factors; protective
    factors)
pregnancy
  and antisocial tendencies, 292
  teenage, 83–4, 116–17
prenatal/perinatal factors, 81, 83–5, 169
  intervention in, 116–18, 182–3
Preparing for the Drug (Free) Years, 184–5
preschool intellectual enrichment, 119–
    20, 171, 183
prevention (see intervention)
Program on Human Development and
    Criminal Behavior, 249–50
Project ALERT, 125
propensity to crime (see criminal poten-
    tial; individual difference factors)
protective factors, 152–4
  elementary school, 172, 174
  high school, 176
  middle school, 174, 176
  preschool, 169

proximate vs. ultimate explanation, 272, 294

race, 160–2, 169, 241–2, 261
rational choice theory, 103, 127
recidivism, 114–16, 121, 239, 261, 262
  (*see also* antisocial personality, continuity; offending, developmental continuity)
reciprocal effects, 151, 153, 178, 199, 201–5, 210, 276 (*see also* interactional theory; transactional effects among problem behaviors)
reinforcement, 156, 161–5, 167, 171, 172, 174, 181
  of antisocial involvement, 176, 178, 179
reproductive effort as adaptive strategy, 270–2
  and age, 282–3
  biological and social consequences, 301
  and gender, 280–2
  maximizing success, 271, 283, 301
  rate, 276, 301
  (*see also* mating/parenting effort)
rewards (*see* reinforcement)
risk factors, 1, 8, 21, 68, 76–7, 80–114, 149, 200
  elementary school, 172, 174
  high school, 176
  middle school, 174, 176
  preschool, 169
  and prevention/treatment, 112–14
  summary, 104–5, 152–4
risk identification, 16
Ritalin, 118
r/K theory, 268, 301–2

Scared Straight Program, 127
school factors, 81, 98–100, 245–6, 252–3
  achievement, 17–18, 69–70, 83–4, 87–8, 111, 153, 169, 176, 238
  behavior, 69, 83
  classroom management, 172, 174, 183–4
  commitment, 211–19, 224, 229–30
  elementary school, 172–4, 183–4
  high school, 186–7
  interventions, 124–5, 183–7
  middle school, 184–5, 174
  (*see also* preschool intellectual enrichment)
School Transitional Environment Program, 185–6
Seattle Social Development Project, 124–5
self-esteem, 215–16
sex differences (*see* gender)
sexuality, 270, 291, 296

and age, 282–5
and gender, 280–2
sexual life history and crime, 279–80
  (*see also* reproductive effort)
sexual selection theory, 280–2
sibling relations, 7, 97, 172, 276, 279–80, 281, 296–97
  number of siblings, 94–5
  (*see also* family factors)
situational factors (*see* opportunities for involvement/interaction; costs/benefits of behaviors)
social bond (*see* bonding)
social control theory, 29, 32–3, 42–4, 57–64, 155, 157, 163, 165, 199, 211, 223–4, 245, 256, 287, 304, 305–6
social development model, 149–88, 201, 203–4
  elementary school period, 172–4
  general model, 160–9
  high school period, 176–8
  and intervention, 181–7
  key features, 154
  middle school period, 174–6
  overview, 156–60
  preschool period, 169–72
  summary, 187–8
  theoretical considerations, 149–54
social disorganization (*see* community factors)
social influences, 72, 74, 153, 276, 293–4, 301 (*see also* community factors; family and parenting factors; sibling relations; peer influences)
social learning theory, 28, 29, 32–3, 37, 42–4, 57–64, 106–7, 109–10, 155–6, 162, 199, 219, 223–4, 287, 289, 293–4
  variables, 219–28, 231
social position, 160, 169 (*see also* socioeconomic status)
social skills, 17, 107, 119, 156, 158, 164, 167
social withdrawal, 4, 17, 86
socioeconomic status (SES), 83, 87–8, 95–7, 160, 169, 215, 241, 268, 290, 299–300, 305
  contextual, 252–5
  deprivation, 81, 96–7, 109–10, 111, 113, 152, 162, 299, 305
  and discipline/child management, 106–7
  intervention, 122–3
specification error, 237
stability effects, 210
static model, 82–3, 199, 205
stealing (*see* theft)
strain theory 162, 214, 305

structural equation model of exposure, belief, and delinquent behavior, 57–60

subculture theory, 305

substance use
    and delinquency, 9–10, 69, 217
    drug use defined, 149–50
    as group behavior, 31
    as an outcome of teenage pregnancy, 83
    during pregnancy, 84
    marijuana, 217, 221, 225–8, 232
    transactional effects, 20

Swedish Adoption Study, 281

syndrome of problem behavior, 76

Syracuse Family Development Research Program, 118

systemic qualities (*see* contextual analysis, emergent properties)

temperament, 4, 11, 78, 153, 166, 169, 306

termination (*see* desistance)

theft, 5, 8, 11, 13, 20, 33–4, 69, 212, 217, 222, 225–8, 269 (*see also* covert behaviors)

theories of delinquency and crime, reviews, 32–3, 105–8, 150–52, 155–6

transactional effects among problem behaviors, 18–21. (*see also* interactional theory; reciprocal effects)

transactional social interaction, 151, 171, 172

transitions, developmental, 179–81

treatment (*see* intervention)

truancy, 5, 11, 69–70, 78, 81, 87–8, 99, 112

ultimate vs. proximate explanation, 272

victimization, 239, 242, 243–4, 259–62

Youth in Transition study, 210, 211, 212, 214, 215, 216, 221, 222, 228